Technology Ethics

The first of its kind, this anthology in the burgeoning field of technology ethics offers students and other interested readers 32 chapters, each written in an accessible and lively manner specifically for this volume. The chapters are conveniently organized into five parts:

- I   Perspectives on Technology and its Value
- II   Technology and the Good Life
- III   Computer and Information Technology
- IV   Technology and Business
- V   Biotechnologies and the Ethics of Enhancement

A hallmark of the volume is multidisciplinary contributions both (1) in "analytic" and "continental" philosophies and (2) across several hot-button topics of interest to students, including the ethics of autonomous vehicles, psychotherapeutic phone apps, and bio-enhancement of cognition and in sports. The volume editors, both teachers of technology ethics, have compiled a set of original and timely chapters that will advance scholarly debate and stimulate fascinating and lively classroom discussion.

Downloadable eResources (available from www.routledge.com/9781032038704) provide a glossary of all relevant terms, sample classroom activities/discussion questions relevant for chapters, and links to Stanford Encyclopedia of Philosophy entries and other relevant online materials.

Key Features:

- Examines the most pivotal ethical questions around our use of technology, equipping readers to better understand technology's promises and perils.
- Explores throughout a central tension raised by technological progress: maintaining social stability vs. pursuing dynamic social improvements.
- Provides ample coverage of the pressing issues of free speech and productive online discourse.

Gregory J. Robson is an Assistant Professor of Philosophy at Iowa State University and a Visiting Assistant Research Professor in the Mendoza College of Business at the University of Notre Dame. His research focuses on ethics (including business and technology ethics) and social and political philosophy.

Jonathan Y. Tsou is a Professor of Philosophy and the Marvin and Kathleen Stone Distinguished Professor of Humanities in Medicine and Science at the University of Texas at Dallas. He has teaching and research interests in philosophy of science, philosophy of technology, and philosophy of psychiatry.

Contents

Contributors

Justin B. Biddle is an Associate Professor in the School of Public Policy at the Georgia Institute of Technology, as well as the director of the Ethics, Technology, and Human Interaction Center (ETHICx) and a Faculty Affiliate in the Machine Learning Center. His research interests are interdisciplinary in nature, drawing on fields such as philosophy of science and technology, ethics of emerging technologies, and science and technology policy. Conceptually, his research explores the relationships between (1) the role of values in science and technology, (2) the epistemic and ethical implications of the social organization of research, and (3) ethics and policy. His current work explores these relationships in artificial intelligence (AI) and machine learning, and he has also worked in the areas of biomedical research and agricultural biotechnology.

Jason Brennan is the Robert J. and Elizabeth Flanagan Family Professor of Strategy, Economics, Ethics, and Public Policy at Georgetown University in the McDonough School of Business. He is the Editor of *Public Affairs Quarterly* and the Associate Editor of *Social Philosophy and Policy*.

David R. Cerbone is a Professor of Philosophy at West Virginia University. His research interests include 20th-century continental philosophy (especially phenomenology) and Wittgestein. He is the author of *Understanding Phenomenology* (Acumen, 2006; republished by Routledge, 2014), *Heidegger: A Guide for the Perplexed* (Continuum, 2008), and *Existentialism: All that Matters* (Hodder-Stoughton, 2015).

Rebekah Cochran is a Law Clerk at the Iowa Supreme Court. She completed a J.D. at the University of Iowa.

Miranda Dam is a Law Student in the College of Law at the University of Iowa.

Emerich Daroya is a Postdoctoral Research Fellow at the Dalla Lana School of Public Health, University of Toronto. He works at the intersection of queer-feminist science and technology studies and HIV prevention technologies. His research interests include queer theory, HIV/AIDS, new materialisms, sexuality studies, and race/racism. His work has been published in *Critical Race and Whiteness Studies Journal, First Monday*, and *The Psychic Life of Racism in Gay Communities*, edited by Damian W. Riggs and published by Lexington Books.

Inmaculada de Melo-Martín is a Professor of Medical Ethics at Weill Cornell Medicine–Cornell University. Her research focuses on ethical and epistemic challenges regarding biomedical science and technology. She is the author most recently of *Rethinking Reprogenetics* (Oxford University Press, 2017), and with K. Intemann, *The Fight against Doubt* (Oxford University Press, 2018).

John William Devine is a Lecturer in Sports Ethics and Integrity at Swansea University and the Chair of the British Philosophy of Sport Association. He is the co-author of the *Stanford Encyclopedia of Philosophy* entry on the 'Philosophy of Sport' and he has written on a wide range of philosophical topics in sport, including 'excellence', 'enhancement', and 'leadership'.

Mihailis Diamantis is a Professor of Law at the University of Iowa. His research focuses on corporate crime, law and technology, and legal theory. He is concerned with how emerging technologies and familiar concepts like mens rea shape corporate incentives. He has also written about privacy law and surveillance.

Val Dusek is the Professor Emeritus at the University of New Hampshire. He has written *Philosophy of Technology: An Introduction, Knowledge in Social World: The Path of Steve Fuller's Social Epistemology*, and *The Holistic Inspirations of Physics* and he co-edited *Philosophy of Technology: The Technological Condition, An Anthology, Critiques of Evolutionary Psychology*, and on the philosophies of C. S. Peirce, Imre Lakatos, and Nikolai Bukharin, as well as the biology of Stephen Jay Gould and Richard Lewontin.

Shaun Gallagher, PhD, Hon DPhil., is the Lillian and Morrie Moss Professor of Excellence in Philosophy at the University of Memphis, and a Professorial Fellow at the School of Liberal Arts, University of Wollongong (AU). His areas of research include phenomenology, philosophy of mind, embodied cognition, social cognition, and concepts of self. His recent publications include *Action and Interaction* (Oxford 2020); *Performance/Art: The Venetian Lectures* (Milan 2021); and *The Phenomenological Mind* (Routledge 2021 – 3rd ed.). He is the editor-in-chief of the journal *Phenomenology and the Cognitive Sciences*.

Axel Gelfert is a Professor of Theoretical Philosophy at the Technical University of Berlin. Much of his work focuses on the intersection of social epistemology and philosophy of science and technology. He is the author of *A Critical Introduction to Testimony* (Bloomsbury 2014) and *How to Do Science with Models* (Springer 2016).

Adam Gjesdal is a Visiting Assistant Professor in the Gabelli School of Business, Ethics, and Law at Fordham University. His research interests include social and political philosophy, social contract theory, and philosophy of law.

Fernando Ilharco is an Associate Professor at the Faculty of Human Sciences (FCH) and the Communication and Culture Research Centre at the Catholic University of Portugal. His research interests include (i) the philosophy of communication and information and (ii) communication and leadership.

Lucas D. Introna is a Distinguished Professor of Organization, Work, and Technology and the Centre for Technological Futures at Lancester University. His research interests include sociomateriality, phenomenology of technology, information and power, privacy, surveillance, IT and post-modern ethics, and virtuality.

Christian B. Miller is the A. C. Reid Professor of Philosophy at Wake Forest University. His main research areas are contemporary ethics and philosophy of religion. His books include *The Character Gap: How Good are We?* (2018, Oxford University Press), *Moral Psychology* (2021, Cambridge University Press), and Honesty: *The Philosophy and Psychology of a Neglected Virtue* (2021, Oxford University Press).

Saura Masconale is an Assistant Professor in the Department of Political Economy and Moral Science and the Center for the Philosophy of Freedom at the University of Arizona. Her research addresses a broad range of topics in the domain of law and political economy.

Adam D. Moore is a Professor in the Information School at the University of Washington and examines the ethical, legal, and policy issues surrounding intellectual property, privacy, freedom of speech, accountability, and information control. He is the author of *Intellectual Property and Information Control* (Routledge, 2001) and *Privacy Rights* (Pennsylvania State University Press, 2010).

David R. Morrow is the Director of Research at the Institute for Carbon Removal Law and Policy and the Forum for Climate Engineering Assessment, both at American University. He is also a Research Fellow at the Institute for Philosophy and Public Policy at George Mason University. His research focuses mainly on the ethics and governance of climate change, especially issues related to carbon removal and solar geoengineering. He is the author of numerous articles and books, including *Values in Climate Policy* (2020, Rowman & Littlefield International).

Daniel Moseley is a Research Instructor in the Department of Psychiatry and a Research Assistant Professor in the Department of Social Medicine at the School of Medicine at the University of North Carolina at Chapel Hill. His research interests include Bioethics, Practical Ethics, Moral Psychology, Philosophy of Mind, Political Philosophy, and Philosophy of Law.

Christina Murray is a UNC Consultation-Liaison Fellow in the Department of Psychiatry at the University of North Carolina at Chapel Hill.

Stuart J. Murray is a Professor of Rhetoric and Ethics in the Department of English Language and Literature at Carleton University. He holds appointments in the Department of Health Sciences and the Institute for Comparative Studies in Literature, Art, and Culture. His work considers biopolitical discourses on health, sexuality, and identity. His recent book is titled *The Living from the Dead: Disaffirming Biopolitics* (Penn State University Press, 2022).

Bjørn K. Myskja is a Professor of Ethics and Political Philosophy at the Norwegian University of Science and Technology. His research interests include Kantian ethics, bioethics, ethics of technology and animal ethics. He has published numerous articles within these research areas.

James R. Otteson is the John T. Ryan Jr. Professor of Business Ethics, the Rex and Alice A. Martin Faculty Director of the Notre Dame Deloitte Center for Ethical Leadership, and the Faculty Director of the Business Honors Program in the Mendoza College of Business at Notre Dame. He is the author of numerous books, including *Adam Smith's Marketplace of Life* (Cambridge University Press, 2002), *Actual Ethics* (Cambridge University Press, 2006), *Adam Smith* (Bloomsbury, 2013), *The End of Socialism* (Cambridge University Press, 2014), *Honorable Business* (Oxford University Press, 2019), and *Seven Deadly Economic Sins* (Cambridge University Press, 2021).

Kate Padgett Walsh is an Associate Professor of Philosophy at Iowa State University. She has research interests in ethics, metaethics, Hegel's ethics, and the ethics of debt.

Joseph C. Pitt is the Professor Emeritus of Philosophy at Virginia Tech. His research interests include philosophy of science, philosophy of technology, and pragmatism. His books include *Doing Philosophy of Technology: Essays in a Pragmatist Spirit* (Springer, 2011) and *Heraclitus Redux: Technological Infrastructures and Scientific Change* (Rowman & Littlefield, 2020).

Megan Rim is a PhD Candidate in Digital Studies in the Department of American Culture at the University of Michigan. Her research interests include race and digital technologies, algorithmic bias, infrastructure, and surveillance. Her current project focuses on the ways that face recognition technologies operate as part of sociotechnical landscapes and reinvigorate racist systems, infrastructures, and logics.

Megan Rim is a PhD Candidate in Digital Studies in the Department of American Culture at the University of Michigan. Her research interests include race and digital technologies, algorithmic bias, infrastructure, and surveillance. Her current project focuses on the ways that face recognition technologies operate as part of sociotechnical landscapes and reinvigorate racist systems, infrastructures, and logics.

Gregory J. Robson is an Assistant Professor of Philosophy at Iowa State University and a Visiting Assistant Research Professor in the Mendoza College of Business at the University of Notre Dame. His research focuses on ethics (including business and technology ethics) and social and political philosophy.

David C. Rose is a Professor of Economics at the University of Missouri–St. Louis and a Senior Fellow at Common Sense Society. He is also a member of the US Commission on Civil Rights. His research interests include behavioral economics, political economy, and organization theory. He is author of *The Moral Foundation of Economic Behavior* (Oxford University Press, 2011) and *Why Culture Matters Most* (Oxford University Press, 2019).

Daniel C. Russell is a Professor in the Department of Philosophy at the University of Arizona. His research focuses on human flourishing: what it is to live well (human well-being), how people do better at living their lives (virtue and moral development), and what people in free societies might aspire to become (social institutions and political economy). He is the author of *Owning Yourself* (forthcoming), *Happiness for Humans* (2013), *Practical Intelligence and the Virtues* (2009), *Plato on Pleasure and the Good Life* (2005), and the editor of *The Cambridge Companion to Virtue Ethics* (2013).

Simone M. Sepe is the Chester H. Smith Professor and Professor of Law and Finance at the University of Arizona. His research interests include business organizations, corporate finance, contract theory, law and economics, law and philosophy, and empirical methods.

Tony Smith is a Professor of Philosophy and Political Science (emeritus) at Iowa State University. His main areas of interest are Marxism, normative social philosophy, and the philosophy of technology. His books include *Technology and Capitalism in the Age of Lean Production* (SUNY Press 2000) and *Beyond Liberal Egalitarianism: Marx and Normative Social Theory in the Twenty-First Century* (Brill 2017).

Şerife Tekin is an Associate Professor of Philosophy and the Director of the Medical Humanities Program at the University of Texas at San Antonio. Her work in philosophy of psychiatry takes place at the intersection of feminist philosophy of science, philosophy of mind, bioethics, and neuroethics.

Jonathan Y. Tsou is a Professor of Philosophy and The Marvin and Kathleen Stone Distinguished Professor of Humanities in Medicine and Science at the University of Texas at Dallas. He has teaching and research interests in philosophy of science, philosophy of technology, and philosophy of psychiatry. He is the author of *Philosophy of Psychiatry* (Cambridge University Press, 2021) and co-editor of *Objectivity in Science: New Perspectives from Science and Technology Studies* (Springer, 2015).

Peter-Paul Verbeek is the Rector Magnificus and Professor of Philosophy and Ethics of Science and Technology in a Changing World at the University of Amsterdam. His research focuses on the relations between humans and technologies and aims to contribute to philosophical theory, ethical reflection, and responsible practices of design and innovation. He is currently one of the six Principle Investigators of a 10-year, multi-university research program on the Ethics of Socially Disruptive Technologies.

Mark A. Walker is a Professor in the Philosophy Department at New Mexico State University where he occupies the Richard L. Hedden Endowed Chair in Advanced Philosophical Studies. His current primary research interests are in epistemology and in ethical issues arising out of emerging technologies, e.g., genetic engineering, advanced pharmacology, artificial intelligence research, and nanotechnology. His published work includes *Happy-People-Pills for All* (Blackwell) and *Free Money for All: A Basic Income Guarantee Solution for the Twenty-First Century* (Palgrave).

Ava Thomas Wright is an Assistant Professor of Philosophy at Cal Poly San Luis Obispo. Wright's main areas of research are in AI Ethics, Ethics, Political Philosophy, and Philosophy of Law, with an emphasis on Kantian moral theory. Some of Wright's recent publications can be found in *Philosopher's Imprint, Kant-Studien,* and the anthology, *Kant and Artificial Intelligence.*

Sally Wyatt is a Professor of Digital Cultures at Maastricht University in the Netherlands. For many years, her work has focused on various social and ethical issues arising from the development and use of digital technologies, particularly in healthcare. Her books include *CyberGenetics. Health Genetics and New Media* (co-authored with Anna Harris and Susan Kelly, Routledge, 2016) and *Virtual Knowledge. Experimenting in the Humanities and the Social Sciences* (co-edited with Paul Wouters, Anne Beaulieu and Andrea Scharnhorst, The MIT Press, 2013).

Qin Zhu is an Associate Professor in the Department of Engineering Education and Affiliate Faculty in the Department of Science, Technology & Society and the Center for Human-Computer Interaction at Virginia Tech. His research interests include engineering ethics, global and international engineering education, engineering cultures, and the ethics of human-robot interaction and artificial intelligence.

Introduction

Gregory J. Robson & Jonathan Y. Tsou

If there is one factor that most characterizes today's changing world, it is perhaps the rise of technology made possible by the growth of scientific knowledge within commercial society. Of course, stunning technological change is nothing new. Computers, artificial intelligence, medical advances, and other innovations are improving human lives today much as anesthesia, cars, and plastics did not so long ago. We develop technologies. Innovations are replicated and spread. Then, we take them for granted like the air we breathe. It is thanks to technological innovation that we have not only the internet but also chairs, pianos, and even indoor plumbing!

We can glimpse the value of various technologies by asking how things would differ in their absence. How would your life change if, awakening one morning, you learned that the internet no longer exists and never will again? Or that there are now no pipes carrying clean drinking water at your convenience? No indoor heating and air conditioning? No mobile phones? No anesthesia for surgery? No cars and planes but only horses and wagons for travel?

Or, imagine your life without computers. How would your daily life change? How would your studies or work differ? With whom would you cease communicating? How would your modes of entertainment alter?

In countless ways, technologies increase the potential for valuable human cooperation. Sadly, though, it is also because of technological innovation that gas chambers operated in Auschwitz and warlords profit from the sale of illicit weapons and drugs. And even the internet, which is immensely valuable and perhaps most people put to good purposes most of the time, has led to severe addiction, depression, and other problems.

Seen as the application of science in the creation of human artifacts, technology interfaces with countless aspects of our individual and social lives, propelling us forward while simultaneously creating special ethical challenges. The ways in which technologies enhance or undermine our capacity to lead good lives are so numerous and varied that no single book can delineate them all. We can, however, identify pivotal ethical questions around our use of technology. We can examine these questions rigorously. And we can thereby come to better understand the promises and perils of technology. This is the central task of *Technology Ethics*.

★ ★ ★

Despite the clear importance of technology ethics for contemporary individuals and societies, many books written in the area are either too narrowly focused for university courses, too generic or unfocused to assist researchers, or too dry to excite the interest of university students. Other books lack consideration of key areas (e.g., business and medicine) that would draw a wide readership. Still others are, simply put, too academic. The language and

DOI: 10.4324/9781003189466-1

analysis employed can be convoluted, imposing a high cost in terms of readers' time and attention. The co-editors of this volume have sought to ensure both that the topics selected are diverse and interesting and that the chapters are written in accessible writing styles that engage a broad audience of readers. This makes for easy citation by researchers and easy learning by students. We have striven to make this anthology thought-provoking, relevant to leading ethical issues today, and accessible. We have aimed to provide a diverse range of arguments and perspectives, which give researchers and teachers a broad range of materials with which to engage critically. And we have endeavored to give ample attention to business ethics, a vital subject often not discussed by technology ethicists.

The ethics of technology is a burgeoning area, but few if any anthologies include multi-disciplinary contributions from leading scholars in both (1) "analytic" and "continental" philosophy and (2) across several hot-button topics of interest. *Technology Ethics* is an anthology of new work to fill this gap. The book covers five main areas. Part I, "Perspectives on Technology and Its Value," addresses topics such as whether technology is value-neutral or value-laden, the relationship between science and technology, and debates over technological determinism. Part II, "Technology and the Good Life," covers normative ethical theories (e.g., Aristotelianism, Confucianism, and Kantianism) and the value and roles of technology in lives well-lived. The essays investigate specific ethical theories and technological topics with reference to influential authors and leading research. Part III, "Computer and Information Technology," addresses issues at the intersection of ethics and computing, such as privacy, internet ethics, and robot ethics. Part IV, "Technology and Business," covers the value and roles of technology in firms and in the economy overall, with discussions of key ethical issues at the intersection of technology, business, and economics. Part V, "Biotechnologies and the Ethics of Enhancement," explores the value or disvalue of technology regarding the human body, addressing issues such as genetic enhancement and performance enhancement in sports.

In this anthology, we have also sought to include a fair amount of discussion on the pressing issues of free speech and productive online discourse. For example, Axel Gelfert's chapter addresses the problem of fake news, its negative societal consequences, and how it might be regulated. And Gregory Robson's essay discusses how social media users avoid gaining exposure to alternative perspectives, rendering online moral, social, and political discourse incomplete or rife with bias. Robson details steps that social media firms and users can take to make online discourse more constructive.

We have also aimed to explore the effects of technology on the social tension between dynamism and stability. A key form of this tension is the conflict between preserving traditional modes of technology (hence, promoting social stability) and trying to improve society with technology (hence, promoting social change and potential instability). Several chapters explore this theme. One example is consider Ava Thomas Wright's chapter on Kantian ethical approaches to autonomous vehicles. Wright highlights ethical complexities in expanding the option set for human modes of travel and association while also dynamically changing those modes, possibly in destabilizing ways. Moreover, Şerife Tekin's chapter on artificial intelligence critically examines the use of smartphone applications (psychotherapeutic chatbots), which are intended to help individuals with mental health issues. Tekin's chapter addresses whether such technologies facilitate or undermine more traditional mental health interventions (e.g., therapy), including the stability of social values. Christian B. Miller's chapter investigates how our use of technology can aid or undermine our cultivation of the virtue of honesty, an important virtue for the promotion of stable and healthy online interactions. And, as a final example, James R. Otteson's essay considers the impacts of digital technology on the formation of moral sentiments. Looking to insights from the philosopher and economist Adam Smith, Otteson examines how our use of social media affects our capacity to lead happy and fulfilling lives in the digital age.

We hope this book will be judged to meet two particular goals. First, we have sought to provide for *students* a set of illuminating essays that will expand and deepen their engagement with key issues in technology ethics. Second, we have endeavored to provide for *instructors* and *researchers* an easy-to-reference guide to existing literature and viewpoints—including many arguments developed specifically for this book. This guide is the culmination of considerable reflection by both rising and distinguished scholars.

The authors gratefully acknowledge the generous support of The John Templeton Foundation, including funding through the Key Challenges Project. We also wish to thank the Institute for Humane Studies for assistance with the funding process and for reviewing much of the manuscript. The editors particularly thank Jonathan Fortier, Maria Rogacheva, and Gregory Wolcott. We also owe thanks to Gavin Oliver, Jayant Shah, and Caroline Stark for their valuable help in reviewing the chapters. We are grateful, as well, to the contributors for their illuminating essays. Finally, we thank our students, with whom we have had the privilege of exploring fascinating and important questions in technology ethics.

Part I

Perspectives on Technology and Its Value

Introduction

Philosophers of technology address questions concerning the nature of technology and its impact on society. What is technology? What is the relationship between technology and science? Is technology applied science? Is technology value–neutral or value–laden? Does technology determine social structures and events?

Instrumentalists argue that technology is a *value-free* tool that can and should be used to achieve various human goals (e.g., facilitating human needs and comforts). Negative uses of technology in society (e.g., the use of weapons to harm people) are due to people misusing technology, rather than the nature of the technology itself. Others argue that technologies (e.g., books and guns) are *value-laden* insofar as they inherently embody certain values that can change persons and societies. The argument that technology is value-laden is closely related to the thesis of technological determinism: technology determines, or causes changes to, society. On this view, the presence of certain technologies, and the values that they implicitly promote, changes society (e.g., the presence of books makes society more concerned with recording information). While instrumentalists argue that society controls technology, technological determinists argue that technology controls society. Martin Heidegger, an important technological determinist, argues that modern technology (i.e., technology since the industrial revolution) has changed society in a specific way: it has driven society to *perceive nature as a resource to be used and exploited*. This mode of perception ('challenging') associated with the modern technological age is related to the 'essence' of modern technology ('enframing'): the human desire to control nature.

The chapters in this part examine the nature of technology and its consequences for society. The chapters are written by prominent contributors to the philosophical literature on technology. The chapters represent a wide range of important perspectives (e.g., philosophy of science, science and technology studies, postphenomenology, and philosophy of mind) on technology.

DOI: 10.4324/9781003189466-2

Chapter 1

The Definition of Technology

Val Dusek

Often, people dismiss investigations of definitions. They say this is "mere semantics" and get on with their presentation or discussion. However, "mere semantics" can be important. If two people are discussing a topic and unbeknownst to them have different ideas of what the topic whose name they share, this can derail the argument or discussion. This is most frequent with what Walter Gallie calls "essentially contested concepts," such as those of freedom, religion, art, or democracy. However, determining a definition can be important in less obviously contested topics, such as that of technology.

There are several definitions of technology. They have implications concerning treatment of other notions. Some of them have inadequacies as well as virtues.

Guidelines for Definitions

Elementary traditional logic texts (see Copi et al., 2019) give various features of proposed definitions to avoid.

1   Definitions should not be circular. Some examples of circular definitions of technology are:

> ...the branch of knowledge that deals with the creation and use of technical means and their interrelation with life, society, and the environment....

Clearly, defining technology in terms of "technical means" is circular. Which is technological or what is technical must be defined to avoid circularity.

> I think it can be a synonym of State of the Technique too. Which means the level of technique or technology.

Again, either technique of technology must be defined or else this characterization falls into circularity.

2   Definitions should not use figurative, emotive, or metaphorical terminology. Some examples of this are:
    "Technology is a gift of God." Freeman Dyson.
    A somewhat different emotive characterization is: "Crap is the essence of innovation and technological advancement. Michael Scott Galegos, "The Pompous Propensity of Poop." Clearly, a more detailed characterization is needed for this to be a rigorous definition.
    Other metaphorical definitions, such as "Technology is the death of nature," or "technology is the opiate of the technorati," don't tell us what technology is but point to some effect of it in a metaphor.

DOI: 10.4324/9781003189466-3

3   Definitions should not be negative. If technology is defined as not art, not religion, not science, or *not* whatever, we aren't told what technology *is*.

4   Definitions should not be too broad or too narrow.

An example of a very narrow definition is implicitly when many people speak of "technology" today meaning electronic or computer technology. "Educational technology" usually means computers or other electronic devices. Yet, an old-fashioned blackboard is also technology.

The commonplace button and buttonhole, seemingly so obvious, was innovative technology. In prehistoric and ancient times, the button, to the early wearer of animal skins or even the early Roman toga wearer, would have been a highly non-intuitive idea whose medieval creator was an imaginative technological inventor.

Below, we shall see several major attempts at general definitions or characterization of technology (as applied science, as hardware and machinery, or as rules of behavior) that are too narrow. We then look at another major, much more complete and adequate definition of technology. This one can be overextended so as not to distinguish technology from any other branch of human culture. The anthropologist Ian Jarvie (1966) ends up defining technology as all of culture, which fails to distinguish technological devices from artworks or to distinguish technological behavior from any other kind of human behavior.

Different Philosophical Approaches Support Different Kinds of Definitions

1   Real Definitions: The so-called conceptual realists, such as the ancient Greek philosophers, Socrates, Plato, and Aristotle, as well as more modern so-called "Platonists" hold that definitions capture the real nature of things. Socrates questioned people in an apparent quest of finding the true definitions of bravery, beauty, and justice. He, his major followers, and other conceptual realists claimed that objects have real natures or essences and that a "real definition" can fully describe that essence of a thing.

2   Nominal Definitions: Many average people today, as well as many eighteenth-century British philosophers, and later groups such as twentieth-century logical positivist philosophers of science, have held that definitions are initially arbitrary. These are also called stipulative or conventional definitions. They are simply laid down by the definer as anything she pleases. In this view, objects have no real natures or essences. Their qualities are simply what the definer defines them to be.

During the Middle Ages 900 years ago, realists and nominalist philosophers argued and disputed, defending one or another of these kinds of definitions. This dispute has continued in various forms and in various fields until today.

Several major philosophers of technology of the mid-twentieth century, such as Jacques Ellul, whose other views we shall later examine, have claimed that there is an essence or real nature of technology. Many more recent philosophers of technology, in the so-called "empirical turn" in philosophy of technology in Holland and the USA, have claimed that we should focus on describing various particular technologies and not attempt to characterize technology as such. "Postmodernist" philosophers of technology, influenced by recent French thought, have likewise denied that technology is a single sort of thing and has emphasized the diversity and plurality of technologies, arguing that each technology has many different purposes and interpretations.

In addition to both real and nominal definitions, there are "lexical" and "precising" definitions.

Lexical definitions of a word are supposed to simply describe what people mean when they utter a word. Often, this is based on the dictionary definition. However, dictionaries often claim to be giving the "correct" or "proper" meaning of a word. A purely descriptive definition would not attempt to give the "correct" definition, often based on literary or upper-class usage of the word. A purely descriptive definition would take into account all the various meanings of the word as used by various geographical and social groups. Most contemporary linguists deny that there is any "correct" or "proper" usage and claim that there are simply different regional or cultural usages. This view vastly complicates any attempt to give a simple lexical definition and would necessitate an extensive statistical survey, which undermines the apparent simplicity and obviousness of lexical definitions if one does not simply stick to the dictionary.

A kind of compromise between the real, the nominal, and the lexical definition is the "precising definition."

Precising definitions begins with a basic lexical definition of some sort, but it cleans up vague boundaries of the applications of a word. To some extent, this cleanup is an arbitrary construction of the definer, but its purpose is to develop a clear and useable definition. The precising definition is only partially arbitrary in that it does start with the commonest and core meaning of the word but sharpens the edges of its range of application for the purpose of making a more rigorous definition for use in further inquiry.

One problem of both the nominal or stipulative as well as the precising definition is that the speaker in the course of discussion or debate and the writer in the course of a long narration may start with the nominal, stipulated, or precising version of the definition, but later unknowingly slips back into the common sense meaning with all its vagueness and ambiguity. This is a difficulty against which the user of a supposedly real, a nominal, precising definition must carefully guard.

Technology as Applied Science

One common definition of technology is that it is applied science. Although much contemporary technology, such as electronics and computer technology, *is* applied science, there are several reasons to reject that definition as a definition of all technology. One reason is that technology in the form of simple tools long predates science. The stone axes and baskets of prehistoric humans were certainly technology, but in all but the most general and overly broad definitions of science these came before science. Only if one defines science as any searching behavior or trial and error behavior can prehistoric humans be said to engage in science. If science is defined as the combination of experimental method with the formulation of laws as it is often defined, then science began no earlier than the sixteenth or, most likely, the early seventeenth century with the "scientific revolution" of Galileo and others. Even if one includes ancient Greek science, Chinese and East Indian science, this would not be broad enough to encompass prehistoric technology. Even if, further, one includes the so-called "ethnosciences" which do include knowledge of plants and animals, early treatments for illnesses, and knowledge of the arrangement of the stars, most of the technological activities, such as cooking, hunting, and building shelters, were not guided by the culture's ethnoscience and the "theories" which with indigenous peoples accompany these practical activities were often mythical stories.

Further, even in more recent technology after the scientific revolution, many technological inventions were not guided by the science of the day. Most of the mechanical inventions that made the Industrial Revolution were not guided by the physics of Newton but were created by tinkerers largely ignorant of such physics. Sometimes, the most advanced mathematical physicists' works on practical technology were not as useful as much simpler treatments.

For instance, Leonard Euler, one of the greatest mathematicians of all time, an important innovator in advanced theoretical mechanics, and major contributor to hydrodynamics in the eighteenth century, produced a two-volume 900-page advanced mathematical work giving few practical applications. It found little practical use for well over a century. In the 1800s, the steam engine was not based on the consolidated physics of the day. Indeed, it has often been said that thermodynamics owes much more to the steam engine than the steam engine owes to thermodynamics. The Carnot Cycle was based on observations concerning the already invented steam engine rather than the other way around.

Even in contemporary science, now extensively based on theoretical science, many technological innovations are based on accidental discoveries. This is particularly true in the chemical and biological sciences. In chemistry, there are numerous innovations that arose by accident. Scotch Guard that protects upholstery was discovered when a chemist Patsy Sherman spilled a chemical on her sneakers and found that they were protected from grime. "Smart dust," programmable silicon particles now used in pollution detections and elsewhere, was discovered by Jamie Link when a computer chip of hers exploded. The discovery of vulcanized rubber by Charles Goodyear and the discovery by Spencer Silver and Art Fry of the Post-it note's weak but reusable glue are among the very many accidental chemical discoveries. In biology, James Olds' award-winning work on the pleasure center of the brain began with a mistaken insertion of an electrical wire that was meant for another location into the part of the brain that turned out to be the pleasure center. Viagra was originally developed as a medicine for heart conditions, when an unexpected side effect was observed and exploited.

Certainly, in contemporary science, there must be not only the recognition of the practical significance of such "accidents" but much further work on perfecting the discovery and producing the result on a large scale. Nevertheless, the process in these cases depended on an accident for its start, not on a prior theoretical description.

Technology as Hardware

Another definition of technology is in terms of hardware. Often, works or slide shows with a focus on technology use images of machinery, oil refineries, and such. Certainly, the Industrial Revolution was characterized by mechanical inventions such as the power loom and the steam engine.

Hardware or machines are more than physical objects. Many of the vibrations of a washing machine or a railroad train are just as much physical phenomena as the circular motion of the washer's water or the rotation of the train's wheels, but in terms of technology, they are simply extraneous imperfections which undermine the efficiency of the machine.

One problem with the hardware definition of technology is that physical hardware is not sufficient for there to be technology. Without knowledge of what the technology is and how to use it, the technology as technology is a meaningless object. Many science fiction scenarios of a world after a devastating nuclear war include the presence of what to us are huge technological devices, but to the now primitive and ignorant post-apocalyptic inhabitants are simply mysterious monuments or objects of worship. Members of the cargo cults in the Pacific during World War II and after saw military airplanes overhead as magical birds that dropped goods for the island inhabitants' reward and enjoyment.

It is not just members of cargo cults that see what we think of as technological devices as something other than technology. The 1984–1985 "Primitive and Modern Art" exhibit at the Museum of Modern Art in New York presented artifacts of African and Pacific Island societies as purely aesthetic objects that were displayed alongside works of modern art that had superficial geometrical resemblance to the indigenous works. There were no dates or context provided for the works. Critics emphasized that the exhibit stripped the works of historical and social contexts as well as original function. It is likely that the aesthetic and technological functions of many of the works were fused, but the viewers saw simply shapes and colors, not the practical uses of many of the artifacts on display. The viewers of these "artworks" were as oblivious to the real practical functions and operations as the objects as were the cargo cult members of World War II warplanes overhead.

We shall see the inclusion of the human operators and maintainers of technology as well as the technological hardware in the systems definition of technology to be discussed later.

A different criticism of the hardware definition of technology is by those who claim technology does not need tools, machines, or hardware at all. One example of this view-point is given by the historian of architecture and technology Lewis Mumford (1974) as the "megamachine." Mumford means by this the huge assemblies of human workers that built the gigantic monumental structures of archaic societies, such as Stonehenge, the Egyptian and Central American pyramids, or the Great Wall of China or the giant statues of Easter Island. Mumford claims that the real "machine" here is the population of workers who are organized and coordinated for the building task. Mumford exaggerates in suggesting that this "megmachine" consists solely of human bodies. Baskets for carrying dirt, ropes and rollers for dragging huge stone blocks, as well as other simple tools were involved. Nevertheless, it is true that the most complex organization in these early, massive construction projects was the command and deployment of human laborers.

Another phenomenon claimed to be technology without hardware is the behavioral "engineering" by the psychologist B. F. Skinner. Skinner during his later career called himself an engineer rather than a scientist. He was interested in changing and manipulating behavior rather than simply neutrally observing it. Skinner did use hardware such as boxes and food pellet dispensing devices. However, behavioral engineering can be performed simply by speech or body language. Certainly, propaganda especially has used the latest technological devices from printed pamphlets and broadsides through Hitler's pioneering use of movies and the airplane, to contemporary television and the internet, but propaganda that channels and manipulates human behavior was done in earlier times simply by public speeches without any technology.

More recently, software in the form of computer programs has replaced hardware in the form of machinery that has become a central image and focus of thought about technology. Computer programs can be embodied in a variety of physical devices. Charles Babbage in the early nineteenth century had built the architecture of a modern computer but used mechanical gears and giant wooden punch cards. Later, there were early mainframe computers with large role tapes and paper punch cards before modern silicon chip personal computers arrived. Yet, the programs themselves are purely formal, not physical, entities allowing numerous physical embodiments. Just as a musical piece can be embodied in the staffs of printed notes, older vinyl disks and tape recordings, CDs, or digital instructions for a computer, so computers themselves can be differently embodied. This aspect of technology can be appealed to by advocates of the rules definition of technology, to which we shall turn.

Technology as Rules: "Technique"

Another definition of technology is as a certain kind of rules of activity. The French writer Jacques Ellul (1964) in his *The Technological Society* is the major theorist of this approach to characterizing technology. Ellul speaks of "technique" not technology. He lists features of technique that make efficiency central: rationality, artificiality, automatism, rationality, artificiality, automatism of technical choice, self-augmentation, monism, universalism, and autonomy. He sees technique as a self-generating entity that grows to take over all aspects of human life. Rather than technology being something humans use for their own purposes, Ellul sees humans having to adapt to technology. For Ellul and later analysts such as Langdon Winner (1977), in a sense technology now uses humans.

Means-end activity is the core of technology. Efficiency of means is the primary value in the technological society. Other values, aesthetics, ethics, and religion are displaced by the emphasis on efficiency.

The early twentieth-century German sociologist Max Weber ([1930] 1958) can also be said to depict how means-end behavior has come to dominate society. Weber called this not "technique" as in Ellul but "rationalization." As society develops, more and more aspects of social life become systematized in terms of systems of rules. Weber examined this at length in world religions as well as in economics, law, and even music. Surprisingly, Weber's extensive surveys of this process hardly discuss science and technology, but his rationalization story applies even more thoroughly to science and technology.

The rules definition of technology gains support from the burgeoning importance of "software," computer programs in contrast to hardware. As noted, programs themselves are non-physical and can be implemented in a variety of mechanisms.

The rules definition has the difficulty of being both too narrow and too wide. It is too narrow in downplaying the physical embodiments of technology, the hardware. It is in danger of becoming too wide in that many kinds of rule-governed behavior can then be included in technology. Psychological self-help books with rules for improving one's emotions or coping will count as technology. Guides for reading body language or guides to sexual technique can be included as technologies. Ellul wrote extensively on propaganda as a form of technology. However, Ellul can retort that indeed everything in life in the technological society during recent decades has, indeed, become a form of technology.

Technology as a System

A more inclusive definition of technology than either applied science, hardware, or means-end rules is technology as a system. A technological system includes not only scientific knowledge, machinery, and rules but also non-human living things, as well as human inventors, operators, and maintainers of the hardware and living things. A number of writers have settled on the systems definition.

A number of writers of texts on philosophy of technology such as Bernard Gendron (1977) and Arnold Pacey (1985) have used slightly different versions of the system characterization. These various versions of the systems definition can be combined as: "the application of scientific and other knowledge to practical tasks by ordered systems that involve people and organizations, production actions and skill, living organisms and machines." Thus, the systems definition of technology includes applied science, hardware, and rules, combining the previous definitions.

The systems definition has a number of advantages in dealing with various disputes in the philosophy of technology. One of these is the debate concerning the neutrality versus biased or "valenced" nature of technology. Many say technology in itself is neutral. "Guns don't kill people. People kill people" is a common slogan of this approach. It is claimed, and often is the case, that any technology can be used for good or for harm. The proponents of the view that many technologies are not neutral note that depending on the particular technology, the easiest or most effective use may be for harm or for good. Atom bombs are most easily and efficiently used for destruction and harm. The "father of the H-bomb" Edward

Teller once tried to use nuclear bombs for mining or releasing gases from the earth, but the long-lasting radiation produced totally undermined this use. Someone once satirized the neutrality view of the "Guns don't kill people...." slogan with "WWII gas ovens don't kill people. People kill people."

With the machine or tool definition of technology, it is easier to claim that that technology is totally neutral. The user is outside the technology and uses it for whatever purpose she wishes.

However, in the system approach to technology, the "user" is inside the technology as a buyer consuming advertising, as a worker enmeshed in the technological system, and so forth. The technological system can use the "user" so to speak, rather than the other way around. Designers, owners, administrators, advertisers, and propagandists channel the technology in one direction rather than another, and workers, consumers, and citizens are themselves channeled in one direction or another. This thesis, called technological determinism or "autonomous technology," is most easily defended from the technological system approach, though as we have seen, the rules approach also held to this.

In recent decades, the systems definition has been used by the so-called social constructionists and the so-called postmodernist philosophers of technology. The social constructionist emphasizes the extent to which the development of knowledge and ideas at the basis of a technology and the building of the hardware of the technology ("facts" and "artifacts") are both made up or constructed. This construction is not the result of a single genius or single inventor but is produced by a social process involving many people over both space and time.

Postmodernist philosophers of technology emphasize the lack of a single nature or essence of technology and the diversity or pluralism of kinds of technology, uses of technology, and groups that interact with and use the technology, who may assign very different meanings of and uses of the technology. The many groups that the systems definition includes in the technology itself, above and beyond the hardware and non-human organisms involved, fit well with the systems definition.

A further extension of the postmodernist use of the systems definition is the "actor network theory" or ANT of Bruno Latour (2007) and his followers. This approach describes all the actors and entities involved in the invention, use, consumption, and interpretation of the technology and all of the intricate web of their interactions. The most controversial part of ANT is that non-human animal and machines or other devices are claimed to be "actants" just as much as the humans involved. Latour included even such apparently passive physical objects as doorstops and speedbumps among his "actants." This addition of non-human actors in the network is a part at which even many postmodernists who accept the network approach balk.

The systems definition has become the "consensus definition" of technology for most contemporary philosophers of technology.

References

Copi, Irving, Carl Cohen, and Victor Rodych. 2019. *Beginning Logic.* 15th ed. New York: Routledge.
Ellul, Jacques. 1964. *The Technological Society,* Translated by John Wilkinson. New York: Knopf.
Gendron, Bernard. 1977. *Technology and the Human Condition.* New York: St. Martin's Press.
Jarvie, Ian C. 1966. "The Social Character of Technological Problems: Comments on Skolimowski's Paper." *Technology and Culture.* 7(3): 384–390.
Latour, Bruno. 2007. *Reassembling the Social: An Introduction to Actor Network Theory.* Oxford: Oxford University Press.

Mumford, Lewis. 1974. *The Myth of the Machine: Vol. 1, The Pentagon of Power.* New York: Harcourt, Brace Jovanovich.

Pacey, Arnold. 1985. *The Culture of Technology.* Cambridge: MIT Press.

Weber, Max. (1930) 1958. *The Protestant Ethic and the Spirit of Capitalism.* Translated by Talcott Parsons. New York: Scribner's.

Winner, Langdon. 1977. *Autonomous Technology: Techniques Out of Control as a Theme in Political Thought.* Cambridge MA: MIT Press.

Chapter 2

Value-Free Technology?

Joseph C. Pitt

There has been a long-standing debate over whether or not technology is value-free. There are two sides to the debate. One side argues that technology is embedded in some way with values. The other side claims that technology is value-free. Part of the reason for the duration of the debate has to do with the way the question was formulated. Asking whether technology is value-free assumes that there is something out there called "technology." When I look around, I see many technologies from pencils to computers to automobiles to refrigerators to lawn mowers, etc. But nowhere can I find Technology *simpliciter*. This situation is similar to the one facing science. We are told that science shows us this, or that science has discovered that. But when we look for Science, we find biology, physics, astronomy, chemistry, microbiology, etc. – but no Science *simpliciter*.

At best, we might want to call Technology and Science names of categories of things. But when you ask for the criteria by which we put something in one of those categories, we are lost. For example, it has often been said that something qualifies as a science because it uses the scientific method. This is sort of what happens in, for example, the introduction to high school biology textbooks. "Biology is a science because it uses the scientific method. The scientific method consists of five steps:

1   Formulate a hypothesis
2   Conduct experiments
3   Make observations
4   Test the results of your experiments
5   Formulate conclusions."

The order in which these five steps are listed varies, but that is the basic idea. The problem is that it really tells us very little. And, among other things, it completely ignores the role of theory. You don't just form a hypothesis – Scientists use theories to guide them in their explorations of the universe – theories give them the intellectual equipment they need to undertake their explorations – vocabulary, ideas about unobservable entities and how things are related, etc.

When it comes to Technology, there is no appeal to a technological method. Sometimes, technology is said simply to mean tools.[1] But what counts as a tool? A hammer seems obvious. But what about an educational system? In *Thinking About Technology* (Pitt, 2000), I attempted to offer a definition: *Technology is humanity at work* (p. 11). I also immediately noted that this definition was much too broad and that using it forces us to look at specific activities and specific technologies, which, as it turns out, is a good thing.

But back to technology – what is it? In *Heraclitus Redux* (Pitt, 2020), I gave up trying to find that perfect definition and, instead, turned my attention to the concept of a technological infrastructure. A technological infrastructure is that set of interrelated things (taken broadly) we

DOI: 10.4324/9781003189466-4

need in order to do the work we want to do. I have often used the example of doing science. The main theme of *Heraclitus Redux* is that in many cases scientific theory change is forced by the development of technological innovations. Get a new instrument that shows you something you couldn't see before and which current theories can't explain, you need a new theory. But the story is more complicated than that. For, at least in the contemporary world, you can't do science sitting alone in an empty room. You need a lab, and that means lots of toys, various instruments, venting for chemistry labs, computers, assistants, and lots of money, which means writing grants to be submitted to granting agencies, which are an integral part of the support system of science. Furthermore, the cost of the building in which your lab is housed is a lot more than an ordinary classroom building, for it needs to be able to handle all this equipment. This is what I mean by a *technological infrastructure* – what needs to be in place in order for us to do what we want to do. If you bring in new instruments, you will need new equipment to support them. This forces you to shift stuff around and restructure the support system. Here, we have one example of change – but let's look further at a very simple component of a technological infrastructure for science. To run your lab, you need graduate students – they come and go, and when new ones appear, things get done differently.

Now, if we concentrate on technological infrastructures, the question of the value-ladenness of technology takes on a very different color. The original formulation of the problem essentially wanted to know if we could say of technology that it was good or bad. The initial move was to claim that a technology was one or the other because it had certain values embedded in it. But technologies rarely, if ever, wear their value, assuming they have one, on their sleeves. A hammer is a good hammer if you can use it to drive nails. It is a bad hammer if you use it to injure someone. But notice, here it is really not the hammer that is good or bad – it is the person using the hammer. If a person does not know how to use a hammer, it is not the hammer's fault if the nails go all over the place. Ok – what about an educational system? We need to educate the young so they can get jobs, support themselves, help build the economy, etc. Take the same educational system and consider two different results. In the one case, our young people emerge ready to become productive members of society. In the other, they emerge ready to follow the orders of their fascist leaders. It is the same system – just used in different ways. It might be objected that the two systems could not be the same because they would vary in the details, such as which textbooks to use.[2] That is correct. But the details such as choice of texts are a function of the person using the system – i.e., the teacher.

The bottom line here is that those who insist on claiming that Technology has values are missing the point. It is not Technology that has the values; it is the people using the technologies who have values. An atomic bomb is not inherently evil. It is the use to which it is put that produces evil or good results. Used to destroy a city – it is evil. Used to facilitate mining – it can be seen as good. In response, it can be argued that if someone built an atomic bomb for the express purpose of destroying a city in wartime, the bomb carries both intent and the values of the maker with it. Ok – show me the intent and values of the maker *in* the bomb. What do they look like? How are they manifested?

As it happens, technologies and technological infrastructures can be used for a variety of purposes. Even if a technology such as the atomic bomb was designed and built for a specific purpose, it doesn't follow that it can't be used for something else. The technologies behind the bomb made atomic power plants possible and are being explored to power inter-galactic space travel. Even if the person or group who built the bomb were specifically guided by a deep-seated hatred of an enemy and wished to obliterate them, that does not make the bomb itself evil – but those who built it may have been.

I want to suggest that values are the sorts of things that people have – more to the point, the values we manifest determine the type of people we are. Things, simple or complicated, do not manifest values. This issue is currently under discussion in the world of machine learning where, it has been noted, the facial recognition programs embody the values and prejudices of their programmers. One of the first pieces of evidence of this was the discovery that facial recognition programs created by White programmers had a hard time identifying Black individuals. Correcting for programmers' biases takes a lot of careful work. And those biases must be detected if we don't want them further manifested when these programs become self-programming.

What about non-material technologies such as language?[3] It strikes me that the way we use language says a lot about us, not the language. We may claim that certain words or phrases are not to be used *because* they express certain values we deem unacceptable, such as the N word. I would claim that the way we speak manifests our values in the most overt fashion. How we talk about the world and other people says a lot about us because we expose our values when we use language.

The fact that our technologies manifest the biases of their makers does not mean that those technologies themselves *have* those biases. I frankly don't even know what it means for a thing to possess a value. If we look again at machine learning, the computers seek out features they are constructed to look for. It is people who build the programs and it is their values and objectives that dictate how they build them. Interestingly, this creates problems for the idea of self-programming machines — how can they create new programs if they have no values — perhaps the values of their original creators determine what programs computers can create.

If we accept the position that it is people who possess values, then we can turn the question away from whether technologies are good or evil and ask the question many in this debate have been avoiding: how do we ensure that the people using the technologies possess the right values, i.e., they are good people or that the results of using the technologies benefit humankind?

Parents have been trying to figure that out since time immemorial. What do you need to do to ensure your children turn into good people? Often, the question is avoided by concentrating on specific actions people undertake. He is a bad person because he killed someone. But what if he killed someone accidentally in order to stop that person from hurting an elderly disabled person? The emphasis on getting individuals to act in certain ways by itself is insufficient. To get people to act in the ways we want them to, to do the right thing, we have to locate doing the right thing in a context that makes doing the right thing more or less obvious.

People cannot live successful lives by themselves. They need the assistance of a lot of other people. They need those people to build and operate the set of technological infrastructures we call society. It seems to me that we spend too much time concentrating on the individual and too little on society. If we start from the simple premise that in order for me to flourish, those around me must flourish, then doing the right thing begins to become obvious. I am doing the right thing when I act to increase the viability of society so that everyone flourishes. Sometimes that may mean I have to make a sacrifice, but if we substitute the ultimate goal, which is for the technological infrastructure in which I live to operate at maximal efficiency, for my personal success, that is doing the right thing. I am suggesting that we spend a lot more time emphasizing the betterment of the whole and deemphasize my personal well-being.

Finally, Andrew Garnar has suggested that technological infrastructures may have values because of the way we put things together in order to facilitate what we can do. Well, two things here. First, some infrastructures develop over time in a somewhat haphazard way. A good example here is the food supply system. We did not intend to develop a large complicated system, including farmers, truckers, food processors, roads, large grocery store chains, clerks, inventory systems, etc. The system we so blithely take for granted today evolved over time and we are now so used to it and how we use it that when there is a breakdown in one section, we all panic. The second type of infrastructure is one that is carefully and deliberately created. A good example of this is the effort to put a man on the moon.[4] The moon project was complicated and detailed and very deliberate. The question was not so much: can we put a person on the moon? As it was: can we put a person on the moon safely and return them to earth safely? The constructure of the infrastructure to bring that about developed in a very different way than the one supporting food delivery.

Back to value-free technology. How we use things has consequences. The only law of technology I have been able to determine is that we cannot predict the consequences of technological development. That is because we are each acting in our individual interests and these most often conflict. But if we see our interest in the context of the best interests of society, we can most probably decrease those conflicts and put our technologies to better use. If we understand that technologies can be used in many ways and there is no inherent value in any of them, only the values we use to advance them, which are our values, then we might free up our technologies to enhance our values and our lives. The bottom line here is that we act based on our values and that we do not all share the same values and that when values conflict, bad things happen. The solution is to learn to identify our values so that we can pinpoint our disagreements and work to resolve them. It is therefore important to see that the values are in us, not in our technologies.

Notes

1 See the work of Emmanuel Mesthene.
2 Thank you Andrew Garnar for this objection.
3 Thank you again, Andrew Garnar.
4 Here, we have an example of how values influence our use of language. Yes, we originally said that we wanted to put a *man* on the moon – but is that the proper way to talk about the objective of the program *today*? Should we not talk about putting a *person* on the moon? But to do that would be to rewrite history. What to do?

References

Pitt, Joseph (2020), *Heraclitus Redux; Technological Infrastructures and Scientific Change*, New York: Rowman and Littlefield, 115 pages.

Pitt, Joseph (2000), *Thinking About Technology; Foundations of the Philosophy of Technology*, New York: Seven Bridges Press, 146 pages.

Chapter 3

The Values Built into Technologies

David Morrow

"A lie can travel halfway around the world," Mark Twain supposedly said, "before the truth gets it boots on." The point is that misinformation spreads more easily and more quickly than the truth.[1] Never have lies traveled faster than in the age of social media, where fake news flourishes as falsehoods leap from one person to the next. These lies can do real damage, too, as evidenced by widespread misinformation about COVID-19 or election fraud.

Social media accelerates the spread of misinformation, but is this a problem with social media itself, or is it just a problem with the way people use it? Is it fair to say that *social media* is bad, at least to some extent, because it accelerates the spread of dangerous misinformation? Or should we insist that the technologies themselves are value-neutral, and that any fault lies with the technologies' users?

Many engineers and scientists, among others, believe that technologies are "value-neutral." There are various ways to understand this claim. Typically, it means something like "a technology is neither good nor bad in itself, even if people use it to do good or bad things."[2]

Many philosophers of technology, however, argue that technologies are not value-neutral; they are value-laden—they have values built into them.[3]

To think carefully about this dispute, we need to get clear about just what we mean when we say that technologies are value-neutral.

I propose that we understand the claim that some particular technology is value-neutral as follows: for a technology to be value-neutral means, roughly, that any bad consequences of using the technology result from blameworthy preferences or ignorance of users and any good consequences result from praiseworthy preferences or happy accidents. (To reiterate, this is not the only way to understand the claim, but of the many things that people can mean by the claim, I think this is one of the most important.) When people say that *technologies* are value-neutral, though, they usually mean that *all* technologies are value-neutral or that technologies are necessarily value-neutral. Putting these ideas together and making them a bit more precise, we have the following thesis:

Value-Neutrality Thesis

All technologies are value-neutral in the sense that any bad consequences of using the technology happen because users have blameworthy preferences with respect to the technology's use, or they use the technology without knowing that it has bad consequences; and any good consequences result from users' praiseworthy preferences with respect to the technology's use or users' ignorance that the technology has good consequences.

In this chapter, I argue that the Value-Neutrality Thesis is false: a non-negligible number of technologies can have bad consequences even if morally decent people use that technology

DOI: 10.4324/9781003189466-5

with full knowledge of the bad consequences of doing so, while other technologies have good consequences even if none of the users have particularly praiseworthy preferences with respect to them. After considering some objections to my main argument, I will briefly explore a number of related questions that arise if we reject the Value-Neutrality Thesis. Can we still blame people for doing bad things with technology? What does the argument imply about how we think about, design, and regulate technologies?

The Main Argument

Here is the gist of my main argument against the Value-Neutrality Thesis:

1   People respond to incentives, in the aggregate and in the long run.
2   Technologies change people's incentives by making it easier, possible, or more appealing to do certain things.
    Therefore,
3   Technologies change people's behavior, on average and in the long run, in particular ways.
4   The behavioral changes that technologies induce can have good or bad consequences.
5   The changes that technologies cause in people's behavior can lead to bad consequences, even without ignorance or blameworthy preferences; or to good consequences, even without ignorance or praiseworthy preferences.
    Therefore,
6   The Value-Neutrality Thesis is false.

Each premise in this argument needs some explanation.

To say that people respond to incentives, in the aggregate and in the long run, is to say that when you make it less difficult, less risky, or more rewarding for people to do something, more people will do that thing or people will do it more often; and conversely, if you make something harder, riskier, or less rewarding, then fewer people will do it or people will do it less often. Not everyone will change their behavior, and people might not change their behavior right away, but looking at a group of people as a whole and giving them enough time to adapt, changing people's incentives will change their behavior.

Some examples will illustrate the idea. Suppose that the instructor of a large class suggests that the students read a specific section from a specific book that is only available in a single library on campus. The section supplements the course material, but nothing in the course depends on completing the reading. Some students may do the extra reading; some will not. Now suppose that the instructor offers extra credit for doing the reading, thereby changing her students' incentive to do the reading. It is very likely that more students will do the reading. Not everyone will do it, and some students might have done it anyway, but on average, students are more likely to do it—or, to put the point differently, more of the students will do it. What if the instructor puts a copy of the reading online, making it easier for the students to do the reading? Presumably, even more students will read it. In each case, changing the students' incentives changes the students' behavior.

This is not a particularly controversial premise, and it would not be difficult to come up with more examples. The idea that people respond to incentives is both commonsense and a bedrock principle of various social sciences—including, most prominently, microeconomics and closely related fields. In fact, it is the cases where people seem *not* to respond to incentives that cry out for explanation. The explanation often turns out to be that we had misunderstood their incentives in the first place. In other cases, the explanation is that people are running up against limits to how well they are able to respond to their incentives, such as limited or inaccurate information or limits to how well they can understand or use the information they have.

The next premise in the argument is that technologies change people's incentives in particular ways by making it easier, possible, or more appealing to do certain things. In a sense, this is just what technologies *are*: ways to do things that humans cannot do (or do as easily) on their own (Kline 1985).[4] This holds not just for sophisticated technologies, like rockets and robots that enable us to explore other planets or apps that let us livestream videos to people all around the globe, but also for very simple technologies, like cups and ramps. Notice, though, that to make something easier or more appealing for someone is a way of changing their incentives: it makes the action less costly or less risky or more rewarding to perform. So, it follows from the very nature of a technology—from *what it is* for something to be a technology—that it changes people's incentives.

Taking the first two premises together, it follows straightforwardly that technologies change people's behavior in particular ways, at least in the aggregate and in the long run. Again, this does not mean that a new technology will *always* change *everybody's* behavior; it means only that introducing new technologies into a *group* of people will change their behavior, *in the aggregate* and *in the long run*. For example, consider the television. Even before streaming services put an endless variety of shows at your fingerprints, television offered people an easy, entertaining way to spend an evening at home; it made it more appealing to stay home by yourself or with your roommates or family. Sociologist Robert Putnam argues that as television became widespread during the twentieth century, more and more people did just that: they stayed home more often than they had before (Putnam 2020). This does not mean, of course, that *everybody* stayed home or that people stayed home *all the time* and never went out again, but only that more people stayed home more often than they would have if they did not have television. (How much more frequently would *you* go out if you didn't have the option of staying home to stream a movie or binge watch your favorite show?)

The argument's fourth premise states that these changes in behavior can have good or bad consequences. This does not yet say anything about whether those good or bad consequences can be attributed to the technologies. It is just stating the obvious: when technologies induce people to change their behaviors, sometimes those changes bring good consequences, and sometimes they bring bad consequences. Ransomware, for instance, makes it easier for people to extort money from others, which brings bad consequences.

It is tempting to say that whenever these behavioral changes have bad consequences, the blame lies entirely with the people who changed their behavior. Here, too, ransomware provides a clear example: even if some technology makes it *easier* to extort money from people, actually using for that purpose demonstrates a moral failing on the part of the user. A morally decent person, we might say, simply would not use the technology for that purpose. This is what the defender of the Value-Neutrality Thesis would have to say: a morally decent person would never respond to a technology by changing their behavior in a way that had bad consequences.

This is precisely what the main argument's fifth premise disputes. The fifth premise asserts that some technologies change people's behaviors in ways that have bad consequences, even when the users do not act on blameworthy preferences (or other moral failings). The fifth premise also rules out the case where users bring about bad consequences out of ignorance, as when people used products containing chlorofluorocarbons without realizing that they would damage the ozone layer. In other words, it asserts that sometimes morally decent people acting on morally acceptable preferences can bring about bad consequences.

How could this be? In the next section, we turn to this crucial question. For now, let us note that *if* it is true that technologies can induce morally decent people to bring about bad consequences while acting on morally acceptable preferences, *then* we will have reached the conclusion of the main argument: the Value Neutrality Thesis is false.

How Morally Decent People Can Bring About Bad Consequences

There are several kinds of cases in which morally decent people can bring about bad consequences while acting on morally acceptable preferences. Here, we identify several of the most important cases and examine how technologies can create new instances of each case.

Collective Action Problems

A collective action problem occurs when a group of people could achieve some good outcome (or avoid some bad outcome) by acting cooperatively, but each individual has a self-interested incentive to behave uncooperatively (Olson 1965). Group projects in school provide a classic example: if everyone in the group works on the project, the project would come out well, but each individual in the group has an incentive to slack off, leaving the other group members to do the work. Of course, when every group member acts on that incentive, the project does not get done, and everyone suffers. Other examples involve higher stakes. For instance, humanity could collectively reduce climate change by reducing our greenhouse gas emissions, but in the absence of good climate policies, most of us have incentives to do things that lead to the burning of fossil fuels and the emission of greenhouse gases from other sources. The most intractable collective action problems occur when individuals cannot make any meaningful difference through their own actions.

Let us grant that any morally decent person will *sometimes* make sacrifices for the sake of others. Still, there are limits to what morality demands of us; there are limits to how much we can be expected to give up, especially when our own sacrifices will not make any noticeable impact. In the face of severe collective action problems, even morally decent people will often fail to act cooperatively; their sacrifice would be too great and the gain too little. In acting uncooperatively, however, they contribute to the bad outcome, such as climate change, that arises from a failure of collective action.

While technologies can solve or reduce some collective action problems, they can also create or exacerbate others. Cars create traffic jams, for instance, and no one person changing their behavior is enough to avoid clogged streets and highways. Similarly, modern fishing technologies make it easy to overfish an area, and no one fishing vessel can prevent overfishing. These are examples of technologies leading to a bad outcome, even if all of the users are morally decent people acting on morally decent preferences.

Short-Term Thinking

People naturally value the present over the future and the near future over the distant future. Economists call this *discounting*: valuing the present and near future more highly than the distant future (Angner 2020). The idea is that a person who attaches less value to something in the distant future—say, a free pizza that you'll get a year from now—than they attach to something in the near future—say, a free slice of pizza that you'll get *right this second*—is "discounting" the thing in the future, much as a store "discounts" something when they sell it at a lower price. Discounting is a normal and in some case perfectly rational thing to do, but, especially in the way that humans do it, it can also induce us to make decisions that lead to very bad outcomes. In general, this is because valuing the present over the future makes it more tempting to do things that are enjoyable today even if that leads to bigger problems later, as well as avoiding things that are unpleasant today even if they would lead to bigger rewards later. For instance, we all know that we ought to exercise regularly and maintain a healthy diet to ensure good health later in life. Many of us, however, exercise less than we should and eat more than we should—and we do so precisely because healthy foods in reasonable portions make us feel good later, but unhealthy foods make us feel good *now*. Less flippantly, many of the things that add enjoyment or meaning to your life, such as developing your talents, learning another language, helping to improve your community, and maintaining your health, require long-term dedication and near-term drudgery. When we discount the future, it can be hard to muster the willpower to make that commitment. Short-term thinking—or, more technically, discounting the future—can therefore lead people to act in ways that bring about bad consequences, even if they would prefer something different. Philosophers sometimes call this "weakness of the will."

Technologies can exacerbate these kinds of problems by providing more means of instant gratification. This makes unhealthy choices and shallow near-term distractions even more palatable. For instance, the invention of high-fructose corn syrup made it even cheaper to sweeten foods, making junk food cheaper and more appealing. Smartphones and social media mean that there is always something more immediately appealing than whatever long-term investment you might be making in yourself. Thus, these technologies make it more likely that people will act in ways that bring about bad consequences.

Accidents

People make mistakes. Some technologies make those mistakes worse, more frequent, or harder to reverse. This can happen in several ways.

Technologies make mistakes worse when they make the consequences of a mistake more severe or harder to reverse. Certain kinds of weapons offer salient examples. Sometimes, people lash out in a fit of anger, and guns make it more likely that such an event turns deadly. Relatedly, sometimes one person shoots first from a mistaken belief that the other person has a gun and will use it. Nuclear weapons raise the stakes of accidental use even higher, as various Cold War movies suggest. Gain-of-function research in virology labs, such as experiments that engineer viruses to be more infectious, can lead to the creation of extremely dangerous viruses, such as the strain of bird flu that a team of Dutch researchers created in 2011 (Enserink 2011), which could have devastating consequences if it escaped into the wild. In these cases, technologies do not necessarily increase the likelihood that people will bring about bad consequences, but they exacerbate the badness of those consequences if they do come about and sometimes make them impossible to reverse.

In addition, technologies can make mistakes more frequent, especially when it can be hard to tell when a particular use of the technology is appropriate. I do not mean to include cases where people are simply ignorant of some general consequences of using a technology, as the general public was long ignorant of the dangers of using leaded gasoline, smoking cigarettes, or emitting greenhouse gases. Instead, I mean cases like sharing misinformation on social media, where it can be difficult for people to tell when a particular piece of information is true, but nonetheless simple and highly rewarding for them to share that information anyway. Even someone who is moderately conscientious about vetting information is likely to share misinformation when technologies incentivize doing so.

An Objection

A defender of the Value-Neutrality Thesis might object that many of these cases, at least, result from weakness of the will, ignorance, irrationality, or downright immorality. If only people were more virtuous, had more self-discipline, were better informed, were more careful, or could think more critically, they would not fall into these noxious behaviors! Thus, the objection goes, the fault really does lie with the technologies' users, and not with the technologies themselves.

It is true for many of these cases—perhaps even all of them—that perfect people could avoid them. This is irrelevant, though: humans make technology for other humans, not for saints or supercomputers. No one would deny that cigarettes are bad for you just because they pose no threat to beings that are radically unlike humans; we would not say, "The problem is not in the cigarettes—it is the weakness of the human body that is to blame!" So why should we say something similar about technologies that have bad consequences because of the way they interact with normal human psychology? Morally decent people fall victim to collective action problems, they discount the future (often more steeply than they should), and they make mistakes. When technologies make those things more likely or more harmful, they can make morally decent people do bad things.

A Case Study

I have mentioned a number of brief examples of the ways in which technologies can lead to bad consequences, even if no one involved acts on bad intentions, but it is worth reflecting more deeply on a particular case. Let us return to the example with which we began: social media.

Consider the software engineers who design social media platforms to maximize user engagement. There is nothing wrong with this goal in itself, but the way to do it, it turns out, is by delivering an unending stream of content that pushes a fairly uniform perspective (which will vary from user to user) and frequently engages negative emotions, such as anger and fear.[5] How are human users going to respond to such content? Will they effectively identify and ignore misinformation? Will they recognize that they have fallen into an echo chamber and seek out opposing viewpoints and reliable sources of information before forming opinions and attitudes about things? For the most part, the answer is no—and predictably so, given humans' well-known confirmation bias. (Confirmation bias is the psychological tendency to seek out or accept information that agrees with or confirms what you already believe, while avoiding or rejecting information that disagrees or conflicts with what you believe.) In short, when exposed to such streams of content, people predictably make mistakes in forming beliefs, and these mistakes can have serious consequences, even if no users act on blameworthy preferences or intentions.

Assuming, as seems plausible, that software engineers could have predicted the effects that their algorithms would have, what should they have done with that prediction? One possible answer is that they should have taken steps to reduce their platforms' polarizing effects, even if that meant failing to maximize user engagement. Some of these steps are easier than others. Many platforms have started to flag misinformation, for example, but finding ways to get users to read and consider conflicting opinions is more difficult. Perhaps engineers could have adjusted the algorithm to direct people toward more balanced and more accurate sources of information or to highlight comments and responses that are more nuanced, less inflammatory, and from a wider range of perspectives. Another possible answer is that the engineers should not have done anything differently—not without different instructions, at least. One might argue that their responsibility is to their employer, who has assigned them to maximize user engagement (although "I was just following orders" is hardly a strong defense of one's innocence). If we adopt this answer, perhaps we ought to regard *the employers* as the real "creators" of the technology and say that the moral responsibility for the platforms' effects rests with the executives who decided to press ahead with maximizing user engagement at all costs. After all, it would be odd to say that the executives made the engineers produce polarizing algorithms but bear no responsibility because they did not actually create the algorithms themselves. Either way, there is a strong case to be made that the platforms' tendency to polarize and misinform people could and should have been reduced.

Implications for Inventors' and Engineers' Responsibilities

Suppose we accept this argument against the Value-Neutrality Thesis. What does that imply about the responsibilities of inventors, engineers, and other creators of technologies? (Recall that, for our purposes, "creators" might also include business executives or policymakers giving instructions to engineers or other more "hands-on" creators.)

It does not mean that a technology's creators bear all the responsibility for any bad consequences that result from their creation. In most cases, at least some of the responsibility rests with the user. In some cases, perhaps all of the responsibility rests with the users. In still other cases, there may be no one to blame, as when creators and users are excusably ignorant of the consequences of using some invention.

Nor does it mean that any technology that brings about bad consequences is bad overall. Many technologies—perhaps most—produce a mixture of good and bad consequences. The question is whether the bad consequences outweigh the good or vice versa. The argument against the Value-Neutrality Thesis implies that for this overall evaluation of technologies, we cannot ignore bad consequences brought about by the technologies' users when we evaluate the technologies themselves.

The argument also implies that creators have a responsibility to think about how their technologies will change people's behavior and whether those changes will be for better or worse, as well as a responsibility to design technologies in ways that minimize bad consequences from those changes in behavior, insofar as that can be predicted. In extreme cases, it might be unethical for someone to complete the technology or make it available.

By analogy, imagine a team of engineers that designed a new kind of brakes for a car, and they determined that although the brakes generally perform better than existing technologies, they have a 50% chance of complete failure when the temperature falls below freezing for more than a week. Suppose that the engineers simply ignored the problem, saying to one another that it wasn't *their* fault; it was simply that the materials used in the brakes were not strong enough to withstand winter weather. This would be a gross dereliction of duty; the engineers would bear at least some of the blame for the accidents and deaths that resulted from their decision.[6] My argument against the Value-Neutrality Thesis suggests that when technologies predictably induce certain changes in behavior in their users, in the aggregate and over the long term, and those new behaviors predictably result in bad consequences, the same kinds of responsibilities apply. Technology creators ought not to ignore such bad consequences simply because users appear in the chain of cause and effect between the technology's invention and the bad consequences.

Notes

1 Ironically, it's not true that this quote originated with Mark Twain, but it's widely attributed to him anyway. Searching for the quote online leads to a mix of simple Web pages and images attributing the quote to Twain and longer, denser, far more boring articles yammering on about how even if Twain did say it, it can be definitively attributed to an English preacher named C. H. Spurgeon in 1855, when Twain was just 20 years old, and that Spurgeon himself described it as an "old proverb," which makes it impossible for Twain to have originated the saying. You can see how much easier it is to just attribute to quote to Mark Twain.

2 For a more detailed look at this position and the arguments for it, see Chapter 2 in this volume.
3 Different philosophers of technology have understood the claim of value-neutrality in different ways and/or offered different arguments for this claim. See, for example, works by Albert Borgmann (1984), Langdon Winner (1986), Ibo van den Poel (2001), Christian Illies and Anthonie Meijers (2009), Hans Radder (2009), David Koepsell (2010), Michael Klenk (2021), and Boaz Miller (2021).
4 For a more detailed look at the definition of technologies, see Chapter 1 in this volume.
5 For a discussion of this phenomenon, listen to the podcast *Rabbit Hole* (Roose 2020).
6 We could imagine cases where the engineers themselves bear little or no responsibility for such accidents. Maybe they try their best to solve the problem but, when they can't do it, they explain the situation to their employer, who decides to include the brakes along with a warning to drivers not to use the brakes in freezing weather. In such a case, the blame arguably lies with the employer, not the engineers. That is not the sort of case I have in mind with this example. I am imagining a case in which the engineers do not make any concerted effort to fix the problem and do not bother to report the problem to their employers.

References

Angner, Erik. 2021. *A Course in Behavioral Economics*. Third edition. London: Macmillan International.

Borgmann, Albert. 1984. *Technology and the Character of Contemporary Life*. Chicago: University of Chicago Press.

Enserink, Martin. 2011. "Scientists Brace for Media Storm around Controversial Flu Studies." *Science*. November 23, 2011. https://www.sciencemag.org/news/2011/11/scientists-brace-media-storm-around-controversial-flu-studies

Illies, Christian & Anthonie Meijers. 2009. "Artefacts without Agency." *The Monist*, 92(3), 420–440.

Klenk, Michael. 2021. "How Do Technological Artefacts Embody Moral Values?" *Philosophy & Technology*, 34, 525–544.

Kline, Stephen J. 1985. "What Is Technology?" *Bulletin of Science, Technology & Society*, 5(3), 215–218. https://doi.org/10.1177/027046768500500301

Koepsell, David. 2010. "On Genies and Bottles: Scientists' Moral Responsibility and Dangerous Technology R&D." *Science & Engineering Ethics*, 16(1), 119–133.

Miller, Boaz. 2021. "Is Technology Value-Neutral?" *Science, Technology, and Human Values*, 46(1), 53–80.

Olson, Mancur. 1965. *The Logic of Collective Action: Public Goods and the Theory of Groups*. Harvard Economic Studies 124. Cambridge, MA: Harvard University Press.

Putnam, Robert D. 2020. *Bowling Alone: The Collapse and Revival of American Community*. Revised and Updated. New: Simon & Schuster.

Radder, Hans. 2009. "Why Technologies Are Inherently Normative." In A. Meijers (Ed.), *Handbook of the Philosophy of Science, Vol. 9: Philosophy of Technology and Engineering Sciences* (pp. 887–921). Amsterdam: Elsevier.

Roose, Kevin. 2020. Rabbit Hole. *New York Times*. https://www.nytimes.com/column/rabbit-hole

Van de Poel, I. 2001. "Investigating Ethical Issues in Engineering Design." *Science & Engineering Ethics*, 7(3), 429–446.

Winner, Langdon. 1986. *The Whale and the Reactor: A Search for Limits in an Age of High Technology*. Chicago: University of Chicago Press.

Chapter 4

Technological Determinism
What It Is and Why It Matters

Sally Wyatt

Introduction

Decades of detailed and thorough scholarship in, among other fields, philosophy and ethics of technology, Science and Technology Studies (STS), and history of technology have not been enough to relegate "technological determinism" to the dustbin of history. The nuances of different types of technological determinism are explored more fully later in this chapter, but for now, let us define it simply as the belief that technologies are independent of society and that they drive the cultural, political and social forms of a society. There are many alternatives to this view, including the idea that technology is neutral and that its social consequences are the result of choices made by people, individually or in groups. There are also various theories that emphasize the complex entanglements between society broadly construed and science and technology, including feminist technology studies (Wajcman 1991), Actor-Network Theory (ANT) (Latour 1987) and the Social Construction of Technology (SCOT) (Bijker, Hughes and Pinch 1987).

All of that thorough research by STS scholars and others has repeatedly demonstrated that technology and society are deeply interwoven, and the processes by which they are developed and used are fundamentally social and relational. Technologies are imagined, designed, built and shaped by people at particular historical moments and in specific locations. Technologies emerge from and are embedded in social practices in university and company labs, on the production line, and in people's homes. Even though those who design and make technologies have their own ideas of what constitutes appropriate use, those who buy and deploy technologies often find new purposes (Oudshoorn and Pinch 2003; Hyysalo, Elgaard Jensen and Oudshoorn 2016).

Arguments against technological determinism may have become taken for granted in much of the scholarly community. Nonetheless, technological determinism continues to be deployed in wider public discourses and by those designing technologies. Opening the pages of any newspaper (or the digital equivalent of searching and clicking online) will quickly turn up phrases about, for example, how artificial intelligence and big data will save lives, make healthcare specialists redundant and reduce crime.

In the next section, I expand on technological determinism. Then, I move on to present different types of technological determinism. The final section contains a renewed plea to continue to take technological determinism seriously, and to look to science fiction for ways of re-imagining the technology-society relationship.

Defining Technological Determinism

"Technological *determinism* is the claim that technology causes or determines the structure of the rest of society and culture", so begins Dusek's (2006, 84, emphasis in original)

DOI: 10.4324/9781003189466-6

chapter on the topic. He goes on to say that in a technologically determinist view, "culture and society cannot affect the direction of technology... [and] as technology develops and changes, the institutions in the rest of society change, as does the art and religion of the society" (Dusek 2006, 84).

MacKenzie and Wajcman ([1985] 1999) also distinguish between these two parts of technological determinism. The first is that technological innovation occurs outside of society, independent of any social, economic or political factors. In other words, "[n]ew or improved products or ways of making things arise from the activities of inventors, engineers, and designers following an internal, technical logic that has nothing to do with social relationships" (Wyatt 2008, 168). The second part is that technological change causes, or *determines*, social change, including the institutions, art and religion mentioned by Dusek (2006).

As mentioned in the opening paragraph of the Introduction, other theories present the relationships between technology and society very differently, drawing on historical and contemporary analyses of the actual practices of scientific and technological development. STS, and more recently, empirical philosophy, have contributed numerous rich accounts of the messy, entangled, relational nature of technical developments, opening the "black box" of technology to reveal the politics, culture and social relationships of both technologies and the ways they come into being (see, e.g., Latour and Woolgar 1986; Bijker, Hughes and Pinch 1987; and the journals *Queer-Feminist Science & Technology Studies; Science as Culture; Science & Technology Studies; Science, Technology, & Human Values;* and *Social Studies of Science*). The various non-determinist accounts, including ANT, SCOT, (post-) phenomenological, feminist, queer and post-colonialist, share a commitment to challenging both parts of technological determinism: technology is very much shaped by the conditions of its design and production, and people have agency regarding how they choose to incorporate technologies into their lives, though of course agency and choice can be unevenly distributed.

In his classic text about the cultural, political and technical history of television, Williams ([1975] 1990) provides nine versions of cause and effect in the relationship between technology and society. I will not reproduce all of them here, just the first in its entirety and elements of the seventh and ninth:

> (i) Television was invented as a result of scientific and technical research. Its power as a medium of news and entertainment was then so great that it altered all preceding media of news and entertainment.
>
> ...
>
> (vii) Television became available as a result of scientific and technical research, was selected for investment as a new and profitable phase of a domestic consumer economy;
>
> ...
>
> (ix) Television... in its character and uses both served and exploited the needs of a new of kind of large-scale and complex but atomised society. (11–12)

By making changes to the cause and effect elements, Williams illustrates both parts of technological determinism. The first is that technologies emerge from scientific and technical research, irrespective of any social context. This is also sometimes described as an internalist account. In other words, technological determinism ignores the social context in which technologies emerge. By the seventh example, Williams points out the importance of economic factors in influencing what technologies may or may not be developed. The second element of technological determinism is that regardless of the origins, technology causes social change. In Williams' examples, the first offers a classic, "technology X leads to social consequence Y". The later examples emphasize the importance of the social conditions necessary to make technologies more or less amenable to being adopted and used.

Similar sets of statements could be made for all sorts of technologies, including twenty-first-century examples of genetics, autonomous vehicles or artificial intelligence. This can be a valuable exercise to develop one's awareness of the pervasiveness of technological determinism. Technological determinism often presents a utopian view of technology as progress, emphasizing the benefits of technology for humanity as, for example, when politicians claim predictive algorithms will reduce crime. But there are also more pessimistic and dystopian uses of technological determinism, as, for the same example, when civil liberties groups point to the ways in which predictive algorithms could be used to increase racial harassment and discrimination. The pessimistic accounts have their roots in the work of philosophers, including Ellul (1980), Marcuse (1964) and the Frankfurt School, with the latter focusing on the negative effects of mass media such as television.

Having set out the basic premises of technological determinism, the next section disentangles eight different forms that have appeared in the literature.

Types of Technological Determinism

It is rare for scholars, especially those in the humanities and the social sciences, to claim the label of "technological determinist" as part of their own scholarly identity. It is more likely to be an accusation, and more usually leveled against politicians, policy makers, industrialists and engineers. To use the technological determinism label unthinkingly as a way of dismissing a political or academic position has two problems. First, it closes down discussion, and misses the important work that is being done when technologically determinist arguments are deployed. I return to this in the final section. Second, it obscures the variety and nuance that can be found in different types of technological determinism. These different types are the focus of this section, in which I briefly outline the following: justificatory, descriptive, methodological, normative, enchanted, technological solutionism, military-economic adaptationism and permissionless innovation. In earlier work (Wyatt 2008, 174–175), I distinguished between the first four types. These are briefly summarized before I proceed to the others.

Justificatory Technological Determinism has already been mentioned earlier in this chapter. It is the kind of determinism deployed by companies rationalizing why they replace human workers with machines, or by politicians when they claim that technologies have/ will revolutionize the ways in which people live and work, or by engineers and scientists when they announce new discoveries that will prolong human life. It is what we ourselves might use when we think about the ways in which the world has changed over the past two hundred years. And, it is what we might feel when confronted with something new.

Descriptive Technological Determinism is akin to what I described in the previous section. This is used by MacKenzie and Wajcman ([1985] 1999) and others (see, e.g., Misa 1988; Smith and Marx 1994) to dismiss the arguments of others. This is the kind of determinism one uses when trying to make sense of the arguments put forward to explain a complex history. In such cases, we may accuse others of overly internalist or Whiggish histories. (Whig histories of science or technology tend to view the present as the outcome of the onward march of progress. Such accounts assume that the present is the best possible world.) Maybe a better label for this kind of determinism is "accusatory".

Methodological Technological Determinism is well presented and robustly defended by Heilbroner (1994). He argues that if one wishes to understand an unfamiliar society or institution, large or small, past or present, then a good place to start is by examining the technologies available to such groups. This is particularly appropriate for those past societies that did not leave a detailed written record. This kind of determinism could be used to describe the work of many archaeologists and anthropologists. Heilbroner presents this as a useful heuristic tool to make sense of the past.

Normative Technological Determinism is the term I used to capture the challenges to democratic accountability posed by the growth and complexity of technological systems. Winner (1977, 1997) certainly recognizes the economic, political and cultural forces that shape technological design, and thus explicitly rejects the first part of technological determinism. But he also suggests that we must consider technology to be autonomous and determining when its development and use are no longer amenable to political discussion or social control, so moving toward accepting the second part of technological determinism. He does so as a warning that society could and should guard against autonomous technology. Hughes (1994, 112) combines methodological and normative determinism in his concept of "technological momentum", and when he suggests that a "technological system can be both a cause and an effect; it can shape and be shaped by society. As they grow larger and more complex, systems tend to be more shaping of society and less shaped by it".

Military-Economic Adaptationism was introduced by Dafoe (2015) in his attempt to rehabilitate technological determinism as an explanation, and not only as something to be explained (the latter is my own position in Wyatt 2008). He highlights the importance of scale, again a point made by Winner (1977) and Hughes (1994); and of constraints or "path dependency". The latter term is used by economists and innovation studies scholars to capture how technologies (or institutions) develop in certain ways, building on past decisions and paths of action. By focusing on larger scale systems (rather than stand-alone artifacts), Dafoe argues that such systems "will evolve to become more adapted to success in the economic and/or military competition" (Dafoe 2015, 1059). This is not dissimilar to Winner's (1977) "autonomous technology" mentioned in the previous paragraph.

Enchanted Determinism is introduced by Campolo and Crawford (2020) in their analysis of the growing use of deep learning within artificial intelligence. They draw on in/famous case studies, including AlphaGo and the attempt to use facial recognition to detect sexual orientation, in order to highlight how theoretical understanding of how machine learning and neural networks actually work is missing. Even when the system is successful, as in the case of AlphaGo, those who have developed such systems do not always understand how or why they work. This aura of "enchantment" is used to create myths about all-powerful algorithms. As Campolo and Crawford (2020, 15) rightly argue, "[w]hen we see discourses of enchanted determinism at work, we should ask whose interests they serve and where the responsibility for the impacts of that system will ultimately rest". In this sense, it is similar to normative technological determinism.

Technological Solutionism has become popular in recent years, since the introduction of the term by Morozov (2014). While the label is new, the sentiment it captures has been around for much longer, by the term "technical fix", for example. Morozov, like Campolo and Crawford, focuses on algorithms and digital technologies. Solutionism captures the tendency to see big data and digital technologies as the solution to all possible societal problems. For example, obesity is widely recognized as a public health problem to which self-tracking devices are presented as the solution. Such devices may have a role to play for some individuals, but redesigning urban environments or introducing taxes on unhealthy foods and beverages may actually be more productive.

Permissionless Innovation is invoked by Dotson (2015) to remind his readers of the ways in which entrepreneurs, particularly those in Silicon Valley, use the rhetoric of technological determinism to avoid democratic decision making and governance. "Move fast and break things" has been attributed to both Jeff Bezos of Amazon and Peter Thiel of PayPal and Palantir. This is clearly a way to avoid regulation and to make technologies facts of life and thus somehow beyond human control. This is the applied version of Schumpeter's "creative destruction" ([1942] 2010) and Marx and Engels ([1848] 1888) "constant revolution of the means of production". However, these were analyses of capitalism, not handbooks for tech entrepreneurs.

These different types of technological determinism are intended as a heuristic to aid readers make sense of the literature. It is not an exhaustive list. There may be other types of technological determinism, yet to be named. Some types overlap. For example, "permissionless innovation" and "technological solutionism" both capture the reckless justification that is a feature of twenty-first-century developments in computing technologies, including artificial intelligence. "Military-economic adaptationism" can be seen as an instance of "methodological determinism" in the way it draws attention to what guides some investment choices technology. In the next and final section, I renew my plea to take technological determinism seriously, and also highlight the power of words and imaginaries found in science fiction.

Continued Need for Vigilance

Technological determinism "is one of a long line and large lexicon of academic insults and prohibitions", suggests Peters (2017, 11). There are some thoughtful and serious defenses of the position (Freeman 1987; Heilbroner 1994), but within academic debates, an accusation of technological determinism is often used to disqualify the author and close down further discussion. This is unfortunate for at least two reasons. First, technologically determinist arguments are still used outside of the academy, usually to justify courses of action that might be unpopular. By invoking an argument akin to "technology made me do it", social actors place their own political and economic choices beyond democratic debate and control.

Second, as some technical systems gain momentum, they certainly might appear to be beyond human intervention, perhaps due to their scale or geographical scope. This is what Winner (1977) warns against with the rise of "autonomous technology". For technologies that cross national borders or that are used in multiple contexts, it can be difficult to know who is responsible for their operation, use and impact. Again, powerful economic and political actors invoke such features to pre-empt discussion. Nonetheless, all technologies are ultimately the responsibility of those engaged in their design, diffusion, regulation and use.

The simplicity of technological determinism can explain its endurance (Wyatt 2008, 169). It is also what makes most sense of people's everyday experiences, as we buy and use technological devices with very little grasp of where they came from and how they work. However, the growing attention for the potentially dangerous and discriminatory uses of big data and artificial intelligence is beginning to open up public debate (see, e.g., O'Neil 2016; Campolo and Crawford 2020) about the technological world in which we all live, and the ways in which technologies are shaped by commercial and political interests and subsequently shape people's lived experiences as citizens, patients, audiences, consumers, etc.

The importance of understanding the rhetorical strength of technologically determinist arguments and justifications remains. Only by understanding technology and technological determinism can we as citizens hope to intervene in strengthening the democratic accountability of economic and political actors as mentioned above. We also need to pay attention to design activities, as that is where decisions are often made about the technical possibilities. There is a real danger that if deterministic accounts prevail in political and economic discourses about technology, such ways of thinking will also pervade design activities. For example, Papoutsi et al. (2021) draw attention to the ways in which designers of technological devices for epilepsy patients predominantly adopt "a highly deterministic, instrumental view of technology.... Patients are mainly cast as sources of attitudinal data, as beneficiaries of the technology or even as obstacles to be overcome" (2021, 943). Such a view has consequences for the eventual usefulness of such devices, and even for whether they will be successfully incorporated into complex sociotechnical contexts, involving people with epilepsy, their families, friends and professional care workers.

To conclude, I want to build on the previous paragraph, with the reminder that our world is made up of a very heterogenous set of elements, including individual people, social groups, organizations, institutions, flora, fauna, rules, knowledges and "things". These things can be stand-alone devices, medical or otherwise; and complex, more or less tightly coupled technological systems. The words we use to describe those "things" are also important, especially the words used to convey present sociotechnical relationships and imagined, future relationships. Much has been written about imaginaries, expectations and metaphors (see Borup et al. 2006; Jasanoff and Kim 2015; McNeil et al. 2017; Wyatt 2021), but I would like to end with a brief reflection or provocation on the importance of science fiction in reinforcing or challenging technologically determinist points of view. Much more could be written about this, and I confine myself to one paragraph with three examples of eminent, prize-winning science fiction authors.

The influential British science fiction writer, Arthur C. Clarke (1968, 255), wrote that "[a]ny sufficiently advanced technology is indistinguishable from magic". This is a rather classic statement of technological determinism, that technology is a black box, unknown and unknowable to its users. It certainly resonates with the enchanted determinism of Campolo and Crawford (2020). William Gibson, one of the first practitioners of cyberpunk, is credited with introducing the term "cyberspace" in *Neuromancer*, published in 1984. This term was much used in early academic studies of the internet. His body of work continues to provide an extraordinary exploration of what Dafoe labels "military-economic adaptationism". Finally, Ursula K. Le Guin ([1988] 2019, 36) moves beyond determinism, to imagine new possible worlds and to "redefine technology and science as primarily cultural carrier bag rather than weapon of domination". Ideas about technologies and their role in our world can be found in many sources, including engineering textbooks, user manuals, news reports and popular culture. Such ideas circulate, and sometimes find their way to the material world.

References

Bijker, Wiebe, Thomas Hughes, and Trevor Pinch, eds. 1987. *The Social Construction of Technological Systems. New Directions in the Sociology and History of Technology.* Cambridge, MA: The MIT Press.

Borup, Mads, Nik Brown, Kornelia Konrad, and Harro van Lente. 2006. "The Sociology of Expectations in Science and Technology." *Technology Analysis and Strategic Management* 18 (3/4): 285–298.

Campolo, Alexander, and Kate Crawford. 2020. "Enchanted Determinism: Power without Responsibility in Artificial Intelligence." *Engaging Science, Technology, and Society* 6: 1–19. doi: 10.17351/ests2020.277.

Clarke, Arthur C. 1968. "Clarke's Third Law on UFO's." *Science* 159 (3812): 255. doi: 10.1126/science.159.3812.255-b

Dafoe, Allan. 2015. "On Technological Determinism: A Typology, Scope Conditions, and a Mechanism." *Science, Technology, & Human Values* 40 (6): 1047–1076.

Dotson, Taylor. 2015. "Technological Determinism and Permissionless Innovation as Technocratic Governing Mentalities: Psychocultural Barriers to the Democratization of Technology." *Engaging Science, Technology, and Society* 1: 98–120. doi: 10.17351/ests2015.009

Dusek, Val. 2006. *Philosophy of Technology. An Introduction.* Oxford: Blackwell.

Ellul, Jacques. 1980. *The Technological System*. Translated by Joachim Neugroschel. New York: Continuum.

Freeman, Christopher. 1987. "The Case for Technological Determinism." In *Information Technology: Social Issues. A Reader*, edited by Ruth Finnegan, Graeme Salaman and Kenneth Thompson, pp. 5–18. Sevenoaks: Hodder & Stoughton.

Gibson, William. 1984. *Neuromancer*. New York: Ace Books.

Heilbroner, Robert. 1994. "Technological Determinism Revisited." In *Does Technology Drive History? The Dilemma of Technological Determinism*, edited by Merritt Roe Smith and Leo Marx, pp. 67–78. Cambridge, MA: The MIT Press.

Hughes, Thomas P. 1994. "Technological Momentum." In *Does Technology Drive History? The Dilemma of Technological Determinism*, edited by Merritt Roe Smith and Leo Marx, pp. 101–114. Cambridge, MA: The MIT Press.

Hyysalo, Sampsa, Torben Elgaard Jensen, and Nelly Oudshoorn, eds. 2016. *The New Production of Users. Changing Innovation Collectives and Involvement Strategies*. New York: Routledge.

Jasanoff, Sheila, and Sang-Hyun Kim, eds. 2015. *Dreamscapes of Modernity. Sociotechnical Imaginaries and the Fabrication of Power*. Chicago: The University of Chicago Press.

Latour, Bruno. 1987. *Science in Action. How to Follow Scientists and Engineers through Society*. Cambridge, MA: Harvard University Press.

Latour, Bruno, and Steve Woolgar. 1986. *Laboratory Life. The Construction of Scientific Facts*. Princeton, NJ: Princeton University Press.

Le Guin, Ursula K. (1988) 2019. *The Carrier Bag Theory of Fiction*. London: Ignota Books.

MacKenzie, Donald, and Judy Wajcman, eds. (1985) 1999. *The Social Shaping of Technology: How the Refrigerator Got Its Hum*. Milton Keynes: Open University Press.

Marcuse, Herbert. 1964. *One-Dimensional Man. Studies in the Ideology of Advanced Industrial Society*. Boston, MA: Beacon Press.

Marx, Karl, and Frederick Engels. (1848) 1888. *Manifesto of the Communist Party*. Translated by Samuel Moore. Multiple editions. https://www.marxists.org/archive/marx/works/download/pdf/Manifesto.pdf

McNeil, Maureen, Arribas-Ayllon, Michael, Haran, Joan, Mackenzie, Adrian, and Tutton, Richard. 2017. "Conceptualising Imaginaries of Science, Technology, and Society." In *The Handbook of Science and Technology Studies*. 4th ed., edited by Ulrike Felt, Rayvon Fouché, Clark A. Miller, and Laurel Smith-Doerr, pp. 435–463. Cambridge, MA: The MIT Press.

Misa, Thomas. 1988. "How Machines Make History and How Historians (and Others) Help Them To Do So." *Science, Technology, & Human Values* 17 (4): 308–331.

Morozov, Evgeny. 2014. *To Save Everything, Click Here. Technology, Solutionism, and the Urge to Fix Problems that Don't Exist*. London: Penguin.

O'Neil, Cathy. 2016. *Weapons of Math Destruction. How Big Data Increases Inequality and Threatens Democracy*. New York: Crown Publishing.

Oudshoorn, Nelly, and Trevor Pinch, eds. 2003. *How Users Matter. The Co-Construction of Users and Technologies*. Cambridge, MA: The MIT Press.

Papoutsi, Chrysanthi, Christian Collins, Alexandra Christopher, Sara Shaw, and Trisha Greenhalgh. 2021. "Interrogating the Promise of Technology in Epilepsy Care: Systematic, Hermeneutic Review." *Sociology of Health and Illness* 43: 928–947. doi: 10.1111/1467-9566.13266

Peters, John Durham. 2017. "'You Mean My Whole Fallacy Is Wrong?' On Technological Determinism." *Representations* 140 (1): 10–26.

Schumpeter, Joseph. (1942) 2010. *Capitalism, Socialism and Democracy*. Abingdon: Routledge.

Smith, Merritt Roe, and Leo Marx, eds. 1994. *Does Technology Drive History? The Dilemma of Technological Determinism*. Cambridge, MA: The MIT Press.

Wajcman, Judy. 1991. *Feminism Confronts Technology*. University Park: The Pennsylvania State University Press.

Williams, Raymond. (1975) 1990. *Television: Technology and Cultural Form*. 2nd ed. London: Routledge.

Winner, Langdon. 1977. *Autonomous Technology. Technics-out-of-control as a Theme in Political Thought.* Cambridge, MA: The MIT Press.

Winner, Langdon. 1997. "Perspectives: Technological Determinism: Alive and Kicking?" *Bulletin of Science, Technology and Society* 17 (1): 1–2.

Wyatt, Sally. 2008. "Technological Determinism is Dead; Long Live Technological Determinism." In *The Handbook of Science and Technology Studies.* 3rd ed., edited by Edward J. Hackett, Olga Amsterdamska, Michael Lynch, and Judy Wajcman, pp. 165–180. Cambridge, MA: The MIT Press.

Wyatt, Sally. 2021. "Metaphors in Critical Internet and Digital Media Studies." *New Media & Society* 23 (2): 406–416.

Chapter 5

Heidegger's Philosophy of Technology

David R. Cerbone

Guiding Ideas

In this chapter, I provide an overview of Heidegger's contributions[1] to the philosophy of technology. My discussion is organized around five core ideas informing Heidegger's interest in technology. The first and most basic idea is that Heidegger's investigation of technology is an inquiry into the *essence* of technology, which he repeatedly stresses is "nothing technological." For Heidegger, the essence of technology involves a distinctive understanding – or, as we shall see, *revealing* – of what there is in general. This focus on the essence of technology points to a second idea, which I will refer to as the *totalizing* character of Heidegger's conception of technology. For Heidegger, technology is not one sector or domain within cultural life broadly construed. Rather, as an understanding of what there is in general, modern technology marks a way in which *everything* is manifest (including ourselves). That technology – or its essence – constitutes a distinctive understanding of what there is points to two further ideas: the *historical* and *discontinuous* dimensions of his conception of modern technology. The former of these concerns Heidegger's placing of technology within a broader account of human history, wherein that (or at least the history of the West) has been marked by different and largely incommensurable ways of understanding what there is.[2] This epochal conception thus involves the idea that modern technology is radically discontinuous with the many and various prior feats of ingenuity and innovation in pre-modern human history. These four theses together point toward a fifth idea: the *danger* that Heidegger associates with technology (or, more precisely, with the essence of technology). Heidegger refers to technology as involving the "supreme danger," thereby indicating the ethical dimensions of his concerns with technology. But he also says that the "saving power" of technology can be found within that danger. In the last section of the paper, I will sketch Heidegger's vision of the interplay between danger and salvation while also noting some of the shortcomings of that vision.

Questioning Technology

After noting at the outset of "The Question Concerning Technology" that his questioning of technology will endeavor to open "our human existence to the essence of technology" and subsequently cautioning that "the essence of technology is by no means anything technological," Heidegger declares slightly further on:

> Technology is therefore no mere means. Technology is a way of revealing. If we give heed to this, then another whole realm for the essence of technology will open itself up to us. It is the realm of revealing, i.e. of truth.

> (Heidegger 1977, 12)

DOI: 10.4324/9781003189466-7

The first sentence summarizes Heidegger's rejection of – or at least dissatisfaction with – what he considers to be standard accounts of technology. Such accounts involve two key ideas, namely, that "technology is a means to an end" and that "technology is a human activity." Heidegger acknowledges that these ideas are "correct," as no one can exactly deny that technological innovations are often driven by finding better means to given ends and that finding those better means is a human activity. The problem for Heidegger is not that these ideas are wrong as that they are superficial. Fixating on them – on their obviousness – can lead us to miss what he regards as essential in modern technology. Hence his pivot in the above passage from the correct-but-superficial ideas he rejects to the notion of "giving heed" to the idea that technology is a "way of revealing." What does this mean?

Heidegger does not merely wave away the correct-but-superficial ideas concerning technology. Although superficial, they do provide clues for finding one's way toward the essence of technology. That is, reflection on the notion of instrumentality – of something's being a means to an end – yields more fundamental insights. Without rehearsing all of Heidegger's reasoning in the opening pages of "The Question Concerning Technology," the basic idea is that instrumentality points toward the more basic idea of *bringing-forth*. Producing something is one way of bringing something forth, which means that the thing produced comes to *appear* and can appear *as the kind of thing it is*. So very quickly, we are led by Heidegger from the superficial idea of instrumentality to the more profound ideas of revealing and truth. We thereby confront the question of just what kind of bringing-forth – what kind of revealing – is at issue in modern technology. As what does modern technology reveal things?

To get to what is distinctive about modern technology, Heidegger encourages us to reflect on earlier forms of bringing-forth (his example is the production of a silver chalice). Heidegger refers to such earlier forms as modes of *poiēsis*, the skillful production that we associate with handicraft and artisanry. The activity of the artisan engages with, and is responsive to, the specifics of the materials at hand – the silver to be hammered and shaped, the wood to be chiseled and sanded, the clay to be turned and molded – so as to bring forth things that bear the traces of their modes of production not just generally but with reference to the particular maker and the occasion of making. *Poiēsis* brings forth things that are unique particulars. Things are thus revealed as crafted; their createdness as such particulars constitutes the truth of what they are. Contrast handicrafts with modern, industrial forms of production. Such modern forms of production center on the idea of *mass production*, the creation of uniform, indistinguishable, interchangeable items. (Compare walking through an Ikea with a tour of an artisan's studio.) The nature and scale of industrial production *require* this kind of interchangeability: the pieces produced in this manner "are piece-for-piece equivalent. Their character as pieces demands this uniformity" (Heidegger 2012, 35). Just consider all the various parts and mechanisms making up an automobile or a cell phone: while there are many specialized parts making up such machines and devices, there ought not be anything unique or special about any particular instance of those parts. Parts ought to – and can – be replaced more or less at will without affecting the workings of the overall machine. The same holds for other mass-produced products, even when they are not parts of something else. In an Ikea, it does not matter whether I reach for the top, middle, or bottom item in a stack: while numerically distinct, they are all the same in keeping with the uniform, mostly hands-off mode of production.

The stark contrast between pre-modern and modern forms of production indicates not just a difference of degree, as though the differences were merely ones of means and scale, but a difference *in kind* in terms of how and what things are revealed as being. Rather than unique particulars, things in modern life are revealed – and so correlatively understood – as what Heidegger refers to as *Bestand*, which is often translated as *standing-reserve*, but might also be rendered as *inventory, stock,* or *resources.* Such terms bring to mind warehouses filled with goods, to be stored and shipped as needed, connected by complicated supply chains that now span the globe. Consider how the use of uniform shipping containers greatly expanded global trade: freighters larger than football fields could be packed and unpacked quickly and efficiently using massive cranes; containers could then be placed directly on or into massive trucks that were standing by to bring goods to their destination. The goods, ships, containers, trucks: all of this is included in what Heidegger means by standing-reserve, as all of it is understood in terms of its availability to serve as nodes in a flexible, adaptable, reconfigurable network. But Heidegger's principal example of *Bestand* is *energy,* which is extracted, captured, stored, and circulated in order to keep that whole supply chain in operation. Energy is the archetypical resource since its circulation is largely indifferent to its means of production: when I flick a switch in my living room to turn on the lights, the electricity flowing through the wires into and throughout my house is the same regardless of whether it was generated through the burning of coal or oil, collected using solar panels or wind turbines, or produced via the damming of a river (as with Heidegger's example of a hydroelectric plant on the Rhine). If electricity is flowing in my house, the light goes on when I flick the switch and that, when flicking the switch, is all that matters.

The modern technological understanding of what there is – the kind of *revealing* at work in modern technology – brings things forth not as particular things at all, but as resources. Many of the principal ideas mentioned at the outset can now be more readily discerned. First, in keeping with the idea of totalization, *Bestand* encompasses not just paradigmatic technological devices such as computers and cell phones. Heidegger's claim is that now *everything* is manifest as resources. He refers to this general outlook as *Ge-Stell,* translated as *enframing* or *positionality*: as resources, everything is positioned or placed in a network, where those positions are indefinitely changeable. Heidegger connects enframing to the idea of *challenging*: as positioned resources, things are persistently refined, redesigned, and repurposed so as to optimize their use as resources. Consider, for example, the explosive growth in computing power, which involves microchips with ever greater processing speeds and ever higher storage capacities, while continually getting smaller and smaller. The constant demand for increased speed and efficiency – the *more, better, faster* thrum of modern life – is indicative of this challenging orientation. But again, while this orientation is eminently evident in the case of devices like computers, it is by no means limited to that domain: challenging happens *everywhere*. To get a feel for this, watch just about any commercial for athletic gear: these ads center upon the idea of *challenging oneself* to be faster, stronger, better; it isn't just the gear that's an optimizable resource, but one's own body as well. Or consider the preoccupation, especially within the tech sector, with indefinitely extending the human lifespan, perhaps so as even to achieve something approximating immortality. Here not just the body but life itself is a resource to be quantitatively optimized.

Second, we can now see the *historical* dimension of Heidegger's conception of the essence of technology: enframing is a historically recent way of revealing or bringing-forth. The ancient Greeks did not understand things as resources, nor did Medieval Christians. For the Greeks, what there is was understood in terms of an upsurge of *physis*, the ebb and flow of nature whose vicissitudes encompassed the fortunes of human life. For Medieval Christians, everything everywhere was revealed as created by God, and so as having an appointed place and purpose. Human beings were understood as themselves created by God and as having a special place in God's creation (we will return to this idea shortly). The idea that things are merely flexible resources to be switched about and re-ordered for the sake of greater efficiency has no place in these earlier understandings of being. Hence the *discontinuity* of modern technology with prior epochs in human history: for Heidegger, history is not a story of continual development or progress, but a series of radically different ways of revealing what there is. While other philosophers, such as Hegel, share a sense of there being discrete stages of human history, Heidegger rejects Hegel's understanding of these stages as rationally linked to one another and as constituting a painful but steady march along a "pathway of despair" toward an ideal condition. Instead, for Heidegger, these understandings are mysterious "dispensations" that "can be neither logically-historiologically predicted nor metaphysically construed as the result of a process of history" (Heidegger 2012, 65).

We need to be careful here to avoid what can feel like a very natural question, namely, which (if any) of these ways of understanding what there is *gets it right*. One problem with this question is that it treats these different understandings as sets of *ideas*, as changing *conceptions* or even *theories* of what there is. Heidegger's emphasis on bringing-forth and revealing is meant in part to dispel that temptation: the changes he is documenting are as much changes in what things *are* as how they are understood (the two notions do not really come apart for Heidegger). In the Medieval era, things *really were* manifest as created by God, just as now things *really are* manifest as indefinitely flexible resources. There is no neutral perspective – outside of any historically configured understanding of being – from which to decide between them. And as we will see, for Heidegger, our *deciding* anything about how things are revealed is an even graver mistake.

Technology and Ethics

It is difficult not to hear Heidegger's characterizations of technology as charged with an ethical fervor. While "challenging" can be understood positively, as when someone is challenged to do their very best or triumphantly overcomes a challenge, Heidegger typically explicates it in ways that give it a more menacing sense: the challenging of nature is a "setting-upon" that "assaults the materials and forces of nature with a conscripting" (Heidegger 2012, 29). Challenging is thus a kind of "violence"[3] that seeks to "exploit the energies of nature" (Heidegger 1977, 18). Beyond destructive processes such as mining, drilling, and fracking, we can also understand Heidegger's appeals to violence in a somewhat more abstract sense: since enframing challenges everything as resources, it thereby effaces the particularity of things. This kind of effacement is evident in the uniformity of mass-produced items: any cup in a stack of red Solo cups is indistinguishable from any other; the charging block that recharges my iPhone can be replaced by any other. As flexible, switchable resources, nothing has anything like an intrinsic nature: what something is is determined by its place in a broader ordering and that place can be changed at any time if doing so better serves the demand for optimization. We can see this even for something as massively present as a modern airliner:

> Yet an airliner that stands on the runway is surely an object. Certainly. We can represent the machine so. But then it conceals itself as to what and how it is. Revealed, it stands on the taxi strip only as standing-reserve, inasmuch as it is ordered to insure the possibility of transportation. For this it must be in its whole structure and in every one of its constituent parts itself on call for duty, i.e., ready for takeoff.
>
> (Heidegger 1977, 17)

Despite its massiveness, the airliner is "on call" for its designated purpose, and that purpose can be indefinitely altered. The very same plane might at one time be a luxury liner for jet-setters and high-flying executives, then refitted to carry primarily economy travelers, and later still be stripped of its seats in order to maximize its cargo capacity. It can thus be retooled, refitted, and repurposed in all manner of ways, and then be sold for salvage or left to deteriorate in an airplane "graveyard" in a remote desert when it is no longer efficient to continue using it (usually when newer, faster airplanes come to market). These changes flow not from anything intrinsic about the airplane, but are a matter of how it is *positioned* in the overall network of standing-reserve.

Heidegger's emphasis on the violence and rapaciousness of modern technology – of enframing – aligns his views with more familiar concerns about the environmental impact of modern industrial technology: the destruction of ecosystems and habitats, pervasive pollution and contamination, and, most ominously, the rising threat posed by climate change (although Heidegger himself was of course not aware of this). For this reason, readers of Heidegger frequently connect his views to the more philosophical strands of ecological thinking, especially the so-called "deep ecology" movement.[4] These connections are especially evident in the essays and lectures that frame what he writes specifically about technology and its essence. In essays such as "The Thing" and "Building Dwelling Thinking," Heidegger develops ideas first formulated in his Bremen lectures about human dwelling that contrast starkly with the kind of challenging and setting-upon he associates with technology. Heidegger spells out his vision of human dwelling in terms of his notion of the *fourfold* of mortals, earth, sky, and divinities. The "simple oneness" of the fourfold emphasizes how its elements are interconnected: to dwell as a mortal is to be grounded on the earth, which involves reaching an accommodation with the specifics of one's environment (rather than, say, bulldozing everything everywhere to create the same level terrain); under the sky, which means living within the rhythms of the seasons and the arc of a human lifespan and the occasions that punctuate it; and before the divinities. This last notion of divinities is the most difficult to articulate in terms of how literally to construe what Heidegger means by "gods" and "the godhead." But at minimum, we can say that dwelling's acknowledgment of divinities marks its dependence on something outside of itself, which we can think of as pointing toward the idea that aspects of one's life be non-metaphorically, non-reductively regarded as *blessings* and *curses*, and where some things stand out as *sacrosanct* and *inviolable* (in contrast to the indefinite flexibility of resources). Mortals, for Heidegger, are charged with a kind of special duty with respect to the fourfold in terms of helping it to "abide." As "shepherds of being," human beings are called upon to preserve and protect the earth, to cultivate and nurture it. "Saving the earth does not master the earth and does not subjugate it, which is merely one step from spoliation" (Heidegger 1971a, 148). There is in this way a clear connection between Heidegger and more recent concerns with environmental ethics.

More broadly, Heidegger frames his investigations of technology with a concern for the loss of *nearness*. In both the lecture and the essay entitled "The Thing," Heidegger begins by remarking on the way that modern technology involves the "frantic abolition of all distances" (Heidegger 1971b, 163). As the modern age has progressed, travel has become faster and more widespread, but the principal driver of this abolition for Heidegger is the growing reach of various media technologies. Heidegger cites the "reach" of radio and film, as well as what he correctly senses as the imminent ascendance of television. We can consider the current dominance of the Internet as a further refinement of the same basic idea. While such technologies abolish distances, they do not establish any nearness. This is because they bring everything equally close. Consider what happens when surfing the web: just by clicking here and there, or typing a few words or phrases, I can place before me all manner of sights and sounds from all over the world and from various points in time. I can almost effortlessly find footage of Thelonious Monk playing piano in 1961, switch to a scene from a Bollywood movie, and then check out my favorite band's latest release. I can move almost seamlessly from pornography to poetry; Syria to San Francisco; fine art to funny cat videos. All of it is uniformly accessible, equally available at pretty much any time. But the absence of distance is not the same as nearness, as the latter requires *differences* in degree of closeness. Not everything can be important to the same degree and at the same time. Insofar as everything is equally important, nothing is. To be near to something is for that thing – things in the preeminent sense – to stand out, to play a special role rather than be interchangeable or substitutable. As Heidegger puts it, human dwelling involves things *thinging*, brought forth as distinctive, meaningful things rather than as flexible, disposable resources.

Although Heidegger never quite says so, it seems clear that dwelling is meant to be ethically charged,[5] as it casts human beings in a more caring and thoughtful role than that found either in the early modern era (e.g. Descartes' casting us as "masters and possessors of nature") or the fully modern technological era epitomized by mindless clicking and consumption. Just how one actually attains to dwelling is far less clear, especially as the currently prevailing technological understanding of what there is throws up particularly severe obstacles. These obstacles concern what Heidegger calls the "supreme danger" of technology. In order to understand what Heidegger means by *supreme* danger, first consider the danger associated with *any* historical understanding of what there is. As we have seen, every historical understanding is a general way of revealing – things appear or are brought forth in accord with that understanding – but as such, every historical understanding is also a way of *concealing* in that it blocks or defeats other ways of revealing. As a matter of how *everything* is revealed, each such understanding makes a claim to universality and finality. The danger here is thus the danger of diminishing our being receptive to new understandings, new ways of revealing how things are. In this respect, the technological understanding of being is no different from its predecessors: that things show up as resources conceals their being created by God, just as their showing up as being created by God concealed their revelation as the upsurge of *physis*. None of technology's predecessors, however, involved the supreme danger posed by technology. What's special – in the sense of especially dangerous – about technology is the particular threat it poses to our being receptive to new understandings of being. As indicated above, the universal revealing of things as uniform resources extends to how human beings appear to themselves (the darkness of the phrase "human resources" was not lost on Heidegger). The technological understanding of being thus conceals the special standing of human beings in relation to being. Compare, for example, the standing of human beings in the Medieval understanding of things as created by God: although being created by God pertained to human beings just as it does to the rest of creation, human beings enjoyed a special status as created in God's image and as endowed with the ability either to gratefully receive God's love or to proudly and sinfully shun it. So understood, human beings remained receptive to the revealing of entities despite the totalizing character of that understanding of being. That special status allowed for us to be receptive to new, post-theological understandings of the kind ushered in by the new sciences and ultimately technology. By effacing any distinctive status for human beings (including for human language and thinking), such receptivity is maximally imperiled within the technological understanding of being: "The rule of enframing threatens man with the possibility that it could be denied to him to enter into a more original revealing and hence to experience the call of a more primal truth" (Heidegger 1977, 28).[6] Heidegger does not think that the threat posed by the "rule of enframing" is insurmountable. Indeed, he claims that the "saving power" lies precisely in that threat: "But what help is it to us to look into the constellation of truth? We look into the danger and see the growth of the saving power" (Heidegger 1977, 33). What could Heidegger mean here? The basic idea is that the only way to overcome the threat posed by the all-encompassing character of the technological understanding of being is to think one's way all the way to its *essence*. Doing that accomplishes two things: first, it preserves and sustains the distinctively human capacity for thinking the essence of things; second, it delineates the essence of technology as (just) one more understanding of being among others. In this way, as Heidegger announces at the outset of "The Question Concerning Technology," his mode of questioning will "prepare a free relationship to" technology, adding that "the relationship will be free if it opens our human existence to the essence of technology" (Heidegger 1977, 3). Such openness will preserve the kind of receptivity that Heidegger regards as fundamental to human existence.

Beyond this kind of receptivity, Heidegger's characterizations of a "free relationship" to technology are disappointingly thin. Heidegger rejects both a "stultified compulsion to push on blindly with technology," but also "what comes to the same thing, to rebel helplessly against it and curse it as the work of the devil" (Heidegger 1977, 25–26); in another essay, after again cautioning against regarding technology as "the work of the devil," Heidegger says that we should only strive to be less "shackled" to our technical devices: "We can use technical devices as they ought to be used, and also let them alone as something which does not affect our inner and real core" (Heidegger 1969, 54). In this way, Heidegger insists that our relationship to technology will be "wonderfully simple and relaxed" (ibid.). Salutary as it may be to "unplug" more often, to venture out without one's phone or spend an evening away from all screens, it is difficult to see how managing this will really address the kinds of depredations of the earth Heidegger himself laments. After all, even the phone that I use only occasionally rather than constantly has to be produced, and its production still involves the kind of global supply chain to which modern technology has given rise. While I might individually be more "relaxed," the kinds of problems posed by modern industrial technology are not adequately addressed by these sorts of correctives within one's own life. The problems are instead structural and collective (and also political), and in this way go beyond what Heidegger prescribes.

For Heidegger, however, the dearth of practical prescriptions might – in current tech parlance – be regarded as a feature rather than a bug. Recall that one of the two ideas about technology that Heidegger rejects as superficial is that "technology is a human activity." This idea fosters the illusion that ways of revealing are susceptible to human mastery. Asking what we can *do* to address the problems posed by technology or, more radically, to bring about a new understanding of being is to remain within the grip of this idea. Insofar as the powers of the will can be harnessed here, it is only to strive (koan-like) to "will non-willing,"[7] and in that way prepare for a new "sending" of being. That this might be enough to ward off ecological disaster appears rather unlikely.[8]

Notes

1 Heidegger 1977, first published in Heidegger 1954, is of paramount importance, especially as it has dominated discussions of his understanding of technology. But we should not lose sight of the way this essay emerged in Heidegger's thinking in tandem with his inquiries into the notion of *the thing*, his interest in a specifically human form of *dwelling*, and his notion of the *fourfold* (earth, mortals, sky, and divinities). These connections are obscured by the scattered appearance of Heidegger's essays on these matters across different collections in English. Heidegger 1971a and Heidegger 1971b were originally published in Heidegger 1954 along with the technology essay; moreover, the ideas in all three essays were initially presented together in Heidegger 2012, which includes his 1949 Bremen Lectures. I will not have space in this essay to follow all of even the most important connections among these ideas, but I will try to document some of them, especially in the final section on the ethical dimensions of Heidegger's account.
2 This is what Wrathall 2019 refers to as Heidegger's "universal and total grounds thesis." I have drawn upon Wrathall's formulation for the first four of the five core ideas I lay out here.
3 See, for example, Heidegger 2012, 29 and 57.
4 See Taylor 1992 for a discussion of Heidegger's thinking in relation to ecology (although much of the paper explores Heidegger's conception of language). For further discussion of Heidegger and deep ecology, see also Zimmerman 2019; and see Glazebrook 2019, which sees connections between Heidegger's thinking and ideas about "local knowledges" and sustainability.

5 There are difficulties here in terms of properly accounting for the normative force of Heidegger's descriptions of dwelling. Recall the futility from Heidegger's perspective of asking what things *really* are apart from how they are revealed within various historical understandings of what there is. It is not clear to me how to square this rejection of any neutral or authoritative perspective with his insistence that some ways of being oriented toward things allow them to appear as what they really are. I discuss this difficulty further in Cerbone 2019; for a much more extensive discussion of the tensions generated in part by Heidegger's historicism, see Westerlund 2020.

6 Sean Kelly has suggested to me in conversation that central to the idea that technology constitutes the *supreme* danger is its effacement of our *dependence* on something outside of ourselves, an idea that Heidegger's appeal to the fourfold emphasizes. Common to the Greeks and the Medievals is some recognition of that dependence – whether on nature or on God – despite their many differences. As I touch on below, for Heidegger, technology involves the illusion of human mastery, while revealing us as resources.

7 See, for example, Part III of Heidegger 1969.

8 Thanks to Henry Cerbone, Lian Dunleavy, and especially Sean Kelly for helpful comments on an earlier draft of this chapter. I am grateful also to the editors of this volume, along with three anonymous referees, for their comments and suggestions.

References

Cerbone, David R. 2019. Review of Wendland, Merwin, and Hadjioannou, *Heidegger on Technology*. *Notre Dame Philosophical Reviews*. https://ndpr.nd.edu/reviews/heidegger-on-technology/

Glazebrook, Trish. 2019. "Letting Beings Be: An Ecofeminist Reading of *Gestell*, *Gelassenheit*, and Sustainability." In Wendland, Merwin, and Hadjioannou 2019, 243–260.

Heidegger, Martin. 1954. *Vorträge und Aufsätze*. Stuttgart: Verlag Günther Neske.

Heidegger, Martin. 1969. *Discourse on Thinking*. Translated by J. Stambaugh. New York: Harper Torchbooks.

Heidegger, Martin. 1971a. "Building Dwelling Thinking." In *Poetry, Language, Thought*, translated by A. Hofstadter, 141–160. New York: HarperCollins.

Heidegger, Martin. 1971b. "The Thing." In *Poetry, Language, Thought*, translated by A. Hofstadter, 161–184. New York: HarperCollins.

Heidegger, Martin. 1977. "The Question Concerning Technology." In *The Question Concerning Technology and Other Essays*, translated by W. Lovitt, 3–35. New York: Harper Torchbooks.

Heidegger, Martin. 2012. *The Bremen and Freiburg Lectures*, translated by A. J. Mitchell. Bloomington: Indiana University Press.

Taylor, Charles. 1992. "Heidegger, Language, and Ecology." In *Heidegger: A Critical Reader*, edited by H. Dreyfus and H. Hall, 247–269. Oxford: Blackwell.

Wendland, Aaron, Merwin, Christopher, and Hadjioannou, Christos. 2019. *Heidegger on Technology*. New York: Routledge.

Westerlund, Fredrik. 2020. *Heidegger and the Problem of Phenomena*. New York: Bloomsbury.

Wrathall, Mark. 2019. "The Task of Thinking in a Technological Age." In Wendland, Merwin, and Hadjioannou 2019, 13–38.

Zimmerman, Michael. 2019. "How Pertinent is Heidegger's Thinking for Deep Ecology?" In Wendland, Merwin, and Hadjioannou 2019, 209–225.

Chapter 6

Postphenomenology and Ethics

Peter-Paul Verbeek

Introduction

How to account for the ethical significance of technology? Technologies have become an intricate part of human existence, and their influence on human beings and society raises many ethical questions and concerns. But does this imply that technology itself is ethically significant? After all, it is human beings who decide about the goals for which they use technologies, not the technologies themselves. It would be odd to blame a car for a traffic accident: it's the driver who has moral agency, not the vehicle. Or would we throw out the child with the bathwater if we drew this conclusion? Should we indeed take seriously the idea that technologies are ethically 'charged', and that there is some kind of ethics 'in' the devices and systems that we use? When Artificial Intelligence helps medical doctors to make decisions about life and death, doesn't that make AI systems 'moral'?

Questions like these have a central place in the postphenomenological approach to technology. This approach takes the relations between human beings and technologies as its starting point. The role of technologies in society, after all, always rests on the relations that human beings have with them: on the basis of human-technology relations, technologies help to shape human practices, perceptions, and interpretations. And exactly this 'shaping' role of technology can be seen as the basis for their ethical significance. After all, ethics is about the questions of 'how to act' and 'how to live', and the influence of technologies on human actions and decisions gives them an explicit role in our answering of these ethical questions. The main challenges this brings for the ethics of technology, then, are (1) how to conceptualize this 'morality of technology'?; and (2) how to deal with it in a responsible way?

In this chapter, I will explain the postphenomenological approach to ethics of technology in three steps.[1] First, I will introduce postphenomenology itself, as a specific way to analyze technology and its role in society. Second, I will discuss the various dimensions of the moral significance of technology that become visible from the postphenomenological approach. I will explain how technologies mediate moral actions and decisions, how they help to shape value frameworks, and how they challenge the concepts with which we can do ethics in the first place. Third, I will move this discussion from theoretical philosophy to practical philosophy, by explaining the approach of Guidance Ethics, which grew out of postphenomenological ethics of technology.

Postphenomenology

The phenomenological tradition in philosophy has always had quite a substantial role in philosophy of technology. Phenomenology focuses on the study on human experience. Its central starting point is the intricate connection between subject and object, human and

DOI: 10.4324/9781003189466-8

world. Human subjects and the world of objects can never be separated, after all: humans are always directed at the world (we always see *something*, hear *something*, feel *something*) and at the same time, the world is what it is for us based on our relations with it. The world 'in itself', therefore, is by definition inaccessible to human beings. As soon as we even ask a question about it, it becomes a world-for-us, which is meaningful on the basis of our relations with it. Phenomenology is a relational approach: it sees humans and world as intricately connected.

On the basis of the phenomenological focus on 'experience', classical phenomenological analyses of technology tended to be quite negative. They typically saw technology as a threat to the primordial role of experience and considered technology to be an alienating force. Karl Jaspers, for instance, considered technology to be alienating in an existential sense: we have become dependent on technology, and the technologization of labor together with the increasingly bureaucratic organization of society turns our social environment into a big 'Apparatus', in which human authenticity is less important than the function of each individual in the system. For Martin Heidegger, technology was alienating in a hermeneutic sense: it affects our understanding of the world and of ourselves. The technology way of thinking approaches all entities in the world as 'raw material' for the human 'will to power'. While an old, wooden bridge over the river Rhine still recognized the river in its own right, Heidegger stated, a waterpower station built into it forces the river to show itself as a supplier of energy (Heidegger 1977, 16–17).

Over time, resistance grew against the romanticism and one-sidedly negative character of these classical positions. Gradually, technology started to be understood as an *element of* society, rather than being *opposed to* it as an alienating force. As I have argued in my book *What Things Do* (Verbeek 2005), classical philosophy of technology typically had a 'transcendentalistic' approach to technology: it reduced technology to its *conditions* and analyzed these conditions rather than the technologies themselves. Jaspers reduced technology to the system of mass production, and Heidegger to the technological way of understanding the world. This resistance resulted in the so-called 'empirical turn' in philosophy of technology: a turn toward studying concrete technological artifacts and systems as a basis for philosophical analysis. Instead of reducing technologies to their conditions, it took them as a *starting point*.

The postphenomenological approach, which developed out of the work of North American philosopher Don Ihde, embodies this empirical turn (Ihde 1990; Selinger 2006; Rosenberger and Verbeek 2015). Postphenomenology leaves the romantic opposition of humans and technologies behind, and approaches technology as constitutive for human existence. Instead of taking 'Technology' as its object of investigation, it focuses on actual technologies and the ways in which they help to shape the relations between human beings and their world. The central idea of the postphenomenological approach is that it does not locate technologies in a realm of material 'objects' which is clearly demarcated from to the realm of human subjects, but in the *relations* between humans and world. When using a technology, humans are typically not only interacting with that technology, but also have a relation with the world via that technology. This means that technologies can bring about new human–world relations, ranging from social interactions to moral and aesthetic experiences, and from scientific observations to religious awe. In short, technologies bring *mediation* rather than alienation. MRI scanners, for instance, help to shape how neuroscientists understand the brain and the mind (De Boer et al. 2020). And Artificially Intelligent systems help medical doctors to understand the symptoms of patients. Technologies are a medium for human–world relations, and this mediation helps to shape the character of these relations, including people's understanding of the world (Verbeek 2015).

To understand this phenomenon of technological mediation, we need to start from technologies themselves, instead of reducing them to their conditions. Don Ihde distinguishes several types of relations human beings can have with technologies. Some technologies are *embodied*, like a pair of glasses: we look *through* it, not *at* it. Others are *read*, like a thermometer, that gives a representation of the temperature which requires human interpretation. Another type of relation is the *alterity relation* in which there is an *interaction* with technologies, as a quasi-other, like interacting with a social robot. And fourth, there is a *background relation*, in which technologies function as a context for human activities and experience, like the functioning of heating and air conditioning systems, that operate without us noticing this.

In all these human–technology relations, technologies are not neutral intermediaries between humans and world, but 'mediators' that help to shape how human beings engage with the world, and how the world becomes meaningful for them. When technologies are used, they contribute to the human practices and perceptions that emerge from that use. And it is on the basis of this mediating role that technologies have an ethical dimension: by helping to shape human practices and interpretations of the world, technologies also help to shape moral actions and decisions, as will become clear below.

The Ethical Significance of Technology

The postphenomenological approach brings a specific contribution to the ethics of technology. First of all, postphenomenology makes it possible to analyze the 'impact' of specific technologies on human beings in a detailed way, as a basis for ethical evaluation: the ethical assessment of technologies can be based on the identification of technological mediations. This results in questions like: to what extent is it acceptable to use speed bumps to make people drive more slowly?; how acceptable is the risk that WiFi tracking in public spaces discourages people to visit these places?; etc.

Such ethical questions address technological mediation 'from the outside', as it were: they apply an ethical framework to assess the moral quality of specific technological mediations. There is a more intricate way to connect ethics and mediation, though: the phenomenon of technological mediation has a normative dimension *itself*. By helping to shape human practices and perceptions, technologies play a mediating role in the central questions of ethics: the questions of 'how to act?' and 'how to live?'. Technologies, in order words, are part of the ways in which humans do ethics. This section will highlight three dimensions of this technological mediation of ethics: the mediation of moral actions and decisions; the mediated character of values and moral frameworks; and the technological disruption of ethical concepts, requiring the development of new concepts to address ethical questions.

Moral Mediation

How to conceptualize the moral significance of technology, in a philosophical discourse which connects ethics only to human subjects, not to technological objects? To qualify as a moral agent, after all, intentionality is needed – a condition that can never be met by technological artifacts. Moreover, attributing agency to things could have the absurd consequence that we could actually blame things for ethically problematic actions. Also, it could reduce our sense of human responsibility: why take responsibility ourselves if we can leave the responsibilities to technology? (Peterson and Spahn 2010; Peterson 2012).

From a postphenomenological point of view, such arguments build on an unjustified separation of humans and technologies: the question seems to be if moral agency can be a property of technologies, just like it is a property of human beings. But from a postphenomenological perspective, moral agency should not be located 'in' technologies themselves, but in the interactions between humans and technologies. Ethics is 'done' on the basis of human-technology relations, in which technologies have a role as 'moral mediators' (Verbeek 2011; Kudina 2019): they play a mediating role in the moral relations in which human beings are engaged. By helping to shape how humans behave and understand the world, technologies-in-use also help to shape moral decisions and moral action.

One of the central examples with which this phenomenon of moral mediation has been investigated is prenatal diagnostics. Sonograms create new moral relations between expecting parents and the fetus. First of all, sonograms make the fetus visible already during pregnancy. This changes the relation between mother and fetus: the mother now becomes the 'environment' of the fetus, while the fetus appears on the screen as a quasi-independent human being. Not the unity of the pregnant woman and the fetus, but a visual depiction of the fetus itself becomes the basis for developing a moral relation to the fetus. Moreover, sonograms make it possible to get information about the health condition of the fetus before it is born, and in countries where abortion is legal this makes parents responsible for getting a child with a specific health condition: what used to be 'fate' now becomes 'choice'. This, as well, affects the moral relations between with the fetus: it informs decisions about parenthood and abortion (Verbeek 2008).

Mediated Morality

Technologies do not only mediate morality at the micro-level of individual human-technology relations, but also at the macro-level of moral frameworks and values. To make this visible, recent studies have expanded the scope of the postphenomenological approach. Besides focusing on technological mediation, these studies also started to include the 'appropriation' of technologies by human beings (Verbeek 2016; Kudina 2019). The initial focus of postphenomenology on what *things* do (Verbeek 2005), also in moral relations, has left underexposed that also *human beings* have an active role in the coming about of human-technology relations. The technological mediation of moral actions and interpretations is not only the result of the characteristics of these technologies, but also of the ways in which human beings 'appropriate' them, as part of their relations with the world. The morally mediating role of sonography, for instance, does not only result from the technological capacity to make the fetus visible, but also from the human appropriation of this capacity as a possibility to investigate the *medical condition* of the fetus, and a potential basis for making decisions to act.

Philosopher Olya Kudina has developed a model to investigate this interplay between mediation and appropriation: the so-called 'hermeneutic lemniscate' (Kudina 2019). This model is an expansion of the figure of the 'hermeneutic circle', which explains the dynamics between interpreter and interpreted (Gadamer 1988). This hermeneutic circle has the following structure: by interpreting the world, the world gets constituted in a specific way for the interpreter; as a result, this newly 'constituted world' becomes a new context for the interpreter, which, then, constitutes her or him in a specific way; on this basis, the interpreter develops a renewed interpretation of the world; etc. As Kudina explains, this circular relation between interpreter and interpreted is in fact mediated by technologies. The resulting 'technologically mediated hermeneutic circle' connects humans, technology, and world via a lemniscate-shaped structure: ∞. Humans interpret a technology in a specific way (human —> technology), which enables the technology to mediate human interpretations of the world in a specific way (technology —> world). Against the background of this specific understanding of the world, the technology acquires a specific role and meaning (world —> technology), which in its turn constitutes the user in a specific way (technology —> human), etc.

Again, the example of sonography is helpful to illustrate this. People have a relation to the ultrasound technology from the intention to make the fetus visible; on the basis of this interpretation of the technology, information about the medical condition of the fetus becomes available, which then constitutes the fetus as a 'potential patient'. Against this background of potential patienthood, and in a society that allows abortion, the ultrasound technology then gets interpreted as a technology that can not only be used to *see* the fetus, but also to *prevent the birth* of children with a specific health condition; and on the basis of this new interpretation of the technology, parents get constituted as being responsible for getting a child with a specific health condition, and therefore as decision-makers about the life of the fetus. Moral mediation appears to be a dynamic process of interpretation, in which technological mediations and human interpretations are closely intertwined.

This hermeneutic lemniscate makes it possible to connect the micro-level of individual human-technology relations to the macro-level of *moral values and frameworks*. Also at this macro-level, technologies play a mediating role. Dutch philosopher of technology Tsjalling Swierstra has indicated this phenomenon as 'technomoral change' (Swierstra et al. 2009): technological developments cannot only be evaluated with the help of moral frameworks, but also affect these frameworks themselves. A good example in this context is the moral impact of the birth control pill, as analyzed by Annemarie Mol (Mol 1997). The pill was not only an outcome of the sexual revolution, but also helped to shape it. By disconnecting sexuality from reproduction, it had a substantial impact on value frameworks regarding sexuality. Before the birth control pill, having sex was intricately connected to the possibility of pregnancy, but the introduction of the pill in fact normalized having sex that was not directed at reproduction. Because of this, the pill contributed to a growing acceptance of sexual relations that cannot result in reproduction, like homosexual relations: it mediated moral frameworks regarding sexuality.

This phenomenon of technomoral change, and its dynamics of mediation and appropriation, can be studied empirically. Olya Kudina, for instance, has investigated online discussions about Google Glass on YouTube, focusing on the implicit and explicit definitions of privacy that play a role in these discussions. Her study shows that Glass invited people to define 'privacy' in new ways that are different from the regular definitions that can be found in textbooks (Kudina 2019). Glass made people understand their privacy as more than the right to be left alone, or to have control over their data: they started to define it as the privacy of being together (is the other person really with you, or looking at something else?), for instance, and of personal memories (will recordings of events from a first-person perspective make memories less 'private'?).

This phenomenon of mediated morality brings an interesting extra dimension to the ethics of technology. The ethical evaluation of technologies appears to not only require anticipation of their future social implications, but also of the impact they might have on the moral frameworks from which they might be evaluated in the future. This can even be seen as a new variant of the 'Collingridge dilemma' in the governance of technology (Kudina and Verbeek 2019). This dilemma, which is also called the 'control dilemma', says that attempts to guide innovation processes always seem to be either too early or too late: at an early stage of the development of a new technology, change is relatively easy, but the potential social implications of the technology are not clear yet, but when these implications do have become clear, changing the path of development of the technology has become hard (Collingridge 1980).

Technomoral change adds an ethical dimension to this dilemma: not only is it hard to anticipate the future impacts of technology, but also the future moral frameworks from which these impacts will be evaluated. To deal with this situation, it is important to create 'threshold situations' for technologies-in-development: situations at which it is already possible to investigate empirically how technologies might induce value change or moral mediation, because of a small-scale, experimental introduction of the technology in society. Such threshold situations make it possible to anticipate future social impacts and moral change with an empirical rather than a merely speculative basis (Kudina and Verbeek 2019).

Conceptual Disruption

A third dimension of the ethical implications of human-technology relations is the phenomenon of conceptual disruption. Here, technologies affect yet another layer of ethics: beyond the micro- and macro-levels of morality, there is also a sub-level or infrastructural level at which technologies have an impact on ethics by disrupting the very concepts with which humans can do ethics in the first place.[2] Several contemporary technologies – like robots, genome editing, and climate engineering technologies – escape the concepts with which ethical theory has been working over the past decades or even centuries. The concept of 'moral agency', for instance, loses its self-evidence when robotic technologies like self-driving cars are equipped with 'learning' algorithms that enable them to make decisions about the lives of human beings in case of a crash. And how to deal with the concept of 'human rights' when the DNA of an organism contains both human and nonhuman elements? Should we consider this organism to have animal rights, human rights, or a blend of both? Or how to understand the concept of 'risk' in relation to climate engineering technologies that could 'dim the sun' (Roeser et al. 2019)? How to use the concept of 'intrinsic value' when nature itself becomes an engineering project? Should risks be acceptable for future generations, or for nature itself? And if so, how to represent them in democratic processes?

Conceptual disruption is not a *direct* result of human-technology relations but is encountered when humans try to deal with ethical questions that arise from our interactions with technologies. Some of these concepts indeed concern the implications of technology for our understanding of the human being itself, where concepts like autonomy, solidarity, empathy, and accountability are challenged in our interactions with technologies. Other concepts concern the relations between technology and *society*, like justice, well-being, and democracy. And yet another set of concepts concerns the relations between technology and *nature*, like naturalness and artificiality, control, and intrinsic value. New and emerging technologies affect ethics at its deepest level: they challenge or even escape the categories with which we can do ethics in the first place. And by doing so, they urge us to revise, expand, or innovate the conceptual infrastructure for ethical analysis and reflection.

Guidance Ethics

Analyzing the moral significance of technologies is not only an interesting academic activity, but also offers many opportunities to connect the ethics of technology to practices of design and innovation. When it becomes possible to analyze how technologies are morally significant, after all, the ethics of technology can also turn itself into an ethics for technology.

In the field of design ethics, several approaches have been developed already, to which the postphenomenological approach adds its own distinct dimension. One of the most influential approaches in the field is Batya Friedman's 'Value Sensitive Design' approach. This interdisciplinary approach enables designers to anticipate the values at stake in the technology they are designing, in order to feed this anticipation back into the design process itself (Friedman and Hendry 2019; see also Van den Hoven et al. 2017).

The postphenomenological approach can be used to expand this program of 'value sensitive design'. First of all, postphenomenology makes it possible to take moral mediation and mediated morality into account when designing technologies. Rather than aiming to 'load' technologies with predefined values, as is often the case in Value-Sensitive Design, the dynamics of the interaction between humans, values, and technologies then becomes the starting point (Verbeek 2013, 2017; Smits et al. 2019). Design then becomes a process of intervention in an ongoing dynamics in which values are not given beforehand, but develop in close interaction with the technologies that are designed and evaluated with the help of these very values.

Second, the postphenomenological approach makes it possible to develop a new, constructive approach in applied ethics. The field of applied ethics has been strongly influenced by bioethics. This branch of ethics focuses on 'ethical assessment', for good reasons: it is often executed by medical-ethical committees that evaluate proposals for research or medical intervention in order to approve or reject them. The bioethical model of ethics is often directed at asking questions of 'yes or no', 'permit or forbid'. In the ethics of technology, though, the possibility to connect ethical reflection to the design, implementation, and use of technologies allows for a broader ethical approach than 'assessment' only. Ethics can also function as 'accompaniment' of technology, aiming to guide technology in society.

The 'Guidance Ethics Approach' (Verbeek and Tijink 2020) is a good example of this accompanying role of ethical reflection. The approach was developed by a Dutch working group on the ethics of digital technologies in which companies, governmental organizations, and academics work together (Verbeek and Tijink 2020, 62). The approach aims to make ethical analysis 'actionable', by connecting it concretely to the development, implementation, and use of new technologies. It aims to be an ethics 'from within' rather than 'from outside': it finds its basis in concrete engagement with technological practices rather than in distant analysis. Moreover, Guidance Ethics has a 'bottom–up' rather than a 'top–down' character: it aims to empower people who are developing the technology or experiencing its impact. Rather than delegating ethical reflection to ethical experts who apply ethical theories to concrete technologies, Guidance Ethics gives a voice to professionals and citizens: their nearness to the technology in the various stages of its development and deployment is a good basis for ethical analysis, and for connecting this analysis to practices of design, implementation, and use. And, finally, Guidance Ethics should be seen as a form of 'positive ethics' rather than 'negative ethics'. This does not imply that the approach is always positive about technologies, but rather that it does not primarily direct itself (negatively) at keeping at bay what we do *not* want, but rather (positively) on helping to shape the conditions for what we *do* want. Just like 'positive psychology' focuses on stimulating well-being rather than 'curing diseases', and 'positive design' focuses on shaping conditions for flourishing rather than 'solving problems', positive ethics focuses on connecting values to technology, rather than defining the boundaries that demarcate what we do *not* want.

The approach has three distinct steps (see Figure 6.1). Its first step ('Case') is a careful analysis of the technology that is at stake, focusing both on its material-technological details and on its concrete context of application and use. The purpose of this step is to get a close understanding of the technology and its social and societal embedding. The second step of the approach ('Dialogue') aims to identify the key values that are at stake in relation to this technology. It arrives at these values by (a) identifying the actors who are involved in the development and functioning of the technology, and who experience the impact of the technology, and (b) anticipating the potential effects ('mediations') that this technology could have on all relevant actors. The third and last step focuses on formulating concrete

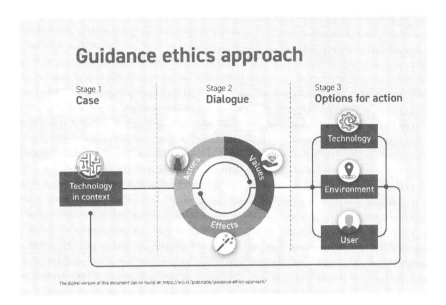

Figure 6.1 Guidance Ethics Approach (ECP | Platform voor de InformatieSamenleving)

'Options for action'. The list of key values that results from step 2 is not used to reach a verdict about the technology, but to formulate concrete options for action regarding the technology itself (is redesign needed to support these values?), its environment (do we need regulation or supporting technology?), and its users (could empowerment of users, education, and communication play a role in supporting the values derived in step 2?).

The Guidance Ethics Approach is not a normative theory itself: it aims to derive its normative content from the people who follow the approach. Yet, this does not take away that the approach is itself basis on a normative starting point: it is directed at emancipation and empowerment, enabling stakeholders in society to anticipate the implications of technology for society, to analyze the normative dimension of these implications, and to translate this analysis into the design, implementation, and use of the technology.

Conclusion

Postphenomenology brings a perspective of human–technology relations to the ethics of technology. By investigating how technologies help to shape human practices, perceptions, and interpretative frameworks, it makes visible a moral dimension of technology itself. Technologies mediate moral actions and decisions, help to shape moral frameworks, and can even disrupt the concepts with which we can do ethics in the first place. This moral significance should not be seen as an intrinsic property of technology itself: postphenomenology does not claim that technologies are 'moral agents' just like humans are. To the contrary: it claims that moral agency should never be seen as something 'purely human', but as intrinsically mediated by technologies.

This moral significance of technology brings an extra dimension to the ethics of technology: it shows that ethical analysis needs to take into account how this analysis is itself affected by the very technologies it aims to analyze. The yardstick is not independent from the things to measure with it – if we can compare ethics to measuring at all. This means that ethics of technology should stay close to the technologies themselves and their concrete implications for human beings, societies, and ethical practices, frameworks and contexts. The Guidance Ethics Approach offers a structure for doing exactly that.

Notes

1 This chapter incorporates reworked fragments from Verbeek, P.P. (2021). The Empirical Turn. In: S. Vallor (ed.), *The Oxford Handbook of Philosophy of Technology*. Oxford: Oxford University Press.
2 This phenomenon of conceptual disruption is the main object of investigation for a large consortium of Dutch researchers that received funding for a 10-year research program (2019–2029) on the 'Ethics of Socially Disruptive Technologies' (www.esdit.nl).

References

Collingridge, David. 1980. *The Social Control of Technology*. New York: St. Martin's Press.
De Boer, Bas, Te Molder, Hedwig and Verbeek, Peter-Paul 2020. Constituting 'Visual Attention': On the Mediating Role of Brain Stimulation and Brain Imaging Technologies in Neuroscientific Practice. *Science as Culture* 29 (4): 503–523.
Friedman, Batya and Hendry, David G. 2019. *Value Sensitive Design: Shaping Technology with Moral Imagination*. Cambridge, MA: MIT Press.
Gadamer, Hans-Georg. 1988. On the Circle of Understanding. In *Hermeneutics vs. Science*, eds. John Connolly and Thomas Keutner, 68–78. Notre Dame, IN: University of Notre Dame Press.
Heidegger, Martin 1977. The Question Concerning Technology. In *The Question Concerning Technology and Other Essays*, trans. W. Lovett. New York: Harper and Row.
Ihde, Don 1990. *Technology and the Lifeworld*. Bloomington: Indiana University Press.
Kudina, Olya 2019. *The Technological Mediation of Morality: Value Dynamism and the Complex Interaction between Ethics and Technology*. Enschede: University of Twente.
Kudina, Olya and Verbeek, Peter-Paul 2019. Ethics from Within: Google Glass, the Collingridge Dilemma, and the Mediated Value of Privacy. *Science, Technology, & Human Values* 44 (2): 291–314.
Mol, Annemarie 1997. *Wat Is kiezen? Een empirisch-filosofische verkenning*. Enschede: Universiteit Twente (Inaugural Lecture).
Peterson, Martin 2012. Three Objections to Verbeek. In *Book Symposium on Peter Paul Verbeek's Moralizing Technology: Understanding and Designing the Morality of Things, Philosophy and Technology*, eds. E. Selinger et al. Philosophy and Technology Vol. 25, 619–625.
Peterson, Martin and Spahn, Andreas 2010. Can Technological Artefacts Be Moral Agents? *Science and Engineering Ethics* 17 (3): 411–424.
Roeser, Sabine, Taebi, Behnam and Doorn, Neelke 2019. Geoengineering the Climate and Ethical Challenges: What We Can Learn from Moral Emotions and Art. *Critical Review of International Social and Political Philosophy* 23 (5): 641–658.
Rosenberger, Robert and Verbeek, Peter-Paul 2015. *Postphenomenological Investigations: Essays on Human-Technology Relations*. Lanham: Lexington.
Selinger, Evan 2006. *Postphenomenology: A Critical Companion to Ihde*. New York: SUNY Press.
Swierstra, Tsjalling, Stemerding, Dirk and Boenink, Marianne 2009. Exploring Techno-moral Change: The Case of the Obesitypill. In *Evaluating New Technologies*, eds. Paul Sollie and Marcus Düwell, 119–138. Dordrecht: Springer.
Smits, Merlijn, Bredie, Bas, Van Goor, Harry and Verbeek, Peter-Paul 2019. Values that Matter: Mediation Theory and Design for Values. *Academy for Design Innovation Management Conference 2019: Research Perspectives in the Era of Transformations*: 396–407.
Van den Hoven, Jeroen, Miller, Seumas and Pogge, Thomas (eds.) 2017. *Designing in Ethics*. Cambridge: Cambridge University Press, 78–94.

Verbeek, Peter-Paul 2005. *What Things Do: Philosophical Reflections on Technology, Agency, and Design*. University Park: Penn State University Press.

Verbeek, Peter-Paul 2008. Obstetric Ultrasound and the Technological Mediation of Morality – A Postphenomenological Analysis. In *Human Studies* 2008–1, 11–26.

Verbeek, Peter-Paul 2011. *Moralizing Technology: Understanding and Designing the Morality of Things*. Chicago: University of Chicago Press.

Verbeek, Peter-Paul 2013. Technology Design as Experimental Ethics. In *Ethics on the Laboratory Floor*, eds. S. van den Burg and Tsj Swierstra, 83–100. Basingstoke: Palgrave Macmillan.

Verbeek, Peter-Paul 2015. Beyond Interaction: A Short Introduction to Mediation Theory. *Interactions* 22 (3): 26–31. ISSN 1072-5520.

Verbeek, Peter-Paul 2017. Designing the Morality of Things: The Ethics of Behavior-Guiding Technology. In *Designing in Ethics*, eds. Jeroen van den Hoven, Seumas Miller, and Thomas Pogge, 78–94. Cambridge: Cambridge University Press.

Verbeek, Peter-Paul and Tijink, Daniel (2020). *Guidance Ethics Approach*. The Hague: ECP.

Chapter 7

Technology and the Extended Mind

Shaun Gallagher

The concept of extended mind involves the idea that the use of various tools, artifacts, or aspects of the environment can facilitate, enhance, or even constitute cognition. The two primary examples of the extended mind given in the now classic paper, "The extended mind," by Clark and Chalmers (1998) involve different types of technology. In one example, a player adjusts the positions of shapes on a computer screen through the manipulation of a computer mouse to supplement or replace the use of the imagination in order to facilitate the playing of the game Tetra. In the second example, Otto, a person with memory problems, utilizes a somewhat older form of technology, pencil and notebook, to record, store, and retrieve his memories. Technologies can operate as vehicles of cognition in ways that supplement or replace neural mechanisms as we attempt to remember, or imagine, or think through solutions to problems. Accordingly, our cognitive abilities (and the cognitive processes themselves) are extended, and perhaps constituted by the use of various aspects of the environment, and more specifically by technologies.

The Parity Principle

Although there are a number of philosophical debates about the nature of the mind in the extended mind literature, technology is consistently understood to play an important role in the various positions defended by extended mind theorists. In the original version of the extended mind hypothesis (EMH), the relevant technology is treated in parity with processes that occur in the head or brain, in conformity with the parity principle, which states:

> If, as we confront some task, a part of the world functions as a process which, were it done in the head, we would have no hesitation in recognizing as part of the cognitive process, then that part of the world is (so we claim) part of the cognitive process.
> (Clark & Chalmers 1998, 8)

According to this account, engagement with a particular piece of technology can be part of the cognitive process, on parity with brain processes. This view is referred to as "active" or "vehicle" externalism, understood in terms of the distinction between the content and the vehicle of cognition (Dennett 1969; Millikan 1991). According to EMH, the vehicles or material mechanisms of cognition are not just neurons, but may include instruments or artifacts in the environment. "Active" externalism registers both "the active role of the environment" and active engagement on the part of the cognizer. To the extent that internal representations play a role, they are action-oriented representations which set the stage for engagement with the material environment (Clark & Toribio 1994). Kirsh and Maglio

DOI: 10.4324/9781003189466-9

(1994) call this "epistemic action." For example, in playing the game Tetris, a player might have the following options:

a   activate neurons in order to mentally rotate the geometric shapes she sees on the computer screen
b   activate a neural implant in her brain to physically rotate the geometric shapes, or
c   physically manipulate the geometric shapes using a rotate button on the computer.

According to the parity principle, these processes would be more or less equivalent. Option (c), as an epistemic action, can simply substitute for (a) or (b).

In response to worries about the reliability of technology and the portability of external tools and artifacts, in contrast to the brain, Clark and Chalmers emphasize that although the brain may come to depend on specific types of technology, it is also the case that the cognizer may have the capacity to couple systematically with a wide variety of elements. This can provide cognitive flexibility. Also, if we can think of language as a technology, it tends to be a reliable and important tool that expands our cognitive capacity (see Rupert 2010).

The most contentious objection to the EMH concerns the idea that the use of an external artifact or piece of technology "constitutes" cognition, or more controversially put, constitutes the mind. What follows from this kind of claim are worries about the boundaries of the mind (where the mind begins and ends), about the "mark of the mental" which would define those boundaries (Adams & Aizawa 2001), and about cognitive bloat, where there seems no limit at all to the mind (Rupert 2004; Rowlands 2009). In contrast to any claim that the mind is constituted not only by brain processes, but also by processes of engagement with whatever equipment might be put in service of cognition, the alternative is to simply take the external technology as causally related to cognition, enabling it but not constituting it. Giving up the constitution claim and retaining the causal claim would still allow one to speak metaphorically about extending the mind without running into ontological difficulties – that is, having to claim the mind includes parts outside of the head. One would thus avoid the causal coupling-constitution fallacy, as Adams and Aizawa define it, a problem of confusing causality with constitution.[1]

Clark (2008, 2010b), retaining the strong claim of constitution, appeals to what are called the "trust and glue" criteria to address some of these concerns. These are criteria that need to be met by external physical processes if they are to be included as part of an individual's cognitive process. He lists three such criteria.

1   That the external resource be reliably available and typically invoked.
2   That any information thus retrieved be more or less automatically endorsed. It should not usually be subject to critical scrutiny (unlike the opinions of other people, for example). It should be deemed about as trustworthy as something retrieved clearly from biological memory.
3   That information contained in the resource should be easily accessible as and when required (Clark 2008, 79).

The Second and Subsequent Waves

A friendlier, or one might say, internal objection to EMH's parity principle leads to a revised version of the extended mind, often referred to as a "second wave" of extended mind theory. Although, in some cases there may be an epistemic-functional similarity or parity between internal neural processes and external tools and technologies, there are also cases that involve significant differences, where the differences offer important and complementary functionality. Complementarity includes the idea that "different components of the overall (enduring or temporary) system can play quite different roles and have different properties while coupling in collective and complementary contributions to flexible thinking and acting" (Sutton 2010, 194; see Gallagher 2018 for further discussion). The balance implied by complementarity between the use of external props or technologies and internal processes like memorization, may alter from case to case or from situation to situation. Indeed, this balance may be modulated by structures or changes in the affordances offered by different environments, as well as differences in agents' bodies and skill levels.

If this is a departure from the parity principle, it is one that Clark allows, since, following Edwin Hutchins (1995) view of distributed cognition, he can say that "the computational power and expertise is spread across a heterogeneous assembly of brains, bodies, artifacts, and other external structures" (Clark 1997, 77), such that disparate components may cooperate to yield an integrated system capable of supporting various (often quite advanced) forms of adaptive success (Clark 1998, 99). Accordingly, there can be a kind of "soft assembly," and sometimes a temporary meshing of neural and non-neural resources to form a "highly integrated," task-specific system. In this respect, technologies, and the practices that surround different technologies, are integrated into cognitive processes, not due to some kind of automatic fit between neural processes and pieces of the environment, but because there is an active coupling through a set of reciprocal causal connections activated by active (sensory-motor) bodily manipulations of the environment (Menary 2007, 2010b). These manipulations include epistemic actions, sensory-motor contingencies (O'Regan & Noë 2001), and self-correcting actions, which may include both the use of technology and cognitive practices which involve "the manipulation of external representational and notational systems according to certain normative practices – as in mathematics" (Menary 2010a, 237; see Menary 2010b, 2012). That is, the use of numbers, diagrams, drawings, maps, charts, etc., operating as external representations, allows for the accomplishment of cognitive tasks. Furthermore, we manipulate our technologies (from pencils and paper to computers), following norms that are culturally established and learned. According to Menary, these practices and normative factors are integrated with the internal activities of our brains and mediated by the movements of our bodies.

The emphasis on social and cultural practices also suggests something that remained implicit in the original proposal of the EMH, namely that those practices, and the social relations they involve, are also extensive for the mind. One can think of this in a bottom-up fashion, in terms of the formation of collective intentionalities emerging from the interaction of agents who, by working together, depend on one another to expand their cognitive capacities and epistemic affordances (see De Boer 2021). One can also think of this in a top-down fashion, in terms of established institutions that provide support for cognitive operations (Gallagher 2013). These are cognitive institutions like the legal system, an educational system, the institution of science, etc., that allow for expansive social organization and the advancement of knowledge. Like the technologies that they typically use, such institutions can both expand possibilities for acting and thinking, or constrain and narrow them.

Changing Your Mind

If we think of the mind as extended by technologies and the practices and institutions that surround technologies, then one clear principle is that changing technology changes the mind. This is nothing new. We find the idea in Hegel as well as Marx; and more recently in post-phenomenology (Ihde 1979, 2009) and material engagement theory (Malafouris 2013). As Ihde and Malafouris (2018, 1) indicate:

> Humans, more than any other species, have been altering their paths of development by creating new material forms and by opening up to new possibilities of material engagement. That is, we become constituted through making and using technologies that shape our minds and extend our bodies. We make things which in turn make us.
>
> (2018, 1)

Technology, in effect, is not neutral; as a product of human activity, it is "always (whether consciously or unconsciously) determined through norms and values" (Loh 2019, 9), and, we might add, determining of norms and values. Since the EMH expresses a form of embodied cognition, it is important to note that, materially, technologies of all sorts have direct effects on our bodies. In one view, expressed by Marx and Engels, the human body is an appendage to the machine (Synnott 1993, 24). In this respect, however, it can be the institutional (social and political) arrangements that make it so. The use of technologies within specific institutional frameworks can in fact constrict cognition and limit our affordances. It's not just the arrangement of task-related operations in the factory, as Marx and Engels were thinking; in more contemporary scenarios, it may be the embodied practices associated with social media and communicative technology that create the constraints on our thinking capacities. Web-based technologies (what Smart (2012) calls "web-extended mind"[2]), for example, can have a direct effect on how we perceive the world, or how we conceive of our social relations. These are technologies that get incorporated; they get "inside our heads" and constrict our abilities to even recognize problems. At the same time, they may be open to manipulation by others, posing a threat to autonomy and privacy (Reiner & Nagel 2017).

Ethical issues aside, such technologies change minds. That is, literally, they change the way that we perceive the world, or change the way that we think about things. A nice example is given by Michael Wheeler (2019) – "North Sense" (now called "Sentero"), a small wearable piece of technology that vibrates gently when it faces magnetic north (https://cybor gnest.net/products/ the-north-sense, last accessed 5 October 2021). As Wheeler explains, first-person reports suggest that North Sense "quickly becomes deeply integrated into the wearer's cognitive life. Most strikingly, orientation and position start to play a bigger-than-usual role in the structuring of memory" (2019, 857). He quotes Scott Cohen, who describes this phenomenon as follows:

> It is hard to put into words only a few hours after attaching the North Sense, but the feeling I am left with is profound. The impact of immediately sensing my position created a permanent memory. I vaguely recall the colours and sounds in the room, but I remember my position vividly.

Wheeler suggests that this alters cognitive processing. Regardless of whether one adopts the constitutional view of extended mind, or simply a causal view, the principle is the same: the mind itself changes as we engage with technology.

According to Clark and Wheeler, however, it is the constitutive relation that allows us to count a piece of technology as part of an extended mind. The example of North Sense can also help us understand how to think of this constitutive relation, since it is an example of a technology that quickly becomes transparent or incorporated. That is, it becomes experientially invisible so that the agent gets directly to the experience without noticing the technology. For Clark, Wheeler, and others, this kind of transparency is a necessary condition for a truly extended mind, i.e., the case in which the agent's engagement with the technology constitutes her cognitive processes (Clark 2008, 27–38; Carter et al. 2018; Wheeler 2019).

The Transparency Requirement

Wheeler summarizes this view with what we can call the transparency requirement:

> When a tool is transparent, that is a necessary condition met for its constitutive incorporation into the user's mental machinery. When a tool becomes visible, due to, for example, damage or malfunction, or when, as in the case of some sensory substitution subjects, a deliberate, conscious effort on the part of the user resets the mind–world boundary at the skin, that means that cognitive extension is no longer operative.
>
> (Wheeler 2019, 862)

There are some technologies that follow the opposite logic. In contrast to the term "incorporation," as it is used to describe how some technologies becomes transparently integrated with the body (Clark 2008; De Preester & Tsakiris 2009; Nourrit & Rosselin-Bareille 2017), Butnaro (2021) argues that some technologies, which are not incorporated or transparent, nonetheless *extend* bodily and embodied mental capacities. She provides a detailed analysis of exoskeletal technology (ET), i.e., robotic enhancements of the body, and argues that these are embodied extensions rather than incorporations. They do not become experientially transparent for the user, as some prosthetics do. In this respect, they are similar to smartphones and computers which are epistemic extensions, allowing us to store knowledge, "outdoors," so to speak, but also allowing easy access to that knowledge. Rather than *ego cogito*, through such technology we engage with *exo-cogitans*.

In contrast to Butnaro, Clark (2008, 37–38; 74ff) and Wheeler (2019) would deny that non-transparent technology can be truly constitutive of extended cognition. On the transparency requirement, transparency is the measure of extension. Clark and Wheeler acknowledge that human cognition employs both kinds of technology, transparent and non-transparent, even if only the transparent kind can be truly constitutive of extended mind. Like Butnaro, Clark appeals to the example of technologies that extend the capabilities of the body to make his point. Experiments show rapid changes in neuronal processing when macaque monkeys learned to use a rake to reach their food. Such neuronal changes, reinforced by behavioral measures, are usually interpreted to mean that perception of peripersonal space changes to include space as far as the rake can reach; this change is also formulated as the tool being incorporated into the body schema, "as if the rake was part of the arm and forearm" (Maravita & Iriki 2004, 79). The idea that one can become fluent or skilled at using such a tool, to the point that it results in plastic changes in one's brain, is evidence that the tool has become transparent or incorporated – part of the body schema, and not just causally related to it. In the same way, that is, appealing to the transparency requirement, Clark suggests, human minds can be "genuinely extended and augmented by cultural and technological tweaks" (2008, 39).

For Wheeler, the issue is framed by a concern about the use of deep-learning AI systems in devices that classify information in ways that are not consistent with the classificatory norms that human agents typically use. On the one hand, the use of such technology may indeed meet the experiential transparency requirement; on the other hand, and at the same time, the technology is not epistemically transparent in so far as the agent does not fully understand how the algorithm works, and is unaware that the technology may be changing his mind in unwanted ways.

> This outcome would surely have epistemic implications and perhaps moral ones too. If a deep neural network application to which I am transparently coupled qualifies as part of my cognitive architecture and thus as part of me, then the classifications in question—classifications that unconsciously guide my behaviour—will be part of what I unconsciously believe to be the case, and thus presumably will have the same status as my more familiar, internally realized unconscious beliefs when it comes to any moral judgments that are made about my resulting thoughts and actions.
>
> (Wheeler 2019, 864)

In such cases, Wheeler suggests, we may not want the technology to meet the transparency requirement; it would be better if we were aware of what the technology was doing or how it was classifying information if it is doing so in an obscure or aberrant way. Rather than the model of the incorporated tool, Wheeler offers a model of conversation, following Usman Haque's proposal for high-tech interactive buildings. For Haque, we would create a rapport with the technology through "conversations," where new possibilities are built on a history of interactions (Haque 2006, 3). Such human-AI interfaces would be modeled on a "constructive interactive dialogue" rather than a smooth transparent coping (Wheeler 2019, 865). One could happily endorse this model, but it comes with the proviso that a dialogical relation with technology would not constitute an extended mind in the genuine sense, specifically because it does not meet the transparency requirement.

It is not clear, however, why the transparency requirement should be the measure of constitutive status or genuine extension. In this respect, the requirement is related to the trust and glue criteria mentioned above (see Clark 2008, 80). Consider, for example, the second of these criteria.

> That any information thus retrieved be more-or-less automatically endorsed. It should not usually be subject to critical scrutiny (unlike the opinions of other people, for example). It should be deemed about as trustworthy as something retrieved clearly from biological memory.

Of course, biological memory is not always trustworthy, although we may not normally give it much critical scrutiny. If we did give it critical scrutiny, would that make it less genuinely a cognitive process? It would seem that on this criterion, as well as the transparency requirement, any type of cognitive activity that required critical scrutiny would simply disqualify the activity from being considered a genuinely extended cognitive process. Even if I usually engage in critical reflection or a metacognitive heedful attitude – perhaps I'm a habitual skeptic – why should that disqualify any processes that would otherwise count as cognitive. Critical reflective scrutiny is simply another cognitive process, so it seems odd to think that by adding a cognitive process like reflection to a process that otherwise would count as cognitive, it suddenly makes that process non-cognitive. Likewise for any use of technology that would normally count as constitutive for extended cognition, the fact that, as I am using it, I take a critical perspective on it, making it less transparent – perhaps, for example, reflecting on, or even conversing with another agent about what the AI device that we are using may be doing to our scientific project – should not undermine its status as an extended cognitive performance. Indeed, in typical instances of problem solving, it is important to take a critical metacognitive perspective on how one is going about solving the problem. Such reflection on methods, tools, or my use of a particular technology will make all such cognitive doings less than transparent. We can also note that such critical processes may sometimes involve certain institutional or collective practices that require conversation or communicative actions, and such practices may be even more trustworthy or reliable, than biological memory.

The upshot, then, is that there is good reason to question the transparency requirement as a measure of the extended nature of cognition. Just as in the process of writing this paper, I may engage in a kind of metacognitive evaluation of the argument I am constructing, so I could also engage in a reflective evaluation of my practice as I am using Google Scholar to locate other arguments, or to trace the development of arguments about the extended mind. Neither kind of reflection, even if it makes the cognitive processes more "visible" and less than transparent, should disqualify those processes from being part of my extended cognition, or make them no longer genuinely cognitive.

Conclusion

I've reviewed several versions of the EMH, and its connection to the epistemic use of technology, as well as issues that pertain to the claim that, in some sense, the use of technology may constitute cognition. It is clear, at least, that the use of certain technologies can change our cognitive processes, including perception, memory, and imagination. I've also questioned whether the transparency requirement is a true requirement for the extended mind, and I've argued that it is not. Cognition, whether extended or not, is not always experientially transparent. We often deliberate, make decisions, and solve problems in ways that involve conscious reflection on our thought processes, and sometimes we make such processes "visible" in collective reflection, conversation, and interaction with others. Indeed, such reflective considerations may be important for evaluating the ethical use of technologies that extend the mind.

Notes

1 The strict distinction between causality and constitution derives from new mechanist theory (Craver 2007). On the latter view, constitution is a mereological relation that requires a simultaneity of parts and whole; causality, in contrast, involves diachronic processes. An alternative definition of constitution as diachronic or dynamical, that does not require a strict exclusion of causal processes, however, dissolves the objection and avoids the fallacy (see Kirchhoff 2012; Krickel 2017, 2018; Gallagher 2019).
2 Smart et al. (2008, 2) call this "network-enabled cognition" and define the "thesis of network-enabled cognition: The technological and informational elements of a large-scale information network can, under certain circumstances, constitute part of the material supervenience base for an agent's mental states and processes."

References

Adams, Fred and Kenneth Aizawa. 2001. "The bounds of cognition." *Philosophical Psychology* 14 (1): 43–64.
Butnaro, Denisa. 2021. *Deviant Bodies. Extended Bodies: How Exoskeletal Devices Reshape Corporealities and Their Phenomenologies in Social Contexts*. Habilitation Thesis. University of Constance.
Carter, Adams J, Andy Clark and S. Orestis Palermos. 2018. "New humans? Ethics, trust and the extended mind." In *Extended Epistemology*, edited by Adams J. Carter et al. (331–352). Oxford: Oxford University Press.
Clark, Andy. 2010a. "Memento's revenge: The extended mind, extended." In *The Extended Mind*, edited by Richard Menary (43–66). Cambridge, MA: MIT Press.

Clark, Andy. 2010b. "Coupling, constitution, and the cognitive kind: A reply to Adams and Aizawa." In *The Extended Mind*, edited by Richard Menary (81–100). Cambridge, MA: MIT Press.

Clark, Andy. 2008. *Supersizing the Mind: Embodiment, Action and Cognitive Extension*. Oxford: Oxford University Press.

Clark, Andy. 1998. "Author's response: Review symposium on *Being There*." *Metascience* 7: 95–103.

Clark, Andy. 1997. *Being There: Putting Brain, Body and World Together Again*. Cambridge, MA: MIT Press.

Clark, Andy and David Chalmers. 1998. "The extended mind." *Analysis* 58: 7–19.

Clark, Andy, and Josefa Toribio. 1994. "Doing without representing?" *Synthese* 101: 401–431.

Craver, Carl. 2007. *Explaining the Brain: Mechanisms and the Mosaic Unity of Neuroscience*. Oxford: Clarendon Press.

De Boer, Bas. 2021. Explaining multistability: Postphenomenology and affordances of technologies. *AI and Society*. https://link.springer.com/article/10.1007/s00146-021-01272-3

Dennett, Daniel. 1969. *Content and Consciousness*. London: Routledge.

De Preester, Helena and ManosTsakiris. 2009. "Body-extension versus body-incorporation: Is there a need for a body-model?" *Phenomenology and the Cognitive Sciences* 8(3): 307–319.

Gallagher, Shaun. 2018. The extended mind: State of the question. *Southern Journal of Philosophy* 56(4): 421–447. DOI: 10.1111/sjp.12308

Gallagher, Shaun. 2019. New mechanisms and the enactivist concept of constitution. In M. P. Guta (ed.) *The Metaphysics of Consciousness*. London: Routlege.

Gallagher, Shaun. 2013. The socially extended mind. *Cognitive Systems Research* 25: 4–12.

Haque, Usman. 2006. Architecture, interaction, systems. *Arquitetura and Urbanismo* 149(Brazil). http://www.haque.co.uk/paper s/ArchInterSys.pdf. Accessed 9 October 2021

Hutchins, Edwin. 1995. *Cognition in the Wild*. Cambridge, MA: MIT press.

Ihde, Don. 1979. *Technics and Praxis*. Dordrecht: Reidel Publishing Company.

Ihde, Don. 2009. *Postphenomenology and Technoscience*. Albany: State University of New York Press.

Ihde, Don and Lambros Malafouris. 2019. "Homo faber revisited: Postphenomenology and material engagement theory." *Philosophy & Technology, 32*(2): 195–214.

Kirchhoff, Michael. D. 2012. "Extended cognition and fixed properties: Steps to a third-wave version of extended cognition." *Phenomenology and the Cognitive Sciences* 11: 287–308.

Kirsh, David and Paul Maglio. 1994. "On distinguishing epistemic from pragmatic action." *Cognitive Science* 18(4): 513–549.

Krickel, Beate. 2017. "Making sense of interlevel causation in mechanisms from a metaphysical perspective." *Journal for General Philosophy of Science/Zeitschrift für Allgemeine Wissenschaftstheorie* 48(3): 453–468.

Krickel, Beate. 2018. "Saving the mutual manipulability account of constitutive relevance." *Studies in History and Philosophy of Science Part A*. 68: 58–67. https://doi.org/10.1016/j.shpsa.2018.01.003

Loh, Janina. 2019. *Roboterethik*. Frankfurt am Main: Suhrkamp.

Malafouris, Lambros. 2013. *How Things Shape the Mind*. Cambridge, MA: MIT Press.

Maravita, Angelo, and Atsushi Iriki. 2004. "Tools for the body (schema)." *Trends in Cognitive Sciences* 8(2): 79–86.

Menary, R. 2012. Cognitive practices and cognitive character. *Philosophical Explorations* 15(2): 147–164.

Menary, Richard. 2010a. "Cognitive integration and the extended mind." In *The Extended Mind*, edited by Richard Menary (227–243). Cambridge, MA: MIT Press.

Menary, Richard. 2010b. "Dimensions of mind." *Phenomenology and the Cognitive Sciences* 9(4): 561–578.

Menary, Richard. 2007. *Cognitive Integration: Mind and Cognition Unbounded*. Basingstoke: Palgrave Macmillan.

Millikan, Ruth. 1991. "Perceptual content and Fregean myth." *Mind* 100(4): 439–459.

Nourrit, Déborah and Céline Rosselin-Bareille. 2017. "Incorporer des objets. Apprendre, se transformer, devenir expert." *Socio-anthropologie* 35: 93–110.

O'Regan, J. Kevin and Alva Noë. 2001. "A sensorimotor account of vision and visual consciousness." *Behavioral and Brain Sciences* 24(5): 939–973.

Reiner, Peter Bart and Saskia K. Nagel. 2017. "Technologies of the extended mind: Defining the issues." In *Neuroethics: Anticipating the future*, edited by Judy Illes (108–122). Oxford: Oxford University Press.

Rowlands, Mark. 2009. "The extended mind." *Zygon* 44(3): 628–641.

Rupert, Robert. 2010. "Representation in extended cognitive systems: Does the scaffolding of language extend the mind." In *The Extended Mind*, edited by Richard Menary (325–353). Cambridge, MA: MIT Press.

Rupert, Robert. 2004. "Challenges to the hypothesis of extended cognition." *Journal of Philosophy* 101: 389–428.

Smart, Paul R. 2012. "The web-extended mind." *Metaphilosophy* 43(4): 446–463.

Smart, Paul, Paula Engelbrecht, Dave Braines, James Hendler, and Nigel Shadbolt. 2008. "The Extended Mind and Network-Enabled Cognition." *The Computer Journal*. https://eprints.soton.ac.uk/266649/

Sutton, J. 2010. "Exograms and interdisciplinarity: History, the extended mind and the civilizing process." In *The Extended Mind*, edited by Richard Menary (189–225). Cambridge, MA: MIT Press.

Synnott, Anthony. 1993. *The Body Social*. London: Routledge.

Wheeler, Michael. 2019. "The reappearing tool: Transparency, smart technology, and the extended mind." *AI and Society* 34: 857–866. https://doi.org/10.1007/s00146-018-0824-x

Part II

Technology and the Good Life

Introduction

Is the life well-lived a life of pleasure? Happiness? Honor? Status? Union with God? Philosophers have long puzzled over the nature of the good life. They have proposed objective list theories according to which the good life is one with goods such as love, friendship, and health. They have proposed desire satisfaction theories on which it is constitutive of the good life to satisfy one's actual desires or rationally and morally defensible desires that one has or could have. Philosophers have also considered, for instance, whether the best life is the hedonistic life in which one secures as much pleasure as possible.

Whatever exactly the good life is, our use of technology has a deep and lasting effect on our prospect of achieving it. It is worth asking, for instance: Are the internet and mobile phones improving our lives by connecting us with other people and resources? Or are they leaving us worse off by, say, distracting users and even causing addiction to the internet and social media?

This part explores such questions by looking to the resources of leading theories of ethics such as Aristotelianism, Confucianism, Kantian, and Utilitarianism. After an overview chapter on leading ethical theories, this part applies ethical theories to everything from issues of online honesty to how technology can contribute to (or detract from) one's pleasure in life. The hope is to help readers answer for themselves how the internet, mobile phones, and other technologies can contribute to their pursuit of the life well-lived if used wisely.

DOI: 10.4324/9781003189466-10

Chapter 8

Ethical Theory and Technology

Jonathan Y. Tsou and Kate Padgett Walsh

Are automated driving cars good for society? To what extent should companies be able to profit from patents for developing innovative technological inventions? Should the use of cognitive enhancing drugs be allowed? Normative ethical theories provide different philosophical reasons for supporting conclusions on these and other ethical issues concerning technology. This chapter provides an overview of influential normative ethical theories and how they can be applied to particular cases in the ethics of technology.

Normative ethics addresses questions concerning what is morally good or right. Normative ethical theories (e.g., utilitarianism, Kantian ethics, and contractarianism) specify different *criteria for moral rightness and wrongness* and how to live a morally good life by appealing to alternative philosophical principles. *Meta-ethics* addresses fundamental philosophical questions concerning the existence and nature of moral norms and judgments (e.g., are moral standards universal or culturally relative? Do moral facts exist? Are there moral truths?). By contrast, normative ethical theories assume that some moral standards (e.g., happiness, equity, and freedom) are universal and articulate criteria for moral goodness based on these assumptions. *Applied ethics* is the application of normative ethical theories to specific cases (e.g., abortion and capital punishment).

Normative ethical theories are typically grouped into three categories: consequentialism, deontology, and virtue theory:

Consequentialism	*Deontology*	*Virtue Theory*
Utilitarianism	Kantian Ethics Pluralism Social Contract Theory	Virtue Ethics

Consequentialists maintain that moral goodness is determined exclusively by the consequences of action (or rules) and that there is nothing *intrinsically* good or bad in action itself. By contrast, deontologists claim that we are morally bound by certain moral duties and that some actions are inherently right or wrong. For deontologists, the morality of action is determined by whether action conforms to specific moral duties (or rules). Rather than focusing on the consequences of action or following moral rules, virtue theorists assert that moral goodness is determined by whether our actions stem from virtuous (i.e., excellent) character traits.[1]

Utilitarianism

Utilitarianism holds that an action (or rule) is morally right if it leads to the best consequences (greatest good) for the greatest number of people. Accordingly, the moral course of

DOI: 10.4324/9781003189466-11

action is to promote the general good by maximizing utility, where 'utility' is the net good created by an action (or rule). In principle, utility can be defined in terms of various human goods (e.g., happiness, health, and freedom). The classic utilitarians, Jeremy Bentham ([1789] 1907) and John Stuart Mill ([1861] 1998), defined utility in terms of happiness or pleasure (Driver, 2014). This is encapsulated by Bentham's 'fundamental axiom' of utilitarianism: 'the greatest happiness of the greatest number … is the measure of right and wrong' (cited in Crimmins, 2021).[2] Compared to *ethical egoism*, which holds that we should act in our own self-interest (Shaver, 2021), utilitarianism holds that we ought to act in the best interests of everyone.[3] Utilitarianism is a consequentialist theory because moral rightness is determined *exclusively by the consequences of action*; there is nothing *inherently* good or bad about *action itself*.

Act Utilitarianism (AU) and Rule Utilitarianism (RU) are two forms of utilitarianism that focus on the consequences of actions and rules, respectively:

Act Utilitarianism (AU): actions that maximize utility are morally good.
Rule Utilitarianism (RU): rules that maximize utility are morally good.

In the philosophical literature, AU and RU are commonly presented as *competing ethical theories* that provide conflicting assessments on the *morality of action*. For example, J. J. C. Smart (1956) presents AU as the theory that moral action is an action that maximizes utility in a specific circumstance, whereas RU holds that moral action is an action that corresponds to a rule (e.g., 'keep promises') that tends to maximize utility. Based on this distinction, Smart argues that it is irrational to endorse RU because it implies that agents should perform an action (e.g., keeping a promise to a dying acquaintance to donate their money to an unsavory institution) even if another course of action (e.g., donating to a charity) would obviously be better for maximizing utility.

While much of the philosophical literature assumes that AU and RU are competing theories that prescribe different normative standards *for evaluating the morality of action*, AU and RU can also be understood as *complementary theories* that have different contexts of application: AU is a theory that assesses the morality of action in specific circumstances, whereas RU is a theory that assesses the morality of general rules (e.g., proposed laws or policies). As such, AU and RU need not be regarded as conflicting theories, but complementary *applications of utilitarian theory*.[4] Applied ethics is typically less interested in evaluating the morality of specific actions and more interested in evaluating the morality of general rules (e.g., policies and laws) regarding a *class of ethical cases* (e.g., abortion, euthanasia, and capital punishment). While AU can assess the morality of action in a specific context (viz., prefer the action that maximizes utility), it provides no specific guidance for *evaluating the morality of general rules*. On this issue, RU maintains that rules (e.g., laws or policies) that maximize utility are morally good.

In ethical cases involving technology, RU can be regarded as an application of utilitarian theory that assesses the morality of policies regarding technology. For instance: Should society tolerate privacy technologies that can virtually secure anonymity online? Should society provide financial incentives for producing electric vehicles? There *are* questions in technology ethics about the morality of a specific action (e.g., was Julian Assange morally justified in publishing confidential US military information on WikiLeaks?). But many questions concern the morality of more general policies (or rules) related to technology (e.g., should democratic societies tolerate media sources that publish classified or confidential information for the sake of public transparency?). RU can be regarded as an application of utilitarianism that assesses the morality of rules in terms of the positive and negative (actual or possible) consequences of adopting such rules.

A strength of utilitarianism is that it provides a concrete method for determining the moral course of action. For a given case, it directs us to operationally define utility (e.g., happiness) and weigh the positive consequences against negative consequences. For cases of policy (e.g., capital punishment), this requires comparing the possible gains of adopting a policy (e.g., vindication for the families of victims, lowering costs of incarceration) against possible losses (e.g., the wrongful killing of innocent suspects). In principle, utilitarianism thus offers a straightforward method for determining the moral course of action. In practice, applying utilitarian theory is more complex. There are alternative ways in which 'utility' can be defined and utilitarianism does not provide explicit guidance on how to weigh conflicting positive and negative utilities. In this regard, there is a tradeoff in how specifically utility is defined and how readily applicable utilitarian theory is. If one assumes a simple definition of utility (e.g., happiness), utilitarianism is more easily applied over a broad range of cases, but it may gloss over nuances regarding utilities (e.g., negative utilities that could be assigned greater value). If one assumes a more sophisticated definition of utility (e.g., a view that places greater weight on certain types of pleasure or pain), then it can better account for nuances, but may be more difficult to apply mechanically over a broad range of cases.

One weakness of utilitarianism is its insensitivity to individual rights. For example, if we adopt a simple definition of utility, wherein each individual human life is assigned a utility value of +1, utilitarianism implies that sacrificing the life of two people (-2) to save the lives of eight people (+8) is not only morally permissible, but morally required (net utility of +6). On this view, it would be acceptable to murder two healthy individuals if their organs could be used to save the lives of eight patients who require organ donation. Similarly, it would be acceptable for a family stranded at sea to eat two family members to save the lives of eight. These somewhat extreme counterexamples are exemplified by 'trolley case' thought experiments, which analyze the ethics of sacrificing innocent lives in order to save a larger number (Wollard & Snyder, 2021). Another drawback of utilitarianism is its neglect of *intentions* and character. Utilitarians regard an action (e.g., creating a vaccine for a deadly disease) as morally good even if the action was motivated entirely by bad reasons (e.g., the inventor acted entirely out of selfish and greedy motives). These considerations suggest that there are other relevant factors (other than consequences) that matter for ethics: certain actions (e.g., violating the rights of others) are *inherently unethical*. While utilitarians hold that there is nothing besides possible or actual consequences that matter for ethics, deontological theories (e.g., Kantian ethics and social contract theory) aim to articulate the theoretical principles that make our actions inherently moral or non-moral.

Kantian Ethics

Immanuel Kant argues that *why* we act is essential to the morality of our actions. Regardless of the consequences of actions, what matters for ethics is our *motives* (or intentions). For Kant, a person who only helps others for self-interested reasons is not truly acting morally. For example, consider the different motives one can have for saving a stranger who is drowning. When we help strangers independent of our own selfish motives (e.g., receiving a reward), we are motivated, Kant says, by good will: the intention to do the right thing just because it is the right thing to do. Good will differs from other motives because it is not self-interested. To translate good will into action, we need a moral principle (or test) for determining the moral goodness and badness of action. Kant calls this principle the 'Categorical Imperative' (CI). CI holds that we have a duty to follow moral rules that could be applied *universally and effectively* by all people in similar situations.

For Kant, the CI is the fundamental moral principle from which all other moral duties are derived. The CI is an 'imperative' because it is a command (or rule) that rational agents have a moral obligation or duty to follow. It is 'categorical' because it prescribes moral duties that apply in all situations without exception. Kant formulates the CI in various ways (Johnson & Cureton, 2021). Kant's first ('Universality') formulation of the CI is perhaps the most important: 'act only in accordance with that maxim through which you can . . . will that it become a universal law without contradiction' (Kant, [1785] 2012, 4: 421). This suggests that we should follow principles of action ('maxims') that could be *consistently and effectively applied as a normative moral rule* ('universal law') by all rational beings.[5] Doing so requires that we first identify the general principles (e.g., tell the truth and do not harm others) that direct our action in particular circumstances. Second, consider whether these principles could serve as universal laws that all people follow. The test of the latter is whether we can conceive of a world where these principles are *consistently applied to everyone* ('without contradiction') *to achieve their intended purposes*.

Several moral duties (e.g., tell the truth, keep promises, do not harm others, and help others) are clearly derivable from the CI. For these duties, we can conceive of worlds where, *if everybody followed these rules*, they would achieve their intended purposes (e.g., supporting the integrity of communication, building social trust, and promoting cooperation). In contrast, if an attempt to universalize a rule results in a contradiction, then acting on that rule is morally prohibited (Korsgaard, 1996). For example, consider a 'promise breaking' principle: 'keep promises except when it is inconvenient.' This principle cannot be a moral duty because universalizing it results in a contradiction. In a world where *everybody* followed this principle, following the promise-breaking principle would cease to be practically effective (since 'promises' would have no credibility in such a world). For the principle of selective promise-breaking to be practically effective, there need to be others in the world who follow a promise-keeping principle to give credibility to promises. What the CI prohibits is following rules that allow us to make an exception of ourselves.

Kant complements his universality formulation of the CI with the second ('Humanity') formulation of the CI: '[a]ct in such a way that you treat humanity, whether in your own person or in the person of another … as an end and never simply as a means' (Kant, [1785] 2012, 4: 429). This formulation suggests that we should never treat other persons *exclusively* as means to an end (i.e., as instruments for achieving our self-interested goals), but as ends in themselves (i.e., as individual beings who possess *inherent value*). This formulation prescribes that all people should be respected *because of their inherent value as persons*. We should not treat persons just as objects or tools (e.g., slaves and child laborers). Doing so is immoral because it violates the basic respect that should be afforded to all persons. According to the second formulation of the CI, coercion and lying are thus paradigms of immoral behavior because they (1) violate the rights of others to consent, and (2) treat other persons (or their beliefs) as mere instruments (Korsgaard, 1996).

A strength of Kantian ethics is that it provides an objective and impartial foundation (i.e., consistency of application) for identifying moral duties. For Kant, the morality of action is determined by whether our motives for action are consistent with the CI, which prescribes that we follow moral principles that can be applied fairly and effectively to govern all rational beings. When we act on principles that could not be followed by everyone, we act immorally because we make an exception of ourselves and exploit rules that we expect others follow. In the context of technology ethics, a Kantian might argue that internet trolling (i.e., participating in internet conversations with the sole intention of upsetting others) is wrong because it violates our duties to be honest and to treat others (as emphasized in Kant's second formulation of the CI) with basic respect.

A weakness of Kantian ethics is its rigidity. Because the moral duties derived from the CI are *categorical*, it is *always* wrong to violate duties prescribed by the CI. Since lying is *always wrong*, it is unethical to tell a lie even if it leads to good consequences (e.g., lying to an assassin to save an innocent person's life or telling a small lie to spare a friend's feelings). In such cases, different Kantian moral duties (e.g., tell the truth and help others) can appear to conflict. Kantians suggest that such conflicts can be resolved by more precisely specifying the principles of our proposed actions so as to include morally relevant details (see Johnson & Cureton, 2021), but the difficulty remains. Relatedly, in its emphasis on universalization, Kantian ethics can sometimes seem overly rationalistic, and thus less sensitive to the particular contexts of ethical cases. In applied ethics and technology ethics, we are often interested in evaluating complex principles that involve numerous conflicting moral duties. For example, questions concerning whether society should tolerate privacy technologies (e.g., encryption or TOR) that can virtually guarantee anonymity online can be reduced to the question of whether the duty to respect everyone's privacy or the duty of governments to protect its citizens (since privacy technologies can be exploited by criminals) is more important. In complex cases, attempts to universalize the relevant principle will not always indicate clearly whether such imagined worlds imply a contradiction.

Ross' Pluralism

An alternative deontological theory is William Ross' intuitionist approach to ethics, which maintains that moral goodness involves following a plurality of moral duties. Unlike Kant, who derives our duties from a fundamental moral principle (i.e., the CI), Ross assumes that our moral duties are fairly self-evident and recognizable ('intuited') by rational agents. Ross conceptualizes our moral intuitions as initial 'intellectual appearances': initial reactions or impressions that seem self-evident (Huemer, 2005). Ross contends that our intuitions reveal a plurality of 'prima facie' moral duties: moral duties that we have an obligation to follow *most of the time*.

Ross' pluralism suggests that we have a number of prima facie moral duties that we are ethically required to follow:

1   Fidelity: keep promises and tell the truth.
2   Reparation: correct wrongdoings that you have inflicted on others.
3   Gratitude: return services to those who help you.
4   Non-injury (Non-maleficence): do not harm others.
5   Beneficence: be kind to others and to try to improve their well-being (e.g., health, wisdom, and security).
6   Self-improvement: improve your own well-being.
7   Justice: distribute benefits and burdens equably and evenly.

In presenting these duties as prima facie obligations, Ross ([1930] 2002) suggests that our moral duties are not categorical duties as Kant assumes, but duties that we should follow most of the time.[6] Moreover, in contrast to Kantian ethics, Ross' moral duties are not organized hierarchically and, in cases where duties conflict, *the context of a case* will determine which moral duty is most salient.

A strength of Ross' pluralism is that it provides a compelling list of moral duties that most people would agree are good moral rules to follow. In this regard, it is worth noting that Ross' duties are derivable from Kant's CI *and* they are principles that a Rule Utilitarian would endorse as good moral rules. Compared to Kantian ethics, a strength of Ross' theory is that it more directly addresses the particular circumstances surrounding ethical cases. For example, in cases where the moral stakes are not particularly high (e.g., a romantic partner asks if they look attractive in a certain outfit), Ross' pluralism would tolerate small lies (i.e., the duty of beneficence outweighs the duty of fidelity). In cases with higher moral stakes (e.g., an assassin asks you whether an innocent person is hiding in your house), pluralism suggests that it is morally permissible to lie (i.e., the duty of non-injury outweighs the duty of fidelity).

A weakness of Ross' pluralism, compared to Kantian ethics, is that moral duties are not systematically derived. This raises the possibility that when applying pluralism to specific ethical cases, one is simply reaching ethical conclusions in an *ad hoc* manner (i.e., using pluralism to justify moral conclusions that we want to reach prior to analysis). Relatedly, it will often be difficult to determine the moral course of action in cases where duties conflict. For example, when hiring job candidates, there will be cases where the duty of justice (e.g., offer the job to the best candidate) and the duty of beneficence (e.g., offer the job to the candidate who will benefit the most) conflict. In such cases, Ross' theory offers no specific guidance on how to settle such conflicts besides looking at the context. Another weakness of pluralism is its reliance on moral intuitions. In recent years, empirical and experimental research into philosophical methodology has suggested that intuitions—including moral intuitions—are an unreliable source of philosophical evidence (Knobe & Nichols, 2017; Pust, 2021). For example, intuitions about prominent ethical thought experiments show a systematic variation across cultures, which suggests that our moral intuitions are determined (or at least strongly influenced) by cultural factors (e.g., moral norms prevalent within a culture). This speaks against Ross' assumption that rational agents can reliably 'intuit' our moral duties and obligations.

Social Contract Theory

More recent deontological approaches draw on social contract theory. Historically, social contract theory was defended in the seventeenth and eighteenth centuries by Thomas Hobbes, John Locke, Jean-Jacques Rousseau, and Kant as a political theory. It was subsequently developed in the twentieth century as a normative moral theory. Social contract theorists aim to provide a rational justification for normative ideals (e.g., justice and moral goodness) by appeal to the idea of a social contract: our political and moral obligations are ultimately justified by *an agreement among rational, adequately informed agents to follow certain contractual rules*. As a moral theory, this implies that our moral duties are not Kantian universal duties nor Rossian-intuited prima facie duties. Instead, they are *contractual duties* that rational agents would mutually agree or consent to. Two distinctive approaches in contemporary social contract theory are *contractarianism* (which follows a Hobbesian tradition) and *contractualism* (which follows a Kantian tradition). These approaches diverge on what grounds rational agreement regarding contractual duties. While contractarians ground this agreement in Hobbes' idea of mutual self-interest, contractualists ground rational agreement in Kant's ideal of the equal moral status of persons (Ashford & Mulgan, 2018; Cudd & Eftekhari, 2021). Prominent contemporary examples include Rawls' contractualist political theory, Gauthier's contractarian moral theory, and Scanlon's contractualist moral theory.

John Rawls is the most important contemporary social contract theorist, and his theory of justice (Rawls, [1971] 1999) spurred a revival of social contract theory in the twentieth century. Rawls' theory is driven by the idea that our political obligations should be governed by a respect for individual rights and a philosophy of fairness. On this view, all individuals possess certain rights in virtue of an implicit social contract with society. For Rawls, this social contract is a not actual, but a hypothetical ideal contract that rational individuals would agree to. Rawls considers what kind of contract individuals would consent to in the 'original position,' where individuals are behind a 'veil of ignorance' and have no knowledge about their personal characteristics (e.g., age, race, and social standing) or the society. Rawls argues that rational agents would agree to a contract that *protects everyone's rights* equally: rules that protect people's rights equally are just. From this perspective, Rawls ([1971] 1999) defends a 'greatest equal liberty principle': 'Each person is to have an equal right to the most extensive total system of equal basic liberties compatible with a similar system of liberty for all' (p. 266). Assuming that freedom and happiness are fundamental basic liberties, individuals have a right to maximize their freedom and happiness, so long as they do not infringe on others' right to these basic liberties. When the interests of groups conflict, Rawls ([1971] 1999) proposes his famous 'difference principle,' in which inequalities in the distribution of goods are justified only if they benefit the least advantaged members of society (p. 266). Rawls' theory implies that justice is fairness insofar as the hypothetical social contract is a *fair contract* that rational individuals would agree to. The veil of ignorance assures that agreement is based on the interests of everyone, rather than self-interest.

In the context of contemporary ethical theory, David Gauthier and T. M. Scanlon defend influential social contract theories that offer alternative justifications for our moral obligations. Gauthier (1986) defends a contractarian ('morals by agreement') theory that justifies our moral duties in terms of self-interest. Like Hobbes, Gauthier assumes a naturalistic view of humans (i.e., as self-interested creatures), an instrumental account of rationality (i.e., as a practical ability to meet agent-relative goals), and a conventionalist account of moral duties (i.e., as rules that promote mutual self-interest). Gauthier maintains that we should be moral because it is in everybody's mutual interest to do so. If everyone followed moral rules (e.g., do not lie and do not harm others) that promote social cooperation and mutual benefit, then everyone would be better off. In cases where self-interest (e.g., earning more money) conflicts with moral action (e.g., paying taxes), morality demands that we *constrain* our self-interested pursuits. The justification and normative force of these constraints stems from their rationality: rational self-interested individuals would agree to constrain their behavior and follow moral rules that are mutually beneficial, so long as others also follow these rules.[7] Scanlon (1998) defends a contractualist theory that justifies our moral obligations in terms of the Kantian ideal (expressed in Kant's Humanity formulation of the CI) that all rational agents should be valued and respected *equally*. According to Scanlon (1998), an act is wrong if it would be prohibited by moral principles that *no rational agent could reasonably reject* (p. 153). An important feature of rational agents is their capacity to recognize and act upon justified reasons. Hence, treating other rational agents as equals requires acting toward them in accordance with principles that they (and we) could not reasonably reject. On this view, actions wrong if they are *unjustifiable* to other rational agents. While Rawls' contractualist theory invokes self-interest behind a veil of ignorance to establish agreements that account for everyone's interests equally, Scanlon's theory maintains that the impetus to respect everyone's interests equally is driven by an intrinsic desire *to justify our actions to others*. Possessing this kind of desire (akin to Kant's 'good will') is part of what it is to be a rational moral agent (Ashford & Mulgan, 2018).

Social contract theories offer useful resources for evaluating complex ethical cases where the interests of different groups conflict. Such theories emphasize identifying and justifying moral (contractual duties) that are *fair* and *impartial*. For example, questions concerning the regulation of encryption and other privacy protection technologies (e.g., TOR and cryptocurrency) concern a conflict between the right of citizens to protect their privacy (e.g., against governmental surveillance) and the right of governments to regulate what technologies are widely available to its citizens (e.g., to protect public safety). One could give a Rawlsian argument that the rights of individuals should take priority in this case because they are the larger and more disadvantaged group. Alternatively, one could appeal to Gauthier's contrarian analysis to evaluate whether a policy (e.g., that the government should have some power to regulate privacy technologies) is fair in the sense of advancing everyone's mutual self-interest. Given the specific questions that social contract theories are formulated to address, one limitation they face is their applicability. Rawlsian analyses are most relevant to issues of social justice and the state within liberal and democratic societies, which is an important, but narrow aspect of ethics. Scanlon's contractualism is most relevant for questions concerning our moral obligations to one another.

Virtue Ethics

In contrast to consequentialist and deontological theories, virtue ethics focuses on understanding how we should live our lives and what sorts of persons we should be. Compared to the moral theories reviewed above, which evaluate the rightness or wrongness of action (see note 1), virtue theorists address broader ethical questions concerning how to live the good life. According to the Greek philosopher Aristotle and the Chinese philosopher Confucius, the ultimate goal of ethics is to cultivate a good character and live a flourishing life, rather than just to decide which actions are right and which are wrong. In the second half of the twentieth century, virtue ethics was revived by philosophers who were disenchanted with the narrow focus on actions within consequentialism and deontology.

Virtue ethics starts with the idea that humans, like all living beings, have lives that can go well or badly. To flourish rather than languish, we need good nutrition and opportunities to be physically active, just like other animals. But because of our complex cognitive abilities and social natures, we also need to have a *strong personal character* to live well. And a strong character is made up of many different virtues (e.g., courage and generosity).

Aristotle (1984, books 2–4) discusses a number of moral virtues, which represent an optimal point ('mean') between two vicious extremes. Some of the virtues proposed by Aristotle include the following:

Vice (deficiency)	Virtue (Mean)	Vice (excess)
Cowardice	Courage/bravery	Rashness/recklessness
Self-indulgence	Temperance/moderation	Abstinence/insensibility
Stinginess	Generosity	Extravagance/prodigality
Undue humility	Pride	Vanity
Indifference	Moderate temper	Irascible/easily angered
False modesty	Truthfulness	Boastfulness
Bashful/ Ashamed	Modesty	Shameless
Quarrelsome	Friendliness	Obsequious/fawning
Rudeness/ boorishness	Wittiness/charm	Foolishness/buffoonery

Aristotle's virtues apply to specific domains ('spheres') of feeling or action. For example, courage applies to the domain of fear and confidence; generosity to the domain of spending money; and wittiness to the domain of social conduct. In this theory, virtues represent an *optimal ('mean') amount of some character trait* that falls between two extremes. For example, someone who has too little courage is a coward, but someone who is courageous to the point of lacking caution is reckless. The rightness or wrongness of actions is, then, determined by whether a person acts in accordance with virtuous or vicious characteristics. When someone drinks excessive amounts of alcohol to get drunk, they act immorally because they act upon the vice of self-indulgence. When someone interacts rudely with others on social media, they act immorally because they act upon vices such as vanity, shameless-ness, and excessive anger.

A strength of virtue ethics is that it offers concrete guidance on how to acquire strengths of character. If we can identify moral virtues that contribute to a flourishing life, then we can attempt to cultivate those virtues ourselves. These virtues are to be developed and improved through experience, rather than by learning a rule and simply applying it. We learn by following virtuous role models and by training ourselves to act virtuously. To become a more generous person, for instance, you could commit to looking for opportunities to donate to charities. Over time, by creating a habit of acting generously, you would slowly begin to think more about helping others and thereby acquire the virtue of generosity. For cases of technology ethics, e.g., a virtue theorist might analyze the ethics of social media use in terms of virtuous characteristics (e.g., moderation, pride, and friendliness).

Like other ethical theories (e.g., Kantian ethics and contractarianism), a weakness of vir-tue ethics is that it is sometimes not obviously applicable to complex ethical cases. When trying to decide how to act, virtue ethics recommends that we do whatever a virtuous person would do; however, in complex cases (e.g., stealing food to say a starving family), different virtues may push us toward conflicting behavior and virtue ethics does not offer a specific procedure of weighing different virtues against one another. Another difficulty concerns the nature of the virtues themselves. Among contemporary proponents of virtue theory, there is disagreement on what the correct moral virtues are and how virtues should be conceptualized (Hursthouse & Pettigrove, 2018). Moreover, given cultural differences, there is a worry that different virtues identified by virtue theorists might reflect *prevalent, culturally relative social norms*, rather than universal virtues (MacIntyre, 1985). For example, among Aristotle's proposed virtues, it seems peculiar to argue that someone acted *immorally* if they were too shy or not witty enough in a social setting. Hence, various moral virtues proposed by philosophers might simply codify and reinforce culturally relative norms (cf. Nussbaum, 1993). In addition, some have challenged virtue ethicists' assumption that char-acter traits are sufficiently stable across time and situations to translate into moral behavior. A growing body of 'situationist' psychological research suggests that many of our character traits are specific to situations (Doris, 2020). For example, someone might be generous whenever they are relaxed, but stingy when stressed out. If character traits are not stable across time and situations, then the project of cultivating virtues is much more complex than it initially appears.

Normative Ethics and Technology

The normative ethical theories discussed in this chapter offer different philosophical rea-sons for thinking that a particular action (or rule) about technology is morally good or bad. Importantly, these theories will often converge upon the same ethical conclusions albeit for different reasons.[8] For example, all theories reviewed in this chapter reach the conclusions that murdering innocent people for fun is morally bad and that helping people in need is morally good. Where they differ is in the principled reasons that justify such conclusions. In the context of ethical cases concerning technology, different ethical theories provide alternative theoretical resources for evaluating and justifying ethical claims about actions or policies related to technology.

The broad summary of canonical ethical theories in this chapter provides a reference point for reading subsequent chapters in this volume. Other chapters provide more detailed examinations of the normative theories discussed, an examination of alternative normative ethical theories not discussed, and applications of such ethical theories to various cases in technology ethics.

Notes

1 Since the revival of virtue ethics in the twentieth century, it has been commonplace to distinguish ethical theory and moral theory in terms of their scope of application (e.g., see Williams, 1985). In this chapter, we follow the distinction that ethical theories are concerned (broadly) with the goodness or badness of the agent's character or dispositions, whereas moral theories are concerned (more narrowly) with the rightness and wrongness of actions.

2 Bentham and Mill are 'hedonistic Utilitarians' who assume that pleasure is the only intrinsic good and pain is the only intrinsic bad (Sinnott-Armstrong, 2021). While Bentham maintains that pleasure and pain only differ *quantitatively* (e.g., in terms of intensity and duration), Mill argues that there are *qualitative* differences between lower-level pleasures (e.g., sensual pleasures and drunkenness) and higher-level pleasures (e.g., intellectual achievements and spiritual gratification) (Driver, 2014; cf. Crimmins, 2021).

3 Mill ([1861] 1998) held that this axiom can include non-human animals, since they are sentient beings who experience pleasure and pain. Peter Singer ([1975] 2009) famously argues for animal rights on the Utilitarian ground that non-human animals experience pleasure and pain (e.g., suffering).

4 This is arguably Mill's view. For a discussion of various interpretations of utilitarian theory, see Lyons (1965) and Sinnott-Anderson (2021).

5 This formulation is complemented by Kant's third ('Autonomy') formulation and the 'Kingdom of the ends' formulation of the CI (Johnson & Cureton, 2021), which both emphasize the universality of our moral duties and their status as potential *laws* that could legislate the morality of rational beings.

6 Ross ([1939] 2019) suggests that 5–7 could be grouped together as a general duty to maximize the overall good (i.e., to promote values that are intrinsically good).

7 Gauthier explicates the (practical) rationality of moral agents in the language of rational choice theory. He presents rational moral agents, alternatively, as 'constrained maximizers' (Gauthier, 1986) or 'rational optimizers' (Gauthier, 2013).

8 Based on this convergence, Derek Parfit (2011) defends a moral theory that combines rule consequentialism, contractualism, and Kantian ethics.

References

Aristotle. (1984). *Nicomachean Ethics*. Translated by W. D. Ross; revised by J. O. Urmson. In *The Complete Works of Aristotle*, The Revised Oxford Translation, vol. 2. Edited by Jonathan Barnes. Princeton: Princeton University Press.

Ashford, Elizabeth and Tim Mulgan. 2018. "Contractualism." *The Stanford Encyclopedia of Philosophy* (Summer 2018 Edition). Edited by Edward N. Zalta. https://plato.stanford.edu/archives/sum2018/entries/contractualism/

Bentham, Jeremy, (1789) 1907. *An Introduction to the Principles of Morals and Legislation*. Oxford: Clarendon Press.

Crimmins, James E. 2021. "Jeremy Bentham." *The Stanford Encyclopedia of Philosophy* (Winter 2021 Edition). Edited by Edward N. Zalta. https://plato.stanford.edu/archives/win2021/entries/bentham/

Cudd, Ann and Seena Eftekhari. 2021. "Contractarianism." *The Stanford Encyclopedia of Philosophy* (Winter 2021 Edition). Edited by Edward N. Zalta. https://plato.stanford.edu/archives/win2021/entries/contractarianism/

Driver, Julia. 2014. "The History of Utilitarianism." *The Stanford Encyclopedia of Philosophy* (Winter 2014 Edition). Edited by Edward N. Zalta. https://plato.stanford.edu/archives/win2014/entries/utilitarianism-history/

Franssen, Maarten, Gert-Jan Lokhorst, and Ibo van de Poel. 2018. "Philosophy of Technology." *The Stanford Encyclopedia of Philosophy* (Fall 2018 Edition). Edited by Edward N. Zalta. https://plato.stanford.edu/archives/fall2018/entries/technology/

Gauthier, David. 1986. *Morals by Agreement*. Oxford: Oxford University Press.

Gauthier, David. 2013. "Twenty Five On." *Ethics* 123(4): 601–624.

Hursthouse, Rosalind and Glen Pettigrove. 2018. "Virtue Ethics." *The Stanford Encyclopedia of Philosophy* (Winter 2018 Edition). Edited by Edward N. Zalta. https://plato.stanford.edu/archives/win2018/entries/ethics-virtue/

Johnson, Robert and Adam Cureton. 2021. "Kant's Moral Philosophy." *The Stanford Encyclopedia of Philosophy* (Spring 2021 Edition). Edited by Edward N. Zalta. https://plato.stanford.edu/archives/spr2021/entries/kant-moral/

Kant, Immanuel. (1785) 2012. *Groundwork of the Metaphysics of Morals*, 2nd ed. Translated and edited by Mary Gregor and Jens Timmerman. Cambridge: Cambridge University Press.

Knobe, Joshua and Shaun Nichols. 2017. "Experimental Philosophy." *The Stanford Encyclopedia of Philosophy* (Winter 2017 Edition). Edited by Edward N. Zalta. https://plato.stanford.edu/archives/win2017/entries/experimental-philosophy/

Korsgaard, Christine. 1996. *Creating the Kingdom of Ends*. Cambridge: Cambridge University Press.

Lyons, David. 1965. *Forms and Limits of Utilitarianism*. Oxford: Clarendon Press.

MacIntyre, Alasdair. 1985. *After Virtue*, 2nd ed. London: Duckworth.

Mill, John Stuart (1861) 1998. *Utilitarianism*. Edited by Roger Crisp. New York: Oxford University Press.

Nussbaum, Martha C. 1993. "Non-Relative Virtues: An Aristotelian Approach." In *The Quality of Life* (pp. 242–270). Edited by Martha C. Nussbaum and Amartya Sen. Oxford: Oxford University Press.

Parfit, Derek. (2011). *On What Matters*. Oxford: Oxford University Press.

Pust, Joel. 2019. "Intuition." *The Stanford Encyclopedia of Philosophy* (Summer 2019 Edition). Edited by Edward N. Zalta. https://plato.stanford.edu/archives/sum2019/entries/intuition/

Rawls, John. (1971) 1999. *A Theory of Justice*, 2nd ed. Cambridge, MA: Harvard University Press.

Ross, W. David. (1930) 2002. *The Right and the Good*. Philip Stratton-Lake, ed. Oxford: Oxford University Press.

Ross, W. David (1939) 2018. *Foundations of Ethics*. Oxford: Clarendon Press.

Scanlon, T. M. 1998. *What We Owe to Each Other*. Cambridge, MA: Harvard University Press.

Shaver, Robert. 2021. "Egoism." *The Stanford Encyclopedia of Philosophy* (Winter 2021 Edition). Edited by Edward N. Zalta. https://plato.stanford.edu/archives/win2021/entries/egoism/

Singer, Peter. (1975) 2009. *Animal Liberation*. New York: Harper.

Sinnott-Armstrong, Walter. 2021. "Consequentialism." *The Stanford Encyclopedia of Philosophy* (Fall 2021 Edition). Edited by Edward N. Zalta. https://plato.stanford.edu/archives/fall2021/entries/consequentialism/

Smart, J. J. C. 1956. "Extreme and Restricted Utilitarianism." *Philosophical Quarterly* 6(25): 344–354.

Williams, Bernard. 1985. *Ethics and the Limits of Philosophy*. Cambridge, MA: Harvard University Press.

Chapter 9

Disagreeing Well about Technology

Daniel C. Russell

In January 2022, Facebook ran this advertisement:

We support updated regulations on the internet's most pressing challenges.

A lot has changed in the last 25 years. But the last time comprehensive regulations were passed was in 1996. We want updated internet regulations to set clear guidelines for addressing today's toughest challenges.[1]

The ad went on to explain that Facebook was already making huge investments in greater security, safety, privacy, and cross–platform compatibility. They asked only that regulators set "clear and fair rules for everyone," so that other social media firms should go and do likewise.

Question: *Would a regulation like that be a good idea?*

The question looks easy: Do we want clear, fair rules or not? But a question like that is actually *two* questions:

- *How is that regulation likely to work out?* and
- *Would it be a good thing if the regulation worked out that way?*

The first question asks for a *prediction*, and the second for an *evaluation*. Once we pry the questions apart, it's clear that the Facebook question doesn't have an authoritative answer one way or another, and not just because of the evaluative question. The predictive question—not whether the outcome will be good, but what the outcome *will be*—doesn't have an authoritative answer, either. Results don't always match intentions.

Call this a *hard question*: a question for which there isn't an authoritative answer. Questions in a calculus textbook aren't hard in precisely *this* sense, since there are authorities who have the answers at the ready.

This chapter is about disagreeing well over hard questions, especially questions about regulating technology firms, where things are routinely more complicated than they seem. Its thesis is that disagreements—about predictions and about evaluations—can improve our understanding of the ethics of technological regulation, provided that we learn to disagree well. Part 1 looks at some of the things that make such predictions so difficult and how we might handle predictive disagreements better. Part 2 is about handling disagreements well when they stem from different values and priorities at a deeper level.

DOI: 10.4324/9781003189466-12

The Prediction Problem

Predicting Well Is Difficult

Technology firms are regulated for good reason. Sometimes, the public would be better off if technology firms changed what they were doing, but the reason they don't is that their interests aren't aligned with public interests. In those cases, it might be possible for functionaries to intervene on the public's behalf to bring firms into better alignment with the public.

Now, much of the time, the hope of profits combined with the risk of loss helps to align interests between firms and consumers. When firms *have* to compete for customers, the purchasing relationship forces firms to seek and provide what customers want to buy, even when no one has discovered what that is yet.[2] But the public can't always exert that kind of pressure. A power plant that sells electricity to people in one place might also emit sulfur oxides that drop acid rain on people somewhere else. Those people can't alter the plant's decisions because they're not the ones in a purchasing relationship with the power plant in the first place. They are bystanders.

Regulation exists for good reason, because the interests of technology firms are not always aligned with ours. However, it still can be extremely difficult to predict *when* a particular regulation would be good for the public. We might expect prediction to be difficult when a technology is new, but it's important to see that what makes prediction difficult has less to do with novelty than with how complicated the world is. It's hard to predict what will make online platforms safer, but it's not much easier to predict what will make lawnmowers safer.

Here are five reasons why prediction is a problem. The list isn't exhaustive, but it should still give you a sense of how complexity makes prediction difficult, and difficult even for technologies that are already familiar.

A.   *It isn't always obvious when firms' interests are out of alignment with public interests in the first place.*

Consider:

Lawnmowers: *Would higher lawnmower safety standards benefit users of mowers?*[3]

Surprisingly, it is hard to say. For one thing, the regulation might not increase overall lawnmower safety. True, people who buy new lawnmowers will now have safer mowers. But safer mowers are costlier to build and more expensive to buy. Safety is important to buyers, but so is price, and different buyers want different tradeoffs between safety and price. So, some users will wait longer to replace their old mowers with new, safer ones. As a result, the mowers *in use* may be less safe overall than if varying levels of safety-for-price had been available. A threshold of mandatory mower safety doesn't mean that consumers will now have safer mowers. It just means that certain tradeoffs between safety and price are now illegal.

For another thing, although such a regulation increases costs, large firms can bear those costs better than their smaller competitors can. Firms may welcome and even solicit the restrictions when they *already* have a good share of the market that is now harder for smaller firms to remain in and for would-be rivals to enter. Unfortunately, a less competitive market eases the pressure on the remaining firms to give consumers new options and better value for money. Interests might not have been misaligned before. But they might be now.

B. *It isn't always obvious what the public intervention should be, even when there should be one.*

Consider:

> **Tailpipes**: *Would a stricter emissions standard for new automobiles be better for air quality than a less strict standard?*

I may prefer a car that is dirtier but cheaper to one that is cleaner but more expensive, but the costly effects of my decision on *other* people aren't factored into the price. Regulation is appropriate here. But *which* regulation?

Everybody would be better off if the cars people drove were a *lot* less toxic than if they were just a little less toxic, but that is not what *Tailpipes* asks. If the stricter standard would make new cars more expensive than the less strict standard would, then many people might wait longer to replace their old, dirtier cars with new, cleaner cars. Paradoxically, the result of the stricter standard could be higher total emissions than would have resulted from the less strict standard.[4]

Or consider:

> **Converter**: *Would requiring automobile manufacturers to adopt the industry's best practice for improving automobile emissions be good for air quality?*

The US in the 1970s started requiring all new cars sold in the US to be fitted with catalytic converters, which were considered the industry's best practice for improving engine emissions. Question: Why not make the best practice mandatory?

Answer: Because enforcing the current best practice might stop people looking for a new best practice. For example, Honda had already developed a new engine with greatly improved emissions even *without* a catalytic converter; once the converter mandate passed, though, there was no way to recover the costs of developing that cleaner engine technology from the US sales, so such innovations didn't pay.[5] This intervention addressed one misalignment of interests between technology firms and the public, but it created another one. The details matter.

C. *It isn't always obvious when interventions will be worth what they cost.*

Consider:

> **Testing**: *Would requiring proof of drug effectiveness be good for patients?*

In 1962, the US Congress required testing to determine that new drugs would be effective at treating whatever they purported to treat, to keep patients from wasting money and—much worse—precious time when they might have avoided needless suffering or even death by using a treatment that was more effective. It can be hard for doctors and patients to know the difference before it's too late, so there was a danger that the interests of drug manufacturers were not aligned with the interests of patients.

And they were not aligned. About a decade later, the economist Sam Peltzman estimated that the new law had indeed saved patients' precious time, and money too, compared with what probably would have happened without the law.[6]

However, Peltzman *also* found that the law had added about two years on average to the drug approval process, time in which those drugs did nothing to prevent suffering and death, for the simple reason that they were unobtainable at any price. So that added delay was costly, too—and Peltzman estimated that the cost of delay was many times greater than the waste it saved. The prior alignment between public interest and the interests of pharmaceutical companies wasn't great, but this intervention to improve that alignment harmed the public even more.

D. It isn't always obvious when regulators' interests are aligned with ours.

Peltzman's tale has an interesting sequel: the US Food and Drug Administration replied that they knew of no less costly way to maximize the effectiveness of new drugs once they hit the shelves.[7] But the problem *just was* that the FDA had tried to *maximize* the effectiveness of drugs, when instead it needed to *optimize* the tradeoff between effectiveness and availability. However, the FDA has its own interests to protect, and *it* has more to lose from visible failures stemming from approval than from invisible losses from delay.[8] Frédéric Bastiat observed that we cannot make good predictions by focusing on the benefits we can see. We must also take account of hidden costs we cannot see, and which are therefore easy to overlook.[9]

Technology firms' interests are not always aligned with ours, but regulators' interests aren't always aligned with ours, either. In fact, sometimes the interests of firms and regulators align with each other and *against* ours. Consider:

Scrubbers: *Would requiring power plants to adopt the industry's best practice for improving emissions be good for air quality?*

In the 1970s, flue-gas desulfurization units—"scrubbers"—were the industry standard for reducing sulfur oxide emissions from coal–fired power plants, a cause of acid rain. So in 1977 the US Congress required that all new power plants have scrubbers working at all times.

A crucial detail: some varieties of coal have more sulfur than others, sometimes by an enormous margin, and in the 1970s that coal was also cheaper. So, to help offset the massive costs of installing scrubbers, power plants turned to cheaper coal. As a result, the 1977 law did reduce sulfur emissions, but it would have been far less costly and at least as effective if plants could have sought other methods, such as switching to coal with less sulfur in the first place.[10] However, in the US, high–sulfur coal is mined mostly in the northeast, and the coal industry there was much better organized and politically connected than the rest of the industry. The law had more to do with stimulating demand for northeastern coal than with the cleanliness of the air.[11]

Because crucial details aren't always obvious in a complicated world, cronyism—a bureaucracy of special favors for privileged groups—can hide behind a veil of public interest and the common good. And that brings us to the final item on our incomplete list:

E. When complexities aren't obvious, bad laws can garner good support.

Good people get duped sometimes. It's no surprise now that the United Mine Workers supported the scrubber mandate, but so did the National Clean Air Coalition, the Environmental Policy Center, and the Sierra Club, as lawmakers connected to the northeastern coal industry were eager to point out. People motivated by public spirit can become allies—without even realizing it—of people with motives of a very different sort. Bruce Yandle calls this strange sort of alliance the "bootleggers and Baptists" phenomenon. The name comes from the temperance movement in the US history, when public-spirited people might advocate a ban on Sunday liquor sales, unwittingly granting a Sunday monopoly to black-market booze runners.[12]

The things we are trying to predict can *be* very complicated and yet *appear* simple. That appearance makes it natural to skip the prediction question, and a hard question masquerades as an easy one: do we want that good outcome or not? Unfortunately, the road to unintended outcomes is paved with easy answers to hard questions.

Why Is Predicting Well So Difficult?

When we assess hard questions like these, we employ a *predictive model*: a strategy for predicting certain outcomes paired with a way of evaluating the outcomes we predict.[13] Two important points about predictive models are clear already: one, even people who have the same values might make different predictions, and two, accurate predictions are hard to make.

Unlike evaluations, predictions might seem unconnected with ethics, but I think Aristotle was right to see predictive skills as a crucial element in ethics. For Aristotle, our virtues constitute our character. But these virtues include not just the good goals we care about but *also* the practical wisdom to predict what it would take to realize those goals through action.[14] The virtue of generosity, for instance, has the goal of helping others with one's resources, but that goal is extremely broad—like saying that a doctor's goal is to heal people. If a doctor is actually to heal a patient, he or she must be skilled in determining exactly what "healing" would amount to in that individual patient's case. So too a person with the genuine virtue—what Aristotle calls the *excellence*—of generosity will also be wise in determining just what it would take to be genuinely helpful. But that wisdom *just is* a skill of making intelligent predictions: "How is my doing this or that likely to work out for the people I'm trying to help?" So learning to predict intelligently is part of character development, just as a doctor's ability to predict is part of the skill of medicine.

Perhaps the chief difficulty for making good predictions about hard questions is that we never have enough information, because so often there is *no possibility* of having enough information. Think about *Lawnmowers*, or *Tailpipes*: if newly produced technology must be safer and cleaner, how will that change the costs of compliance, and how will those costs change consumers' access to safer technology, cleaner technology, and a competitive marketplace for technology? Think about *Testing*: how will the resulting tradeoff between effectiveness and availability affect consumers, and how will the industry change if only large firms with armies of administrators can afford to navigate the regulatory process? Think about *Scrubbers*: how will power plants be fueled after the mandate, and what will those fuel choices mean for air quality? To answer any of these questions, we rely on a predictive model. But to make a prediction, we make simplifying assumptions about unknowable variables—and yet it is just those variables that will determine the actual outcome.

So, how do predictive models ever improve? The answer is through *joint discovery*.

Surprisingly, the answer is *not* through finding a savant. It is tempting to say that a firm that brings out a winning innovation does so because it is a predictive savant. It would be more correct, though, to say that it is not the individual *firm* that makes the discovery, but the dynamic *process* of innovation and competition, planning and readjusting, in which the firm is a participant.[15] That process discovered that people wanted the smartphone, say, only by discovering first that they didn't want the Blackberry. What's more, even the firm that produced the smartphone didn't know that that was what it was. They thought it was an updated MP3 player that could take pictures and run apps, including an app for making telephone calls.[16] The process, not the producer, decided what the product actually was.

The same point holds for you and me. The way to improve our predictive ability is also by participating in a dynamic process of discovery. That discovery process we call disagreement and debate. The reason to compare our many different predictions is not that it increases our odds of finding a savant that gets all the unknown variables right, though. The reason is that someone whose predictions are different from yours just might have a point that you can learn from, and vice versa, even if neither of you has the whole picture. Where you get stuck on a problem, someone else might see a way forward, and then you might go on to return the favor when he or she gets stuck somewhere down the line. Disagreement now becomes a boon, since people who look at things in the same ways are likely to get stuck in the same places. By pooling different perspectives, the *process* starts to generate better informed predictions than *any* of its members ever could have made by working alone or with only like-minded people.[17]

The key, though, is that the people in the process have to be ready to accept that someone who disagrees might be someone they can learn from, someone who might help them get unstuck. For that reason, they must also accept the possibility of being stuck without realizing it. The simplest way to get ready to see someone else's point is to recognize that disagreements very often stem from different predictions, and no one's predictions can ever be complete. We need each other, not in spite of disagreeing but because of it.

The Evaluative Impasse

Disagreement Is Personal

Hans Rosling once gave a public talk in which he put it to the audience that there is something magical about washing machines. He showed a picture of his mother and grandmother washing clothes together, by hand, with water they had carried from a stream and heated with fire. When the two women washed this way, it took an entire day for them to wash, every week of their lives. Then after years of saving, Rosling's parents bought a washing machine. Now the machine did the washing, and Mrs. Rosling would spend that day taking young Hans to the library instead. Rosling demonstrated the magic on stage: he loaded laundry into a machine, pushed the button, and when he reached in again, he pulled out books.[18]

Rosling has a point: technology is about more than gadgetry. It changes the frontier of possibilities for what we might do with our lives and who we might become. It did that for the Roslings, and it does it for the rest of us, too—so well, ironically, that we don't notice anymore.

But a dear friend of mine, Jane, saw something in Rosling's story that I hadn't: washing day was no longer a day for Rosling women to spend together. When machines do laundry, Jane pointed out, people do have more time for other things, but they also lose an occasion to gather, to share stories and work and tips and emotional support and fun. Such losses have an impact on people, too, and on tradition and community and future generations. Washing machines have costs of their own, although again we probably don't notice.[19]

Both viewpoints are legitimate, but look: there is *tension* between them. I look at washing machines in these two ways and I'm not sure how to piece them into a single point of view. This is not like the tension between wanting to attend a concert and a play that happen to fall on the same night. I can't do both, but it's not as if appreciating music makes it harder to appreciate theater. By contrast, when I think about the washing machine in the first way, the second seems a bit curmudgeonly. When I look at it in the second way, the first seems a bit frivolous.[20]

Here is a first point: evaluative disagreement stems from the underlying tensions between different evaluative viewpoints that compete for attention.

Here is a second: evaluative viewpoints are deeply personal. Sometimes, people evaluate things differently because they use different *standards*—they care about different things. In other cases, people might *apply* their evaluative standards differently, because they prioritize things differently and assign them different weights. Another, subtler possibility is that people might not notice the same *features* of a situation as being relevant to their evaluative standards.[21] That, I think, is why Jane and I disagreed. She was reminding me of something that we both thought was important, but that in my enthusiasm I just hadn't stopped to notice.

What different people are inclined to value, to prioritize, and to notice can be the result of all sorts of things that make them different.[22] Jane studied public health among indigenous populations, so her bread-and-butter was the complex interplay of culture, health, and technology. No wonder she spotted immediately something that I had to have pointed out to me! The effect runs in the other direction, too: people who evaluate things differently might then pursue different paths that bring them different experiences. People's evaluative viewpoints cannot be neatly separated from the experiences that have made them the people they are, and those viewpoints are part of their *way of thinking about the world*, of *making some sense* of it all.

Now put these two points together: *the tension between different evaluative viewpoints can feel deeply personal when those viewpoints come into disagreement.* Small wonder that hard questions about what is a better or worse idea create tensions that put people "on the defensive."

Think back to our examples of regulating technology firms: *Lawnmowers, Tailpipes*, and the others. I said that the interests of technology firms are not always aligned with our interests, as a public. I also said that the interests of those who regulate technology firms are not always aligned with our interests, either. These two statements can both be true. I think they *are* both true. In practice, though, it can be very difficult to piece them into a single viewpoint, and that tension can feel like a threat to one's very way of making sense of the world, at least the world of technology. Starting from the one, we see the world as a place where regulators keep us safe from firms that thrive at our expense. Starting from the other, we see the world as a place where regulators create the very opportunities for firms to thrive at our expense. Neither viewpoint is wrong, only incomplete, but it is hard to see things in both ways at once.

Disagreeing well, therefore, cannot be easy. But it also follows that *disagreeing well is a matter of managing tension*, the tension between different evaluative viewpoints that makes it so difficult to capitalize on that disagreement, to learn from others who might have a point. So, if we can understand better how people manage evaluative tensions well, we might learn something about how people can disagree productively.

Making Peace with Tension

We have looked at two types of evaluative tension. One is intrapersonal tension experienced by a single person caught between two evaluative viewpoints—the frontiers that technology opens up, say, and the traditions that don't survive technological change. The other is interpersonal tension, which arises between people who (are more inclined to) bring one or the other of these evaluative viewpoints to the discussion.

Start with intrapersonal tension. People's values change, often in ways that change those people. They become parents, or lovers of great music, and only then can they really know what it is like for *them* to be people who value those things. Sometimes, people have changes thrust upon them, but sometimes people seek out change. Sometimes, they "just choose" something different, but not for any reason.[23] Sometimes, their reason is the thrill of change itself.[24]

But sometimes people change because they already begin to glimpse the value of being someone who loves parenting or great music, and they make choices *to cultivate* those values. Agnes Callard observes that when that happens, a person experiences tension: I *begin* to see *some* value in enjoying great music, but right now, I *do* in fact enjoy lower-grade music. These values compete for my attention: as my attention is drawn to either of them, the grasp of the other weakens. So I become conflicted between these two values and I do not have either of them entirely. When I am so conflicted, appreciating either is compromised to the extent that I also appreciate the other.[25] You may recognize a similar tension between the two reactions to Rosling's lecture, above.

Callard also argues that it is possible to manage these tensions intelligently. We do it all the time. We seek exposure, little by little, to new experiences and points of view. We seek the advice of people who better appreciate what we are still learning to appreciate. We keep our options open for changing course or turning back. We don't give up too quickly in the face of tension and discomfort. We experiment, we trust, we seek guidance, we think critically.

Notice: people are capable of *holding more than one evaluative viewpoint at a time*, and of *exploring evaluative viewpoints that they don't fully grasp yet.*

Now consider interpersonal disagreement again, such as my disagreement with Jane over how to evaluate the changes that technological innovation—like a washing machine—can make in people's lives. Perhaps she and I value different things, or prioritize them differently, or notice different features. In any case, Jane brings to the discussion one evaluative viewpoint and I bring another. There is tension between these viewpoints, and the tension feels personal. But recall: we are capable of *holding more than one evaluative viewpoint at a time,* even though they compete with each other. And we are capable of *exploring an evaluative viewpoint intelligently and openly,* even when it is one we are only just beginning to see. In that case, the evaluative viewpoint that Jane brings to the discussion is one *that I can begin to appreciate and explore, too*—even if only a little bit at first, and in a way that is compromised by the fact that I also see things from a competing viewpoint. Jane's viewpoint and mine are in competition for my attention, but that doesn't mean that I must have one or the other. It will create tension within me, but I *can* begin to see her point, even if this is only a beginning.

From there, Jane and I might resolve the disagreement, as I come to resolve the tension within me, between my current viewpoint and the one she is helping me to begin to see. Having seen things from her point of view, I might come around to that viewpoint after all—or I might stick with the other viewpoint instead. Either way, the tension within me might be resolved well, if I stay open-minded, don't rush to judgment, listen carefully, think critically.

However, I think it can also be productive for some tensions to *remain* unresolved. I might *continue* to disagree with myself—I might remain in a state of intrapersonal tension—and that might be where I should stay. It can be okay for people to look at things in one-sided ways. Perhaps there is good that I might do *because* I see things as I do, just as there certainly is a lot of good that Jane has done by looking at things as *she* does. Something good might be lost if either of us ever changed the other's mind—*and* if we didn't have others around to remind us that there *are* other ways of looking at things. Sustaining that tension could be a good thing for us.

A deeper point, I think, is that some evaluative viewpoints might be in tension because some *values* are in tension, so we would resolve such a tension only by trivializing it. The world is a complicated place. Why should we assume that everything that is worthwhile in the world should *sit comfortably in human attention* with everything else that is worthwhile?

Mrs. Rosling bought a washing machine. The washing machine did her some good. The washing machine also cost her some good. Was she better off, all things considered? I don't know. Even if I did, I still wouldn't know how to generalize the point to other people and their washing machines, much less to technological innovation as a general phenomenon. The question might even be wrong-headed. Two pounds and two miles don't make four of anything, "all things considered." In order to consider such questions well, we must consider them from viewpoints that *just do* compete for our attention, with no way to combine them into an "all things considered" total. We want an authoritative answer, but we shouldn't always want that.

Conclusion

The world is a complicated place. It isn't always obvious how to make things safer, either at our computers or behind our mowers. It isn't always obvious how to make things cleaner or more effective. It isn't always obvious who wins and who loses, or who is on whose side. And it isn't always obvious what standards we should evaluate things by, or how we should prioritize the standards, or even what things we should notice as relevant to the standards in the first place. As a result, the world of technology is full of hard questions. Technology always stands at the frontier—not just of what is technically possible, but of what is possible for public action and even for ethical reflection. The world of technology has no monopoly in hard questions, of course, but it is little wonder that so many of the predictive and evaluative questions in the world of technology turn out to be as hard as they are.

When questions are hard, definitive predictions and definitive evaluations risk trivializing the very complexities that make those questions hard in the first place. Perhaps the first thing to learn about predictive models—in both their predictive and their evaluative elements—is how to use them carefully, humbly, slowly—and with each other. It is tempting to see disagreement as a bad thing. Not so. When questions are hard, good answers require different points of view. We don't need to disagree less. We need to disagree well.

Notes

1 https://about.facebook.com/regulations/, accessed 3 January 2022. Their emphasis.
2 See Munger and Russell (2018).
3 See Yandle (2007).
4 See Rhoads (1985, 16f). See also Russell (2014).
5 Yandle (2007).
6 Peltzman (1974). See Russell (2018) for a discussion.
7 See Peltzman (1974, 88f).
8 See Peltzman (1974, 83); Malani and Philipson (2012).
9 Bastiat (1848/1995).
10 That law also stifled innovation in emissions-reducing technology (recall *Converter*): Burtraw and Szambelan (2009).
11 See Ackerman and Hassler (1981). See also Yandle (2007); Russell (2018).
12 Yandle (1983, 2007); Smith and Yandle (2014).
13 Page (2007, Chapter 4).
14 See Aristotle, *Nicomachean Ethics* book VI, Chapters1 and 12, 13. For a discussion, see Russell (2009, Chapter 1; 2014, 2018).
15 See Kirzner (1973, Chapter 2).
16 Brownstein (2019).
17 See Page (2007, Chapters 6–8). See also Vonnegut (1976), a novel of two siblings of ordinary intelligence who constituted one genius when they (literally) put their heads together.
18 Rosling (2010).
19 Vonnegut (1952) is a tale about what can be lost when we lose the necessity of working.
20 See Callard (2018, Chapter 3).
21 See Gaus (2016, 43f).
22 See Page (2007, Chapters 11, 12).
23 Ullmann-Margalit (2006).
24 Paul (2014, Chapter 4).
25 Callard (2018, esp. Chapter 3).

References

Ackerman, B. and Hassler, W. 1981. *Clean Coal/Dirty Air*. New Haven, CT: Yale University Press.
Bastiat, F. 1848/1995. "What is Seen and What is not Seen," in S. Cain and G. B. de Huszar, eds., *Frédéric Bastiat: Selected Essays on Political Economy* (pp. 1–50). New York: Foundation for Economic Education.

Brownstein, B. 2019. "Steve Jobs's Unveiling of the iPhone Holds a Timeless Economic Lesson," www.intellectualtakeout.org.

Burtraw, D. and Szambelan, S. J. 2009. "US Emissions Trading Markets for SO_2 and NO_x," *Resources for the Future*, Discussion Paper 09-40.

Callard, A. 2018. *Aspiration: The Agency of Becoming*. New York: Oxford.

Gaus, G. 2016. *The Tyranny of the Ideal: Justice in a Diverse Society*. Princeton: Princeton University Press.

Kirzner, I. 1973. *Competition and Entrepreneurship*. Chicago: University of Chicago Press.

Malani, A. and Philipson, T. J. 2012. "The Regulation of Medical Products," in P. M. Danzon and S. Nicholson, eds., *The Oxford Handbook of the Economics of the Biopharmaceutical Industry*. Oxford: Oxford University Press.

Munger, M. C. and Russell, D. C. 2018. "Can Profit-Seekers be Virtuous?," in E. Heath, B. Kaldis, and A. Marcoux, eds., *The Routledge Companion to Business Ethics*. Abington: Routledge.

Page, S. E. 2007. *The Difference: How the Power of Diversity Creates Better Groups, Firms, Schools, and Societies*. Princeton: Princeton University Press.

Paul, L. A. 2014. *Transformative Experience*. Oxford: Oxford University Press.

Peltzman, S. 1974. *Regulation of Pharmaceutical Innovation: The 1962 Amendments*. Washington, DC: American Enterprise Institute for Public Policy Research.

Rhoads, S. 1985. *The Economist's View of the World*. Cambridge: Cambridge University Press.

Rosling, H. 2010. "The Magic Washing Machine," https://www.ted.com/talks/hans_rosling_the_magic_washing_machine

Russell, D. C. 2009. *Practical Intelligence and the Virtues*. Oxford: Oxford University Press.

Russell, D. C. 2014. "What Virtue Ethics Can Learn from Utilitarianism," in B. Eggleston and D. Miller, eds., *The Cambridge Companion to Utilitarianism*. Cambridge: Cambridge University Press.

Russell, D. C. 2018. "Practical Unintelligence and the Vices," in P. Kontos, ed., *Evil in Aristotle*. Cambridge: Cambridge University Press.

Smith, A. and Yandle, B. 2014. *Bootleggers and Baptists: How Economic Forces and Moral Persuasion Interact to Shape Regulatory Politics*. Washington, DC: Cato.

Ullmann-Margalit, E. 2006. "Big Decisions: Opting, Converting, Drifting," *Royal Institute of Philosophy Supplements* 81: 157–172.

Vonnegut, K. 1952. *Player Piano*. New York: Dell Publishing.

Vonnegut, K. 1976. *Slapstick, or Lonesome No More!* New York : Dell Publishing.

Yandle, B. 1983. "Bootleggers and Baptists: The Education of a Regulatory Economist," *Regulation* 12: 12–16.

Yandle, B. 2007. "Bruce Yandle on Bootleggers and Baptists," www.econtalk.org

Chapter 10

Technology and the Virtue of Honesty

Christian B. Miller

Technology today provides many opportunities for deception and other failures of honesty. But in surprising ways, it also helps to keep our tendencies to deceive in check, so that we do not lie or cheat nearly as much as we are capable of doing. In this chapter, we will look at some of the recent empirical data on honesty and technology, and consider some of the ethical issues that often come up.

We shall proceed in the following order by looking at (i) the nature of honesty, (ii) some ways we tend to be dishonest using technology, with a focus on online dating, LinkedIn, Facebook, and text messaging, (iii) some ways we tend to be confronted with dishonesty using technology, with a focus on deepfakes and fake news, and finally (iv) some ways technology might be used to promote greater honesty.

What Is Honesty?

When we are talking about "honesty" we could be referring to a lot of different things. For instance, we could be describing an action:

> Smith's post on Facebook was an honest representation of what really happened.

But we also talk about someone being an "honest person":

> West is really honest and trustworthy. You should definitely hire her for the new IT position.

When calling a person "honest," we are describing her character in a certain positive way. Our character is how we are disposed to think, feel, and act. So an honest person is disposed to think honest thoughts (e.g., I shouldn't cheat on my taxes), have honest feelings and motivations (e.g., I don't want to cheat on my taxes, because that would be the wrong thing to do), and do honest things (e.g., I do not cheat on my taxes).

It follows that just because a person performs a bunch of honest actions, that alone does not make him an honest person. The thoughts and feelings behind those actions need to be virtuous as well. For instance, if someone doesn't cheat on his taxes, that is an honest action, but if the only reason why he does not do this is fear of being punished by the IRS, then that would not be an expression of the virtue of honesty. Hence, honest actions do not automatically imply acting from honesty.

The virtue of honesty covers a lot of moral ground. Most straightforwardly, it has to do with matters of lying, as an honest person would not knowingly tell lies. But it also extends further to include not intentionally:

DOI: 10.4324/9781003189466-13

- making misleading statements to try to get someone to arrive at a false conclusion.
- cheating and breaking the rules.
- stealing from others.
- breaking promises.

And more as well, such as engaging in bullshitting, hypocrisy, fraud, and self-deception.

In my own work, I have tried to clarify in more detail what the nature of being an honest person involves (Miller 2021a). On my way of thinking, it starts with this:

> An honest person has virtuous thoughts and feelings which lead to her not intentionally distorting the facts, from her own perspective.

To use our tax example again, someone who reports a $100 donation to charity on his taxes, when from his perspective he knows he never made such a donation, is misrepresenting or distorting what happened. He is failing to act honestly in this instance. That does not automatically make him a dishonest person in general, but in this case his behavior falls short.

There is much more to be said about the virtue of honesty, but this will be enough to allow us to look at some of the connections to technology. Our focus will be on two questions:

> Is the behavior we are discussing dishonest?
> If it is dishonest, is it all-things-considered wrong?

Initially, it might seem puzzling to raise this second question. After all, if an action is dishonest, doesn't it *have* to be wrong?

Many philosophers would be doubtful about this. Consider the famous case of the Nazi-at-the-door:

> *Hiding Jews.* You are hiding a Jewish family in your basement in a Nazi occupied territory during World War II. A Nazi soldier is doing a routine patrol of the neighborhood, asking where any Jews are. The Nazi comes to your door. You know that if you lie and say you don't know where any Jews are, the Nazi will move along to the next house. If you tell the truth, though, the Nazi will kill the family and likely you as well.

Many people would say that in this case, lying to the Nazi would be a dishonest action, but all-things-considered morally permissible, and maybe even morally required.[1]

So it is worth taking seriously the question of both whether a certain behavior using technology is dishonest, and also whether it is wrong.

Our Own Honesty Using Technology

In this section, we will look at the extent to which people tend to behave honestly (or not) using technology. Our focus will be on online dating sites, LinkedIn, Facebook, and text messaging.[2]

Honesty and Online Dating

Online dating websites allow users to create a profile, often with a picture and biographical details, that others can then examine and potentially initiate contact with if they are interested. Popular examples include eharmony and Zoosk.

Should we expect there to be widespread dishonesty in the creation of dating profiles? One reason to think so is that users of these websites are typically highly motivated to start a relationship with someone, and so could be willing to bend the truth to make themselves appear attractive and facilitate greater interest. Two features of dating profiles can help with this process. One is unlimited time – a user can take as much time as she wants in crafting a profile, with no fact checking involved. She can engage in selective self-presentation (Ellison and Hancock 2013; Hancock and Guillory 2015). The other is editability – the profiles are not set in stone when they are published, and so can always be tweaked as needed (for these two features, see Toma et al. 2019, 588).

However, there are also features of online dating which could lead people to be honest about themselves. The most important is the expectation that there will be face-to-face interactions with prospective relationship partners in the future. Presumably, online dating is just a means to an end for most people of connecting in real life. But then if someone has exaggerated his height, weight, and age a lot, for instance, those deceptions will become immediately apparent. Also, another feature of online dating which could curb temptation to be deceptive is recordability. Anything published on these websites is stored, and so could be used as documentation to check against what a person is actually like or says in face-to-face interactions (Toma et al. 2019, 588).

Combining all these features together, then, we might predict that many people will not lie on their online dating profiles, or if they do lie, it will be relatively moderate (Ellison and Hancock 2013). And this is in fact what studies have found so far. For instance, Catalina Toma and her colleagues found that 80% of participants with online dating profiles lied about their height, weight, or age, but usually only to a small extent (i.e., less than one inch off on height and 0.55 years on age, Toma et al. 2008). Summing up the existing research, Toma writes that, "online daters used deception in a limited way to rectify shortcomings, rather than lying indiscriminately simply because technology makes lying effortless" (Toma et al. 2019, 589).

Consider someone who reported himself to be an inch taller than he really is (and knows himself to be – he wasn't just confused). What do our two questions imply in this case? Is he being dishonest, and is he doing something wrong?

Clearly, he is doing something that is not honest. He is intentionally distorting the facts as he sees them. Less clear, though, is whether he is doing something all-things-considered wrong.

On the one hand, the deception by itself counts against the action. It is morally bad, as it is disrespectful of others and a violation (even if a minor one) of their dignity and worth as persons. Furthermore, if this person ends up in a relationship with someone who later finds out about the deception, that could have negative consequences for their level of trust and perceived truthfulness going forward.

On the other hand, it is unlikely that the deception would ever be discovered. And if the improved dating profile does play a role, even if minor, in helping to meet that special someone and start a very fulfilling long-term relationship, would it really be such a bad means to this good end?

All-things-considered, then, are minor deceptions in online dating justifiable or not?

LinkedIn

Instead of a dating website, how about a professional networking site? LinkedIn is probably the leading such site today, where profiles are created that highlight one's education, skills, and current as well as previous positions. Profiles default to being publicly viewable by anyone, including potential employers and current bosses.

What is your expectation about the amount of dishonesty on LinkedIn? I would expect it to be rather low. Yes, there is unlimited time to create a profile, and yes there is complete editability after the profile is created. Plus there is pressure to look as impressive as possible, especially when job seeking, so as to stand out from the crowd.

But all this seems to be counterbalanced by the publicity of the profile. Many of the claims about education, work experience, and so forth are verifiable. Lies can be caught and exposed by others who know the person, such as past employers or current colleagues. Plus, LinkedIn is recordable, and so there can be an online electronic trail (Hancock and Guillory 2015, 280–281).

What do the data suggest? A study by Guillory and Hancock (2012) had participants come to the lab to make either a traditional paper resume, a LinkedIn profile that was only viewable by the experimenter, or a publicly viewable LinkedIn profile. It turned out that rates of lying were roughly equal in all three groups, with about three lies on average per resume.

Taking this one step further, the researchers also compared the subject matter of the lies. LinkedIn resumes were more deceptive, not about clear-cut information like users' degrees, but about more private information such as interests and hobbies. Of the things to lie about or exaggerate, these made the most sense since not many people would be able to spot a lie there. However, more traditional resumes which are not publicly visible had a greater number of distortions about previous work experience and about job responsibilities (Hancock and Guillory 2015, 280–281).

These results suggest that people will be strategically deceptive with their resumes based upon what they take their audience to potentially know. This is clearly dishonest behavior, and it also implies motivation which does not fit with the virtue of honesty either.

Furthermore, it is hard to make a case for such lies being all-things-considered acceptable. The only way I can see to do so is to argue that pursing your own short-term self-interest (such as by increasing your chances of getting a job) is the most important thing in these cases, more so than being moral and potentially even your long-term self-interest if the deception is discovered. That is a hard argument to make.[3]

Facebook

Facebook shares some important similarities with LinkedIn. Profiles are created which can have a picture and various facts about a person. There is unlimited time to make the profiles, and they are editable. You can create a network of "friends," who would be the main ones to interact with the profile. All this allows a person to be identified (and so not be anonymous), and enables the profile to be publicly scrutinized and potentially recorded (Toma et al. 2019, 586).

Initially, two different hypotheses about dishonesty were proposed for social network sites like Facebook. According to the extended real-life hypothesis, because one's friends would likely spot deception, Facebook profiles would be largely truthful. Whereas according to the idealized virtual-identity hypothesis, the unlimited time to craft a profile and subsequent ability to edit it could fuel motivation to enhance one's appearance to others and thereby lead to less than truthful profiles (Toma et al. 2019, 586).

If the parallel with LinkedIn holds, then we would expect both hypotheses to be true in certain respects as Facebook users will be strategic about their dishonesty. So far, this is indeed what the data support. As Toma and her colleagues note, "Publicness indeed curbed deception on issues that were easily verifiable by the audience, such as users' physical attractiveness, but not on more subjective issues, such as how 'cool' or humorous users were" (587).[4]

Similarly, if the relevant parallels hold between LinkedIn and Facebook, then the ethical analysis should too. It is hard to count Facebook profile embellishments as honest. It is also hard to justify them all-things-considered. This is especially so since employment and hiring are not central to what Facebook is about, unlike in the case of LinkedIn, and so any embellishments would have to be justified on other grounds.

Text Messaging

Texting via a phone or computer application like iMessage and WhatsApp also has features that could both facilitate and mitigate dishonest behavior. On the one hand, you can often take your time in writing a text. The communication partner is not present physically, visually (as on Zoom), or auditorily (as by phone).

But texts are not editable. Once they are sent, there is no getting them back, and there is now an electronic trail. Plus a record remains on your own phone or computer. In these ways, they share many of the same features of email messages.

Given these points, we might expect a similar pattern to online dating profiles – some dishonest behavior, but to a limited extent. And that is what studies have found, albeit mainly focusing on college students. These studies tend to use self-reports – participants look at some of their recent texts, report how many involved lies, and rate how deceptive they were. This method is not ideal (should we trust that they are truthful about their lying?), but it is simple and straightforward.

Summarizing the results of a variety of studies, Toma and her colleagues report that participants said roughly 10% of their texts were deceptive, and on a scale from 1 (slightly deceptive) to 5 (extremely deceptive) they are on average rated around 2.5 to 3 (Toma et al. 2019, 585). Across different studies between 20% and 33% of the lies were the so-called "butler lies," named this way "because they serve the function of managing one's availability for current or future interpersonal contact with one's interlocutor, in the same way that a butler would."[5] Have you ever texted "On my way" when you haven't left yet, or "Got to run to class/a meeting/the doctor" when you don't have to? Those are examples of butler lies.

Lies like this are clearly dishonest. In my terms, they are intentionally distorting the facts as the person sees them. They also look to be all-things-considered wrong. They are disrespectful of the other person. They can damage the relationship if they are discovered. They seem to be mainly self-serving.

Can a case be made for it sometimes being okay to text these butler lies to other people?

Being Confronted with Dishonesty Using Technology

The previous section concerned how we might be the agents of deception online. In this section, the perspective shifts from being agents of deception to being passive *recipients* of others' deception. Our focus will be on deepfakes and fake news.

Deepfakes

In April 2020, then President Trump retweeted an obviously manipulated image of Joe Biden that makes his tongue and eyebrows do strange things. Other famous examples of deepfakes include an altered video which made Nancy Pelosi appear drunk, and a video of Mark Zuckerberg, head of Facebook, talking about "whoever controls the data, controls the future."

Deepfakes are intentionally manipulated pictures, videos, and audio files which substitute someone else's image or words for the original. The vast majority of deepfakes are used in the pornography industry, where, for instance, a celebrity's face is switched with that of a pornographic actor or actress. But as the examples above show, they can also be used to spread misinformation in society at large and to try to influence politics and culture. With increasingly sophisticated AI technology, it is becoming harder and harder to distinguish a deepfake from the real thing.

Deepfakes by their very nature involve intentionally distorting the facts, and producing them is thereby dishonest if the goal is to pass them off as real. But is producing and distributing a deepfake for public consumption all-things-considered wrong?

In many cases, it seems that the answer is yes. When someone else's face or recorded words are altered without their permission, that seems like a violation of the person's autonomy. Also, some viewers will inevitably think that a deepfake is *real* if it is carefully done with no warning label attached, thereby enabling more disinformation and deception to spread in society. This, in turn, facilitates audiences being manipulated to believe things for all kinds of purposes. Related to this, deepfakes can become embedded in memory and later make one more susceptible to believing fake news.[6]

The ethical question here seems to be not whether creating and distributing deepfakes is typically wrong, which it clearly seems to be, but whether it is *always* wrong.[7] A case can be made for exceptions that are relatively innocuous or even all-things-considered beneficial. For instance, there are deepfake videos of sing-offs between Boris Johnson and Theresa May. Sometimes, the people involved are dead, so consent is not an issue, and the consequences of seeing them doing something entertaining such as singing a popular song might be positive overall if it causes a lot of laugher and amusement. Plus it is clear to viewers in these cases that these are not real videos. So perhaps certain kinds of deepfakes might be permissible after all.[8]

Besides amusing songs, are there other kinds of deepfakes which could be okay as well? What kind of test could we use to tell if a deepfake is acceptable overall or not?

Fake News

Deepfakes can be classified as a kind of fake news. Following the definition offered by Gordon Pennycock and David Rand, fake news is "news content published on the Internet that aesthetically resembles actual legitimate mainstream news content, but that is fabricated or extremely inaccurate" (Pennycook and Rand 2021, 389). Deepfakes would fit this definition, but fake news encompasses far more. Examples include stories spreading disinformation about the COVID-19 pandemic and the 2020 US presidential election.

The topic of fake news has generated an enormous amount of discussion in recent years, but given that another chapter in this volume is devoted to the topic, we will only consider it briefly here.[9] Our focus is on the ethics of producing and sharing fake news. While this might seem to be a straightforward case of dishonesty, matters are more complex.

A lot depends on what the person who produces or shares the piece of fake news believes. Consider a story about how the election results in the 2020 US presidential election were fraudulent, and that the vote counts in Michigan and Wisconsin were rigged. If the person writing the story genuinely believes that this is the correct conclusion to draw on the basis of his investigative work, then even though it might be extremely inaccurate and so count as "fake news" based on Pennycock and Rand's definition, it is not obviously a case of dishonesty. The author is not intentionally distorting the facts *as he sees them*, even if objectively he is getting the facts wrong as they really are. Note as well that saying he is not being dishonest is compatible with saying that the author is still failing in other areas of his character. For example, one might fault the author for being too close-minded or gullible, either of which is illustrative of a failure to develop the traits necessary to become a responsible journalist.

However, suppose the author is lying in the story, by communicating what he thinks is false with the intention of deceiving his audience about what happened with the election. Or alternatively, he could be bullshitting, which, following the philosopher Harry Frankfurt's famous characterization, is a matter of lacking a concern for the truth in the first place (Frankfurt 1988). If the author of the article is bullshitting, then he is making things up to suit his agenda, regardless of whether any of it is true or not.

Regardless of whether he is lying or bullshitting, such a person would fail to be honest in writing this chapter. So a lot depends on the state of mind of the person at the time who is producing the fake news.

Much the same applies to someone who *shares* a piece of fake news by retweeting it on Twitter or posting it on Facebook. Consider the following case:

> *Committed Trump Supporter.* Ron is a committed supporter of Donald Trump. He has attended MAGA rallies and donated to his campaign. After the 2020 election, he came to sincerely believe that the results in states like Michigan and Wisconsin were fraudulent, and that Trump actually won the election. When he reads an article supporting these claims, he shares it on social media.[10]

On the approach being proposed, it would follow that Ron is *not* being dishonest in sharing the story. He is not intentionally distorting the facts; from his perspective, he is helping to promote the facts. However, if a different person knew that the story was bogus but shared it anyway, thereby acting as if it were true and newsworthy, then that would be dishonest.

Does this sound right? Can someone produce or share fake news and still be honest in the process?

Promoting Honesty Using Technology

Let us end by thinking more constructively about ways in which online technology can be used in a positive manner to help promote greater honesty both online and in our lives in general. Here, we will consider two suggestions.

Remote Proctoring

In an educational context, one of the most tempting opportunities for students to cheat is with closed-book take-home exams. With no one watching and easy access to the answers in the course materials or online, it is no wonder that many professors are reticent to offer this form of assessment.

But matters became more challenging for professors due to COVID-19 and the shift to online education for one or more semesters. Some courses lent themselves to paper assignments, but other courses such as in math and science are naturally geared to problem solving and factual examination.

Enter remote proctoring to the rescue. A company can be paid to monitor a student's test behavior via the student's own camera, and can report to the professor if any suspicious behavior is observed. Access to certain websites can also be blocked during the taking of the exam. And as Sarah Silverman and her colleagues note:

> Current remote proctoring technology has become more sophisticated, combining artificial intelligence, automated proctors, wearable cameras, environmental scans, keystroke tracking, gaze and eye tracking, and head movement detection…with multi-biometric systems for authentication, such as facial recognition.
>
> (Silverman et al. 2021)

However, even if remote proctoring is effective in reducing dishonest behavior, it is not clear that it would help to actually foster the virtue of honesty. It would seem that student cheating would be curbed primarily for reasons having to do with punishment avoidance. But that is an egoistic form of motivation, concerned only with what would benefit the student. To grow in honesty, one does need to act dishonestly less and less, but one also needs to do the honest thing more and more for the right reasons and motives.

There are also plenty of other concerns with remote proctoring that do not have to do with honesty per se. Worries have been raised about infringing on a student's privacy in the home environment. Plus if students need to buy a webcam and have high speed Internet, then there are equity concerns. And to the extent to which the proctoring increases test anxiety for some students, that is not a good thing either.

So the question becomes, can remote proctoring be carried out in such a way as to actually foster honesty in students?

Moral Reminders

When it comes to using the Internet, there are several ways users might be nudged into being more honest with the help of moral reminders. Some of these reminders are more subtle, whereas others are more explicit.

An example of a subtle reminder is the use of eye images. In a few studies *not* involving being online, images of eyes on a wall have been found to reduce theft and littering. There is some evidence that the same effect can show up online, with eye spots staring at users from ads, for instance, although the results are preliminary and somewhat mixed.[11]

An example of a very explicit reminder is the use of warning messages. This has been found in various studies to increase recognition of fake news and also reduce sharing. But it is a slow process, and one which is only used on a small scale, thereby not addressing many cases of false news (Pennycock and Rand 2021, 395–396).

In between these two approaches is the strategy of "getting people to slow down and reflect about the accuracy of what they see on social media" (Pennycock and Rand 2021, 397). This can be done through accuracy prompts, say by asking users to assess the accuracy of a headline before sharing it on social media. One study found that this approach was effective in bringing about a 51% reduction in the sharing of false headlines as compared to a group that had no accuracy prompting (Pennycock et al. 2021). Public service announcements, ads, and other tools could be used as well (Pennycock and Rand 2021, 397).

These moderate reminders can be applied more widely than just to cases of fake news. Returning to the topic of exams delivered remotely, for instance, a school's honor code can serve as a moral reminder to help keep the perspective of a student where it needs to be. Honor codes in general have been found to be effective in curbing cheating behavior (Miller 2020).

Do any of these moral reminder approaches seem promising to you, and can you think of other ways in which honesty reminders might be used online?

Conclusion

Clearly, we are only scratching the surface in understanding the relationship between technology and honesty. We need many more empirical studies to get a better picture of what the situation is like. And we need to think more about whether what we are doing online is honest or dishonest, as well as all-things-considered wrong or not. These issues are not going away anytime soon, and hopefully this chapter can help to spur on further work in this area.[12]

Notes

1   Not everyone agrees, though. For a recent defense of lying always being wrong, see Tollefsen (2014).

2   Each of these will be examined independently. It is also interesting to compare them. For instance, do people tend to be more dishonest when texting than on Facebook? For a relevant study, see Drouin et al. (2016).

3   Although see Marcoux (2006), who argues that, "[t]o the extent that one knows or reasonably suspects that a significant number of others are embellishing non-verifiable information on their résumé's, one ought prudently and ought morally to embellish non-verifiable information on one's own résumé, as well" (185). Thanks to an anonymous reviewer for this reference.

4   A longer discussion would also look at honest behavior on Facebook besides one's profile, such as posting on other friends' walls. For a relevant study, see Spottswood and Hancock (2016).

5   Toma et al. (2019, 585). See also Hancock and Guillory (2015, 285).

6   For this last point, see Liv and Greenbaum (2020).

7   For an extensive discussion of the costs and benefits of deepfake technology, see Chesney and Citron (2019).

8   An anonymous reviewer noted that deepfakes are often parodies, and they might be related to other forms of fiction that are morally acceptable. These seem to be important points worth further exploration.

9   See the chapter by Marc-André Argentino and Adnan Raja.

10 This example and the surrounding discussion draw from Miller (2021b), with permission.

11 See Ellison and Hancock (2013, 87), Hancock and Guillory (2015, 275), and Spottswood and Hancock (2016).

12 I am grateful to Gregory Robson and Jonathan Y. Tsou for inviting me to be a part of this volume, and to Robson and several anonymous reviewers for helpful comments. Work on this paper was supported by a grant from the John Templeton Foundation. The opinions expressed here are those of the author and do not necessarily reflect the views of the Foundation.

References

Chesney, B. and D. Citron. 2019. "Deep Fakes: A Looming Challenge for Privacy, Democracy, and National Security." *California Law Review* 107: 1753–1820.

Drouin, M., D. Miller, S. Wehle, and E. Hernandez. 2016. "Why Do People Lie Online? 'Because Everyone Lies on the Internet.'" *Computers in Human Behavior* 64: 134–142.

Ellison, N. and J. Hancock. 2013. "Profile as Promise: Honest and Deceptive Signals in Online Dating." *IEEE Security & Privacy Economics* 11: 84–88.

Frankfurt, H. 1988. "On Bullshit." *Raritan* 6. Reprinted in *The Importance of What We Care About*. Cambridge: Cambridge University Press, 117–133.

Guillory, J. and J. Hancock. 2012. "The Effect of LinkedIn on deception in Resumes." *Cyberpsychology, Behavior, and Social Networking* 15: 135–140.

Hancock, J. and J. Guillory. 2015. "Deception with Technology," in *The Handbook of the Psychology of Communication Technology*. Ed. S. Sundar. Hoboken: John Wiley, 270–289.

Liv, N. and D. Greenbaum. 2020. "Deep Fakes and Memory Malleability: False Memories in the Service of Fake News." *AJOB Neuroscience* 11: 96–104.

Marcoux, A. 2006. "A Counterintuitive Argument for Résumé Embellishment." *Journal of Business Ethics* 63: 183–194.

Miller, C. 2020. "Just How Dishonest Are Most Students?" *The New York Times*. https://www.nytimes.com/2020/11/13/opinion/sunday/online-learning-cheating.html

Miller, C. 2021a. *Honesty: The Philosophy and Psychology of a Neglected Virtue*. New York: Oxford University Press.

Miller, C. 2021b. "Honesty and Radically Opposing Views: Flat-Earthers, Apocalyptic Preachers, and 2020 American Election-Deniers." *Open for Debate Blog*. https://blogs.cardiff.ac.uk/openfordebate/2021/01/25/honesty-and-radically-opposing-views-flat-earthers-apocalyptic-preachers-and-2020-american-election-deniers/

Pennycook, G. and D. G. Rand. 2021. "The Psychology of Fake News." *Trends in Cognitive Sciences* 25: 388–402.

Silverman, S., A. Caines, C. Casey, B. G. de Hurtado, J. Riviere, A. Sintjago, and C. Vecchiola. 2021. "What Happens When You Close the Door on Remote Proctoring? Moving Toward Authentic Assessments with a People-Centered Approach." *Educational Development in the Time of Crises* 39: 115–131. DOI: 10.3998/tia.17063888.0039.308.

Spottswood, E. and J. Hancock. 2016. "The Positivity Bias and Prosocial Deception on Facebook." *Computers in Human Behavior* 65: 252–259.

Tollefsen, C. 2014. *Lying and Christian Ethics*. Cambridge: Cambridge University Press.

Toma, C., J. Bonus, and L. van Swol. 2019. "Lying Online: Examining the Production, Detection, and Popular Beliefs Surrounding Interpersonal Deception in Technologically-Mediated Environments," in *The Palgrave Handbook of Deceptive Communication*. Ed. T. Docan-Morgan. Camden: Palgrave Macmillan, 583–601.

Toma, C., J. Hancock, and N. Ellison. 2008. "Separating Fact from Fiction: An Examination of Deceptive Self-Presentation in Online Dating Profiles." *Personality and Social Psychology Bulletin* 34: 1023–1036.

Chapter 11

Confucian Ethics of Technology

Qin Zhu

Introduction

As the single most influential Chinese school of thought (Shun and Wong 2004), Confucianism has historically affected human (inter-)action and social organization in China and other Asian cultures. In recent decades, philosophers have employed various approaches to engaging Confucian ethics ranging from overtly historical or textual approaches to comparative approaches that put ideas from the classical period into conversation with contemporary Western ethical, social, and scientific theories (Mattice 2019). Scholars have also tried to understand Confucian ethics as a species of deontology, virtue ethics, or care ethics (Mattice 2019). Until only recently, scholars generally attempted to theorize Confucian ethics as a kind of role-based moral theory (Ames 2011, Rosemont and Ames 2016).

More recently, studies in Confucian ethics have increasingly demonstrated *global* characteristics. As an alternative to dominant Western ethical theories, Confucian ethics has been employed by philosophers and engineers from both the Chinese and Western cultures to tackle extensively complex sociotechnical issues encountered by humanity as a whole such as robotics, AI, and climate change (Vallor 2016, Wong 2019, Bay 2021, Teng 2021). As pointed out by Vallor (2016), Western ethical theories such as deontology and consequentialism often struggle to accommodate diverse, unstable, and complex contexts of emerging technologies. Furthermore, an increasingly globalized environment of engineering practice requires engineers to be able to navigate ethical issues arising from cross-cultural professional contexts (Zhu and Jesiek 2020). Given the critical role of Cultures of Confucian Heritage (CHCs) in global economy (Tu 1989), future competent engineers need to develop moral competency for working with professionals, including engineers who are influenced by (or from) CHCs. Responsible engineers today have a special kind of *global responsibility* to design technosocial experiences sensitive to diverse cultural backgrounds of people and conducive to their unique developmental goals. In particular, non-Western ethical resources such as Confucian ethics are able to help engineers working in the global context cultivate moral imagination and develop creative resolutions to complex sociotechnical problems in culturally responsive ways.

This chapter briefly discusses how Confucianism as an important non-Western intellectual resource can provide useful insights into discussions in the ethics of technology. The chapter first provides a concise introduction to Confucian ethics with a specific focus on three interrelated key concepts: roles, rituals, and the harmonious society. It then discusses the implications of Confucian ethics for the design of *technological artifacts*, including emerging technologies.

DOI: 10.4324/9781003189466-14

Confucian Ethics: Rituals, Roles, and the Harmonious Society

To a large extent, Western ethical theories, especially deontology and consequentialism (this essay focuses on these two theories), can be perceived as "rule-based" ethics. For instance, deontology is concerned about whether one's action is in accordance with some moral rules or "categorical imperatives" that can be universalized. Consequentialism especially utilitarianism emphasizes the unity principle or "rule," that is, good actions are those that can bring the maximum amount of net utility (e.g., happiness, pleasure, and welfare) to the greatest number of people. Both deontology and consequentialism are mainly interested in "defining what good is" and worry about "how one can come to know the good." In contrast, Confucian ethics or Chinese philosophy in general is mostly concerned about the problem of "how to become good" (Ivanhoe 2000).

However, some scholars may challenge this idea of perceiving deontology and consequentialism merely as "rule-based" ethics. Instead, they may further argue that even Confucian ethics includes etiquette or *li* (rituals, 礼) which may seem to be "rule-based." For instance, it is quite common that Confucian classics such as the *Analects* include passages on *li* which might be considered as "rules" such as "not instructing while eating" and "not continuing to converse once one has retired to bed" (*Analects*, 10.10). Nevertheless, compared to moral rules in a more traditional Western sense, Confucian *li* often has a much stronger emphasis on the "centrality of ritual performance in the ethical cultivation of character" (Wong 2014, 180). The *performative* aspect of *li* underscores that what matters is what rituals do rather than what they are (Sun 2013). *Li* creates a world of social convention and authority that help to organize a given messy society. It serves as a crucial way of integrating already appropriate styles of interaction, social convention, and norms into the everyday life in the community. By practicing *li*, we are able to ensure that our daily actions and interactions are aligned with normative expectations in the community. With persistent practice of *li*, our moral selves are gradually cultivated. Such emphasis on the importance of *li* for the moral self is not very much discussed in either deontology or consequentialism. In quite a few passages in the *Analects*, *li* is often considered as a means of cultivating and expressing virtues such as *ren* (benevolence, 仁).

Sometimes, even established ritual practices may be subject to change if the implementation context of rituals has changed. However, what remain unchanged are the virtues or the "essential meaning" that the practice of rituals aims to cultivate. For instance, passage 9.3 in the *Analects* demonstrates well the contextual flexibility of ritual practice:

> The Master said, "A ceremonial cap made of linen is prescribed by the rites, but these days people use silk. This is frugal, and I follow the majority. To bow before ascending the stairs is what is prescribed by the rites, but these days people bow after ascending. This is arrogant, and – though it goes against the majority – I continue to bow before ascending".
>
> (*Analects*, 9.3)

Confucius accepted the change of ritual practice that replaced the linen cap with the silk cap as most of his contemporaries did. Making such a change does not really change the basic function of the ceremonial cap. In fact, making such a change would express and cultivate the virtue of frugality. In contrast, Confucius did not agree with his contemporaries who bow after ascending as he argued that such a change will hurt the essential meaning of the ritual. Furthermore, the extensively practical, context-dependent, and aesthetic aspects of rituals in the *Analects* may not be well captured by deontological or consequentialist rules.

Another interesting comparison between deontology and consequentialism and Confucian ethics is that the two Western ethical theories often assume an idea of *ethical impartiality*, whereas Confucian ethics places a much stronger emphasis on *ethical partiality*. Deontological impartiality represented by Kantian ethics requires that "moral judgments be universalizable" and these moral judgments "be independent of any particular point of view" (or any particular person) (Jollimore 2018). Consequentialist impartiality is "strictly impartial in a very direct manner and in a very rigorous sense" and a consequentialist agent is thus "not permitted to prefer herself, nor any of her loved ones, in choosing a distribution of benefits and burdens" (Jollimore 2018). In contrast, Confucian ethics advocates the idea of love with distinction. In other words, our moral concerns toward others decrease as our relationships with them weaken.

While both deontology and consequentialism place a strong emphasis on the value of following rules (e.g., Kantian categorical imperatives and the consequentialist rule to maximize utility) for moral actions, Confucian ethics argues that the key to become a good person is to live and reflect on the social roles (e.g., parent, child, citizen, and engineer) one assumes in specific communal contexts. By nature, humans are social, interdependent, and related to each other after birth (Yu and Fan 2007).

According to Confucian ethics, the moral actions we take in different situations are influenced by the specific roles we take in these situations. We as humans all assume different roles which are determined by the relationships we have with others. These different relationships and social roles affect the ways we choose to interact with others. The tone you use when speaking to your parent is different from the one you use when communicating with a stranger. The nature of a particular role relationship often evokes feelings and expectations characteristic of that relationship (Ames 2016). Through living and reflecting on these social roles, one gets to cultivate virtues that define the ideal forms of these social roles.

Differentiation and fulfillment of these different social roles are critical for a harmonious and flourishing society. In Confucian ethics, five cardinal role-based relationships are of critical importance; these are the relationships between parents and children, husband and wife, older and younger siblings, rulers and ministers, and friends (Cottine 2020). The five relationships belong to three social spheres: (1) *the family sphere*: the parent-child relationship, the husband–wife relationship, and the relationship between siblings; (2) *the intermediary sphere*: friendship; and (3) *the social/political sphere*: the ruler and minister relationship. Cottine (2020) argues that family relations are foundational for individual moral development and state governance. Arguably, being a filial child provides a paradigmatic case for being a loyal minister. In particular, Mengzi connects specific virtues with the five different cardinal role-relations:

> Between father and children there is affection; between ruler and ministers there is righteousness; between husband and wife there is distinction; between elder and younger there is precedence, and between friends there is faithfulness.
>
> (*Mengzi*, Book 3A4.8)

Similarly, to live and reflect on the role as a medical doctor, one gets to cultivate virtues (e.g., benevolence) that are required by an ideal medical doctor. Nevertheless, such process of cultivating virtues cannot be completed solely by the doctor but must be done by both the doctor and the patients they take care of. Therefore, Confucian role ethics advocates a kind of relational moral epistemology: becoming benevolent is something we either do together or not at all (Ames 2011). Moral conduct thus refers to behavior that "conduces to growth in the roles and relations we live together with others, and immoral conduct is the opposite" (Ames 2020). Confucian ethics acknowledges the value of social roles in making an agent the person they are (Nuyen 2007). What characterizes the personhood is not so much about one's innate and inalienable individual human rights as most Western political and ethical theorists would emphasize. Instead, Confucian role ethicists insist that what defines one's personhood is one's intentional efforts to actively live out one's social roles.

Therefore, Confucian ethics defines humans as "the sum of the roles we live in consonance with our fellows" (Rosemont and Ames 2016, 122). Confucian role ethics appeals to the actual life experience we are living with others both cognitively and affectively. A critical way of becoming virtuous persons in the Confucian tradition is to observe how others practice *li* (rituals) that are required by the social roles they assume. Practicing *li* appropriately can be conducive to the reinforcement of human relationships and associated communal roles. Ritual practices require us to be both physically and emotionally engaged (Hagen 2010). Emotions and feelings are thus critical for us to demonstrate our commitment to the practice of *li* and the fulfillment of our role-based moral obligations. A truly caring nurse can never be one who knows only how to follow rules. They develop the virtue of benevolence by feeling what their patients are suffering. Arguably, their emotional engagement with patients' experience allows and encourages them to develop qualities and dispositions that define a truly caring nurse. Thus, one possible way of evaluating whether we fulfill our communal roles well is to examine whether we have any emotional investment in these roles.

Relationships, contexts, and social roles are crucial in Chinese philosophy especially Confucian ethics. Nuyen (2007) conceptualizes a systematic framework that integrates a set of key concepts in Confucian ethics, including relationships, social roles, moral obligations, *li* (rituals), and virtues:

1   A person is a self who stands in a network of social relationships.
2   Social relationships define social roles with more or less specific obligations.
3   To stand in a social relationship (to be a mother, a son, a wife, etc.) is to stand under a set of obligations specified by *li*.
4   If names are rectified (or if one is sincere), a person is a self who places himself or herself under (undertakes) obligations to behave in a certain way specified by *li*.
5   A person is obligated to behave in accordance with *li*.
6   A person ought to follow the rules and cultivate the virtues according to *li* (Nuyen 2007, 321).

In summary, Confucian ethics is mainly concerned about social relationships which determine our social roles and associated role-based moralities. Rituals or *li* in the Confucian sense provide behavioral guidelines for how to live these roles and relationships well. We get to cultivate our virtues that are required by different social roles while practicing rituals. A harmonious society is therefore based on everyone in the society living their assigned social roles, practicing rituals required by these roles, and cultivating their virtues and moral selves. Such a practical orientation in Confucian ethics affects the ways humans engage with the world especially through technological means.

Confucian Ethics and Technological Design

From the Confucian perspective, technology is *never* value-neutral. Good technologies should always help promote the values respected and maintained in the communities, such as harmony. Therefore, the Confucian approach to the ethics of technology evaluates to what extent and in what ways technology contributes to a process of harmonization. Reliable technological development often leads to "a continuous negotiation and adjustment of relationships between human beings, society and technology" (Wong 2012, 81).

More specifically, a major task for the Confucian ethics of technology is to investigate whether practices engendered by technology "are conducive or detrimental to our performance of the social roles" (Wong 2012, 83). In this sense, the development of technologies such as artificial intelligence (AI) can and should be encouraged by our political communities if these technologies help us realize our constitutive commitments or moral obligations prescribed by our social roles (e.g., child and parent). Similarly, technologies that undermine the realization of our constitutive commitments should be restricted (Bell and Wang 2020). Daniel Bell and Wang Pei (2020) imagine two examples involving AI and robots that can be assessed by Confucian ethics:

- If an AI-enabled technology can free us from socially necessary work so that we can spend more time caring for our parents with love and compassion, then such technology should be supported.

- If a cute-looking robot relieves all of our caring obligations and our parents are convinced that the robot truly cares about their well-being, then the parents care more about the robots than their own children. Such robotic technology should be restricted, from the Confucian perspective.

The two scenarios demonstrate that the moral quality of technology is assessed based on the extent to which technology helps us practice our role-based obligations and cultivate virtues for better living these social roles. Such role-based morality in Confucian ethics has been integrated into recent efforts to design ethical guidelines for socially integrated robots. JeeLoo Liu argues that a robot inspired by Confucian ethics "must first and foremost fulfill its assigned roles" and needs to "render assistance to other human beings in their pursuit of moral improvement" (Liu 2017). In this sense, to design and evaluate moral agency in a robot is to: (1) assess to what extent such robot well assumes its assigned social roles (e.g., a social companion robot working with elderly people); and (2) what capabilities and dispositions are required to define a good robot that fulfills its assigned roles.

Also, as suggested earlier, Confucian moral development is a social and collaborative process between a moral learner and others. This social, interactional aspect of Confucian ethics opens a creative possibility for artifacts such as robots to serve as a kind of "others" in helping people behave morally (Hung 2021). In contrast to Western philosophies, which often romanticize robot rights or agency, Confucian ethics is more flexible in assigning personhood to robots insofar as these robots have put efforts to cultivate virtuous tendencies among themselves and others. A truly socially integrated robot has the obligation to offer assistance to other humans in their moral development projects. Nevertheless, it is worth noting that the social roles we assume and the relationships we have with others are taken by Confucian role ethics to be "natural." Such an assumption in Confucian role ethics can be problematic. It is unclear who gets to decide the roles we should play. The challenge becomes more visible when we introduce the Confucian role-based morality to the design of human-robot interaction. It seems even more challenging to answer the question of who gets to decide what roles robots should play and what kinds of role-based moralities they should employ.

Technologies such as AI and robotics can improve the efficiency of work and free us from some role obligations. Yet, philosophers also feel concerned that these technologies may also lead to "technology-driven moral deskilling" (Vallor 2016, Wong 2019), negatively affecting our moral cultivation. For instance, robot caregivers are morally questionable as they reduce the precious opportunities for nurses to exercise and cultivate the virtues defined by their role as professional nurses. One implication for the design of AI and robotics is whether engineers can be creative enough to design technologies that allow or create opportunities for users to develop their moral skills and cultivate role-based virtues.

Confucian ethics that focuses on role-based morality and relationship also has profound implications for assessing biomedical technologies such as gene editing technology. For instance, moral assessment of gene enhancement technology for children raises at least two questions: (1) what is the appropriate role of children in the familial context? and (2) what are the role-based moral responsibilities of parents? In the Confucian tradition, children are perceived as gifts from ancestors (Fan 2010). They are critical for promoting the family's prosperity and integrity (Li and Zhang 2019).

Confucian ethics emphasizes the sociocultural practicality of genes (Fan 2010). Confucians may accept some types of genetic enhancement while reject others. Again, the single most important criterion for assessing the moral quality of technology is whether and how such technology helps to promote the values upheld by a Confucian community and how it helps community members realize and live their assigned social roles and associated moral obligations. Ruiping Fan (2010) invites us to consider the following thought experiment. Suppose a genetic enhancement technology for changing skin and hair color is possible, and a Confucian Chinese wants genetically to change his children's skin color from yellow to white, or hair color from black to blond. Is it morally acceptable to do so? Such a gene enhancement technology that can change the skin or hair color may rightly be rejected by Confucian ethics. The reasoning behind such rejection is quite straightforward. In the Confucian tradition, a child is considered as a gift from ancestors. Such gift is not from a *particular* ancestor but from all the ancestors of the family (Fan 2010). As a child, our moral obligation is to respect and love our ancestors, including our lives given as their gifts and continue the family lineage. As parents, our moral responsibility requires us to respect all of the ancestors of the family and not to change the appearances of our children. As our ancestors had yellow skin and black hair, we do not want our children to look more like the image of other people (Fan 2010).

However, it is worth noting that a much deeper reason why Confucian ethics may reject certain genetic enhancement technologies that change children's skin and hair colors is not simply that these technologies change children's resemblance to their ancestors. Instead, what is at stake here is how the changes made by these technologies (or others) "stand in relation to our respect to ancestors or our virtue of filial piety" (Fan 2010, 69). In other words, it can be totally okay for a family to adopt a child from a different family insofar as the inclusion of the adopted child demonstrates and enhances a set of core values of the Confucian family: (1) venerating ancestors, (2) strengthening basic human relations, (3) promoting the continuity, integrity, and prosperity of the family, and (4) practicing family determination on important issues of family members. Adopting a child especially in a family that, say, cannot have their own children will likely enhance these values if the family is following appropriate Confucian rituals. In particular, in the Confucian culture, promoting the continuity, integrity, and prosperity of the family is the key to the cultivation of the virtue of filial piety. Given the valuable role of the adopted child in promoting the continuity of the family, it is ethically justifiable and required that the parents should treat the adopted child as their own. Similarly, the adopted child is expected to treat the adoptive parents as their own. Through such a reciprocal relationship, both the adoptive parents and the adopted child can cultivate virtues related to their familial roles, and such cultivation of virtues in the familial context is critical for a harmonious society.

However, some gene enhancement technologies might be approved by Confucian ethics. These technologies can enhance certain abilities of the children which demonstrate the respect for the gifts granted by the ancestors and the promotion of family fame (Fan 2010).

For instance, Confucian ethics may approve a gene enhancement technology that is able to improve children's IQ (intelligence quotient). The Confucian ethics of "giftedness" further leads to some interesting questions for future research. For instance, let us imagine a scenario where a child born in a non-Chinese culture was adopted by a Chinese couple. In this scenario, some questions merit further philosophical exploration:

- whether this child can and should still be considered as a gift given by the ancestors of the adoptive family;
- if so, how to understand and justify the connection between a child adopted from a non-Chinese culture and the ancestors of the adoptive family;
- to what extent this adopted child is culturally Confucian despite the fact that this child was not born in a culture of Confucian heritage.

Both the robotics and gene editing technology cases here discussed have demonstrated that ethical assessment of technology needs to examine more than simply the values embedded in technology. Moreover, engineers are encouraged to consider two additional relational and communal factors in technological design: (1) how the users with unique and diverse cultural backgrounds comprehend and interpret the values revealed by the use of technology and in technologically mediated interactions; and (2) the moral impacts of technology on the already appropriate styles of interaction, social conventions, and norms in a community (Wong 2020).

Conclusion

In conclusion, a Confucian approach to the ethical assessment of technology focuses on how and how far a technology affects our moral relationships with others, the social roles we live, and the role-based moral obligations we hold in communal contexts. In contrast to Western philosophies that treat humans as rights-bearing individuals, Confucian ethics considers humans as "blood and flesh" role-bearing persons. Rituals provide behavioral guidance on how we should live our roles, although rituals may change as their contexts change. The fulfillment of our diverse social roles is fundamental for an orderly, harmonious society. Good or ethical technologies are always conducive rather than detrimental to the appropriate living of our social roles. However, when assessing the moral quality of technology, we need to take a more *historical* or *contextual* approach to examining the impacts of technology on social roles and role-based moralities, as our normative expectations about these roles may change if temporal and spatial contexts change. In general, Confucian ethics requires neither *technological optimism* nor *technological pessimism* but *technological pragmatism*. Understanding the ethics of technology calls for specific empirical tests to carefully examine how a technology affects our life goals and relationships, whether positively or negatively.

References

Ames, Roger T. 2011. *Confucian Role Ethics: A Vocabulary*. Hong Kong: The Chinese University Press.

Ames, Roger T. 2016. "Theorizing 'Person' in Confucian Ethics: A Good Place to Start." *Sungkyun Journal of East Asian Studies* 16 (2): 141–162.

Ames, Roger T. 2020. *Human Becomings: Theorizing Persons for Confucian Role Ethics*. Albany, NY: SUNY Press.

Angle, Stephen C. 2012. *Contemporary Confucian Political Philosophy: Toward Progressive Confucianism*. Malden, MA: Polity Press.

Bay, Morten. 2021. "Four Challenges to Confucian Virtue Ethics in Technology." *Journal of Information, Communication and Ethics in Society* 19 (3): 358–373.

Bell, Daniel A., and Pei Wang. 2020. *Just hierarchy: Why Social Hierarchies Matter in China and the Rest of the World*. Princeton, NJ: Princeton University Press.

Bell, Daniel A., and Thaddeus Metz. 2011. "Confucianism and Ubuntu: Reflections on a Dialogue between Chinese and African Traditions." *Journal of Chinese Philosophy* 38 (supplement): 78–95.

Cottine, Cheryl. 2020. "That's What Friends Are For: A Confucian Perspective on the Moral Significance of Friendship." In *Perspectives in Role Ethics: Virtues, Reasons, and Obligation*, edited by Tim Dare and Christine Swanton, 123–142. New York, NY: Routledge.

Fan, Ruiping. 2010. "A Confucian Reflection on Genetic Enhancement." *The American Journal of Bioethics* 10 (4): 62–70.

Hagen, Kurtis. 2010. "The Propriety of Confucius: A Sense-of-Ritual." *Asian Philosophy* 20 (1): 1–25.

Hung, Ching. 2021. "Technological Mediation in and for Confucianism-Based Cultures." *Harmonious Technology: A Confuscian Ethics of Technology*. Edited by Pak-Hang Wong and Tom Xiaowei Wang, 50–65. Abingdon: Routledge.

Ivanhoe, Philip J. 2000. *Confucian Moral Self Cultivation*. 2nd Edition. Indianapolis, IN: Hackett.

Jollimore, Troy. 2018. "Impartiality." *The Stanford Encyclopedia of Philosophy*. Edited by Edward N. Zalta. Accessed December 15, 2019. https://plato.stanford.edu/archives/win2018/entries/impartiality/

Li, Jianhui, and Xin Zhang. 2019. "Should Parents Design Their Children's Genome: Some General Arguments and A Confucian Solution." *Philosophies* 4 (3): 43. https://doi.org/10.3390/philosophies4030043

Liu, JeeLoo. 2017. Confucian robotic ethics. Paper presented at the international conference on the relevance of the classics under the conditions of modernity: humanity and science. Hong Kong: The Hong Kong Polytechnic University.

Mattice, Sarah. 2019. "Confucian Role Ethics: Issues of Naming, Translation, and Interpretation." In *The Bloomsbury Research Handbook of Early Chinese Ethics and Political Philosophy*. Edited by Alexus McLeod, 25–44. London: Bloomsbury Academic.

Nuyen, A. T. 2007. "Confucian Ethics as Role-based Ethics." *International Philosophical Quarterly* 47 (3): 315–328.

Rosemont, Henry, and Roger T. Ames. 2016. *Confucian Role Ethics: A Moral Vision for the 21st Century?* Göttingen: V&R Academic.

Shun, Kwong-loi, and David B. Wong,. 2004. *Confucian Ethics: A Comparative Study of Self, Autonomy, and Community*. New York: Cambridge University Press.

Sun, Anna. 2013. *Confucianism as a World Religion: Contested Histories and Contemporary Realities*. Princeton, NJ: Princeton University Press.

Teng, Fei. 2021. "Climate Change and Moral Responsibility toward Future Generations: A Confucian Perspective." *Philosophy East and West* 71 (2): 451–472.

Tu, Weiming. 1989. *Centrality and Commonality: An Essay on Confucian Religiousness*. Albany: State University of New York Press.

Vallor, Shannon. 2016. *Technology and the Virtues: A Philosophical Guide to a Future Worth Wanting*. New York: Oxford University Press.

Wong, David B. 2014. "Cultivating the Self in Concert with Others." In *Dao Companion to the Analects*. Edited by Amy Olberding, 171–197. Dordrecht: Springer.

Wong, Pak-Hang. 2012. "Dao, Harmony, and Personhood: Towards a Confucian Ethics of Technology." *Philosophy & Technology* 25 (1): 67–86.

Wong, Pak-Hang. 2019. "Rituals and Machines: A Confucian Response to Technology-Driven Moral Deskilling." *Philosophies* 4 (4): 59. https://doi.org/10.3390/philosophies4040059

Wong, Pak-Hang. 2020. "Why Confucianism Matters in Ethics of Technology." In *Oxford Handbook of Philosophy of Technology*. Edited by Shannon Vallor, 609–628. New York: Oxford University Press.

Yu, Erika, and Ruiping Fan. 2007. "A Confucian View of Personhood and Bioethics." *Journal of Bioethical Inquiry* 4 (3): 171–179.

Zhu, Qin, and Brent Jesiek. 2020. "Practicing Engineering Ethics in Global Context: A Comparative Study of Expert and Novice Approaches to Cross-Cultural Ethical Situations." *Science and Engineering Ethics* 26: 2097–2120.

Chapter 12

Utilitarianism and Happy-People-Pills

Mark A. Walker

Introduction

This chapter offers a moral argument that we should make and take drugs (of a certain sort) to make ourselves happier. In outline, the argument is simple enough: taking drugs to make ourselves happier will improve our lives, and we have a moral duty to improve our lives. Admittedly, the argument may not sound plausible. However, my aim here is not to secure your *belief* that we should create and take drugs to make ourselves happier; rather, I hope after reading this chapter you will have a better *understanding* of the issues.

Hedonism

I'll come to the question of drugs in a bit. First, we need to get some idea about the good life so that we can assess the claim that drugs might help to improve our lives. The term the "good life" is ambiguous. In one sense, it means the "prudentially good life," and in another it means the "morally good life." The prudentially good life is a life good for the person whose life it is. Examples of prudentially good but morally bad lives include very happy and successful Mafioso bosses. Their lives are not morally good lives—they inflict horrendous suffering on others—but they may be prudentially good lives. We might imagine them waking up each morning happy and with an extra spring in their step as they contemplate all those whom they will rob, torture, and kill that day. We can also imagine the opposite: morally good lives that are not prudentially good. Picture a person who spends her entire life in service helping masses of desperately hungry and poor people even though this causes her much anguish and distress. We might describe her living a morally good life precisely because of sacrificing her (prudential) good for the sake of others.

The "crib test" may be used to investigate the question of what makes for a prudentially good life (Feldman 2004). Imagine looking at your newborn child sleeping peacefully in her crib. What sort of life should you wish for her? Let us imagine that her fairy godmother allows you to gaze into a crystal ball and choose for your daughter one of two lives. The first is one where your daughter turns out to be a high achiever as a world-renowned mountain climber, a competitive tennis player, a great violinist, a fabulous painter, and a prodigious mathematician. The crystal ball reveals a magazine article published forty years in the future that describes her as a "Renaissance Woman" of the twenty-first century. Your initial enthusiasm for this life begins to wane when you discover that your daughter is not happy in this life. By "happy," we mean experiencing positive moods and emotions. In this sense, a happy person is one who experiences frequent positive moods and emotions like joy, interest, and contentment. Of course, even though she is generally unhappy, your daughter has brief moments in this life where you would describe her as happy, for example, after she wins a tough tennis game. But, by and large, her mental life is an unhappy one: she

DOI: 10.4324/9781003189466-15

frequently experiences "down" moods and emotions. The other possible life the fairy god-mother shows you is the exact opposite. In this life, your daughter is a happy couch potato. She has an ordinary job that provides little challenge and spends almost all her free time watching mindless tv. Despite this unremarkable life, she is almost always buoyant and in a good mood. She is very happy.

If the fairy godmother insists you must choose one, which life would you choose for your daughter: the life of great achievement with little happiness, or the life of little achievement but much happiness? If your answer is the happy life with little achievement, then you side with the hedonist. The hedonist says that happiness is what makes a life prudentially good. The happier a person is, the better her life is. If your answer is the life of great achievement with little happiness, then you side with the perfectionist. Perfectionists believe that the best life for people is one where they achieve in important domains of human activity. These domains include athletic, musical, artistic, and intellectual accomplishment (Hurka 1993). The more a person accomplishes, the better the life. (It is worth noting that the term "perfectionism" has unfortunate connotations of people obsessed with achieving some im-possibly high standard. A better term than "perfectionism" might be "accomplishmentism," but "perfectionism" is the standard way to refer to this view.)

In my experience, given the choice, most people side with the hedonist. In a typical first-year introductory philosophy course, perhaps 80% of students choose the happy life for their daughter. We will return to the question of whether hedonism is correct, but for the moment we will assume it is.

Utilitarianism

We will examine the question of using drugs to make ourselves happier using utilitarianism—a well-known but controversial moral theory. The utilitarian answer to the question of what makes for a morally good life is as follows: a morally good life is one where your actions do the most to maximize net utility. The technical words of this definition need a little unpacking. The word "utility" in this context usually means "happiness." So "net utility" means "net happiness" where this is understood as the difference between the hap-piness generated by an action minus the unhappiness generated by the action. For example, suppose your parents ask you to take your little sister to the dentist and you wonder if a utilitarian would approve of this action. You might think to yourself:

> The trip to the dentist will cause my sister lots of unhappiness: she *hates* going to the dentist. So, this action is not one the utilitarian would approve. On the other hand, my sister *loves* candy, so, as a good utilitarian, I should take her to go buy some candy instead.

What this thinking ignores is that utilitarians are concerned with *net* happiness. Utilitarians would advise having your sister put up with the lesser short-term unhappiness of the dentist visit for greater long-term happiness. Another aspect of utilitarianism is its impartiality: everyone's happiness counts when deciding which action to take—not just your happiness, or the happiness of your friends and loved ones. Imagine as you are driving your sister to the dentist, you see a car accident. A utilitarian might recommend that you stop and help complete strangers to escape the burning wreckage even if it means missing your sister's dentist appointment. The minor unhappiness caused by the missed dental appointment is more than offset by the future happiness of strangers you help to safety.

Stepping back, we can see that utilitarianism defines the morally right action in terms of two components. One of these is a conception of "the good." As you may have noticed, this conception of the good is the same as the hedonist's happiness. The second component is a "mathematical rule," namely: the idea that we should maximize the good. So, utilitarians enjoin us to maximize the good in the world, that is, to make it such that our actions maximize net happiness. We will look at challenges to these two components below.

What Makes Us Happy?

Utilitarians are very interested in the question of what makes us happy. Why? The best way to realize the aim of maximizing anything, including happiness, is to use limited resources as efficiently as possible. Or to put the point the other way around, using resources inefficiently in the present means that there will be fewer resources in the future which can be devoted to maximizing happiness.

At the most basic level, the question of what makes us happy can be divided into environmental influences and genetic influences. We are most familiar with environmental influences on happiness, e.g., winning an award makes people happy, whereas losing a loved one makes people unhappy. People are much less aware of genetic influences on happiness. Consider the following report by psychiatrist Dr. Friedman about a woman who came to his office seeking advice. In the previous year, she had lost her husband to cancer and also lost her job. However, she was not seeing Dr. Friedman for her sake, but for advice about her son who was having great difficulty coping with the loss of his father. Dr. Friedman was intrigued and surprised about the woman's resiliency in the face of such terrible circumstances:

> Despite crushing loss and stress, she was not at all depressed–sad, yes, but still upbeat. I found myself stunned by her resilience. What accounted for her ability to weather such sorrow with buoyant optimism? So I asked her directly. "All my life, "she recalled recently, "I've been happy for no good reason. It's just my nature, I guess." But it was more than that. She was a happy extrovert, full of energy and enthusiasm who was indefatigably sociable. And she could get by with five or six hours of sleep each night.
> (Friedman 2002)

This "happy by nature" view is confirmed by scientists, but it needs some careful clarification. The first point is about the strength of this genetic influence. According to some, the influence is almost as strong as the influence of genes on our height (Lykken 1999). The term "influence" is very important here. Genes influence how tall someone is, but genes alone do *not determine* adult height. Environmental influences like serious childhood disease or malnutrition can cause diminished growth, while other environmental influences, like the injection of growth hormone in children, can increase height. Behavioral geneticists express the "gene influence" idea as a heritability measure. A heritability measure "fixes" the environment and then asks what explains variation of a trait from the average. So, for example, the heritability of adult height in the US is about 90%. The environment here is "fixed" as the US. What this means is that if someone is say five inches taller than the average height in the US, 90% of the difference is explained by the person's genes, and 10% by environmental influences. If we "fix" a different environment, for example, where half the children suffer from malnutrition while the other half are well-fed, much more of the differences in height would be explained by environmental factors. For our purposes, what is important is that happiness in developed nations has a high level of heritability— somewhere between 40% and 80% (Lyubomirsky 2008). Genes influence how happy we are, but genes alone do not determine how happy we are.

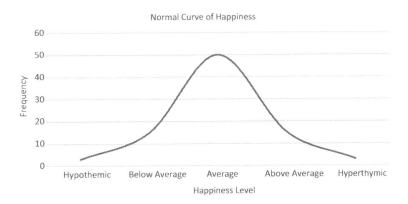

Figure 12.1 Normal Curve of Happiness

Second, scientists have confirmed that people have a disposition to a certain level of happiness, and this variation can be described by a normal curve. The notion of a "disposition" here means something like a tendency to happiness or unhappiness. Everyone has happy and unhappy moments. People with a happy disposition tend to have more frequent positive moods and emotions, while people with an unhappy disposition tend to have more frequent negative moods and emotions. We will call those who experience the greatest tendency to frequent positive moods and emotions—like the woman in Dr. Friedman's office—the "hyperthymic," and those who experience frequent negative moods and emotions the "hypothymic." (To remember the difference between these, it helps to think about the word "hyper" in hyperthymic.) The graph above shows that people in the average range of happiness—those who experience an average amount of positive moods and emotions—are most frequent in human populations, while the hyperthymic and the hypothymic are relatively rare.

Utilitarians think that it is a tragedy that more people aren't hyperthymic, "happy by nature" like the woman in Dr. Friedman's office. And, as intimated, genes influence where we land on the happiness curve. So our genetics are an obvious target for utilitarians seeking to improve happiness.

Happy-People-Pills

The question is, could we use technology so that more of us could become like the woman in Dr. Friedman's office? The answer here is yes—or, at least, there is room for much optimism. Let me describe two research programs to achieve this goal using analogies with current scientific investigation into the treatment of diseases.

It is well established that many diseases have a genetic component: for example, if both of your parents develop Alzheimer's disease, you are much more likely to develop it yourself as compared to people whose parents do not develop it. Thus, scientists hope to identify the relevant genes that influence the disease and then develop pharmacological agents to help patients whose genes give them a propensity to Alzheimer's. Naturally, the hope is that some sort of therapy can be developed using this information. The treatment might involve developing pharmaceutical agents (pills) or, perhaps in the future, using advanced genetic technologies (like CRISPR) to change the genes of patients.

The same type of research program could be undertaken for happiness. The idea would be to look at the genetic differences between the hyperthymic and the rest of us. (For some indication of how research is progressing at genetic correlates for happiness, see Walker 2013.) Using knowledge about what, genetically speaking, separates the hyperthymic from the rest of us, the hope would be to bring advanced pharmaceuticals or genetic technologies to the task of permitting the rest of us to become hyperthymic.

We will call these "happy-people-pills" (HPP) to indicate that these are supposed to provide for us in pill form what the hyperthymic have due largely to their genes. HPP will not make you feel "high" or unable to drive, or impair your consciousness. Perhaps you know among friends or family the hyperthymic and hypothemic. The hyperthymic—like the character Tigger from the Winnie the Pooh series—might be described as "up" or having a "spring in their step," not "wasted" or "high."

The second research program using some of our current "anti-depressant" drugs could be carried out much more rapidly, but, as we shall see, it has limitations. Anti-depressants are normally thought of as improving happiness for those who do suffer from depression. Dr. David Healy relates how surprised he was to discover that they had an effect on those in the non-depressed range of happiness. Healy had healthy volunteers—mostly from the medical profession—try two anti-depressants in a "cross-over" study. Either Zoloft or Reboxetine were randomly (and blindly) given to participants for two weeks, followed by a "clean out" period of two weeks where subjects took nothing. The study concluded with participants "crossing over": taking the other anti-depressant for two weeks. Here are Healy's surprising findings:

> Our focus group met two weeks after the study ended. We already knew that almost everyone preferred one of the two drugs. But two-thirds rated themselves as "better than well" on one of the two drugs. Although this was a study of wellbeing, antidepressants weren't supposed to make people who were normal feel "better than well." Not even Peter Kramer had said this. The argument of his famous *Listening to Prozac* was that people who were mildly depressed on Prozac became better than well.
>
> (Healy 2004)

The fact that two-thirds of these "normal and healthy" people felt better than well offers some hope that anti-depressants might help those in the "normal" range of happiness move closer to the hyperthymic end of the scale.

I can't stress enough that this is a research proposal. It is definitely not a suggestion that people (not under medical supervision) should start taking anti-depressants. One very important reason for this is that anti-depressants have unwanted side effects for some individuals, including reduced interest in sexual activity, nausea, constipation, and weight gain. The most disturbing result of Healy's healthy volunteers study is that Zoloft dramatically increased the risk of suicidal ideation, specifically; two of the healthy volunteers began to have thoughts of suicide while on Zoloft. The Healy study illustrates the need to answer two important research questions before utilitarians could endorse the use of anti-depressants: Do they boost the moods of healthy volunteers? What short- and long-term side effects do anti-depressants have on healthy volunteers? To date, there is surprisingly little research on how anti-depressants affect healthy persons. (For some summary of what little research there is, see Walker 2013.)

Preliminary Conclusion

We said that the utilitarian aims to create as much happiness as efficiently as possible. So this leaves the question of how much it would cost to create HPP. The cost of the first research program is somewhere on the order of 1 billion dollars per year, and basic research for ten years would be necessary. So, a total of $10 billion dollars. This figure is based on analogous estimates for similar research programs examining the genetics and pharmacological remediation of diseases like Alzheimer's. Obviously, 10 billion dollars is a lot of money, but on a national level it doesn't amount to all that much. To put this in some perspective, the US spends about $4,000 billion a year on health care, and $700 billion on its military. So, a billion a year is a tiny fraction of these budgets. The anti-depressant research program would cost a fraction of this since these drugs are already available. A budget of less than $100 million would be more than adequate to finance clinical trials.

So, our preliminary conclusion is that there are very good utilitarian reasons to pursue the creation of HPP. Just to be clear, this is not the only sort of reform that utilitarians might like to spend resources addressing. Food and health care for the needy are some obvious targets that could improve the happiness of many that utilitarians would like to address. This does not change the fact that addressing shortfalls in our biology should be of great concern to utilitarians. There are two "oars" that we need to pull to make us as happy as possible: genes and the environment. Utilitarians instruct us to pull both.

To bolster the case for creating HPP, it will help to consider a number of objections to the argument.

Hedonism Redux

The first objection questions hedonism. As noted in the discussion of the crib test, not everybody agrees with the idea that the best thing for our future child is the hedonistic life. Some people think achieving excellence is far more important than happiness. But there's a much more serious problem here. Maybe one that has already occurred to you: the crib test seems to offer us a false dilemma: we are asked to make a choice between just two alternatives. There's a third alternative that we should consider: it seems we might wish for our child to be both happy *and* achieve excellence. You might think this is the best choice, for it combines the best of what the hedonist and the perfectionist have to offer. We will call this combined view "pluralism."

We can see the challenge pluralism offers to hedonism by spelling out its implication for the crib test. Let us imagine that we have some way of quantifying happiness and achievement such that we can assign the following numbers to the expanded crib test:

A   Your daughter has 100 units of happiness over the course of her life, and 5 units of achievement.

B   Your daughter has 5 units of happiness over the course of her life, and 100 units of achievement.

C   Your daughter has 100 units of happiness over the course of her life, and 100 units of achievement.

The A and B options summarize, in quantitative terms, our original two choices. The new C option combines the achievement of life A with the happiness of life B. Most people find C the most attractive option for their child. The trouble for the hedonist is that she has no reason to prefer the C life over the A life. The hedonist says that the only thing of ultimate value is happiness, so it doesn't matter (at least for your daughter's sake) whether she lives the A or C future. Each life has exactly the same amount of happiness. You might as well flip a coin to decide. Similarly, the perfectionist has no reason to think that the C life is better than the B life: a coin flip would be as good as any means to decide between these. Only the pluralist has a reason to non-arbitrarily prefer the C life that offers both happiness and achievement.

We can see how this line of thinking might prove a major challenge to the argument:

If there is more to a (prudentially) good life than happiness, then the adoption of HPP will be counterproductive. Instead of striving for achievement, people will be happy with their lot in life: they won't strive for anything worthwhile. A world with HPP would be a world where people would achieve very little. The use of HPP will lead to a world of happy couch potatoes.

I hope to show that the objection fails because even perfectionists and pluralists should endorse HPP.

The objection presupposes a false view of human psychology. Consider this question: Does achievement cause happiness or does happiness cause achievement (or both)? An example might help clarify the question. Suppose you are an excellent philosophy student. Perhaps you have written a fantastic term paper and received an A+. You are likely to be very happy. Everyday examples have been confirmed by scientific studies: in general, achievement causes happiness.

Scientists have also, however, discovered something that surprises many people: happiness causes achievement. I'll explain what this means first with an example, and then tell you about some of the scientific findings. Imagine you study high school students intending to go to college in terms of their GPA and where they fall on our happiness curve. From your sample, you randomly select 50 students with a 3.0 GPA who are in the lower half of the happiness curve—those at the hypothemic end—and 50 students with a 3.0 GPA who are in the upper half of the happiness curve—those at the hyperthymic end. What should we predict about their GPA upon graduating college? There are three possibilities: (i) there is no difference in their college GPA, (ii) the hypothemic have a higher average, and (iii) the hyperthymic have a higher average GPA. The couch potato objection favors (ii). Recall that the objection is that since the hyperthymic are already happy, they are not motivated to achieve. Since they are not motivated to achieve, they will likely have a lower GPA as compared with the hypothemic. What scientists have found, however, is that (iii) is true. Those at the hyperthymic end of the scale have a higher college GPA. A happy disposition leads to greater academic success (Lyubomirsky, King, and Diener 2005).

Scientists have found this same causal relation—happiness causes success—across our social lives, work lives, and health. In terms of work, a happy disposition leads to better success at securing job interviews and jobs, to being better evaluated by supervisors, to success at managerial jobs, being more creative, and earning a higher income. In terms of social life, a happy disposition leads to having more friends, better friendships, and more cooperative, prosocial, and charitable behaviors. Finally, a happy disposition leads to greater mental and physical health (Lyubomirsky, King, and Diener 2005).

What this means is that pluralists, and even perfectionists, should be enthusiastic about HPP. We might imagine the perfectionist saying the following: "Well, we don't agree with the hedonist about the value of happiness. Nevertheless, we endorse HPP because they are a good instrument for achieving human excellence." Obviously, pluralists should also be enthusiastic about HPP because HPP promote both things that they think are important in a good life, namely, happiness and perfection.

The upshot here is that we don't need to decide the hedonism versus perfectionism versus pluralism question when it comes to HPP. Whether you support any of these three views of the prudentially good life, you should be an enthusiastic proponent of HPP.

Emotional Appropriateness

Imagine someone objects to HPP as follows:

We would lose out on something of great value in life if we were always happy. There are times for sadness: if your dog gets run over, if your partner dumps you, or you lose a loved one. These are appropriate times for humans to be unhappy. With HPP we will be like "happy robots"—not emotionally responsive to what is happening in our lives.

Recall, however, the aim is to make a pill that makes the rest of us more like the hyperthymic. But even the hyperthymic are sad on occasion. Recall the woman who went to see Dr. Friedman. She was saddened by the loss of her husband, but she was not overwhelmed by this negative emotion. Scientific evidence backs this up. A survey of college students found that even the happiest college students had experienced some negative moods or emotions in the last week (Diener and Seligman 2002). Even Tigger doesn't laugh it up at funerals.

False Happiness

We might imagine someone objecting to HPP as follows:

HPP might make me feel happier, but this wouldn't be my happiness, it would be a false happiness caused by HPP. I want an authentic happiness, not an artificial happiness.

To reply to this objection, consider that there are many things we do to our bodies which are artificial in this sense of "artificial." We use artificial means to relieve headaches when we take aspirin. We artificially restore our vision when we wear glasses or contacts. People get artificial hips to replace worn out ones, etc. But just because something is artificial in this sense does not mean that it is inauthentic. It is easy to imagine that someone like Eeyore (a hypothemic character from Winnie the Pooh) might take HPP and find that they help him realize his true self. He might say something like:

Before taking HPP, I often felt that I was very lucky, and that I should have been happier about my lot in life. Now I understand that the reason I did not feel happy has a lot to do with the genes I inherited. Thanks to HPP, I can finally experience the joy that I think is appropriate.

Certainly, there is no guarantee that everyone will feel as Eeyore does when taking HPP. Some may believe that to be authentic means not taking HPP, just as some refuse to take pain pills because they do not want the pills to alter them. So, the mere fact that HPP are artificial does not show that taking them will automatically lead to an inauthentic life. And so long as we allow people the choice (see below) to take HPP, there is every reason to suppose that more people will be able to lead an authentic life, since HPP will give people more control over their moods and emotions.

Freedom

An important objection has to do with our freedom to choose.

People should be free to choose whether they take HPP, drink alcohol, or smoke pot. However, if we accept the utilitarian argument, then everyone should be forced to take HPP, which violates our rights and our freedom.

This objection raises a frequent criticism of utilitarianism, namely, that utilitarianism is too quick to sacrifice individuals and their rights for the collective good. A famous sort of example makes this point: a utilitarian, it seems, would recommend sacrificing a healthy person to save five people who need an organ donation. The idea is that the utilitarian should think it is a good idea to remove the heart, liver, kidneys, and lungs from the healthy person for the sake of the five who each need one of the organs. The sacrifice of the future happiness of one person is worth the gain in happiness of the other five. But, the critic of utilitarianism says, this "sacrifice" is plainly morally objectionable.

This line of objection raises big issues that we can't explore here. However, at least in this instance, utilitarians are not likely to think that we should force people to take HPP. The reason is very general: just because doing some action X will increase happiness, it does not follow that forcing someone to do X will increase happiness. Applying punitive measures typically generates unhappiness, and so this will have to be factored in. Utilitarians are not likely to endorse "pill police" who hold people down and force HPP down their throats, since this would generate massive amounts of unhappiness. Even if you think HPP are a great idea, and you are thankful that you can take HPP, you may be very unhappy if your next-door neighbor is roughed up on a weekly basis by the pill police. So, utilitarians will agree that people should not be forced to take HPP.

Distributive Justice

The last objection we will consider may be stated as follows:

> *If HPP are as wonderful as you describe, then HPP will only exacerbate existing economic inequalities. The poor will not be able to afford HPP. The rich will use HPP to increase their advantage over the rest of us in things like getting a higher GPA and getting better jobs.*

To respond, we need to consider two cases: HPP are available either as generics, or as patented drugs. If HPP are available as generics, then their cost is likely to be quite low. For example, you can buy generic formulations of many anti-depressant drugs now for less than $1 per day. This would be affordable for most. And for those who cannot afford it, utilitarians would be strong supporters of public assistance for such folks.

If HPP are under patent, this means that their cost could be quite high. Patent holders have, in effect, a monopoly, and so they can charge whatever they like. So, if HPP are under patent, then they are likely to be very expensive. And so, the objection is a real worry for the utilitarian.

Fortunately, drug patents in the US last only twenty years. It often takes eight years or more for a drug to go through clinical trials, so often patent holders can charge exorbitant rates for their drugs for a dozen years or so. So, if HPP are patented, then the same pattern we see for the distribution of technology may hold: only the rich will be able to afford initial offerings, but over time, the price comes down to the point where the average person can afford it. This is the pattern we saw, for example, when computers and cellphones first appeared in the market: only rich individuals or well-financed business could afford cellphones and computers. Short of changing the economic system to distribute happiness more efficiently, utilitarians should reluctantly agree that the initial inequalities generated by patented HPPs are tolerable for the long-term good consequences for the rest of us.

Conclusion

As noted above, the aim here is not to convince you to be an enthusiastic supporter of HPP, but to provide some understanding of what is at stake in using technology to take more control over our moods and emotions. As we have seen, there are very deep questions at stake involving what makes for a good life, and what obligations we have to improve others' lives.

The last point—our obligations to improve the lives of others—connects in a way with HPP that we have not yet discussed. Recall in the "Hedonism Redux" section, it was noted that scientists have found that happiness is correlated with "prosocial behavior": the happier you are, the more likely you are to engage in prosocial behavior. (Scientists sometimes refer to this as the "feel good, do good" phenomenon. The causal relation also works in the opposite direction. Scientists have found that you can make yourself happier by doing good for others: do good, feel good (Lyubomirsky 2008).) Many of the behaviors that social scientists examine under the "prosocial behavior" category might be described by ethicists as "morally good deeds." For example, volunteering one's time to help the less fortunate might be described as "prosocial behavior" by social scientists, and a "morally praiseworthy" action by ethicists. This raises the interesting possibility—which I can only mention here, but not discuss in any detail—of encouraging the use of HPP as a way to encourage people to engage in more morally praiseworthy actions (Walker 2007).

We have examined these issues through the lens of utilitarianism. One of the advantages of using a moral theory to examine such issues is that it helps us keep a track of our deepest moral commitments. Many moral theories, including utilitarianism, build these deep commitments into the very structure of the theory. In the end, you may disagree with the deepest commitments of utilitarianism, for instance, the claim that happiness is the one and only ultimate value in life. But even so, you might find some value in studying the question of HPP through a utilitarian lens precisely because it helps us see what your fundamental commitments are, and whether these commitments suggest a different verdict. As we have noticed, even perfectionists and pluralists who differ from hedonists and utilitarians on the question of the prudentially good life have reason to be supportive of HPP. If you are familiar with other ethical theories, e.g., Kantianism or Virtue Ethics, you may want to consider what they might say about the permissibility of the HPP proposal.

References

Diener, E., and M. E.P Seligman. 2002. "Very Happy People." *Psychological Science* 13 (1): 81–84.

Feldman, F. 2004. *Pleasure and the Good Life: Concerning the Nature, Varieties, and Plausibility of Hedonism*. Oxford: Clarendon Press.

Friedman, R. 2002. "Born to Be Happy, Through a Twist of Human Hard Wire." *The New York Times*, December 31, 2002, sec. F.

Healy, D. 2004. *Let Them Eat Prozac: The Unhealthy Relationship between the Pharmaceutical Companies and Depression*. New York: New York University Press.

Hurka, T. 1993. *Perfectionism*. New York: Oxford University Press.

Lykken, D. T. 1999. *Happiness: What Studies on Twins Show Us about Nature, Nurture, and the Happiness Set-Point*. New York: Golden Books.

Lyubomirsky, S. 2008. *The How of Happiness: A Scientific Approach to Getting the Life You Want*. New York: Penguin Books.

Lyubomirsky, S., L. King, and E. Diener. 2005. "The Benefits of Frequent Positive Affect: Does Happiness Lead to Success?" *Psychological Bulletin* 131: 803–855.

Walker, M. 2007. "Happy-People-Pills and Prosocial Behavior." *Philosophica* 71 (1): 93–111.

Walker, M. 2013. *Happy-People-Pills for All*. West Sussex: John Wiley & Sons.

Chapter 13

Marxist Perspectives on Technology

Tony Smith

The Standard View of Technology and Capitalism

The basic ethical defense of capitalism is straightforward enough. Suppose you have more than you need of something, but less of what you want of something else, while I have more than I want of what you need but not enough of what you have too much of. Let's make a deal! If you and I freely agree to exchange, we can both be better off. Similarly, if sales are freely made at prices that give monetary profits to capitalist producers, while buyers obtain products that help them live the lives they have chosen, both gain. If freedom and human well-being are important ethical values, wouldn't a good society allow transactions to continue until there are no more mutual benefits to be won, as capitalism does?

If we add technological change to the story, the case for capitalism seems even stronger. Companies that introduce innovative products addressing the wants and needs of customers better than competitors' products tend to succeed in market competition. So do companies that figure out how to make products more efficiently; they have lower unit costs than competitors, allowing them to lower prices and capture market share without sacrificing profits. Thanks to market incentives, no other way of organizing economic life has ever been as technologically dynamic as capitalism. Human well-being has been furthered in countless ways, from extended life expectancy to the ability to communicate across the globe cheaply and instantaneously (Baumol 2003).

It might surprise some to learn that Karl Marx also affirmed freedom and human well-being as core ethical values (Smith 2017). In an early writing, he called for a society where "the free development of each is the condition for the free development of all" (Marx and Engels 1976, 506). Decades later, Marx endorsed a society where "the full and free development of every individual forms the ruling principle" (Marx 1976, 739). Marx also acknowledged capitalism's technological dynamism:

> The bourgeoisie, during its rule of scarce one hundred years, has created more massive and more colossal productive forces than have all preceding generations together. Subjection of Nature's forces to man, machinery, application of chemistry to industry and agriculture, steam-navigation, railways, electric telegraphs, clearing of whole continents for cultivation, canalisation of rivers, whole populations conjured out of the ground—what earlier century had even a presentiment that such productive forces slumbered in the lap of social labour?
>
> (Marx and Engels 1976, 489)

The ethical problem for Marx is simply that technological change in capitalism does not adequately further "the full and free development of every individual."

DOI: 10.4324/9781003189466-16

Marx's Critical View of Capital

For Marx, the freedom from personal domination that in principle (if not always in practice) sets capitalism apart from slavery or feudalism is accompanied by the rule of an *impersonal* power over human life. In capitalism, producers *must* sell their output for money or else lose their investment and be unable to continue operating. They *must* in fact strive to obtain monetary returns exceeding initial investment to avoid being in a disadvantaged position. If they fail, their competitors will be better able to purchase more advanced productive inputs, increase marketing expenditures, develop promising new product lines, respond to new market opportunities, meet unexpected market fluctuations, retain old investors, attract new ones, and so on.

It follows that units of production and distribution that do not systematically direct their endeavors to monetary returns (M') exceeding initial investment (M) tend to be pushed to the margins of social life, when not forced out of existence altogether. They *must* therefore systematically subordinate all other ends to the end of obtaining monetary returns, including the goal of using products to further human well-being: "Use-values must therefore never be treated as the immediate aim . . . nor must the profit on any single transaction. [The] aim is rather the unceasing movement of profit-making" (Marx 1976, 254).

Turning from producers to consumers, the latter certainly want to use products to address their needs. But in capitalism, these "use-values" are commodities offered for sale. Where does the money required to purchase them come from? In general, individuals *must* acquire it through association with units of production or distribution whose "aim is . . . the unceasing movement of profit-making." For a relative few returns on investments are sufficient. Most must work for a wage or salary. Either way, the ability of humans to acquire the goods they need to pursue their ends is ultimately dependent upon M being successfully transformed into M'.

The imperative that M be transformed into M' is, as Marx says, "unceasing." There is *something* that persists over time, some power, some force, some drive, that maintains its identity as individuals, firms, other sorts of beings, communities, and states come and go out of existence. Marx's name for this strange sort of "thing," lording over the society from which it emerges, is *capital*.

The "father" of modern economics, Adam Smith, asserted that "consumption is the sole end and purpose of all production," regarding this thesis as "so perfectly self-evident that it would be absurd to attempt to prove it" (Smith 1976, 155). For Marx, however, "the end and purpose" in capitalism is *not* in fact consuming products to meet needs or any other human good. It is *capital's* good, the endless accumulation of *surplus value* (the difference between M' and M), an inhuman ("alien") end in itself.

This is a difficult – and absolutely essential – point to comprehend. Perhaps an analogy may make Marx's claim clearer. Suppose a thermostat system set to maintain a temp of 65 degrees; it shuts off the furnace when it gets warmer, kicks in when the temp goes below 65. Yes, the social acts of social agents set the imperative "The temperature must be 65 degrees!" in place. But once it has been established, it imposes itself on those in the house until they dismantle it. Before that happens, we can refer to a non-human system with an impersonal end. That is not merely a metaphor. Maintaining the temperature is truly the goal of the system.

Capital too is established by the social acts of social agents. Its emergence is an unintended consequence of the historical transition to generalized commodity production and exchange. Capital too can be dismantled through social action. But once it has emerged as established, it imposes its imperative ("M must become M'!") on social life. In a non-metaphorical sense, M' greater than M is the true goal of this system, subordinating human ends. Neither the thermostat system nor the capitalist system could have been established without human agency. But once established, the impersonal end of both systems is pursed automatically until the system is dismantled. Technological change in capitalism is not primarily about producing better products more efficiently so that human needs can be addressed more effectively. It is instead primarily a means for the accumulation of capital. As the following examples show, human needs tend to be addressed when doing so is compatible with that goal, neglected when they aren't.

Technology and Commodification

Capital is accumulated through the production and sale of commodities. Vast amounts of social resources are devoted to developing technologies that increase the production, transportation, and sale of commodities. Human needs that cannot be effectively addressed by commodity purchases – for clean air, meaningful work, standing as a true equal in social life – tend in contrast to be treated as secondary matters when not ignored altogether.

That would be less of an ethical concern if commodity production for profit were directed to the most pressing social needs that can be addressed by commodities. But the demand that matters in market societies is *effective* demand, backed up with purchasing power. The needs of those lacking purchasing power simply do not count. Billions are spent to on developing technologies to provide the wealthy an opportunity to be propelled into space; next to nothing is devoted to developing technologies to clean up environmental wastes in poor communities. This is a systematic pattern, and it is the pattern, rather than the narcissism of billionaires, that is more troubling. From Marx's standpoint, there is no mystery why a study of nearly four million scientific articles found that "The global burden of disease accounts for *none* of the distribution of total health research" (Evans, Shim, and Ioannidis 2014). The market for medicines for afflictions of the wealthy is far more profitable than for the diseases of those in poorer regions. We also do not need to ask why the rate of product innovation has been so rapid in the financial sector, where devices now allow a trade order in Sydney to be delivered to Chicago in four billionth of a second (Sprothen 2016). Being able to make a speculative bet a nanosecond before competitors matters very much to wealthy investors.

One of the most striking examples of the commodification imperative in the contemporary economy is the commodification of knowledge goods through the extension of intellectual property rights in scope and enforcement. Knowledge goods are inherently collective, a point Marx emphasized in his discussion of "the general intellect" (Marx 1987, 92). The production of knowledge goods depends on our shared cultural heritage. As Isaac Newton famously remarked, if he saw further, it was only because he stood on the shoulders of giants, and the same is surely true of those advancing the scientific-technological frontier today. Further, as we shall discuss below, the most important investments in the development of scientific-technological knowledge today are publicly funded. And once the initial costs of establishing an information network have been expended, knowledge goods can be made freely available to anyone at close to zero additional cost. The state's coercive powers are required to transform knowledge into a privately owned commodity.

There are obvious downsides to this commodification. More and more social resources must be defending intellectual property rights claims in court, attacking the claims of others, and amassing vast stockpiles of patents (often just to prevent competitors from developing them). A handful of corporations have amassed unprecedented power over society due to the monopolies granted by their intellectual property holdings, while their investors have become obscenely wealthy from the rents they have been able to extract from those holdings (Boldren and Levine 2008). Intellectual property rights have played their part in returning us to levels of inequality not seen since the 1920s (Columbo 2019).

We are told that all this is simply the price we must pay to provide an incentive to innovate. But the set of those who actually innovate, and the set of those benefitting the most from the commodification of knowledge and knowledge goods, do not overlap very much. Most of the former are forced to sign away their intellectual property rights as a condition of employment. While most scientific-technical researchers want to have a decent life in return for their contributions to innovation, few contribute because of the prospect of becoming another Gates or Bezos. The astounding successes of open-source innovation have established conclusively that plenty of knowledge workers are even willing to freely cooperate with others to produce knowledge goods for anyone to use without any monetary incentive whatsoever, motivated by the intrinsic pleasure of mobilizing their creativity, meeting challenges, and winning the respect of their peers (Benkler 2006).[1]

Not all knowledge goods are commodified. Google's search engine and Facebook and many other apps are freely available for anyone to download and use. People share information, opinions, stories, pictures, and articles freely with each other, thanks to contemporary information technologies. But this too is distorted by capitalist commodification. In business models of platform capitalism, products are offered for free in order to collect as much data about users as possible ("surveillance capitalism"). The data is then processed by the algorithms of artificial intelligence systems to predict the sort of commodities users might be convinced to buy and the sort of solicitations that might be most effective at getting them to pull the trigger. The right to display ads on websites these users visit are then auctioned off electronically to marketers the instant a webpage is opened, employing massive amounts of computing power. Untold billions are spent to convince people to purchase commodities they might not otherwise purchase. For all the blather about "consumer sovereignty," contemporary capitalism employs the most extensive and technologically sophisticated system for manipulating subjective dispositions in human history. Marx's theory helps us comprehend why.

Technology and the Workplace

In the standard view, the labor contract is essentially just another free agreement for mutual benefits. For Marx, this overlooks the social coercion underlying the capital/wage labor relationship. Those lacking extensive monetary reserves are forced to put their human capacity to act at the disposal of some capitalist enterprise or other if they hope to have even a minimally decent life. Impersonal coercion is still coercive.

In capitalism, workers would not be hired unless owners or their agents foresaw that their labor would create more economic value than what they received back in the form of wages or salary. Much technological change in the workplaces aims at increasing the difference between the two, which Marx termed the rate of exploitation. Machines governing the assembly line can be speeded up, at the costs of health-impairing stress, avoidable injuries, and even death (Marx 1976, 533–564). Technologies that deskill workers are also sought, since they enable more costly skilled workers to be replaced with cheaper options.

If workers are sufficiently organized, they can resist intensification of the labor process and deskilling. Technologies automating production tend to be introduced as soon as they are feasible in order to lessen the risk of such resistance (Marx 1976, Chapter 15). In *Capital*, Marx paid special attention to the use of the technologies as part of a "divide and conquer" strategy dividing workers along gender lines (Marx 1976, 601). Generalizing, Marx writes:

> (M)achinery does not just act as a superior competitor to the worker, always on the point of making him superfluous. It is a power inimical to him . . . It would be possible

to write a whole history of the inventions made since 1830 for the sole purpose of providing capital with weapons against working-class revolt.

(Marx 1976, 562–563)

The sort of technological changes affecting workplaces in the twenty-first century – technologically induced speed-ups, technologies enabling deskilling, automation of good paying jobs, transportation technologies enabling capital flight away from regions where workers are relatively well paid and labor organizations are relatively strong, and so on – is clearly analogous to those Marx discussed in *Capital*. The main difference is that now technologies can be used to shift the balance of power in the capital/wage labor relationship in capital's favor far more quickly and on a far greater global scale than the technologies of the nineteenth century were able to do.

The process continues as artificial intelligence begins to take over routinized forms of professional knowledge work. As workers are forced out of well-paid positions, the supply competing for the remaining positions expands, putting intensified downward pressure on wages. New platform technologies enable new forms of precarious employment to emerge, including supposedly "independent" contractors that are connected to customers through the mediator of the platform owner, who takes a significant cut without having to provide health care, pensions, or other benefits.[2]

You do not have to be a Marxist to acknowledge the pernicious social consequences of technological change over the last decades. At the turn of the century, Alan Greenspan, then the the right-wing chair of the Federal Reserve Board, referred to "the traumatized worker" as a key to developments in the US economy (Woodward 2000, 168). As the prestigious business magazine *The Economist* notes, this has been a global trend: "Labor has been on the losing end of technological change for several decades. ... Over the last thirty years or so ... the share of income going to labour has fallen steadily the world over" (*The Economist* 2014, 7).[3]

Finally, there is ample evidence that past a certain point, the well-being of workers is furthered more by having time for relationships with family, friends, and acquaintances, participating in community life, projects of one's own choosing, and so on, than by increased material consumption. In capitalism, however, productivity advances that could enable the same output to be produced with a shorter workday tend to be used instead to increase the output to be sold for profit ("surplus value").

> John Stuart Mill says ... 'It is questionable if all the mechanical inventions yet made have lightened the day's toil of any human being'. That is, however, by no means the aim of the application of machinery under capitalism. Like every other instrument for increasing the productivity of labour ...The machine is a means for producing surplus-value.
>
> (Marx, 1976, 492)

The level of output that took workers 40 hours to produce in 1990 now requires 29 hours or less (Rauch n.d.). A system that aimed at human well-being would not continue to condemn most adults to spend most of their adult-waking lives in workplaces that had "the unceasing movement of profit-making" as their aim.

Ownership and control of capital grant its holders the power to initiate and direct the innovation process in the workplace. As long as that power is in place, technological change will generally tend to reinforce the structural coercion and exploitation at the heart of the capital/wage labor relation, subordinating human flourishing broadly to the flourishing of capital.

Technology and Global Inequality

Units of capital need a steady stream of commercializable innovations to be successful. Generating that stream requires not only corporate labs, but extensive public investment in basic scientific research and long-term research and development, an education system capable of producing adequate numbers of knowledge workers, financing to support new high-tech companies before they are profitable, a legal system to resolve disputes about intellectual property rights, and so on. All of this is quite costly.

This creates a serious "chicken and egg" ["Catch 22"] problem: it takes wealth to generate innovations that are the basis for success in markets, but it takes success in markets to obtain the wealth required to establish an effective national innovation system. Wealthy regions have a good chance to establish a virtuous circle of investment, where the wealth to establish, maintain, and expand the national innovation system makes success in the world market possible, and success in the world market provides the national economy with the funds to develop the next generation of innovations. Poorer regions, in contrast, tend to find themselves in a vicious circle. Unable to fund the development of innovations today, their firms cannot enjoy the market success today required to fund innovations for tomorrow.

Marx concluded that technological change in capitalism tends to systematically reproduce severe global inequality (Marx and Engels 1976, 488). Interestingly, a leading mainstream theorist of economic development agrees with this thesis, still overlooked by most philosophers of global justice:

> (I)nvestment in innovation widens the gap between rich and poor countries. The output gains of the industrial countries exceed the output gains of the less-developed countries. We therefore conclude that *investment in innovation in the industrial countries leads to divergence of income between the North and the South.*
>
> (Helpman 2004, 85; emphasis added)

A handful of countries did escape from the vicious circle after World War II, thanks to the US aid to allies in the front lines of the Cold War (Westra 2012, 59–60). More recently China has escaped by leveraging access to what seemed like an endless supply of cheap and skilled workers and a vast internal market in return for extensive technology transfers. These exceptional cases have not established a blueprint other regions can follow. The salient fact about technological change in global capitalism is not that some countries have approached the scientific-technological frontier in some sectors, but rather how few there have been in the last centuries.

Technology and the Environment

All living things – and all human societies – extract resources from their environment and emit wastes into it. What sets capitalist societies apart is the relentless competitive pressures that force capitalist producers to make as much profit as possible, as fast as possible. This generally requires using technologies to produce and sell as many commodities as possible, as fast as possible. This use of technologies necessarily tends to deplete resources at a faster rate than they can be replenished, and to generate wastes at a faster rate than they can be processed, by the planet's ecosystems. As long as capital's imperative – "M must become M'!" – governs human life, it would be quite mistaken to hope for a "technological fix" to environmental difficulties (Marx 1976, 638).[4]

Many societies in human history have used technologies that have harmed the ecosystems those societies depended on. But the harm was limited to specific regions. Only capitalism, however, has done so on a planetary scale. Of the 31 crucial variables making up "planetary viral signs," 18 are at new all-time record lows or highs. These changes "largely reflect the consequences of unrelenting business as usual" (Ripple et al. 2021, 896). The term "Anthropocene" has become widely accepted as the proper term for the present period of the earth's history, after human actions have profoundly affected the state of the planet as a whole.[6] But a far better term would be "Capitalocene." It is not humanity in general that has caused planetary states to approach or already begin to exceed the boundary conditions required for the "viability of contemporary human societies" (Rockström et al. 2009, 473). It is capital, specifically, the "Grow or die!" imperative imposed by the property and production relations of capitalism.

Conclusion

As long as capitalism continues, there will be rapid technical innovation that furthers freedom and human well-being in important respects. But technological change in capitalism is ultimately a means to further capital's good; the freedom and well-being it provides will be limited and distorted. Needs that cannot be addressed through the consumption of commodities will be systematically neglected. Technologies that could significantly help address social needs, but aren't sufficiently profitable, will suffer the same fate. Massive economic and political power will continue to be concentrated in a relative handful of individuals and corporations, thanks to rents extracted from intellectual property. Technologies will continue to contribute to overwork and worker surveillance, the reproduction of massive global inequality will continue to be unchecked,[5] and extreme weather events, species eradication, and a host of other environmental harms will continue to intensify.[7]

State legislation and regulations address these problems in certain circumstances in limited ways. But trying to deal with the ethical problems raised by capitalism is like playing a whack-a-mole game that cannot be won. It is too easy for concentrated economic power to be translated into disproportionate political power, whether by direct influence on the political process (campaign contributions, lobbying, the "revolving door" between government and industry) or indirectly (by using privately owned media and the funding of think tanks to shape political discourse, insisting on policy concessions in return for investments in a political territory, or simply relying on political elites' self-interest in appropriating a cut of surplus value for their political projects). Capitalist societies have an oligarchical core covered by a democratic surface.

There is no space here to sketch a socialist alternative to capitalism where technological change would take different paths with different social consequences. It might surprise those who have not studied Marx's works that in his most detailed account of a postcapitalist society, all positions of authority are elected, subject to recall, and paid average workers' wages, democratic measures absent in the regimes that have misleadingly invoked his name (Marx 1986b, 331). Social needs, and the priorities among them, are determined in open democratic deliberation; managers in workplaces are elected by those subject to their authority; social investments are directed toward units of production effective at providing the goods and services addressing democratically determined needs.

It is reasonable to wonder whether such a society would be able to generate anything like the innovative dynamism of capitalism. There are many reasons to be confident of an affirmative answer, beginning with the tremendous contributions to innovation of those who have signed away intellectual property rights and those who freely deploy their creative intelligence in open-source projects without monetary reward. There is only space to mention one other relevant consideration here; technological change is already "socialized," albeit in a perverted manner.

Capitalist firms and investors happily invest in research foreseen to have profitable results within a relatively short timeframe. But they generally have little interest in costly basic research and long-term development projects that may not be successful, or if successful may not generate commercializable results, or if there are commercializable results they may not arise within the timeframe relevant to investors, or if they do occur within that timeframe, it is uncertain whether effective demand will be sufficient to make them sufficiently profitable. As a result, basic research and long-term R&D will tend to be poorly funded when left to private investment. And yet if basic research and long-term R&D are underfunded, there can be no steady stream of innovations for units of capital to commercialize.

It is a "dirty secret" of capitalism that public funds are at the heart of the technological change process. While only one-third of R&D in the US is publicly funded, almost all the truly breakthrough innovations fall in this group (Block and Keller 2011). Public funds also prop up high-tech start-ups in the crucial period before venture capitalists are willing to risk their own funds. And they provide demand for high-tech products when they are too costly to attract buyers in the private sector, enabling high-tech companies to attain economies of scale that lower unit costs and prices to the point where market demand can take over.

Apple is widely seen as a paradigmatic high-tech company. But its genius has been to design attractive products integrating technological breakthroughs, not to make those breakthroughs itself. There are 12 core technologies in i-Phones and other i-products. 12 out of 12 were developed with public monies (Mazzucato 2013). The story is similar for the pharmaceutical industry. Funding from the National Institute of Health was essential to the development of every one of the 210 new drugs approved by the Food and Drug Administration from 2010 to 2016 in the view of those applying for approval (Cleary 2018). The threat of the Trump administration to cut funding to the National Institute of Health forced companies to publicly admit something they would prefer to keep quiet: their business plans are entirely dependent on the costly and risky basic research and long-term R&D being funded by public money. They prefer to put their own money to advertising, duplicating existing profitable drugs ("(I)n the US, 78% of new medicine patents between 2005 and 2015 were related to drugs that are already on the market" Mazzucato 2018) and stock buybacks to boost share prices and the stock options of their executives ((Mazzucato 2018).

Our society gives quite a bit of lip service to "investors' rights." Yet, the most important investors in technological change, the public at large, have their fundamental interests systematically sacrificed for the interests of capital in the ways Marx described. What we have today is a limited and distorted form of socializing technological development. What we need is a socialization beyond the limits and distortions imposed by reign of capital. Technological change can then be a means to the full and free development of every individual, rather than a means for an insane end, "the unceasing movement of profit-making."

Notes

1 On the successes of open source, see Haff (2021), who writes, "The manner in which open source allows innovations from multiple sources to be recombined and remixed in powerful ways has created a situation in which a huge number of the interesting innovations are now happening *first* in open source" (23). He mentions cloud computing, bid data, and AI as specific examples.

2 In a recent study of the "advanced" capitalist countries belonging to OECD (the Organisation for Economic Co-operation and Development), McKinsey Global Institute found that

> Part-time paid work was the primary driver of the increase of overall employment between 2000 and 2018. Its share rose ... by an average of 4 percentage points, equivalent to 29 million jobs, while that of full-time employment declined by 1.4 percentage points.
>
> (Manyika et al. 2020, 5)

3 In the "advanced" OECD countries, median wealth was 23% lower in 2018 than it was in 2000, "eroding the welfare of the bottom three quintiles of the population by income level (roughly 500 million people in 22 countries)" (Manyika et al. 2020, vi; 1). Any attempt to explain this social pathology must surely include the social consequences of technological change in capitalism.

4 Technical change in capitalism generally introduces more "sustainable" technologies over time, that is, technologies that use fewer resources and emit fewer wastes. In the course of the industrial revolution, for example, each generation of the steam engines burned less coal per unit of output. Nonetheless, the economists Jevons noted, the aggregate amount that was burned greatly increased. The solution to the "Jevons Paradox" is straightforward: the increase of aggregate output overwhelmed the decrease of coal used per unit.

5 In the last four decades, the richest 1% have earned more than double the income of the bottom half of the global population (*World Inequality Report 2018*).

6 "Anthro" is derived from the ancient Greek word for 'human being', anthrōpos.

7 There is no space to address other issues of ethical import in Marx's critical account of technological change in capitalism here. The role of technological change in industrial and financial crises and the ever-more destructive technologies of the "military industrial complex" are perhaps the two most important of these issues.

References

Baumol, William. 2003. *The Free-Market Innovation Machine: Analyzing the Growth Miracle of Capitalism*. Princeton, NJ: Princeton University Press.

Benkler, Yochai. 2006. *The Wealth of Networks*. New Haven, CT: Yale University Press.

Block, Fred and Matthew R. Keller. 2011. "Where do Innovations Come From?" In *State of Innovation: The US Government's Role in Technology Development*, edited by Fred Block and Matthew R. Keller, 154–172. Boulder, CO: Paradigm Publishers.

Boldren, Michele and David Levine. 2008. *Against Intellectual Monopoly*. Cambridge: Cambridge University Press.

Cleary, Ekaterina Galkina, Jennifer M. Beierlein, Navleen Surjit Khanujaa, Laura M. McNamee, and Fred D. Ledley. 2018. "Contribution of NIH Funding to New Drug Approvals 2010–2016." *Proceedings of the National Academy of Sciences* 115 (10): 2329–2334.

Columbo, Jesse. 2019. "American's Inequality is at Roaring Twenties Level." *Forbes*, February 28. https://www.forbes.com/sites/jessecolombo/2019/02/28/americas-wealth-inequality-is-at-roaring-twenties-levels/?sh=690978ad2a9c

Evans, James, J. Shim, and J. Ioannidis. 2014. "Attention to Local Health Burden and the Global Disparity of Health Research." *Plos One*, April 1. https://doi.org/10.1371/journal.pone.0090147

Haff, Gordon. 2021. *How Open Source Ate Software*. New York: Springer Science+Business Media.

Helpman, Elhanan. 2004. *The Mystery of Economic Growth*. Cambridge, MA: Belknap Press.

Manyika, James, Anu Madgavkr, Timan Tacke, Jonathan Woetzel, Sven Smit, and Abdulla Abdulaal. 2020. *The Social Contract in the 21'st Century*. New York: McKinsey Global Institute.

Marx, Karl. 1976. *Capital, Volume I*, translated by Ben Fowkes. New York: Penguin.

Marx, Karl. 1986a. Economic Manuscripts of 1857–58. In *Marx and Engels Collected Works, Volume 28*. New York: International Publishers.

Marx, Karl. 1986b. "The Civil War in France." In *Marx and Engels Collected Works, Volume 22*. New York: International Publishers.

Marx, Karl. 1987. *Economic Manuscripts of 1857–58*. In *Marx and Engels Collected Works, Volume 29*. New York: International Publishers.

Marx, Karl and Frederick Engels. 1976. *The Communist Manifesto*. In *Marx and Engels Collected Works, Volume 6*. New York: International Publishers.

Mazzucato, Mariana. 2013. *The Entrepreneurial State: Debunking Public vs. Private Sector Myths*. London: Anthem Press.

Mazzucato, Mariana. 2018. "Putting the Public Back in Public Health." *Project Syndicate*, Dec. 3. https://www.project-syndicate.org/commentary/big-pharma-health-care-costs-by-mariana-mazzucato-2018-12

Rauch, Erik. n.d. "Productivity and the Workweek." *MIT Productivity and the Workweek Project*. http://groups.csail.mit.edu/mac/users/rauch/worktime/

Ripple, William J., et al. 2021. "World Scientists' Warning of a Climate Emergency." *BioScience* 71 (#9): 894–898. https://doi.org/10.1093/biosci/biab079

Rockström, John, et al. 2009. "A Safe Operating Space for Humanity." *Nature* 461: 472–475.

Smith, Adam. 1976. *An Inquiry into the Nature and Causes of the Wealth of Nations*. Oxford: Clarendon Press.

Smith, Tony. 2017. *Beyond Liberal Egalitarianism*. Leiden: Brill.

Sprothen, Vera. 2016. "Trading Tech Accelerates Toward Speed of Light." *Wall Street Journal*, Aug. 8. https://www.wsj.com/articles/trading-tech-accelerates-toward-speed-of-light-1470559173

The Economist. 2014. "The World Economy: Third Great Wave." October 4: 3–18.

Westra, Richard. 2012. *The Evil Axis of Finance*. Atlanta: Clarity Press.

Woodward, Bob. 2000. *Maestro: Greenspan's Fed and the American Boom*. New York: Simon and Schuster.

World Inequality Report 2018. https://wir2018.wid.world/

Chapter 14

Technology and Trust – A Kantian Approach

Bjørn K. Myskja

Introduction

We do not know the people who do the quality controls for transport systems, cars, buses, trains, and airplanes. The same is the case with those who make the control systems for food safety or those who check that these systems are followed. Most people have some idea of what goes on, but we do not *know* that the systems are well-designed or that the routines for following them are adequate – or that the people who have made the systems and those who ensure the controls are actually competent and reliable. We just assume that they are, since these tools and systems usually function well, others seem to trust them, and we have some idea that there are quality controls taking place.

Modern society is a complex, technological society. Life in it is dependent on a wide variety of technologies, helping us to deal with the challenges of complexity. At the same time, technology itself is a significant aspect of this complexity. We regularly interact with, and depend on, people we do not know, as well as with technologies whose workings we lack the resources to fully understand. We are not competent to check that the technologies function as they should. Trust is a way to handle the complexities of modern life (Luhmann 2014). Unless most of us have this trust, modern society cannot function well (Fukuyama 1995), and a well-functioning society is a condition for having good lives, as Aristotle (1985) pointed out.

Trust is also a fundamental aspect of human interaction independent of societal and technological complexities. Trust is key in the relationships between parents and children, spouses, friends, and even strangers. We learn from ancient texts such as the Bible, the Greek tragedies, or the Norse *Hávámál* that trust and distrust are timeless topics. Trust is also a concept that is difficult to define or delimit. Many have tried, but their attempts are either said to cover phenomena that ought not to be included or are undermined by examples not covered by the definition.

In this essay, I will first give an overview of trust in general, based on a framework adapted from the ethics of Immanuel Kant. Although the ethics of trust is often thought to be mainly about trustworthiness, I will also discuss why we often have a duty to trust, although not blindly. We must take responsibility for our choices, expressed in a duty to display reflexive trust. This will be a key element in the second part of the essay, where I discuss trust as an ethical challenge in the context of some controversial technologies, such as self-driving cars and genetically modified (GM) food.

Trust and Ethics

What is trust? As we have seen, trust is a form of reliance. I rely on others to act in a certain way regarding something that has value for me. This also means that I make myself

DOI: 10.4324/9781003189466-17

vulnerable, lower my guard, and "refrain from taking precautions" (Elster 2007, 344) in a situation where there is something at stake for me. In this sense, trust is an act. I risk something by letting others have power over me. To trust is to enter an asymmetrical relationship, although trust is also an important element in contract theories that builds on reciprocity (Hollis 1998). Trust is not just an act, though. Trust is also an attitude containing a specific expectation that those I trust have the required competence and are motivated to act in a way that takes care of my interests. It is also common to emphasize the significant emotional component in at least some instances of trust, for example, in close interpersonal relations (Potter 2002).

Trust is usually thought to occur in the context of a three-part relationship: "A trusts B with valued item C" (Baier 1986, 236) or "A trusts B to do X" (Hardin 2002, 9). When the expectation is fulfilled, the trusted party – the trustee – is shown to be trustworthy. I can trust someone who is not trustworthy, just as I may distrust someone who is trustworthy. However, some argue that trust is at its core a two-part relationship: "A trusts B" (Domenicucci and Holton 2017), with specified trust as a derived variety. Many philosophers have been concerned with discussing why we should trust others, but some have claimed that trust is the default position and what needs justification is distrust (Løgstrup 1956). The reason for default trust would be that humans are social beings, and our lives are fundamentally intersubjective. We are completely dependent on others for survival, at least during the first part of our lives, and trust is descriptive of most close relationships. As exemplified above, we also trust total strangers in our everyday lives. In her influential analysis, Annette Baier (1994, 98) wrote that "we notice trust as we notice air only when it becomes scarce or polluted" (Baier 1994, 98). Trust, then, is the default position in human life. This explains why breaches of trust are usually a source of indignation and condemnation.

Trust is not necessarily a moral good. Criminals must trust each other, and many misdeeds exploit trust. Being trustworthy may also be exploited by evil-minded people. I will discuss neither these "unethical" varieties of trust, nor trust in contract-based cooperation where the trustor has the power to sanction the trustee. I will explore trust as an ethical relationship. Arguably, the most important *ethical* aspect of trust concerns trustworthiness and the trustee's motivation. Some hold that trustworthiness is motivated by self-interest (Hardin 2002). Others say that it requires good will toward the trustor (Baier 1986). Still others have argued that trustworthiness is a virtue (Potter 2002). One important characteristic of trust that distinguishes it from other cases of reliance is that the trustor feels betrayed or let down when the trustee does not live up to the expectations. When I rely on my bike to bring me home safely, and it breaks down on the way, I do not feel betrayed but disappointed – and annoyed at myself for misjudging the quality of the equipment. But when I trust my neighbor to help me fix the bike and he fails to show up, I feel let down. If my trust was based on what I took to be my friend's self-interest, feeling let down is not the appropriate reaction. I should not blame him for having other interests than what I expected. It is more appropriate to be disappointed, like I would be when I rely on my bike to function well. This means that understanding the motivation for trustworthiness to be self-interest fails to capture the essence of a relationship of trust. What is missing in the self-interest approach is the ethical element in trust. Regarding trustworthiness as a matter of good will or virtue better captures this aspect of trust.

A Kantian Account of Trust

There are several possible moral frameworks for describing trust and trustworthiness. Immanuel Kant's moral philosophy seems to be particularly appropriate for modern society, as its key concept is autonomy, our ability to act according to our own reasons and motives, independent of outer forces. If I blindly follow the advice of some authority or just act according to my desires or impulses, I am not acting freely. For an act to be autonomous, I must take responsibility for the act by basing it on a reasoned decision. I must be the one deciding what is right to do. This decision may be to follow what the authorities told me to do or to follow my desires, as long as I am the one deciding that this is the right thing to do. But how, according to Kant, do I know what is right? This is when I follow what Kant calls a "categorical imperative." The basic formulation of this imperative is that we should act according to a rule that we would want to be a universal law (Kant 1965, 42). Another way of saying this is that we should not make exceptions for ourselves or those we happen to sympathize with. Onora O'Neill (2002, 86–89, 97) said that this formulation of the categorical imperative primarily prohibits coercion and deception of others, and that these are the key elements in trustworthy behavior.

In the virtual reality of social media, it is easy to present yourself as somebody completely different from your everyday self. Some use fictitious characters to seek advantage from others, either innocently to gain friendship or, more sinisterly, when older men use it to try to lure young people into a relationship. Both kinds of deception are morally wrong as we cannot want this deceptive behavior to become a universal law. Then nobody would fall for such deception, because we would not trust each other. Deceptive behavior is only possible if it is an exception rather than the rule (Myskja 2011).

Another formulation of the categorical imperative states that we should treat every rational being as an end in itself, never as a mere means (Kant 1965, 52). This follows from the idea that autonomy is decisive for an act to be morally good. If I treat someone as a mere means, I undermine their autonomy by denying them the possibility to decide for themselves what is right to do. It follows that this formulation, as well, is contrary to the use of coercion and deception even if the intention is to benefit those I deceive or coerce. This Kantian account seems compatible with theories of trust that understand trustworthiness as expressions of good will. Kant states that good will is motivated by respect for the autonomy of rational agents. He had a view of virtue as the strength of will to act according to the demands of morality, which is not fully in keeping with standard virtue ethics but draws out the significance of moral character for being trustworthy.

Nancy Potter argued that the Kantian approach misses the important particularity and depth of a trusting relationship and cannot provide an adequate account of trust. She admitted that one can "reasonably be able to be well-treated by a Kantian moral agent, but it would seem not to have to do with her or his attitudes or feelings toward me or with the particularities of who I am" (Potter 2002, 6). It is correct that the Kantian approach prohibits exceptions based on self-interest or unreflective feelings, such as immediate sympathies or likings. But it does not overlook the special moral requirements in particular relations such as friendship and family. I have other moral duties to my close relations than to those I merely pass by, and this affects what kind of trust and trustworthiness is adequate. I should not leave my baby in the care of a total stranger, but I should let my close relatives or friends do the baby-sitting, and they should not betray the trust. Even if we grant that the Kantian account has not worked out the details of trust in close relationship, this account is highly relevant when we talk about trust and technology. When I buy something on eBay, take a genetic test on MyHeritage, or turn on Tesla's self-driving Autopilot, I trust someone I do not know and with whom I have no relationship involving special duties of trust.

In describing the traditional philosophical discussions of trust and trustworthiness, I have argued that people should be motivated to trust one another. But trust is also about action (Faulkner 2011, 150). When I trust, I act in a way that makes me vulnerable, and when I am trusted, I am expected to act in a way that protects the values of the trustor. Likewise, when I distrust someone, I take precautionary measures. The categorical imperative is also about how we act, although Kant made it clear that you should not be blamed for things you cannot control, meaning that the intention or motivation for action is decisive for evaluating the act. We trust a person, or an institution, based on how we regard their character. We usually get to know their character by seeing how they act.

Reflexive Trust

The categorical imperative also makes demands on the trustor. As Pedersen (2012) pointed out, Kant's tract on the idea of enlightenment (Kant 1996) emphasized that autonomy does not imply that we should blindly trust others. That would be a form of moral laziness. Kant said that it "is reckoned a universal maxim of prudence" to put "a limit upon trust in the mutual confidences of even the best friends" (Kant 1960, 28–29), meaning that the moral demand of trust is not unconditioned. Full enlightenment means a reflexive trust in others, based on an assessment of their trustworthiness. Accordingly, a key issue is how to place trust well (O'Neill 2020). All else equal, I am morally obliged to respect the autonomy of others through trusting them, but this gives no excuse for laziness – I am responsible for the act of placing trust, taking into account the weaknesses of human nature. For example, I may trust someone I meet on Facebook to tell the truth about her life. But when she asks me to help her enroll others in crowdfunding to cover debt run-up in her name by an ex-boyfriend, it is my responsibility to double-check the story before getting involved. Likewise, I can trust internet search engines to deliver the information I seek. However, many of them collect private information from my activity and sell it to advertising companies. It is my responsibility to find out what kind of information they generate from my search history and choose search engines that sufficiently respect my privacy.

O'Neill wrote that "since much public, professional and commercial life takes place in large and complex institutions and involves transactions that link many office-holders and many parts of many institutions to unknown others, it can be much harder to judge trust-worthiness" (O'Neill 2020, 21). This makes it more challenging to take responsibility for trust in contemporary institutions, compared to private relations. The paradigmatic cases of trust usually analyzed in the philosophy literature have person A trusting person B with some X. Yet, the reality of institutional trust is that B consists of a non-specific number of individuals, most of whom we know nothing about. Still, as said earlier, it is exactly this complexity that makes trust necessary in modern societies.

Trust, Distrust, and Social Institutions

The basis for trust in technologies and institutions, according to Luhmann (2014), is that the procedures and activities exercised by the institution are controlled by using an approach of systematic distrust. When I trust that my flight is safe, it is because I know that someone has checked all crucial aspects that are required for a safe flight, as if they expected that something is wrong, that is, as if they distrusted the technologies and systems. This is not a moral distrust of the kind I have when I engage with someone I take to be untrustworthy. It is a rational approach to controlling the elements of procedures and machineries according to an assumption that they do not function as they should. This is a way to discover unreliable elements, from broken parts to sloppy procedures and reckless colleagues. This means that the systematic distrust is as much a check of general reliability as of ethical trustworthiness, which is reasonable. Trust is seldom merely a question of motivation; technical competence is usually at stake, too. This means that institutional distrust provides us a basis for reflexive trust demanded by morality, even if we have not examined the control systems ourselves.

Institutional distrust is an essential part of a complex relation between trust, distrust, and autonomy (Grimen 2009, 101).

Modern society is a highly complex lifeform demanding advanced institutions, sophisticated infrastructures, and technologies that ideally improve life conditions for people in general. The development of technology and society is interwoven. They are co-produced in that technology, like science, "embeds and is embedded in social practices, identities, norms, conventions, discourses, instruments and institutions" (Jasanoff 2004, 3). Technology includes more than machines, software, processes, and so forth. In a certain sense, it may encompass even the social practices that constitute the basis for the artifacts as well as the social practices that are shaped by these artifacts. If we think of technology in this broad way, this can explain why talk about trusting technology means more than just counting on the reliability of an artifact. Accepting that technologies are also social systems, it is meaningful to say that we can trust them in a moral sense. I can be angry because a technology or technological system betrayed me or let me down. Blame may be an appropriate response if a technology fails to live up to my trust. In most cases, we will blame some unspecified expert or public authority, but usually they are just representatives for the technological system that has itself failed.

Trust in Self-Driving Cars

When people are killed by self-driving cars, it is reasonable to say that the technology was untrustworthy. Sometimes it is possible to pinpoint one cause of the failure, usually some form of human error. However, a common argument for trusting self-driving cars in the first place is that they will *remove* human error. Accepting this, the occurrence of human error is a shortcoming of the technology. Then, we fall back on the question of whether this is a moral shortcoming, or merely a lack of reliability. It is an ethical shortcoming since this technology is a human artifact made to solve a moral problem. But suppose that there is no specific human being responsible for the failures that do occur. So how do we place trust if no one is responsible?

This lack of specific trustees is a common feature of modern technologies. The self-driving car technology is a good example, as it is a collective work but also because it involves artificial intelligence (AI), of which machine-learning is an essential component (Rao and Frtunikj 2018). If the cause of harm is a failure due to AI, who is to blame? This form of AI is very much an emerging technology, which illustrates the ethical challenges of developing technologies in a real-world context. It is to be expected that something will go wrong when the technology is transferred from a controllable experimental setting to a complex environment. But if we do not try the technology outside of the laboratory, we will never discover in what ways it may be harmful, so we have to do it if we want the long-term benefits. Still, the harm is foreseeable and, hence, blameworthy. If we do something that we should realize will lead to harm, it is our responsibility.

This means that we have to decide how to handle the issue of responsibility in order to build conditions for trust in technology. AI, through machine-learning, is a matter of social learning, as "society has not yet worked out the terms of responsibility, the distribution of liability, the thresholds of acceptable safety or the lines dividing recklessness from negligence" (Stilgoe 2018, 26). A part of this learning process is to work out the normative issues involved in regulation of the technology. In other words, we need to rethink the issue of responsibility in order to give an adequate account of the issue of trust and trustworthiness of self-driving cars (Coeckelbergh 2016).

In some cases, it is reasonable to say that technologies such as AI have characteristics that are analogous to human reflection, and so we can reasonably judge this technology a proper object of trust or distrust. In other cases, however, technology that fails is merely unreliable. We cannot blame it for failing to live up to our expectations and it is a mistake to feel betrayed or let down. So how do we draw the distinction between a technology being reliable in a non-moral sense and as morally trustworthy?

Trust in Food Biotechnology

One way to try to draw this distinction between mere reliability and trustworthiness is to analyze other technologies in which the issue of trust has been a crucial part of the discussion, and in particular look closer at the human aspects of the technology. An illustrative example is the challenges of trust in food biotechnology. It is a standard claim, at least by European research institutions and political authorities, that there is a need to build or rebuild trust in food biotechnology (Meijboom 2020, 379). Many people perceive this food as unnatural and say that it may harm health or the environment, regardless of the assurance by producers and experts that it is as safe as other forms of food.

In this case, the object of potential trust is not the technology understood as the products we usually call GM food, or the processes involved in producing them. The public distrust is directed at the institutions involved in the development and promotion of GM food. This includes the scientists and technologists developing these products, the companies owning the patent rights and producing the GM products, and the regulatory authorities responsible for controlling their safety for environmental and human health. A significant portion of the public expresses their distrust in debates or through surveys or other forms of engagement, making it problematic for regulatory authorities to approve the products. Even if they are approved, farmers may be reluctant to grow them, and food retailers may refuse to include them in their product range for fear of loss. They also risk organized boycotts or even sabotage, due to the strong sentiments in the debate.

One may wonder why many who distrust the biotechnology industry and experts have such strong concerns (one should also note that the concerns run high among the proponents, as well), making it a risky venture to introduce the products. One reason may be the special role of food in human life, as food is not only essential for survival, "but has strong social, cultural, religious and emotional aspects" (Meijboom 2020, 382). This is evident in a number of social movements and classification systems, such as local food systems and organic farming, with clear implications for the issue of trust in food (Myskja and Myhr 2020, 2615). The current GM food products are made by large-scale industrial farming, with no connection to the traditions and practices that provide food with social and cultural meaning.

The proponents of food biotechnology usually claim that the skepticism is primarily due to a lack of knowledge, and that people wrongly believe that GM food is unsafe. If they knew the safety control system, for example, the one administered by the European Food Safety Authority, they would realize that there is an adequate trust-building system in place.[1] However, it is unlikely that this distrust is merely a matter of public lack of knowledge. There is no obvious correlation between knowledge and a trustful attitude to biotechnology. The knowledge deficit model is problematized in numerous studies. It is well established that the model is inadequate to account for the complexities of public lack of trust in the expertise on food risks (Hansen et al. 2003). It is likely that the proponents fail to grasp the significance of the cultural aspects and other non-safety issues, such as who is controlling and reaping the benefit from patented food products (Tait 2001).

Meijboom (2020, 385) argued that the core issue in the ethics of food biotechnology should be trustworthiness rather than trust. The trustees should carry the burden of proof in a situation where they have the power and the trustor, the general public, is the vulnerable party. Accepting the moral responsibility for demonstrating trustworthiness rather than demanding trust based on expertise status expresses respect for the autonomy of the trustor, in accordance with Kant's categorical imperative.

Trust, Interests, and Values

The trust relations in using modern technologies are complex versions of Baier's standard scheme "A trusts B with something of value." This complexity leads to problems that we do not find in standard trust-based relations. Since these technologies involve many people and institutions, it is unclear who is the person or body we should trust. One suggestion is that the public body approving applications for production and sales, based on a thorough risk assessment, be the right object of trust or distrust. They do the risk assessment according to the principle of systematized distrust, thus enabling trust and autonomy. However, they are concerned with avoiding health and environmental risks, usually based on information from the producers or research institutions. Therefore, other parties, such as researchers and producers, must be drawn into the trust evaluation. They provide information for the risk assessments, while having economic interests in the product. Can we trust their information? That depends on how we perceive their interests and values.

The review on public trust in food expertise (Hansen et al. 2003) suggested that trust in food biotechnology is not merely a matter of risk as it is understood by biotechnology researchers and producers. Many are concerned with what they take to be the primary concerns of the potential trustee. This is not different from the simple cases of trust. When I trust someone, it is not because she justifies to me why I should trust her based on her own conception of what is at stake. I trust her when I perceive her to take seriously what I consider to be of value, and implicitly or explicitly, promises to take care of that. In a Kantian framework, we should not do as Lisa in the movie *Casablanca* did, and let others do the thinking for us. Reflexive trust means knowing when to trust and when to question the trustee. It is the trustee that must convince the trustor that they are trustworthy. For example, biotechnology researchers and producers must accept that they alone cannot decide what should be the relevant values in discussions on GM food. They need to listen to the public concerns rather than dismiss them as expressions of deficient knowledge.

Conclusion – Trust in Trustworthy Technologies

The philosophical literature on trust has exploded over the last thirty years, indicating that this is an important issue in contemporary society. One reason is the ubiquity of trust in complex modern technology-driven societies. Another reason is the new arenas of trust created by these technologies. Trust is difficult to define and delimit, but there are good reasons to view it as an ethical category. In this text, I have presented a Kantian framework based on the notions of autonomy and ethical demands as expressed in categorical imperatives. By looking at cases such as self-driving cars and food biotechnology, I have argued that we need a social understanding of technology. We must also emphasize the responsibility of technology proponents and regulators to take seriously the perspective of stakeholders, including the public. But technology users are also responsible for avoiding blind trust and unjustified distrust. A critical, reflective approach is required for ethically well-placed trust.

Acknowledgments

I would like to thank the anonymous reviewers and Greg Robson for comments and suggestions greatly improving this chapter.

Note

1 GMO applications: regulations and guidance | EFSA (europa.eu).

References

Aristotle. 1985. *Nicomachean Ethics*. Indianapolis: Hackett.

Baier, Annette. 1986. "Trust and Antitrust." *Ethics* 96 (2): 231–260.

Coeckelbergh, Mark. 2016. "Responsibility and the Moral Phenomenology of Using Self-Driving Cars." *Applied Artificial Intelligence* 30 (8): 748–757.

Domenicucci, Jacopo and Richard Holton. 2020. "Trust as a Two-Place Relation." In *The Philosophy of Trust*, edited by Paul Faulkner and Thomas Simpson, 149–160. Oxford: Oxford University Press.

Elster, Jon. 2007. *Explaining Social Behavior. More Nuts and Bolts for the Social Sciences*. Cambridge: Cambridge University Press.

Faulkner, Paul. 2011. *Knowledge on Trust*. Oxford: Oxford University Press.

Fukuyama, Francis. 1995. *Trust. The Social Virtues and the Creation of Prosperity*. New York: The Free Press 1995.

Grimen, Harald. 2009. *Hva er tillit [What Is Trust]*. Oslo: Universitetsforlaget.

Hansen, Janus, Lotte Holm, Lynn Frewer, Paul Robinson, and Peter Sandøe. 2003. "Beyond the Knowledge Deficit: Recent Research Into Lay and Expert Attitudes to Food Risks." *Appetite* 14 (2): 111–121. https://doi.org/10.1016/S0195-6663(03)00079-5

Hardin, Russell. 2002. *Trust and Trustworthiness*. New York: Russell Sage Foundation.

Hollis, Martin. 1998. *Trust within Reason*. Cambridge: Cambridge University Press.

Jasanoff, Sheila. 2004. "The Idiom of Co-production." In *States of Knowledge: The Co-Production of Science and the Social Order*, edited by Sheila Jasanoff, 1–12. London: Routledge.

Kant, Immanuel. 1960. *Religion within the Limits of Reason Alone*. New York: Harper & Row.

Kant, Immanuel. 1965. *Grundlegung zur Metaphysik der Sitten*. Hamburg: Felix Meiner Verlag.

Kant, Immanuel. 1996. "An Answer to the Question: What is Enlightenment?" In *The Cambridge Edition of the Works of Immanuel Kant. Practical Philosophy*, edited by Mary J. Gregor. Cambridge: Cambridge University Press.

Luhmann, Niklas. 2014. *Vertrauen. 5. Auflage [Trust. 5th edition]*. Konstanz: UVK Verlagsgesellschaft.

Løgstrup, Knud E. 1956. *Den Etiske Fordring [The Ethical Demand]*. Copenhagen: Gyldendal.

Meijboom, Franck L. B. 2020. "Trust and Food Biotechnology." In *The Routledge Handbook of Trust and Philosophy*, edited by Judith Simon, 378–390. New York: Routledge.

Myskja, Bjørn K. 2011. "Trust, Lies and Virtuality." In *Trust and Virtual Worlds: Contemporary Perspective*, edited by Charles Ess and May Thorseth, 120–136. Bern: Peter Lang.

Myskja, Bjørn K. and Anne I. Myhr. 2020. "Non-Safety Assessments of Genome-Edited Organisms: Should They be Included in Regulation?" *Science and Engineering Ethics* 26 (5):2601–2627. https://doi.org/10.1007/s11948-020-00222-4

O'Neill, Onora. 2002. *Autonomy and Trust in Bioethics*. Cambridge: Cambridge University Press.

O'Neill, Onora. 2020. "Questioning Trust." In *The Routledge Handbook of Trust and Philosophy*, edited by Judith Simon, 16–27. New York: Routledge.

Pedersen, Esther O. 2012. "A Kantian Conception of Trust." *Sats. Northern European Journal of Philosophy* 13 (2): 147–169. https://doi.org/10.1515/sats-2012-0009

Potter, Nancy N. 2002. *How Can I be Trusted? A Virtue Theory of Trustworthiness*. Lanham: Rowman & Littlefield.

Rao, Qing and Jelena Frtunikj. 2018. "Deep Learning for Self-Driving Cars: Chances and Challenges." In *SEFAIS '18: Proceedings of the 1st International Workshop on Software Engineering for AI in Autonomous Systems*, 35–38. https://doi.org/10.1145/3194085.3194087

Stilgoe, Jack. 2018. "Machine Learning, Social Learning and the Governance of Self-Driving Cars." *Social Studies of Science* 48 (1): 25–56. https://doi.org/10.1177/0306312717741687

Tait, Joyce. 2001. "More Faust than Frankenstein: The European Debate about Risk Regulation for Genetically Modified Crops." *Journal of Risk Research* 4 (2): 175–189. https://doi.org/10.1080/13669870010027640

Part III

Computer and Information Technology

Introduction

The computer and information revolution in the second half of the twentieth century has drastically changed many aspects of human life—education, employment, business, medicine, transportation, security, entertainment, and more. Moreover, the information revolution has undoubtedly had both positive and negative effects on community life. Our increasing reliance on computers in the information age highlights the importance of ethical and regulatory issues concerning information technology (e.g., artificial intelligence, privacy technologies, social media, and internet censorship). The world is changing, it sometimes seems, as quickly as some of these technologies themselves.

The chapters in this part examine salient issues in computer and information ethics. Topics addressed include the ethics of artificial intelligence (e.g., self-driving cars and psychotherapy bots), how screens-as-mediums have changed our lives, the tension between online privacy and public safety, issues of race and gender in cyberspace, and the problem of misinformation and fake news.

DOI: 10.4324/9781003189466-18

Chapter 15

Values in Artificial Intelligence Systems

Justin B. Biddle

Introduction

Artificial intelligence (AI) systems are all around us. They recommend movies, music, and social media posts to us. They assist in driving our cars (and, in some cases, drive them entirely). They screen job applications for companies looking to hire new employees. They alert us if we might have come into contact with someone who has tested positive for an infectious disease. They tell a judge how likely someone is to skip bale or commit another crime.

These systems can bring significant benefits. Compared to human beings, they process information at a faster rate, and they can avoid some decisional irregularities that affect us due to factors such as mental fatigue and emotional stress. Judges, for example, have been found to give more lenient parole decisions at the beginning of the day or after a food break than at the end of a session (Danziger et al. 2011). Judges in Louisiana (US) have been found to give longer sentences to juvenile defendants in the week after an upset loss by the Louisiana State University football team (Eren and Mocan 2018). AI systems do not get tired or hungry, and they do not get angry when a football team loses.

At the same time, it would be a mistake to believe that AI systems are unbiased or value-free. This essay will argue that values (including ethical values) are inextricably embedded in AI systems.[1] AI systems are not – and cannot be – value-free, and they are not necessarily less prone to bias than human decision makers. Rather, AI systems encode human values, because they are developed by human beings in ways that require value judgments throughout the design process. This is not to say that AI systems are flawed and should not be used. Rather, because AI systems invariably encode human values, it is crucial that we scrutinize whose values are embedded, which priorities they reflect, and how those values support or undermine those who are impacted by these systems.

Concepts and Terminology

As this essay is on values in AI systems, it is important to clarify how these terms will be used. Let's begin with "values." Some people use the term "values" to mean subjective preferences. On this account, values are things that exist only in the minds of individual persons, and they are not subject to rational scrutiny or evaluation. ("I prefer pistachio ice cream to peppermint ice cream" is an example of a value as subjective preference.) This is not how I am using the term. Using Elizabeth Anderson's work as a springboard, I construe values not in terms of subjective preferences but rather in terms of standards. I will define the values of an individual as the standards that it employs for evaluating other individuals, actions, or things (where an individual might be a person, an organization, or some other entity). Evaluation is the act of judging the extent to which an individual, action, or thing

DOI: 10.4324/9781003189466-19

meets some standards. The values of an object (such as an artifact) are the "properties it has, in virtue of which it meets various standards of value" (Anderson 1993, 3).

There are several implications of these definitions that are worth emphasizing. First, persons are not the only things that can have values; technological systems can also have values, according to the extent to which they employ standards of evaluation. For example, if a social media platform prioritizes incendiary posts in a newsfeed over ones that are more nuanced and qualified, then it has this (prioritizing incendiary posts over others) as a value. Second, individuals can have values that they are not aware of or that they do not rationally endorse. A person who laughs at a racist joke is employing a particular standard for evaluating things (in this case, jokes); they are employing that standard, even if they are not conscious of it or if they regret what they have done after the fact (Anderson 1993, 2). Third, technological systems can have values that are not intended by those who create them; there are a variety of possible reasons why this might be, including that creators have values of which they are unaware.

Finally, if values are explicated in terms of standards, then it is evident that there is a plurality of different values, as there is a plurality of different standards. Predictive accuracy is a value that many scientists employ to evaluate scientific hypotheses. Respect for persons is a value that many people employ to evaluate actions or policies. These two values are very different from one another; one might think of the former as a kind of scientific value and the latter as an ethical value.[2] The argument of this paper is that ethical values are inextricably embedded in AI systems. The boundaries between ethical values and other values can be fuzzy, and different people might mean different things by "ethical values." However, I take it to be reasonably uncontroversial that a sufficient condition for a value being ethical is that it involves standards about how people should be treated or impacted.[3]

Let us turn to the term "artificial intelligence." For the purposes of this essay, "AI systems" will refer to non-biological computing systems that can perform tasks that typically require human intelligence. Such tasks might include recognizing images or speech and making decisions. The related concept of machine learning applies to a set of methods for producing AI systems. These methods, roughly, involve training systems in a bottom-up, iterative manner, on the basis of data; these systems "learn" to perform tasks on the basis of these data.

Given these discussions of values and AI, what does it mean to say that there are values in AI systems? We can distinguish between values that are embedded in a technological system and values reflected in the processes for designing that system. Different organizations have different processes for designing AI systems; some might be more inclusive, incorporating feedback from diverse researchers or diverse publics from an early stage; others might be less diverse or inclusive. While these different processes will likely impact the resulting technological systems in important ways, we can distinguish between values that guide technology development processes and values embedded in resulting systems. Both process and product discussions are important, but this paper will focus on the latter.

The Argument in Brief

All technological systems are limited in some respect or other. In the case of AI, there is no system that can perform all possible tasks; researchers must make decisions about which tasks to perform and which may be neglected. Once a range of tasks has been specified, researchers must make further decisions about how good the system needs to be in performing these tasks, and which errors and error rates are acceptable (among other decisions). All of these decisions involve values. These include value judgments about which tasks should be prioritized and which may be deemphasized, about "how good is good enough" and which errors or inadequacies are tolerable. To put this another way, all systems involve tradeoffs, and how tradeoffs are navigated reflects values. In some cases, tradeoffs have significant impacts on people. In these cases, the values are ethically relevant.[4]

Consider the example of facial recognition systems. In developing these systems, researchers prioritize one set of problems/questions over others. Researchers must also make decisions about how to design these systems, including which data to use to train them. If they are trained largely on the faces of lighter-skinned people, then they will likely perform better on lighter-skinned faces than on darker-skinned ones – as has been shown to be the case (Buolamwini and Gebru 2018). The value that it is acceptable to train the system on primarily lighter-skinned faces thus becomes embedded in the system and is evident in its performance and error rates – and given that these systems have the potential to impact people, the values embedded in them are ethically relevant.

Not only are AI systems value-laden – they are inextricably value-laden. All systems must prioritize some tasks over others; in so doing, they embed values about which tasks should be prioritized. Moreover, all systems embed values about "how good is good enough." The facial recognition systems discussed above involve the standard that is acceptable to have error rates that are higher for darker-skinned faces than for light-skinned ones. If different facial recognition systems were developed – systems that were trained using different data sets – these systems would embed different values. There is a "tapestry" of different values that could be embedded in AI systems – but there is no AI system that is value-free (Elliott 2017).

The Argument Elaborated

To articulate the argument further, it is useful to distinguish between four phases in creation and deployment of AI systems: problem identification/framing, design, implementation, and monitoring. While these phases overlap to some degree, it is useful to distinguish them conceptually in order to illustrate the range of ways in which values are embedded in AI systems. In this section, I will discuss the first two of these phases in some detail; the third and fourth will be addressed briefly in the conclusion. In discussing these phases, I will draw on several examples of AI systems, including recidivism-prediction algorithms, systems for disease tracking and tracing, and social media platforms.

Problem Identification/Framing

In developing an AI system, researchers must make decisions about which problem (or question) is to be addressed and how this problem is to be framed. By "framing," I mean specifying what falls within the scope of the problem and what does not. Because no AI system can address all problems, the choice to address one problem involves a tradeoff; it implies a choice not to address another problem, and the decision that one problem is more important than another is a decision that involves values. Furthermore, the decision to address one problem rather than another, and the decision to frame a problem in a particular way, implies values about what kinds of errors or inadequacies are more or less tolerable. To see this, let's consider a couple of examples.

Consider, first, the development in the US of recidivism-prediction systems, or data-driven systems that predict the risk that someone accused or convicted of a crime will "reoffend" (Biddle 2020). These tools have been developed (at least in part) to address the problem of bias in the US penal system, which has one of the highest incarceration rates in the world and imprisons disproportionate numbers of black and brown people.

Recidivism-prediction systems can be thought of as a way of addressing this problem by providing objective assessments of risk, which, in turn, can decrease bias in sentencing. Setting aside the question of whether these systems actually provide such objective assessments, it is important to note that there are other possible ways of addressing the problem of bias in the US penal system. For example, instead of developing systems that predict the behavior of purported offenders, researchers could develop systems that identify bias in the decisions of judges. Developing one system rather than another involves a value judgment about which problem is more important to address. Of course, one might wish that both systems could be developed, but it is still the case that a particular system, which can only address one problem or the other, embeds a standard about which is more important.

As a second example, consider data-driven technologies for reducing the spread of an infectious disease – many of which have been developed across the world during the COVID-19 pandemic. Some of these technologies are framed in terms of tracking the spread of a disease through a population, for example, by identifying "hot spots" that individuals might want to avoid. Others are framed in terms of identifying contacts between individuals and then directly informing those who might have come into contact with someone who has tested positive. Framing the problem in terms of tracking individuals versus tracking a disease through a population embeds different standards about which problem is more important to address.

Different ways of framing a problem impact different groups or individuals in different ways. Recidivism-prediction systems directly impact purported offenders who are being assessed; these impacts are especially significant when the systems err, for example, by overestimating the risk of reoffending. Systems that attempt to identify biases in the decisions of judges, on the other hand, directly impact those judges. Thus, the decision to develop one system rather than another implies, among other things, a judgment that it is more acceptable to impact one group in a particular way than another. The contact tracing technologies discussed above also impact different groups and individuals in different ways. Those that track diseases through populations cannot tell a given individual whether they have come into contact with a diagnosed person. They cannot do this because they do not track individuals – but because they do not track individuals, they are not susceptible to the kinds of privacy concerns that other systems might have.

There is an additional aspect of problem identification/framing that is laden with values, namely the operationalization of fundamental concepts. For example, once a decision has been made to develop a recidivism-prediction system, researchers must decide how the concept of "recidivating" or "reoffending" is to be defined. At first glance, it might seem obvious how to do this – to recidivate or reoffend is to commit a crime, be punished, and then commit another crime. But people can commit a crime and avoid arrest, and they can be arrested and convicted for crimes that they did not commit. So how should "recidivism" be operationalized? As being convicted of a crime, punished, and then convicted again? Or convicted, punished, and then re-arrested? Or merely arrested and re-arrested? There are similar questions that arise in the context of contact tracing systems regarding the operationalization of "contact"; how close does one need to be to make "contact"? For how long? And which sources of data should be used to establish contact?

How these concepts are operationalized embeds values, and the resulting systems impact different groups in different ways. For example, most developers of recidivism-prediction tools have opted to define recidivism solely in terms of arrest and re-arrest, due to the relative convenience of obtaining large data sets about arrest as opposed to conviction. But defining recidivism in this way impacts the types of errors that the system will tend to make and who is impacted by these errors. An individual who is arrested and re-arrested will count as a recidivist – even if that individual was wrongly arrested on both occasions. And given that some groups are disproportionately subject to policing and arrest than others, members of these groups will be disproportionately likely to be mistakenly classified as recidivists.

A common refrain in the ethics of technology is, "just because we can, doesn't mean that we should." Before we proceed to investigate a problem, it is crucial that we ask whether we have identified the right problem. Any given technological system reflects a decision that the problem addressed by the system is an appropriate one to address – indeed, that it is a better one to address than the alternatives. In so doing, the system involves values.

Design

Once a problem has been framed and the decision made to create an AI system, researchers must make numerous decisions about how the system is to be designed, and these decisions impact the values embedded in the resulting systems. This section will focus on three broad categories of design decisions: (1) decisions about data collection, use, and storage, (2) decisions about which data to use to train AI systems, and (3) decisions about algorithmic fairness. These categories are not exhaustive, but they are important, and they involve ethical values in significant ways.

For many people, the first ethical value that comes to mind when considering AI systems is privacy. AI systems that involve the collection, use, and storage of data about human beings – including social media platforms, personal digital assistants, and contact tracing systems – have design features that significantly impact privacy. In creating a system, designers must choose which data is collected and whether any of these data are "personal," which is defined as data that can directly or indirectly identify an individual, including data about identification numbers, locations, or other identifying features (EU GDPR 2016, Chapter 1 Article 4). Designers must decide how data is used – for example, by determining whether they are only used in specified ways that are required for a given purpose (such as reducing the spread of a disease) or whether they can be used in other ways (such as being sold to third parties for unspecified purposes). Designers must also decide how data are stored – for example, whether they are stored on centralized servers that have the potential to be hacked or only on physical devices held by individuals (such as cellphones) – and how long they are stored. Each of these decisions reflects values about privacy and how privacy considerations should be weighed relative to other values (Zastrow 2020).

But as the mention of "other values" implies, privacy is not the only ethical value that is relevant to the design of AI systems – values such as safety, human rights, political liberty, respect for persons, and many others are also relevant. Consider contact tracing systems that determine whether contact has occurred between diagnosed and undiagnosed individuals (Gasser et al. 2020; Morley et al. 2020). Designers must choose which data to collect to establish whether contact has occurred. This could be done via GPS location data, which could be used to personally identify individuals, or via Bluetooth proximity data, which does not involve location tracking. The latter option can establish whether contact has occurred without collecting personal data, which helps to preserve privacy; the former option, however, could potentially lead to repurposing for repressive means, such as surveilling political dissidents and policing human rights activists. Consider, as another example, the decision by a social media company whether to sell user data to third parties for unspecified purposes. This could potentially lead to harms to users that they do not anticipate, such as being denied health insurance coverage due to social media posts that they make about preexisting health conditions.

Design choices about data collection, use, and storage are intimately connected with the overarching ethical values of respect for persons and informed consent. Some designs make it easy for users to make informed decisions for themselves, providing accessible and comprehensible information to users without requiring them to read (and agree to) long license agreements written in complicated legal language. Other designs make it difficult or impossible for users to do this. Still other designs might facilitate informed consent but fail to provide viable alternatives to users. For example, many social media platforms collect data about users that are then sold to advertisers. These platforms might inform users about this and, at the same time, refrain from providing them viable alternatives – such as the alternative to pay a subscription fee to use the platform without giving away their data (Véliz 2021). Different stakeholders have different views on how these design decisions should be made – but whatever the views are, they reflect standards about how these systems should and should not impact people.

The second broad category of design decisions concerns which data to use to train AI systems. We have seen one example of how decisions about training data can impact the accuracy of AI systems for different people (facial recognition systems). We can illustrate the ways in which data decisions embed values by noting that many decisions about data involve tradeoffs. Suppose that we have data about a population of people, and we want to know which features of the data we should use to train an AI system; for example, we might want to know whether to use race as a feature of the training data. In some contexts, it might be deemed appropriate to include race; doing this might, for example, help to expose racial disparities in society. In other contexts, it might be deemed inappropriate; it might be that including race as a variable could disproportionately harm a particular racial group. But one cannot both include and exclude race as a variable; the decision to include it (or not) involves tradeoffs, and how one manages these tradeoffs reflects values.

Designers of recidivism-prediction systems face a tradeoff similar to the one just discussed – though it pertains not to race but to socio-economic status (Biddle 2020). These systems are trained on data that include factors such as criminal history, age at first arrest, current age, and antisocial behavior (race is not included). Many include socio-economic status as well, and there is a debate over whether it is equitable to do so. Those who defend the inclusion of data about socio-economic status do so because they believe that it improves the predictive accuracy of the systems; evidence suggests that people of lower socio-economic status are at a higher risk of recidivating (all else being equal). Those who oppose it do so because they believe it violates the ideal of equal protection under the law; if people of lower socio-economic status are assessed to be more likely to recidivate, and if people who are assessed to be more likely to recidivate are given longer sentences, then people of lower socio-economic status will (all else being equal) tend to be given longer sentences, which seems to be a straightforward violation of the notion that everyone (rich or poor) should receive equal protection under the law. The decision of whether to include this feature of the data involves a tradeoff – in this case, a tradeoff between the ideals of predictive accuracy and equal protection – and how one manages this tradeoff reflects value judgments about which of these ideals should be prioritized.

The third broad category concerns design decisions about algorithmic fairness. This is a concept that is relevant to any AI system that has the potential to impact different groups in different ways. Systems that classify people into categories are examples of this – including systems that classify people into risk categories for criminality, or risk categories for failing to pay back a loan, or into employment or admissions categories. Ideally, these systems would treat different groups fairly; they would avoid unjustly disadvantaging one group at the expense of another. However, there are multiple conceptions of fairness, and in some cases, these conceptions conflict with one another.

Consider a system that universities might use to evaluate student applications for admission. One conception of fairness might require that it make recommendations that are proportional to population demographics; that is, the percentage of candidates recommended from a particular group should be approximately equal to the percentage of that group among the overall population. A different conception might require that students are recommended solely on the basis of high school grades and standardized test scores, taking no account of gender, race, ethnicity, or other demographic factors. These are distinct and incompatible conceptions of fairness, and designing an algorithm to satisfy one or the other embeds into the system a value about which is preferable.

The issue of algorithmic fairness has risen to prominence in part due to controversies surrounding a recidivism-prediction system used widely in the US. A study of this system concluded that it was racially biased; more specifically, it found that it systematically overestimated the risk of recidivism for black populations and systematically underestimated the risk for white populations (Angwin et al. 2016; Biddle 2020). The company that created and sold the algorithm disputed this conclusion, stating that it was not racially biased, because it correctly predicted recidivism at equal rates for black and white populations. Further analysis revealed that, in some sense, both were correct. According to one conception of fairness (namely, correctly predicting recidivism at the same rates for black and white populations), the system was fair. According to another (namely, ensuring equal distributions of different types of error for black and white populations), the system was unfair to black populations. And in this case, the two types of fairness are mathematically incompatible; ensuring that one is satisfied will ensure that the other is violated.

In creating an AI system that classifies individuals into categories, designers must decide which type of fairness they wish to encode into the system – which conceptions of fairness they wish to prioritize and which they are willing to violate. Such decisions embed values – including standards about whom may be impacted and how.

Conclusion

This paper has argued that values, including ethical values, are inextricably embedded in AI systems. It has done this by examining decisions about problem identification/framing and design and showing how these decisions reflect values or standards about how AI systems should or should not impact people.

There are a number of important topics that this paper has not addressed. These include questions about process and governance, as well as about implementation and monitoring.[5] For example, which laws or regulations (if any) should ensure privacy rights and structure data collection, use, and storage? Should there be laws or regulations that ensure that the workings of AI systems are transparent and open to public scrutiny? Should some AI systems be forbidden? Or mandated? Who should be held accountable in the case of errors, failures, or violations? These questions are, first and foremost, questions about the social and legal environment in which AI systems are developed; they are not, first and foremost, questions about AI systems themselves, and as such, they fall outside of the immediate scope of this paper. But they are nonetheless extremely important. Given the ubiquity of AI systems and our increasing reliance on them, it is vital that we rigorously examine these systems not only from technical perspectives, but from ethical ones as well.

Notes

1 The argument of this paper draws on Biddle (2020).
2 Some have argued that values such as predictive accuracy differ in kind from ethical values. McMullin (1983), for example, argues that former is an "epistemic value," because it is truth conducive, while the latter is a "non-epistemic value," because it is not truth conducive. Many have

challenged the view that there is a strict distinction between epistemic and non-epistemic values, but I will not pursue these arguments here (see, for example, Rooney 1992; Longino 1996).

3 Some ethical values might not involve standards about the treatment of people; some might, for example, involve standards about the treatment of non-human animals or ecosystems. I take it, however, that if a value involves standards about how people should be treated or impacted, then it is an ethical value. Thanks to an anonymous reviewer for their comments on this point.

4 There is a large literature on the role of values in science and technology. For a few examples, see Biddle and Kukla (2017), Brown (2020), Douglas (2009), Elliott (2017), Tiles and Oberdiek (1995), Verbeek (2011), Winner (1989), among many others.

5 See, for example, Floridi and Cowls (2019), Jobin et al. (2019), Schiff et al. (2020), (2021).

References

Anderson, Elizabeth (1993). *Value in Ethics and Economics.* Cambridge, MA: Harvard University Press.

Angwin, Julia, Jeff Larson, Surya Mattu, and Lauren Kirchner. 2016. "Machine Bias." *ProPublica.* May 23. Available at: https://www.propublica.org/article/machine-bias-risk-assessments-in-criminal-sentencing

Biddle, Justin (2020). "On Predicting Recidivism: Epistemic Risk, Tradeoffs, and Values in Machine Learning." *Canadian Journal of Philosophy.* doi: 10.1017/can.2020.27.

Biddle, Justin B. and Rebecca Kukla. 2017. "The Geography of Epistemic Risk." In Kevin Elliott and Ted Richards (Eds.). *Exploring Inductive Risk: Case Studies of Values in Science* (pp. 215–237). Oxford: Oxford University Press.

Brown, Matthew. 2020. *Science and Moral Imagination: A New Ideal for Values in Science.* Pittsburgh: University of Pittsburgh Press.

Buolamwini, Joy and Timnit Gebru. 2018. "Gender Shades: Intersectional Accuracy Disparities in Commercial Gender Classification." *Proceedings of Machine Learning Research* 81: 1–15.

Douglas, Heather (2009). *Science, Policy, and the Value-Free Ideal.* Pittsburgh: University of Pittsburgh Press.

Elliott, Kevin (2017). *Tapestry of Values.* New York: Oxford University Press.

Eren, Ozkan and Naci Mocan (2018). "Emotional Judges and Unlucky Juveniles." *American Economic Journal: Applied Economics* 10(3): 171–205.

EU General Data Protection Regulation (GDPR) (2016). *Regulation (EU) 2016/679 of the European Parliament and of the Council of 27 April 2016 on the Protection of Natural Persons with Regard to the Processing of Personal Data and on the Free Movement of Such Data, and Repealing Directive 95/46/EC (General Data Protection Regulation), OJ 2016 L 119/1.*

Danziger, Shai, Jonathan Levav, and Liora Avnaim-Pesso (2011). "Extraneous Factors in Judicial Decisions." *PNAS* 108(17): 6889–6892.

Floridi, Luciano and Josh Cowls (2019). "A Unified Framework of Five Principles for AI in Society." *Harvard Data Science Review.* doi: 10.1162/99608f92.8cd550d1.

Gasser, Urs, Marcello Ienca, James Scheibner, Joanna Sleigh, and Effy Vayena (2020). "Digital Tools against COVID-19: Taxonomy, Ethical Challenges, and Navigation Aid." *Lancet Digital Health.* doi: 10.1016/S2589-7500(20)30137-0.

Jobin, Anna, Marcello Ienca, and Effy Vayena (2019). "The Global Landscape of AI Ethics Guidelines." *Nature Machine Intelligence* 1(9): 389–399. doi: 10.1038/s42256-019-0088-2.

Longino, H. (1996). Cognitive and Non-Cognitive Values in Science: Rethinking the Dichotomy. In Lynn Hankinson Nelson, & Jack Nelson (Eds.), *Feminism, Science, and the Philosophy of Science* (pp. 39–58). Dordrecht: Kluwer.

McMullin, Ernan (1983). Values in Science. In P. D. Asquith, & T. Nickles (Eds.), *PSA 1982, Vol. 2* (pp. 3–28). East Lansing, MI: Philosophy of Science Association.

Morley, Jessica, Josh Cowls, Mariarosaria Taddeo, and Luciano Floridi (2020). "Ethical Guidelines for COVID-19 Tracing Apps." *Nature* 582: 29–31.

Rooney, P. (1992). On Values in Science: Is the Epistemic/Non-Epistemic Distinction Useful? In David Hull, Mickey Forbes, and Kathleen Okruhlick (Eds.), *PSA 1992, Vol. 2* (pp. 13–22). East Lansing: Philosophy of Science Association.

Schiff, Daniel, Justin Biddle, Jason Borenstein, and Kelly Laas (2020). "What's Next for AI Ethics, Policy, and Governance? A Global Overview." In *Proceedings of the AAAI/ACM Conference on AI, Ethics, and Society* (pp. 153–158). New York. doi: 10.1145/3375627.3375804.

Schiff, Daniel, Jason Borenstein, Justin Biddle, and Kelly Laas (2021). "AI Ethics in the Public, Private, and NGO Sectors: A Review of a Global Document Collection." *IEEE Transactions on Technology and Society* 2(1): 31–42.

Tiles, Mary and Hans Oberdiek (1995). *Living in a Technological Culture*. London: Routledge.

Véliz, Carissa (2021). *Privacy is Power*. New York: Melville House.

Verbeek, Peter-Paul (2011). *Moralizing Technology*. Chicago: University of Chicago Press.

Winner, Langdon (1989). *The Whale and the Reactor*. Chicago: University of Chicago Press.

Zastrow, Mark (2020). "Coronavirus Contact-Tracing Apps: Can They Slow the Spread of COVID-19?" *Nature*. May 19. doi: 10.1038/d41586-020-01514-2.

Chapter 16

A Kantian Course Correction for Machine Ethics

Ava Thomas Wright

The central challenge of "machine ethics" is to build autonomous machine agents that act morally rightly.[1] But how can we build autonomous machine agents that act morally rightly, given reasonable disputes over what is right and wrong in particular cases? In this chapter, I argue that Immanuel Kant's political philosophy can provide an important part of the answer. The problem that Kant's political philosophy attempts to solve is how to rightfully resolve reasonable disputes between moral equals in cases where their rights and duties with respect to each other come into conflict. Kant argues that only a legitimate *public* authority under laws to which everyone can consent can settle such disputes in a way that respects everyone's moral equality. The judgments of the legislative, executive, and judicial institutions of such an authority, therefore, take moral priority over private ethical opinions about how to resolve such disputed cases. Hence to act morally rightly, autonomous machine agents must, first of all, act in accordance with justice and legitimate public laws.

The chapter has four main sections. In the first section, I criticize what I regard as a misguided approach to the problem of reasonable disputes in machine ethics, which is to build agents that act in accordance with what most people would prefer the agents to do in controversial cases. This approach would result in immoral machines that fail to respect the moral equality of persons. In the second section, I set out Kant's approach to the problem of reasonable disputes. I review Kant's statement of the problem, his solution, and its main implication, the Kantian priority of right.

In the third section, I show how appeal to the Kantian priority of right resolves the conflicts between rights in the famous "trolley problem," which has attracted significant attention in machine ethics because self-driving cars may face analogous conflict cases. Finally, in the fourth section, I consider how autonomous machine agents should handle unresolved conflicts between narrow legal obligations, since appeal to the priority of right cannot resolve them. I conclude with a summary of my main claims.

Introduction: (Im)moral Machines

Machine ethics traditionally has been approached from one or some combination of three main moral theoretical frameworks: (1) Consequentialism (e.g. utilitarianism), (2) virtue ethics (e.g. Aristotle's virtue ethic), or (3) deontology (e.g. Kantian ethics).[2] Each moral theory may indicate a different action to take in particular situations, and applied ethicists are often tasked to work out how each theory would resolve controversial cases. But dispute runs wide and deep in ethics. While some agreement on the morally right action in particular cases might sometimes be achieved among those who accept the same moral theoretical framework, disputes over which framework to adopt in the first place are notoriously intractable. Designers of autonomous machine agents thus seem left with the

DOI: 10.4324/9781003189466-20

perplexing problem of which moral theory to adopt as well as how to implement behavior that conforms with that theory in the agent.

One answer is to build agents that act in accordance with what most people would prefer the agents to do in controversial cases. In the online "Moral Machine Experiment," millions of subjects were asked what a self-driving car should do in various accident scenarios where its only choices were to swerve or maintain its lane (Awad et al. 2018). Subjects were asked to decide who lives or dies among characters who varied by nine attributes such as their age, gender, whether they were jaywalking, whether they were passengers or not, etc. Subjects' decisions in these scenarios were then aggregated and analyzed in order to determine the relative strength of collective ethical preferences with respect to these attributes, all other things being equal. While the strongest such ethical preferences found were to spare more rather than fewer lives, and to spare humans over animals, the Moral Machine Experiment also found strong ceteris paribus preferences to spare those of higher status over those of lower status, younger over older people, females over males, and the "fit" over the "large" (Awad et al. 2018, 61–62).

When reporting these results, the authors of the Moral Machine Experiment did not argue that autonomous vehicles should be programmed to act in accordance with the popular ethical preferences they had collected. Their aim, instead, was to initiate a "conversation" that might help us decide as a society what self-driving cars should do in such controversial cases (Awad et al., 63). In a companion paper, however, some of the original authors of the Moral Machine Experiment review the philosophical literature on moral conflicts and raise the question, "[H]ow can society agree on the ground truth [correct ethical decisions]—or an approximation thereof—when even ethicists cannot?" (Noothigatthu et al. 2018, 1). They then propose a solution: "We submit that [moral] decision making can, in fact, be automated, even in the absence of… ground-truth principles, by aggregating people's opinions on ethical dilemmas" (Noothigattu et al. 2018 1).[3]

This proposal is both naive and misguided. It is naive of a long social contract tradition in political philosophy that addresses the problem of reasonable disputes in such cases; and it is misguided because it ignores two obvious objections.[4] First, popular ethical preferences about how to resolve controversial cases may be wrong. There is no necessary connection between what is ethical and what a popular majority in society believes is ethical; for example, the majority's preferences in Nazi Germany or in the antebellum American South were egregiously unethical. Nor are the preferences of a global majority such as those that the Moral Machine Experiment or Delphi attempts to capture necessarily ethical; in past epochs, a global majority likely would have rejected the equal rights of ethnic, racial, and religious minorities, women, and LGBT people, as well as many other modern values; indeed, a global majority may not accept such rights and values today.[5]

Second, even if a popular majority were correct about how controversial conflict cases affecting rights should be resolved, the direct translation of the majority's raw ethical preferences into action in such cases would often be unjust. The rationale for doing so seems rooted in a vague background sense of the moral legitimacy of democratic rule. But the legitimacy of majority rule in a democracy depends, at a minimum, on its respect for rights of freedom and equality, as well as a number of other institutional and procedural safeguards to establish the rule of law such as representative government, the separation of powers, due process guarantees, etc. The tyranny of a majority acting outside the rule of law is no more morally legitimate than the tyranny of a king. Consider again the preferences found in the Moral Machine Experiment: While acting on popular preferences to spare more rather than fewer lives, or humans over pets, seems morally unobjectionable, acting on preferences to spare higher over lower status people, the fit over the large, females over males, or the young over the old are morally problematic. These latter preferences raise a strong intuition that acting on them would fail to respect the moral equality of persons. Autonomous vehicles that acted in accordance with them in accident scenarios would, therefore, act unjustly.

Machine ethics seems to me to need a course correction. The direct application of popular ethical theories or opinions to determine how autonomous machine agents should act in cases of conflict subject to reasonable dispute is illegitimate and ill-advised. Machine ethics should turn, instead, to meet the moral demands that justice and the rule of law impose on us to build autonomous machine agents that act in ways that respect the freedom and moral equality of everyone.

The Kantian Priority of Right

The authors of the Moral Machine Experiment raise the right question for machine ethics, even if their proposed answer is misguided. Recall their question, "[H]ow can society agree on the ground truth [correct ethical decisions]—or an approximation thereof—when even ethicists cannot?" The cases of concern are those in which our rights with respect to each other are in *conflict*, and where the correct ethical resolution of that conflict is subject to *reasonable* dispute. If there were no such conflict cases, or if there were no reasonable disputes over how to resolve them, then we could just consult ethicists to clarify their correct resolution. There would also be no problem to solve if everyone were not morally *equal*. What moral equality means is that no one has any more natural moral authority than anyone else does to rule over others. If someone had the natural moral authority to settle disputes over our rights—for example, a divinely ordained king—then we would have a duty to defer to the judgment of that superior authority, even if we were to reasonably disagree with it.

This problem of *reasonable disputes* between *moral equals* over their *respective rights and duties in conflict* cases is precisely the problem of justice that Kant's political philosophy attempts to solve. How can we resolve such disputes rightfully, in a way that respects everyone's moral equality? In the next three subsections, I set out Kant's statement of the problem, his solution, and its main implication, the Kantian priority of right.

The Problem of Justice: Reasonable Disputes over Natural Rights

Kant defines the "innate right of freedom" as follows:

> *Freedom* (independence from being constrained by another's choice), insofar as it can coexist with the freedom of every other in accordance with a universal law, is the only original right belonging to every [person] by virtue of [her] humanity.
>
> (DR: 6:237)

Freedom is thus "independence from being constrained by another's choice," and the *right* of freedom is that freedom systematically limited by everyone else's equal freedom under a universal law. Kant elaborates that the innate right of freedom includes a number of constituents such as "innate *equality*" that are "not really distinct from it" (DR: 6:237–8). The innate right of freedom, moreover, entails that we have powers to acquire rights in property, contract, and in status relations such as marriage or parenthood, Kant argues (see DR: 6:250–1).

The problem that Kant's theory of justice confronts is how to rightfully resolve disputes over the order, scope, and limits of our rights in a system of equal freedom under a universal law. The problem arises as a result of two main claims: First, according to Kant, reason cannot by itself completely specify what our rights and duties with respect to each other are (DR: 6:312). While reason may be capable of determining our respective rights in clear cases, the precise order, shape, and scope of our rights with respect to each other in many or most cases cannot be determined by appeal to reason by itself.[6] Reasonable disagreements over our rights are thus unavoidable. The problem is acute in cases of dispute over acquired rights to property or in contract. Kant stresses that any such rights are merely "provisional" in a state of nature lacking a public authority because they are subject to reasonable dispute (DR: 6:264).

Second, the innate right of freedom is equivalent to innate *equality*. What innate equality means, Kant says, is that everyone has her "own [natural] right to do what seems right and good to [her] and not to be dependent on another's opinion about this" in cases of reasonable dispute over rights (DR: 6:312). Like others in the social contract tradition, Kant rejects the superior natural right of divinely ordained kings to rule over others. No one individual or group has the natural moral authority to unilaterally define everyone's rights and duties with respect to others (i.e., legislate them), or to enforce them (i.e., execute them), or to resolve disputes over them (i.e., adjudicate them).

Kant concludes that morally rightful relations with others are impossible in a state of nature. While the state of nature may not devolve into a Hobbesian civil war, "it would be a state devoid of justice (status justitia vacuus)," Kant says, because "when rights are in dispute (ius controversum), there would be no judge competent to render a verdict having rightful force" (DR: 6:312). Hence, rightful relations in the state of nature are impossible, Kant says, even if everyone were committed to acting perfectly ethically with respect to each other (DR: 6:312).

Its Solution: Lawful Public Authority

The solution, Kant argues, is

> . . . *a system of laws for a people . . . which because they affect one another, need a rightful condition under a will uniting them, a constitution (constituto), so that they may enjoy what is laid down as right.*
>
> (DR: 6:311)

Only a *united* will constituted in a system of legitimate public laws and institutions has the moral authority to define, enforce, and adjudicate our respective rights and duties in cases subject to reasonable dispute (see DR: 6:313–14). Why does the united will have such authority? Kant appeals to an idea central to the social contract tradition, consent:

> when someone makes arrangements about another, it is always possible for him to do the other wrong; but he can never do wrong in what he decides upon with regard to himself (for *volenti non fit iniuria*). Therefore only the concurring and united will of all, insofar as each decides the same thing for all and all for each, and so only the general united will of the people, can be legislative [i.e., sovereign].
>
> (DR: 6:313–14)[7]

When we agree to unite our wills with others by forming a civil state under the rule of law, we agree to be ruled by the law of that state, even in cases where we may reasonably disagree with it. Its coercive enforcement in such cases, therefore, is not wrongful. The united will settles our disputes on behalf of the parties to the dispute as well as everyone else in the political community. Kant refers to the action of the united will as "omnilateral" to distinguish it from the "unilateral" action of a private, individual will (DR: 6:256).

The only way to respect everyone's innate right of freedom under universal law in conflict cases is to unite our wills and enter a "civil condition" under the rule of law. We therefore have a duty to do so, Kant concludes:

> [Every human being] must leave the state of nature, in which each follows its own judgment, unite itself with all others (with which it cannot avoid interacting), subject itself to a public lawful external coercion, and so enter into a condition in which what is to be recognized as belonging to it is determined by law and is allotted to it by adequate power (not its own but an external power); that is, it ought above all else to enter a civil condition.
>
> (DR: 6:312)

Main Implication: The Kantian Priority of Right

The judgments of the institutions of a lawful public authority that determine our respective rights and duties in cases subject to reasonable dispute, therefore, take *moral priority* over private ethical judgments about what those rights and duties should be in such cases. I will refer to this priority as the Kantian "priority of right." To reject the judgments of legitimate public authority in such cases is to do wrong "in the highest degree," Kant says, because one rejects the basis of rightful relations with others to "hand everything over to savage violence…" (DR:6:308n).

What distinguishes Kant's political philosophy from traditional social contractarian justifications of public authority is that the priority of right is not established by reference to its good consequences. Thomas Hobbes, John Locke, and Jean-Jacques Rousseau all argue in different ways that we should respect the state's authority to settle our disputes because, otherwise, we would suffer significant negative consequences, individually and collectively.[8] But this instrumental rationale for public authority will not satisfy a deontologist like Kant who holds that doing what is morally right is qualitatively more important than doing what has the best consequences. If my duty is to do what is right *irrespective of the consequences*, and I reasonably believe that the law's judgment in some disputed case is wrong, then it seems that I should reject that judgment and do what I believe is right in the case, even if such disregard for the law's authority may eventually result in the violence or insecurity that Hobbes and Locke fear. Kant explains why respecting the priority of the law's judgment in such a case *is* the morally right thing to do irrespective of its consequences.

Kant's main insight into political theory is that the problem of reasonable disputes over rights can be solved by appealing to the moral authority of the united will as constituted in the tripartite institutions and public laws of a legitimate civil state. Only the united will can settle reasonable disputes over our rights in a way that respects the freedom and equality of everyone. Hence, we must respect the rule of law in cases of reasonable dispute over our rights, even when we believe that the law's judgment is wrong.

Now, there are indeed cases in which one's duty is to resist unjust law and stand on what is morally right. Kant would agree that when positive laws clearly violate fundamental rights of freedom and equality, then one has no duty to obey them; for example, Kant rejects a constitution establishing a caste system because it could not secure everyone's consent (T: 8:397). The duty to respect the priority of right depends on the prior duty to respect the innate right of equality. Hence when a law clearly violates the innate right of equality, the Kantian priority of right does not operate.

Kant's political philosophy thus provides a partial answer to the question of how to program autonomous machine agents to act morally rightly in cases where what is right is subject to reasonable dispute.[9] We should program them to respect the Kantian priority of right. The behavior of an autonomous machine agent that obeys the law in order to respect the Kantian priority of right will thus sometimes diverge from a merely legal machine that obeys the law in order to minimize its legal liability. A rightful autonomous machine agent would ignore laws that violate fundamental rights of freedom and equality, whereas a merely legal machine agent would likely comply with them. Conversely, while a merely legal machine might ignore or evade legitimate laws that are unlikely to be enforced, a rightful machine would still respect them.

In the next section, I show how appeal to the Kantian priority of right resolves the conflicts of rights in the (in)famous "trolley problem" for autonomous machine agents.

The Kantian Priority of Right and the Trolley Problem

Consider the following hypothetical accident scenario ("Driver") (Foot 1967, 3): Suppose you are the driver of a trolley whose brakes have failed. The trolley is approaching a junction in the tracks. On the track ahead are five people who will be struck and killed if you maintain course, while on a side track is one person who will be killed if you turn the trolley. Should you maintain course or turn the trolley? Most people (about 85%) say they would turn the trolley (see, e.g., Mikhail 2007). Contrast this scenario ("Footbridge") (Thomson 1976, 207–208): Suppose you are standing on a footbridge overlooking the trolley's track. The five are still stranded below, but now there is no side track. Standing next to you on the footbridge is a large man. If you push him off the footbridge onto the track, then he would be struck and killed, but the collision would stop the runaway trolley, saving the five. Should you push the large man or not? Most people (about 90%) say they would *not* do so (Mikhail 2007).

The original trolley "problem" posed by Phillipa Foot is the problem of how prevailing moral intuitions in Driver can be reconciled with those in cases like Footbridge, since most people are willing to kill one person to avoid killing five in Driver but not in Footbridge (Foot 1967, 3). How can prevailing moral intuitions in Driver and in cases like Footbridge be simultaneously rational? Foot argues that the answer is that "negative" duties such as to avoid killing others are more important than "positive" duties such as to aid them (Foot 1967, 5–6).[10] In Driver, the conflict is between negative duties not to kill one and not to kill five, Foot says, and since you must, therefore, violate a negative duty not to kill regardless of what you do, it is rational to turn the trolley so as to violate the fewest negative duties (Foot 1967, 5). In Footbridge, by contrast, the conflict is between a negative duty not to kill one (the large man) and a *positive* duty to aid the five, Foot says. In such a case, the negative duty should take priority over the positive duty (Foot 1967, 6). It is therefore rational to kill one to spare five in Driver but not do so in Footbridge, according to Foot.

The Solution to the Original Trolley Problem

Judith Jarvis Thomson criticizes Foot's analysis, pointing out that Foot needs to provide some account of how and why "negative" duties to avoid acts such as killing others should take priority over "positive" duties to perform acts such as aiding others (Thomson 2008, 372). I argue that appeal to the Kantian priority of right can provide this account. Negative duties not to kill in Foot's trolley problem take moral priority not because they are negative duties but because they are *legal* duties authoritatively determined in public law, whereas positive duties to aid others in cases like Footbridge are *ethical* duties. Foot's distinction between negative and positive duties roughly correlates with Kant's distinction between legal and ethical duties, since legal duties are often negative and some important positive ethical duties cannot be legal duties.[11] But the relevant distinction is between legal and ethical duties.

Consider Footbridge again: Suppose you are one of the 10% who believes that your ethical duty is to push the large man because that would save the most lives. But the large man's right to his life has already been authoritatively determined by public law to include at least the right not to be coerced to die in order to aid others. The Kantian priority of right, therefore, controls. Your moral duty is to defer to the legitimate determination of the law concerning the scope of the large man's right to his life, whatever your private ethical judgment in the case may be. To do otherwise is to reject the basis of rightful relations with others. The prevailing intuition that one should not push the large man in Footbridge is, therefore, rational.

Now contrast Driver: Just as you had a legal duty not to kill the large man in Footbridge by pushing him, so here in Driver you have a legal duty not to kill the one on the sidetrack by turning the trolley. But *because you are the driver,* you also have a legal duty not to kill the five on the main track by maintaining the trolley's course. As the driver of the trolley, you are subject to a legal duty of reasonable care when driving that includes at least some duty to avoid collisions that injure or kill people. To see this prior legal duty of care more clearly, suppose there is *no one* on the sidetrack.[12] Or compare an analogous case where you are the driver of a car on a multilane highway (Thomson, 2008, 369). If five people were stranded in the lane ahead, and you could safely change lanes to avoid them, then choosing to maintain course and kill them would violate a legal duty to drive with reasonable care (see Thomson, 2008, 369).[13]

These comparison cases show that the driver is subject to *some* legal duty of reasonable care with respect to the five; the question is one of its scope and shape. In cases of conflict between *legal* duties such as in Driver, the priority of right does not control, and this is what distinguishes Driver from Footbridge. The question of the scope of the driver's duty to drive safely in a case such as Driver has not been authoritatively resolved in public law. There is a reasonable legal case for holding the driver responsible for the injuries of those the trolley kills, regardless of what choice the driver makes. Since the resolution of the conflict between the driver's legal duties in Driver is unclear, it seems rational (as Foot suggests) to minimize harm.[14] The prevailing intuition to turn the trolley in Driver is thus also rational. This solves Foot's original trolley problem.[15]

The Autonomous Trolley Problem

While the analysis of the trolley problem is somewhat different for autonomous machine agents, its solution by appeal to the Kantian priority of right remains the same. In Footbridge, if the manufacturer of an autonomous robot programmed it to push the large man into the trolley's path because that would minimize lives lost, then the manufacturer would be legally liable for battery and, perhaps, murder. Hence, the manufacturer's legal duty to program the robot to avoid killing the large man in Footbridge is clear and takes priority over the ethical duty the manufacturer may have to program the robot to aid the five.

In Driver, the manufacturer is subject to legal liability regardless of what it programs the autonomous trolley to do. If the manufacturer programs the trolley to turn in Driver, then the manufacturer will be liable for battery (or murder) of the one on the sidetrack. The defense that the killing is necessary in order to avoid the greater evil of killing five will likely fail because the doctrine of legal necessity typically does not excuse intentional acts that cause bodily injury or death (Wu 2020, 9). If, however, the manufacturer programs the trolley to maintain course, then the manufacturer likely would be held liable for the deaths of the five on the main track on a theory of strict product liability. Survivors of the five killed would argue that the car is subject to a design defect, since a reasonable alternative design that kills one to spare five would achieve a better balance of expected utility than the (defective) design that killed five to spare one (see Wu 2020, 8). Since the manufacturer's legal duty is unclear in Driver, the priority of right does not control. It is therefore rational for the manufacturer to program the trolley to turn in Driver in order to minimize harm. This solves the trolley problem for autonomous machine agents.

Resolving Dilemmas: "Driver" Redux

Now, one might object that my appeal to minimizing harm to resolve Driver seems ad hoc, and indeed, my analysis of Driver was too quick. Let us assume, as indeed Foot and Thomson both do, that the conflict in Driver is between narrow, negative duties not to kill each of the five by maintaining course, and a narrow, negative duty not to kill the one on the sidetrack by turning the trolley. Foot argues that it is better to violate only one such negative duty not to kill rather than five, and that this is why you should turn the trolley in Driver (Foot 1967, 5).

But while minimizing violations of legal rights of the same kind seems rational, doing so may be contestable as a principle of justice. It may not be clear why it is just to allow the violation of one person's rights in order to achieve the greater good of avoiding violating five people's rights. The one whose rights are violated is wronged, regardless. The conflict in Driver therefore appears to be a genuine dilemma cast between narrow legal duties, where no matter what the driver does, she may reasonably be understood to have acted wrongly. How should agents act in dilemmas cast between two authoritative legal obligations? What is the role of ethical principles such as harm minimization in resolving such conflicts?

I argue that the Kantian priority of right makes two demands relevant to how agents facing such dilemmas may appeal to such principles[16]: (1) First, the agent should try to formulate the dilemma by way of some legal analysis of the duties in conflict. Only after determining that one's legal obligations are indeed in intractable conflict may the agent resort to private ethical principles or preferences to determine right action. (2) Second, any decision taken in a dilemma case must be justified by reference to a rational legal argument. Public laws that determine rights are just only if everyone can consent to them, but one cannot consent to a law that lacks any rational basis whatsoever (T: 8:297). Completely irrational laws are incompatible with the consent needed to unite our wills under the rule of law.

The moral reasoning component of an autonomous machine agent thus should (1) formulate alternative consistent sets of enforceable law applicable to its goals, and then (2) make a choice between these sets, justifying its choice by citing qualifications on applicable legal rules as necessary to form a consistent set. The choice between consistent sets of law should be made by appeal to some principle of justice, if possible, but failing that, may then be made by some fallback ethical principle such as harm minimization. A machine that resolved dilemmas in this way would respect both the moral priority of public laws over private ethical theories or preferences and the demand that its decisions have some minimal rational legal justification.[17] Contrast a merely legal machine that would resolve legal conflicts by calculating which action would reduce the risk of liability or culpability. This calculation likely would be driven by a prediction as to how a court would resolve the conflict case if it were litigated. For a rightful machine, such conflict cases would be resolved by principles of justice, and failing that, principles of ethics.

Conclusion

I have argued the following four main claims:

1   Autonomous machine agents programmed to enact a popular majority's ethical prefer-
    ences in controversial cases involving rights would be *immoral* machines that often act
    in ways that violate the moral equality of persons.
2   Autonomous machine agents must respect the moral priority of the judgments of legit-
    imate public authority over private ethical preferences in cases where rights are subject
    to reasonable dispute. To act morally rightly, autonomous machine agents must respect
    the Kantian priority of right.
3   Appeal to the Kantian priority of right solves the original "trolley problem" by show-
    ing how prevailing intuitions that it is permissible to kill one to spare five in the Driver
    variation, but not to do so in cases like the Footbridge variation, are simultaneously
    rational. The priority of right controls in Footbridge, but not in Driver.
4   The rationale for the priority of right illuminates how to handle dilemmas in the law.
    Dilemmas should be resolved into competing consistent sets of applicable law, and if no
    further principle of justice indicates which to select, then the machine may select one
    by applying supplemental ethical principles or preferences.

Notes

1   The challenge is not to build machine agents that act *morally autonomously* in the Kantian sense of
    that term. While autonomous machine agents can be programmed to do what is right, they can-
    not be programmed to freely choose to do what is right for the reason that it is right, which is what
    Kantian moral autonomy requires (G: 4:397). In artificial intelligence contexts, machine agency
    consists in the ability to act on an external environment, and machine agent autonomy consists
    in the ability to progressively alter how the agent acts on the environment as it learns more about
    it (Russell and Norvig 2010). Autonomous machine agents are programmed with a set of objec-
    tives, rewards and punishments, constraints, inference rules, or other performance measures, and
    then programmed to learn how to act in ways that optimize or satisfy those measures across a
    wide range of situations and environments. Hence while autonomous machine agents might be
    understood to have various "incentives" for action oriented toward achieving competing perfor-
    mance measures, they are not capable of freely choosing for themselves which such incentives to
    take as their motivating reason for action. They will always act in accordance with whatever such
    incentives best optimize or satisfy their performance measures in the ways that they have been
    programmed. See Anderson and Anderson (2011) for a general introduction to machine ethics.
2   Kant distinguishes legal duties ("duties of right") from ethical duties ("duties of virtue") and
    argues that in controversial cases, legal duties take priority (see DV: 6: 379). I discuss the Kantian
    priority of right in the second section.
3   In another recent effort along the same lines ("Delphi"), a deep neural network was trained
    on 1.7 million human-labeled examples as well as a number of other sources in order to model
    "common sense morality," defined as "ethical criteria and principles to which a majority of
    people instinctively agree" (Jiang et al. 2021, 6). Delphi's creators then assert that autonomous
    machine agents should be programmed to act in accordance with some model of popular ethical
    preferences like that of Delphi (Jiang et al. 2021, 2–4).
4   The social contract tradition begins with Thomas Hobbes and includes John Locke, Jean Jacques
    Rousseau, Immanuel Kant, and in recent times, John Rawls, among others. The tradition has
    two strands, a Hobbesian strand in which coercive state power is justified because it is necessary
    to avoid the insecurity that disputes over our rights will otherwise generate in a "state of nature,"
    and a Kantian strand in which state power under the rule of law is justified because it is necessary
    to meet our prior natural duty to treat each other as free and equal persons.
5   Note that the Moral Machine Experiment does not collect preferences with respect to the race,
    ethnicity, or LGBT status of characters in its accident scenarios. The experiment thus appears to
    implicitly assume that acting on preferences with respect to these attributes would be unethical,
    regardless of what the global majority prefers.

6   The libertarian idea that rights of freedom might be naturally self-limiting in a system of equal freedom has been subjected to decisive criticism (Hart 1973, 543, 547–550; Rawls 1993, 291–292). See Wright (2022) for criticism of an effort to revive this idea in a Kantian context.

7   Kant argues that the legislative power is sovereign over the executive and judicial powers (DR: 6:313).

8   The classic texts are Hobbes' *Leviathan*, Locke's *The Two Treatises of Civil Government*, and Rousseau's *The Social Contract*.

9   The answer is only partial because there may still be reasonable disagreement over what action is ethical in cases that do not involve rights. Principles of justice do not apply to such cases (see DR: 6:230).

10   Foot rejects the "Doctrine of Double Effect," which she says she had previously thought resolves the problem (Foot 1967, 6).

11   I do not mean to imply that all legal duties are negative; for example, one has a positive legal duty to pay one's taxes. And it is obvious that many ethical duties such as avoiding lying are negative duties (which are also sometimes legal duties such as to avoid fraud or libel). There is a rough correlation between negative duties and legal duties because justice requires that legal duties precisely specify the actions that will satisfy them. This is easier to do when the duty is negative. At the same time, many positive ethical duties to take up ends such as others' happiness or one's own perfection cannot be precisely specified.

12   This alternative reveals the flaw in the defense that the driver who fails to turn takes no "action" to cause the death of the five. This defense will reduce to the claim that the driver has no prior legal duty of reasonable care with respect to the five. If there is such a duty, then failing to perform it is what causes their deaths (i.e., it is an "action by omission"). But as the scenario where there is no one on the side track makes clear, the driver is subject to some prior duty with respect to the five.

13   In this case, if changing lanes would also kill someone, then the "sudden emergency" doctrine may shield the human driver from liability (Wu 2020, 10).

14   I discuss the relationship between the ethical principle of minimizing harm and the legal duties in the case in the next main fourth section.

15   I ignore another popular variation of the trolley problem ("Bystander") because it is a bad thought experiment. Bystander is the same as Driver, except that instead of being the driver of the trolley, you are a bystander standing next to a lever that you could pull (or not) in order to turn the trolley to the side track, so killing one and sparing five. Bystander is posed ambiguously. In Footbridge, unlike Driver, you have no prior legal duty requiring you to prevent the trolley from killing the five, because there is no general legal duty to help or protect others. But since the "bystander" in this thought experiment exercises a level of control over the trolley's operation as complete as that of a driver, it is plausible to think that the bystander might be subject to a legal duty similar to the driver's prior duty of reasonable care to operate the trolley safely. If the bystander is subject to such a prior legal duty, then the case is like Driver and there is a conflict between legal duties. If, however, the bystander is not subject to such a prior legal duty, then the case is like Footbridge and the priority of right controls. Perhaps the bystander is not subject to a duty of reasonable care here despite her control over the trolley because unlike the driver, she is presumably not employed to operate it. While control is the most important factor establishing the duty of reasonable care, other factors should be weighed as well. Rational intuitions in Bystander will thus shift according to whether subjects draw an analogy with Footbridge or with Driver. In experiments where a case like Footbridge, rather than Driver, is presented to subjects before Bystander, many fewer would choose to turn the trolley in Bystander, and those who still would are less sure about their decision to do so (see Petrinovich and O'Neill, 1996, 156–158). Such "ordering" effects confound intuitions in every variation of the trolley problem except Driver and Footbridge (Liao et al. 2007). Thought experiments where rational intuitions shift because the problem is posed ambiguously are bad thought experiments. Any conclusions drawn from them will rest on equivocation.

16   These normative demands are somewhat similar to the demands that John Rawls' doctrine of public reason makes of citizens engaged in political activity (see Rawls 1993, 212–254).

17   For some discussion of a deontic logic appropriate for handling legal dilemmas in this way, see Wright (2021, 233–235).

References

Anderson, M., & Anderson, S. L. (Eds.). (2011). *Machine Ethics*. Cambridge: Cambridge University Press.

Awad, E., Dsouza, S., Kim, R., Schulz, J., Henrich, J., Shariff, A., Bonnefon, J. F., et al. (2018). The Moral Machine Experiment. *Nature* 563, 59–64.

Foot, P. (1967). The Problem of Abortion and the Doctrine of Double Effect. *Oxford Review* 5, 5–15.

Hart, H. L. A. (1973). Rawls on Liberty and Its Priority. *The University of Chicago Law Review* 40(3), 534–555.

Jiang, L., Hwang, J. D., Bhagavatula, C., Bras, R. L., Forbes, M., Borchardt, J., et al. (2021). Delphi: Towards Machine Ethics and Norms. *arXiv preprint* arXiv:2110.07574.

Kant, I. (1992). In P. Guyer and A. Wood (Eds.), *The Cambridge Edition of the Works of Immanuel Kant*. Cambridge: Cambridge University Press. All references to Kant's work are from the Cambridge edition unless otherwise noted. Citations are made according to standard Academy pagination.

The Doctrine of Right, Part One of The Metaphysics of Morals, trans. M. Gregor [DR]

The Doctrine of Virtue, Part Two of The Metaphysics of Morals, trans. M. Gregor [DV]

Groundwork of the Metaphysics of Morals, trans. M. Gregor [G]

On the Common Saying: 'That May Be Correct in Theory but It Is of No Use in Practice', trans. M. Gregor. [T]

Liao, S., Wiegmann, A., Alexander, J., & G. Vong. (2012). Putting the Trolley in Order: Experimental Philosophy and the Loop Case. *Philosophical Psychology* 25(5), 661–671.

Mikhail, J. (2007). Universal Moral Grammar: Theory, Evidence, and the Future. *Trends in Cognitive Sciences* 11(4), 143–152.

Noothigattu, R., Gaikwad, S., Awad, E., Dsouza, S., Rahwan, I., Ravikumar, P., & Procaccia, A. (2018). A Voting-Based System for Ethical Decision Making. In *Proceedings of the AAAI Conference on Artificial Intelligence* 32(1). https://doi.org/10.1609/aaai.v32i1.11512

Petrinovich, L., & O'Neill, P. (1996). Influence of Wording and Framing Effects on Moral Intuitions. *Ethology and Sociobiology* 17, 145–171.

Rawls, J. (1993). *Political Liberalism*. New York: Columbia University Press.

Thomson, J. (1976). Killing, Letting Die, and the Trolley Problem. *The Monist* 59, 204–217.

Thomson, J. (2008). Turning the Trolley. *Philosophy & Public Affairs* 36(4), 359–374.

Wright, A. (2021). Rightful Machines. In H. Kim and D. Schönecker(Eds.). *Kant and Artificial Intelligence*. Walter de Gruyter GmbH & Co KG.

Wright, A. (2022). Kantian Freedom as "Purposiveness". *Kant-Studien* 113(4): 1–19.

Wu, S. S. (2019). Autonomous Vehicles, Trolley Problems, and the Law. *Ethics and Information Technology* 22 (1), 1–13.18

Chapter 17

Ethical Issues Surrounding Artificial Intelligence Technologies in Mental Health

Psychotherapy Chatbots

Şerife Tekin

The last few decades have witnessed a substantial increase in the number and needs of individuals with mental disorders and other mental health concerns. Unfortunately, the increase has not been met with a parallel rise in treatments and interventions available to these communities. Consider the 2016 statistics in the US: 18.3% of all US adults were diagnosed with a mental disorder, and of these, only 43.1% received some kind of treatment, e.g., inpatient or outpatient counseling or prescription medication (Substance Abuse and Mental Health Services Administration 2017).

The need–availability gap widened during the COVID-19 pandemic (KFF analysis of US Census Bureau, Household Pulse Survey, 2020–2021). For example, about four in ten adults in the US reported symptoms of anxiety or depressive disorder, up from one in ten reporting these symptoms from January to June 2019. Reasons for the gap between the rising demand for mental health treatment and available resources include the stresses of the pandemic, shortage of mental health professionals, especially in remote and rural areas, individuals' inability to recognize their mental health problems, high cost of mental healthcare, stigma attached to having mental disorders, and increased needs of vulnerable populations, such as refugees, immigrants, or veterans.

In the face of these problems, recent advances in applications of artificial intelligence in medicine and psychiatry give some reason for optimism, as their proponents believe these technologies will fill the need–availability gap by enhancing resources for mental healthcare.

One technology that has generated significant enthusiasm is the artificially intelligent chatbots, or what I will call *Chat_Bots*. *Chat_Bots* are purported to provide Cognitive Behavior Therapy (CBT) to their users with the aim of helping them improve their mental health and/or address their mental disorders. In the face of the increased interest in these technologies among researchers and the public at large, a plethora of connected questions has emerged: Are *Chat_Bots* effective tools for mental disorder diagnosis and treatment? Which ethical standards should guide their development and use? Must research on the artificial intelligence–assisted behavioral intervention technology be prioritized over improving other diagnostic and treatment strategies, such as in-person psychotherapy? Should this technology be funded publicly or privately?

This chapter will examine some of the ethical issues concerning the use of *Chat_Bots*. First, I will review what *Chat_Bots* are and the contexts in which they are used, with some examples. Second, I will critically evaluate the promises of the proponents of *Chat_Bots* technology and address the ethical concerns lying therein.

Digital Phenotyping and *Chat_Bots*

Artificially intelligent psychotherapy chatbots, or *Chat_Bots*, are downloadable smartphone applications that purport to offer CBT to users with the aim of helping them improve their

DOI: 10.4324/9781003189466-21

mental health or address their mental disorders. Advantages of using *Chat_Bots* for mental health problems include their comparatively low cost, wide accessibility through personal cell phones, and ability to offer therapy in different languages, making them an ideal tool, especially in areas where there is a shortage of therapists who speak the native language of individuals requiring mental healthcare, such as refugees (Luxton et al., 2011; Becker et al. 2014; Tekin 2021). Before evaluating whether and how *Chat_Bots* might be effective in these contexts, let's review the technology underlying their development and see how they purport to provide CBT.

Deploying this type of artificial intelligence technology to address mental disorders relies on the assumption that people's patterns of smartphone use are indicative of their mental health. Tracking individuals' smartphone use and their interaction with various apps is considered to have advantages over existing tools of diagnosis and treatment where, by the time individuals seek treatment from healthcare professionals, the symptoms and signs of their condition may have significantly progressed. Instead of detecting and then treating mental disorders in the clinic, artificial intelligence technologies promise to detect and intervene in mental states before anomalies become full-blown mental disorders. In other words, the goal is to preempt mental illness and intervene before the illness fully develops (Proudfoot et al. 2013).

The technology that purportedly tracks declining mental states is known as digital phenotyping, a process that involves converting individuals' daily behavior to data. Phenotype refers to individuals' observable traits, e.g., height, gender characteristics, biochemical and physiological composition, and behavior. Phenotypes are the product of our genetics, our environment, the interplay between the two, and the social influence on both. Digital phenotyping is moment-to-moment quantification of the individual-level human phenotype *in situ* using data from personal digital devices (Jain et al. 2015; Onnela et al. 2016; Coghlan & D'Alfonso 2021). For example, digital phenotyping gathers data on our location, movement, the route we take to work, our voice patterns and speech, length or frequency of texts/calls, number of times visiting a certain app, etc. Although data from such moment-to-moment activities may appear trivial and mundane (Martinez-Martin et al. 2018), some argue that they could yield valuable knowledge of hidden current and future ill-health as they provide information about our mental states of behavior (Insel 2018).

Digital phenotyping is made possible through digital sensing, i.e., the activity of digital devices in collecting and storing data about individuals (Coghlan & D'Alfonso 2021). Digital sensing allows passive, continuous, and quantitative information and can yield much more data and more finely grained data than methods such as periodic questionnaires, interviews, tests, and observations. Electronic activities and digital sensors (Saeb et al. 2015) include accelerometers, GPS, Bluetooth, phone calls, microphone, voice, and text capture (e.g., on social media), skin conductance, gestural sensing, email use, web browsing, and interaction with screens (e.g., swiping, typing, locking, and unlocking).

Digital phenotyping collects two kinds of data. Active data require active input from users in response to prompts for those data. For example, questions can be periodically posed by devices to individuals (e.g., "How are you feeling?"). Passive data include unprompted data received from sensors, such as heart rate. Because smartphones collect both active and passive data, they are thought to reflect the user's mental health status. For example, individuals who are sliding into depression may talk with fewer people, speak slowly, say less, and use a smaller vocabulary, return fewer calls, texts, emails, Twitter direct messages, and Facebook messages, spend more time home and go fewer places, and experience disturbed sleep patterns (Dobbs 2017). All these can be sensed by a phone's microphones, accelerometers, GPS units, and keyboards. The specificity of these findings still needs to be defined; yet, avid proponents of the view that digital phenotyping is the future of the intervention into and treatment of mental disorders are optimistic. For example, Thomas Insel, the former director of the National Institute of Mental Health, writes:

> Putting sensor data, speech and voice data, and human-computer interaction together might provide a digital phenotype that could do for psychiatry what HgbA1c or serum cholesterol has done for other areas of medicine, giving precision to diagnosis and accuracy to outcomes.
>
> (Dobbs 2017)

Now let's see how *Chat_Bots* bring together digital phenotyping technology with the core tenets of CBT. In terms of technology, *Chat_Bots* rely on active data collected by digital phenotyping, whereby users download *Chat_Bots* and interact/communicate with the app using its prompts. From a clinical standpoint, *Chat_Bots* are designed as if they were psychotherapists who provide CBT to individuals with mental health challenges and disorders.

CBT is a popular, evidence-based, problem-focused, and time-limited therapeutic approach developed by psychologist Aaron Beck (Beck 1975; Ratnayake 2021). It rests on the assumption that individuals feel bad not only because of events but also because of how they think about those events. It postulates a causal relationship between feelings, thoughts, and behavior that can be summarized as follows: *Thoughts create feelings, feelings create behavior, and behavior reinforces thoughts.* For example, thinking we are not worthy of love may cause us to feel bad about ourselves in social situations. Consequently, we may isolate ourselves from our friends. We will receive less attention from our friends, and this, in turn, will exacerbate our negative feelings. CBT aims to break this vicious cycle by helping people change their thoughts, or feelings, or behavior. To achieve this goal, a CBT therapist helps individuals understand that their perceptions of events may be exaggerated or false and encourages them to first re-evaluate and then reframe their interpretations. For example, "I'm never going to make any friends" is an example of distorted thinking in the form of "all-or-nothing." Removing the (all-or-nothing) distortion leads to a more balanced thought. Rephrasing the thought as "I haven't made any friends yet" or "I'm sure I'll make one or two friends eventually" takes the negative and devastating feeling out and helps individuals cope with the reality of their situation in a more constructive way.

For CBT to be effective, people need to repeatedly record their thoughts and challenge them, again and again, before the new thought pattern becomes natural. This is especially difficult at the moment when they would benefit most from doing it – i.e., when they are experiencing strong emotions.

Let's now examine how *Chat_Bots* are thought to implement CBT. Consider one smartphone psychotherapy chatbot, Woebot. Woebot was created by psychologists and AI experts who aimed to address the mental health needs of those with no access to basic healthcare. They built Woebot to provide CBT to its users. It is currently available via Facebook Messenger. It has over 17K likes, and its standalone mobile application has around 60K downloads to date. The public interest seems to have turned into a significant user base as well. According to the company's website, Woebot has more than 2 million conversations per week, across more than 120 countries (Woebot website; https://woebot.io. Accessed September February 2, 2021). Woebot uses digital phenotyping through brief daily chat conversations, a mood tracking facility, curated videos, and word games to help people manage their mental health. The goal is for people to talk to Woebot when they are feeling emotionally unwell.

Consider this scenario. Suppose Jane has been experiencing a lot of anxiety lately. She is behind in her course work at school, and her boss at the grocery store where she works just scheduled extra shifts for her over the busy holiday season. She cannot say no because she needs this job to pay for her college tuition, and she does not want to disappoint him. But she is also worried about being able to finish her assignments on time. All this has led her to ignore the household chores, and now her roommates are upset with her. Jane is overwhelmed. She has heard about Woebot from her friends at school and decides to download it to see if it can help her with her stress and anxiety. After she registers and enters her data into the app, a little robot person appears on her screen and gives her an orientation on how to use Woebot. The robot person, or *Chat_Bots*, explains to Jane that Woebot is grounded on CBT, and it teaches its users the skills to help themselves. *Chat_Bots* then proceed to explain to Jane that Woebot "tracks her mood," "gives her insight," can "teach her stuff," "help her feel better," and "be there 24/7." Jane starts responding to *Chat_Bots*'s prompts about what and how she is feeling. It is assumed that the more Jane interacts with Woebot, the better the *Chat_Bots* will get to know her mental states and provide strategies that will reduce her mental health burdens.

The ostensible advantage of using Woebot is its ability to guide people in challenging their thoughts (Fitzpatrick et al. 2017). Woebot does not develop solutions to individual problems, such as Jane's ability to dedicate enough time for her school work, but it asks questions, so users can find answers on their own. Woebot's prompts are modeled on CBT; they invite people to recast their negative thoughts in a more objective light, encouraging them to talk about their emotional responses to life events and then to stop and identify the psychological traps causing their stress, anxiety, and depression. Its creators argue that Woebot is not only more affordable than seeing an actual therapist every week (or more frequently); it is also more effective because the person using it does not feel stigmatized. Alison Darcy, one of the psychologists who developed Woebot, said in an interview, "[T]here's a lot of noise in human relationships... Noise is the fear of being judged. That's what stigma really is" (Dobbs 2017). For Darcy, when users are talking to an anonymous algorithm, they will not fear judgment. However, these promises are not warranted, as they sidestep the complexity of the experience of mental disorder, and *Chat_Ters* raise some important ethical concerns.

Ethical Problems with *Chat_Bots*

The first ethical problem is what I call the "bot is not a therapist" problem, namely, that it is incorrect to call what *Chat_Bots* do "therapy," nor can we call *Chat_Bots* "therapists" – even though they are promoted and advertised this way by their developers. The word "therapy" has Greek origins. The verb form *therapeuo* means "to serve, to attend, to be servant," "to worship (gods)," and "to take care of something or someone (people, animals, the mind, etc.)". It also means "to heal, to cure," a meaning developed in the fifth century by Hippocrates, the father of modern medicine. It is important to highlight that *therapeuo* is a transitive verb and is thus directional; it implies multiple agents or persons participating in the process of healing or taking care. The noun form *therapeia* means "healing," "curing," "service done to the sick," and "a waiting on." A feminine noun, *therapeia*, is directional and assumes a giver and a receiver. In modern psychology, medicine, and psychiatry, therapy has been used to address something taking place between (at least) two agents: the healthcare professional and the patient. Thus, calling *Chat_Bots* therapists implies calling them persons or agents, but they are far from that. If *Chat_Bots* are not agents or persons, they cannot be expected to be in charge of addressing mental health concerns of the individuals using them. This poses an ethical problem: by implying users will receive therapy from an agent, a *Chat_Bots* gives a false promise and thereby overstates its potential benefit.

The "bot is not a therapist" problem has negative clinical and ethical ramifications because a fundamental component of recovery or improvement facilitated by therapy is the therapeutic alliance between patient and therapist, but it is hard to speak about such an alliance between an individual and a bot. The alliance represents a process where the patient and the therapist work together to determine the goals of treatment based on the patient's existing problems and expectations from psychotherapy. Thinking together, they identify the steps to achieve that goal, forming a connection in the process. Research suggests that the therapeutic alliance is a strong predictor of successful outcomes (Ardito & Rabellino 2011; Capaldi et al. 2016). Building a therapeutic alliance is a relational process in which the therapist is attentive to the patient's concerns, and the patient feels recognized and cared for. *Chat_Bots* are unlikely to offer patients the crucial therapeutic experience of feeling that someone else, despite knowing their flaws and vulnerabilities, cares about them. Perhaps people will seek help from a bot but such help may not bring them the results they need or desire.

The "bot is not a therapist" problem has other implications as well. An important component of successful psychotherapies, or other healthcare treatments in medicine for that matter, is the trust built between the patient and healthcare professionals (Collier 2012). Research indicates that both medical professionals and patients perceive trust to be the fundamental ingredient of a successful treatment program. Some even say, "Without trust, physician–patient interactions could become more like consumer transactions at a shopping mall" (Collier 2012). For example, Rita Charon, the founder of narrative medicine, argues that the clinician must acquire the skills to listen, interpret, and reflect on the patient's stories with an "engaged concern" to achieve therapeutic outcomes because this is the fundamental way in which the patient learns to trust the clinician (Charon 2006). Giving uptake is necessary to build trust. In the field of mental health, this is crucial. Such alliances cannot be formed between a person and a bot as their interactions are mediated by prompts designed by an AI technology rather than a person who cares for the patient, and the patient who feels recognized and respected by a therapist. In light of this, it is hard to imagine a patient building a trusting relationship with a chatbot.

The second problem is the "trackability assumption," i.e., the assumption that a psychotherapy chatbot will accurately track individuals' feelings, moods, and behaviors and will reflect the status of their mental health. There are multiple reasons why this assumption may be false. First, not everyone is equally self-reflective; individuals may not be aware of their moods, the changes in those moods, or how various triggers may affect their moods and behavior. This might lead them to not accurately relay these to *Chat_Bots*. In fact, one advantage of in-person CBT is the psychotherapist's ability to challenge patients and encourage them to notice the connection between their moods and their behavior. Because *Chat_Bots* like Woebot are self-directed and the users themselves are in charge of tracking and reporting their feelings and moods, they may be limited in fully observing and tracking mental and behavioral phenomena. Second, *Chat-Bots* only know as much as users reveal to them, and they can only help as much as users decide to help themselves. Third, some individuals with mental disorders suffer from anosognosia, which leads them to deny that they have a mental health problem (Amador & David 2004; Tekin 2016). If they do not think they have a problem, they will be less likely to monitor their moods and behaviors. Finally, there is increased awareness worldwide of various concerns about the use of private data by businesses; this may lead users of *Chat_Bots* to self-censor and not report everything about their mental states and behavior. As I discuss below, public awareness of various data businesses' (such as Facebook) manipulation and selling of private data may lead the potential users of these chatbots to lose trust in their effectiveness, thus hampering their ability to benefit.

The third problem is what philosophers Joshua August Skorburg and Phoebe Friesen have called the "evidence gap." More specifically, no conclusive data show *Chat_Bots* to be efficacious for diagnosis and treatment (Becker et al. 2014; Skorburg & Friesen 2021). The number of tested evidence-based mental health apps is small, and studies usually rely on small, non-controlled, and non-randomized samples. Moreover, only a few of them report sustainable results for a period of more than three months, try to replicate these results, or test the effects of mobile interventions on everyday life, work, or social functions in general (Donker et al. 2013; Fiordelli et al. 2013). In fact, the majority of commercially available mental health apps are not supported by robust empirical evidence (Skorburg & Friesen 2021). For example, while 73 of the most downloaded mental health apps in the iTunes and Google Play stores claim to be effective at improving symptoms, only one includes a citation to a published study (Larsen et al. 2019). The efficacy data are even slimmer for CBT delivered by *Chat_Bots*. The best available evidence suggests that *Chat_Bots* may be effective as adjuncts to traditional forms of psychotherapy, but they fail to offer significant benefit on their own. Some may even lead to worse outcomes (Weisel et al. 2019). The technology is advancing so fast that research seems unable to keep up. In addition, there are important questions about evidence. For example, some apps are marketed directly to consumers, who seem less vigilant in relaying evidence of the apps' effectiveness or limitations. Others, especially apps developed by clinicians, seek endorsement by therapists for their patients and are therefore more forthcoming about their limitations.

The fourth and final problem is the ethical problem of "data privacy." *Chat_Bots* collect a great amount of demographic and medical information by urging users to enter a lot of personally identifiable data, for example, name, phone number, email address, age, gender, and even photos. They frequently catalogue lifestyle information, such as food consumption and exercise habits, or information related to diagnoses and treatments (e.g., chronic health/mental health problems, screening results, and medication dosages). Moreover, when using the app, people usually create a record of their daily routines and practices (e.g., diet, exercise, and mood). Even if the developer has a privacy policy, there are usually no regulations[1] to protect the privacy and security of personal health information; once sensitive information is made public via social media, users have little to no control over it. In addition, there is a strong possibility that *Chat_Bots* will lack reliable security; they might transmit unencrypted personal data over insecure network connections or allow ad networks to track users, raising serious concerns about their ability to protect the privacy and confidentiality of user information (Harris 2013; Njie 2013). Personal health information is of great value to cyber-criminals and can be used to obtain medical services and devices or bill insurance companies for phantom services in the victim's name. As there are few legal protections, victims are forced to pay or risk losing their insurance and/or ruining their credit ratings (Dolan 2013). Fraudulent healthcare events can leave inaccurate data in medical records about tests, diagnoses, and procedures that could greatly affect future healthcare and insurance coverage (Dolan 2013). Erroneous mental health information could even influence a person's social life or work opportunities (Tekin 2014; Hoffman & Zachar 2017).

Conclusion

This chapter laid out some ethical concerns about the use of artificial intelligence technology in addressing mental health problems by examining one such technology that promises to provide CBT to its users. Going against the popular wave of enthusiasm for *Chat_Bots*, the chapter raised four ethical problems concerning their use, labeling them "bot is not a therapist" "trackability assumption," "evidence gap," and "data privacy." Given these problems, to the extent the technology is experimented on, developed, and used, it should be funded by private funds instead of public money, as the latter option would take much-needed funds away from the development of efficacious diagnostic and treatment methods.

In addition, more regulation is needed on the use of these technologies. No clear measures and certifications (from federal or other third-party institutions) are in place to guarantee their effectiveness.

Time is of the essence: smartphone psychotherapy chatbots are already becoming integrated into routine healthcare (e.g., logging data, checking, and updating patient status), so we must create strong ethical guidelines for the technology and certification programs for mental health apps worldwide (Ozdalga et al. 2012; Tomlinson et al. 2013), and we must do so quickly. Given my concerns, I suggest that research funding should be allotted cautiously. As it stands now, *Chat_Bots* should not be used as a substitute for person-level interventions.

Note

1 Note that researchers working on developing and using this technology in the US must abide by the statutes of the Health Insurance Portability and Accountability Act (HIPAA) legislation, which requires data privacy and security provisions for safeguarding medical information. However, if the researchers are not in the US, they may be exempt from such requirements. At this point, there are no universal guidelines.

References

Ardito, R. B., & Rabellino, D. (2011). Therapeutic alliance and outcome of psychotherapy: Historical excursus, measurements, and prospects for research. *Frontiers in Psychology*, 2, 270. DOI: 10.3389/fpsyg.2011.00270

Amador, X. F., & David, A. S. (2004). *Insight and psychosis.* New York: Oxford University Press.

Beck, A. T. (1975). *Cognitive therapy and the emotional disorders.* Madison, CT: International Universities Press, Inc.

Becker, S., Miron-Shatz, T., Schumacher, N., Krocza, J., Diamantidis, C., & Albrecht, U. (2014). mHealth 2.0: Experiences, possibilities, and perspectives. *JMIR Mhealth Uhealth*, 2(2): e24.Becker, S., Miron-Shatz, T., Schumacher, N., Krocza, J., Diamantidis, C., & Albrecht, U. (2014). mHealth 2.0: Experiences, possibilities, and perspectives. *JMIR Mhealth Uhealth*, 2(2): e24. DOI: 10.2196/mhealth.3328

Capaldi, S., Asnaani, A., Zandberg, L.J., Carpenter, J.K., & Foa, E.B. (2016). Therapeutic alliance during prolonged exposure versus client-centered therapy for adolescent posttraumatic stress disorder. *Journal of Clinical Psychology*, 72(10): 1026–1036.

Charon Rita. (2006). *Narrative medicine: Honoring the stories of illness.* New York: Oxford University Press.

Coghlan, S., & D'Alfonso, S. (2021). Digital phenotyping: An epistemic and methodological analysis. *Philosophy and Technology*, 34(4): 1905–1928.

Collier, R. (2012). "Professionalism: The importance of trust." *Canadian Medical Association Journal = Journal de l'Association Medicale Canadienne*, 184(13): 1455–1456.Dobbs, D. (2017). The smartphone psychiatrist. *The Atlantic*. https://www.theatlantic.com/magazine/archive/2017/07/the-smartphone-psychiatrist/528726/. Accessed 18 Feb 2022

Dolan, P.L. (2013). Health data breaches usually aren't accidents anymore. http://www.amednews.com/article/20130729/business/130729953/4/. Accessed 18 Feb 2022.

Donker, T., Petrie, K., Proudfoot, J., Clarke, J., Birch, M. R., & Christensen, H. (2013). Smartphones for smarter delivery of mental health programs: A systematic review. *Journal of Medical Internet Research*, 15: e247.

Fiordelli, M., Diviani, N., & Schulz, P. J. (2013). Mapping mHealth research: A decade of evolution. *Journal of Medical Internet Research*, 15: e95.

Fitzpatrick, K.K., Darcy, A., & Vierhile, M. (2017). Delivering cognitive behavior therapy to young adults with symptoms of depression and anxiety using a fully automated conversational agent (Woebot): A randomized controlled trial. *JMIR Mental Health*, 4(2): e19.

Harris, K.D. (2013). *Privacy on the go: Recommendations for the mobile ecosystem*. California Department of Justice. http://oag.ca.gov/sites/all/files/agweb/pdfs/privacy/privacy_on_the_go.pdf. Accessed 18 Feb 2022.

Hoffman, G., & Zachar, P. (2017). RDoC's metaphysical assumptions: Problems and promises. In J. Poland & Ş. Tekin (Eds.), *Extraordinary science and psychiatry: Responses to the crisis in mental health research* (pp. 59–86). Cambridge: MIT Press.

Insel, T. (2018). Digital phenotyping: A global tool for psychiatry. *World Psychiatry*, 17(3): 275–277.

Jain, S.H., Powers, B.W., Hawkins, J.B., & Brownstein, J.S. (2015). The digital phenotype. *Nature Biotechnology*, 33(5): 462–463.

Larsen, M.E., et al. (2019). Using science to sell apps: Evaluation of mental health app store quality claims. *NPJ Digital Medicine*, 2(1): 1–6.

Luxton, D. D., McCann, R. A., Bush, N. E., Mishkind, M. C., & Reger, G. M. (2011). mHealth for mental health: Integrating smartphone technology in behavioral healthcare. *Professional Psychology: Research and Practice*, 42(6): 505–512. DOI: 10.1037/a0024485

Njie, C.M.L. (2013). *Technical analysis of the data practices and privacy risks of 43 popular mobile health and fitness applications*. Privacy Rights Clearinghouse. https://www.privacyrights.org/mobile-medical-apps-privacy-technologist-research-report.pdf. Accessed 18 Feb 2022.

Onnela, J., & Rauch, S.L. (2016). Harnessing smartphone-based digital phenotyping to enhance behavioral and mental health. *Neuropsychopharmacology*, 41(7): 1691–1696.

Proudfoot, J., Clarke, J., Birch, M.R., Whitton, A.E., Parker, G., Manicavasagar, V., et al. (2013). Impact of a mobile phone and web program on symptom and functional outcomes for people with mild-to-moderate depression, anxiety and stress: A randomised controlled trial. *BMC Psychiatry*, 13: 312.

Ratnayake, S. (2021). 'I will never love anyone like that again': Cognitive behavioural therapy and the pathologisation and medicalisation of ordinary experiences. *Medical Humanities*. Published Online First: 29 November. DOI: 10.1136/medhum-2021-012210

Saeb, S., Zhang, M., Karr, C. J., Schueller, S. M., Corden, M. E., Kording, K. P., & Mohr, D. C. (2015). Mobile phone sensor correlates of depressive symptom severity in daily-life behavior: An exploratory study. *Journal of Medical Internet Research*, 17(7): e175. DOI: 10.2196/jmir.4273

Skorburg, J.A., & Friesen, P. (2021). Mind the gaps: Ethical and epistemic issues in the digital mental health response to Covid-19. *Hastings Center Report*, 51(6): 23–26. DOI: 10.1002/hast.1292

Substance Abuse and Mental Health Services Administration. (2017). *Key substance use and mental health indicators in the United States: Results from the 2016 National survey on drug use and health*. HHS Publication No. SMA 17-5044, NSDUH Series H-52. https://www.samhsa.gov/data/

Tekin, Ş. (2021). Is big data the new stethoscope? Perils of digital phenotyping to address mental illness. *Philosophy & Technology*, 34: 447–461. DOI: 10.1007/s13347-020-00395-7

Tekin, Ş. (2016). Are mental disorders natural kinds? A plea for a new approach to intervention in psychiatry. *Philosophy, Psychiatry, and Psychology*, 23(2): 147–163.

Tekin, Ş. (2014). Self-insight in the time of mood disorders: After the diagnosis, beyond the treatment. *Philosophy, Psychiatry, and Psychology*, 21(2): 139–155.

Weisel, K.K. et al. (2019). Standalone smartphone apps for mental health—A systematic review and meta-analysis. *NPJ Digital Medicine*, 2(1): 1–10.

Woebot website. https://woebot.io. Accessed 18 February 2022.

Chapter 18

Privacy, Security, and Surveillance

Adam D. Moore

We have become a nation of watchers and the watched. Don't trick yourself by thinking that you are a watcher as well. No, you lack the computing power and advanced algorithms that can cull through the terabytes of information stored in ever-growing databases. For example, take three or four seemingly innocuous data points; a 50–something-year-old male, with a PhD, who once lived in Michigan, and plays recreational hockey. Crunch the numbers – and poof – yours truly is pulled like a rabbit from a hat. Even anonymized databases provide little security in the face of surveillance technology.

Not that it is impossible to engage in some watching. We can now spy on our kids, spouses, neighbors, and friends. It always seems to be for a good cause. Our spouse might cheat, the neighbors might be robbed, or our kids might need to be protected from a dangerous world. But this watching, however morally suspicious, is hardly systematic, affects few people, and is employed by individuals who are loved ones or friends.

There is a qualitative difference between monitoring one's kids or partner and the sorts of watching we are subject to by governments or corporations. My partner does not deploy facial recognition technology or big data analytics to monitor my daily activities. Additionally, she does not deploy re-identification software or have access to predictive analytic tools that could accurately determine what I might doing tomorrow or next week.

A defender of current surveillance norms might counter with claims such as, "But if you have 'nothing to hide' why should you care if someone is watching?" Only criminals or deviants should be worried about surveillance. A second justification for a *watcher society* is based on security. We need surveillance because there are bad people in the world who will do bad things. Video monitoring, data analytics, predictive policing, and a host of other surveillance technologies are needed to provide security from terrorists and criminals. Being monitored from a distance and without your knowledge is a small price to pay for security of life and limb. On this view, security trumps privacy. Lastly, there is nothing wrong with surveillance when those being monitored have consented. Most of us cast off gigabytes of data by just living our lives. We voluntarily offer information, even private information, on social media sites, email, web-pages, blogs, smart phones, and the like. By stepping into the public domain or using different technologies, we are consenting that governments and corporations may watch.

In this chapter, I will argue that none of these argument strands, considered individually or taken together, are strong enough to override individual privacy rights. Before considering these arguments in more detail, a definition of privacy will be offered along with an analysis of why privacy is morally valuable. Lord Acton claimed that "power tends to corrupt, and absolute power corrupts absolutely."[1] If information control yields power and total information awareness radically expands that power, then we have good reason to pause before trading privacy for security.

DOI: 10.4324/9781003189466-22

Privacy: Its Meaning and Value[2]

Privacy has been defined in many ways over the last century. Samuel Warren and Louis Brandeis, following Judge Thomas Cooley, called it "the right to be let alone."[3] Roscoe Pound and Paul Freund have defined privacy in terms of an extension of personality or personhood. An individual's feelings, thoughts, or private information is as much a part of personality as her limbs, philosophical outlook, or capacities.[4] Alan Westin and others have described privacy in terms of information control.[5] Julie Inness defined privacy as "the state of possessing control over a realm of intimate decisions, which include decisions about intimate access, intimate information, and intimate actions."[6] Judith Wagner DeCew has proposed the "realm of the private to be whatever is not, according to a reasonable person in normal circumstances, the legitimate concern of others."[7] Anita Allen describes privacy as an act of "self-care" and a moral obligation of individuals to society.[8] This brief summary indicates the variety and breadth of the definitions that have been offered.

I favor what has been called a "control"-based definition of privacy.[9] A right to privacy is a right to control access to, and uses of, places, bodies, and personal information. For example, suppose that Smith wears a glove because he is ashamed of a scar on his hand. If you were to snatch the glove away, you would not only be violating Smith's right to property (the glove is his to control); you would also violate his right to privacy – a right to restrict *access* to information about the scar on his hand. Similarly, if you were to focus your x-ray camera on Smith's hand, take a picture of the scar through the glove, and then publish the photograph widely, you would violate a right to privacy. While your x-ray camera may diminish Smith's *ability* to control the information in question, it does not undermine his *right* to control access.

Privacy also includes a right over the downstream *use* of bodies, locations, and personal information. If access is granted accidentally or otherwise, it does not follow that any subsequent use, manipulation, or sale of the good in question is justified.[10] In this way, privacy is both a shield that affords control over access or inaccessibility and a kind of use and control right that yields justified authority over specific items – like a room or personal information.[11]

Turning to why we might think that privacy is valuable, biologist Peter Watts suggests that there is an instinctual inclination to seek privacy and to feel discomfited by surveillance. Watts writes:

> What we see, in short, is stalking behavior— and I mean that in the biological sense, not the sexual-harassment one. Corporate entities do it for profit, political entities for power, but in both cases what we see is stealth and concealment. We'd hear things rustling behind us even if there was nothing there; that's just the way we're wired. But it gets worse when someone invokes hackers and terrorists and creepy men in trench coats to justify poking around in our private lives . . . Many critics claim that blanket surveillance amounts to treating everyone like a criminal, but I wonder if it goes deeper than that. I think maybe it makes us feel like prey.[12]

Lewis Mumford notes similarities between rat overcrowding and human overcrowding.

> No small part of this ugly urban barbarization has been due to sheer physical congestion: a diagnosis now partly confirmed by scientific experiments with rats—for when they are placed in equally congested quarters, they exhibit the same symptoms of stress, alienation, hostility, sexual perversion, parental incompetence, and rabid violence that we now find in [large cities].[13]

These results are supported by numerous more recent studies.[14] Household overcrowding and overcrowding in prisons have been linked to violence,[15] depression,[16] suicide,[17] psychological disorders,[18] and recidivism.[19] Monitoring your children too much increases the probability of early drug use, dropping out of school, teen-pregnancy, and violence.[20] Businesses that use various covert and overt surveillance techniques tend to have higher employee turnover. Employees view various forms of electronic monitoring as harmful intrusions of privacy, and this perception increases aggression, destructive behavior, and employee turnover.[21] Workplace drug testing deters highly qualified workers from applying, has a negative impact on workplace morale, and has been indicated in reduced productivity.[22]

Cultural universals have been found in every society that has been systematically studied.[23] Based on the Human Relations Area Files at Yale University, Alan Westin has argued that there are aspects of privacy found in every society – privacy *is* a cultural universal.[24] Barry Schwartz, in an important article dealing with the social psychology of privacy, provides interesting clues as to why privacy is universal.[25] According to Schwartz, privacy is group-preserving, maintains status divisions, allows for deviation, and sustains social establishments. As such, privacy may be woven into the fabric of human evolution.

While privacy may be a cultural universal necessary for the proper functioning of human beings, its form – the actual rules of association and disengagement – is culturally dependent.[26] The kinds of privacy rules found in different cultures will be dependent on a host of variables, including climate, religion, technological advancement, and political arrangements. It is important to note that relativism about the forms of privacy – the rules of coming together and leave-taking – does not undermine the claim regarding the objective need for these rules. We have strong evidence that the ability to control access to and uses of our bodies, capacities, and powers, and to sensitive personal information, is an essential part of human flourishing or well-being.

Providing a defensible definition of privacy and establishing a clear connection to flourishing or well-being allow us to more insightfully address the pro-surveillance arguments previously mentioned. There are compelling reasons in present social and political contexts to resist trading privacy for security.

The Nothing to Hide Argument

According to this argument, we shouldn't care if our security providers are watching because we have nothing to hide or fear. Only criminals would care and we should not let them determine surveillance policy. The basic rationale of the nothing to hide view is that objecting to surveillance is admitting some sort of guilt. Eric Schmidt, former CEO at Google, sums this up nicely. "If you have something that you don't want anyone to know, maybe you shouldn't be doing it in the first place…"[27]

While this argument is voiced frequently, it is, nonetheless, rather weak. There is sensitive personal information that we each justifiably withhold from others, not because it points toward a criminal activity, but because others simply have no right to access this information. Imagine upon exiting your house one day you find a person searching through your trash painstakingly putting the shredded notes and documents back together. In response to your stunned silence, this person proclaims, "you don't have anything to worry about – there is no reason to hide is there?" Consider someone's sexual or medical history. Imagine someone visiting a library to learn about alternative lifestyles not accepted by the majority. Hiding one's curiosity about, for example, a gay lifestyle may be important in certain contexts. This is true of all sorts of personal information like religious preferences or political party affiliations. If we understand privacy as the right to control access to and uses of bodies, locations, and certain sorts of information, then the fact that someone has "nothing to hide" is simply irrelevant in most cases.

Additionally, it is easy to turn the "nothing to hide" argument on its head. Suppose the politician, police chief, and NSA agent have nothing to hide. Resistance to this sort of monitoring would indicate guilt on their part. If individual citizens have nothing to hide and therefore nothing to fear from surveillance and monitoring, why wouldn't this be true of those doing the watching? Imagine a group of secretive, powerful, and unaccountable university professors watching over the NSA, CIA, and FBI. Suppose these professors had the power and means to deploy secretive surveillance technologies against security agents that are deemed suspicious or threatening. This case highlights hidden assumptions – that we owe each other transparency and that there is no difference between "can" and "should." In our imaginary case, just because this group of secretive professors can unilaterally deploy surveillance technologies to watch NSA, CIA, and FBI agents does not mean that this level of access is owed or appropriate. Simply put, if individuals have privacy rights, then the issue of having something to hide is irrelevant. Additionally, no one would consider a "nothing to hide" view compelling if we were considering body cavity examinations or sneak-and-peak searches of random citizens.

The "Security Trumps" View

According to what might be called the "security trumps" view, when privacy and security conflict, security should win – that is, security is more important than privacy. In the typical case, security protects fundamental rights like the right to life or property. Privacy may protect important interests but these will never be as important as the security of life and limb.

First, it is not clear why a "security trumps" view should be adopted over a "privacy trumps" view. Bodily privacy—the right to control both access to and uses of one's body—seems at least as fundamental or intuitively weighty as security. In fact, one could argue that security only gets its value derivatively based on what it is protecting. On this view, security would be an instrumental value, something used to promote intrinsic values, while privacy would be understood as an intrinsic value.

Second, given that we generally promote individual security by authorizing others, it would be advantageous to maintain certain checks against those who provide security. Privacy is one of these checks. The point is not that privacy is absolute. Rather, the point is that before we set aside privacy for security, it would be prudent to put certain accountability safeguards in place. Giving governments too much power undermines the mission of providing for security – the government itself becomes a threat. The point was put nicely by John Locke in his response to Thomas Hobbes. Hobbes thought that humans were by nature liable to deceit, violence, and overly selfish behavior. Hobbes's solution was to set up a powerful government to scare individuals into doing the right thing.[28] Locke replied, "This is to think, that Men are so foolish, that they take care to avoid what Mischiefs may be done them by *Pole-Cats*, or *Foxes*, but are content, nay think it Safety, to be devoured by *Lions*."[29] If Hobbes was correct, then those in government would be just as likely to be lying selfish thugs as those they are policing. It is also important to note the risk of mischief associated with criminals and terrorists compared to the kinds of mischief perpetrated by governments – even our government. In cases where there is a lack of accountability provisions and independent oversight, governments may themselves pose the greater security risk.

Here, we are rejecting the rule that security trumps in every case, independent of process or procedure. In fact, it seems odd to maintain that any increase in security should be preferred to any decrease in privacy. Such a view would sanction massive violations of privacy for mere incremental and perhaps momentary gains in security. Also, given that others will provide security and that power is likely a necessary part of providing security, we have strong prudential or self-interested reasons to reject the "security trumps" view.

It is false to claim that in every case more privacy means less security or more security entails less privacy. Security arguments actually cut the other direction in some cases – it is only through enhanced privacy protections that we can obtain appropriate levels of security against industrial espionage, unwarranted invasions into private domains, and information warfare or terrorism. Privacy also protects us from overzealous government watchers. Consider how privacy protections enhance security when considering encryption standards for electronic communications and computer networks. Although the NSA's position is that the widespread use of encryption software will allow criminals a sanctuary to exchange information necessary for the completion of illegal activities, consider how this security argument actually cuts the other direction. National security for government agencies, companies, and individuals actually *requires* strong encryption. Industrial espionage and cyber-crime costs over 400 billion annually.[30] In 2007, a cyber-attack took down government communications and banks in Estonia.[31] A report from the CSIS Task Force on Information Warfare and Security notes that "cyber terrorists could overload phone lines . . . disrupt air traffic control . . . scramble software used by major financial institutions, hospitals, and other emergency services . . . or sabotage the New York Stock Exchange."[32] Related to information war, it would seem that national security requires strong encryption and more privacy.

One marker of power is the ability to demand information disclosures from others while keeping one's own information secret. As data mining and profiling have become the norm, many have become frustrated and alarmed with a perceived loss of power. Governments and corporations control vast amounts of information, including sensitive personal information about citizens, and use this information for their own ends. The average information target or citizen has little power to demand disclosures from governments and corporations and even less power to control the vast amounts of information being collected and stored.[33] Unless our security providers are saints, and we know that they are not, it would be irrational to give power without fairly precise accountability rules in place. This is just to say that a necessary condition for robust security is accountability. The problem is that it is the cats who are writing the rules for the mice, and one rule that most individuals in power demand is they not be watched.

Finally, those who defend the "security trumps" view rarely discuss the consequences of the surveillance policy they are promoting or whether an alternative might exist that better protects both privacy and security. Consider, just for example, almost any predominately developed "isolationist" country – perhaps Switzerland. These sorts of countries seem not to have much terrorist activity and likely do not have higher crime rates than the US.[34] Just imagine if the US did not try to be the world's policeman, engage in democracy building wars, or involve itself in any issue some politician has decided affects our "national interest." Our security providers create various security threats and then demand, on grounds of security, that the US citizens give up privacy and liberty. One way to obtain more security would be to change our selectively interventionist policies and, in this way, protect both security and privacy.

The Consent Argument

According to the consent argument, by voluntarily offering information, even private information, on social media sites, email, web-pages, blogs, smart phones, and the like, we are *agreeing* that others may watch. In living our lives, we each cast off vast amounts of data that others may notice. Given that all this information is freely shared, it would seem odd to complain that others are watching.

But this argument strand is just as weak as the others. Consider how difficult it would be to opt out of the vast array of information gathering systems that surround us. Wearing a disguise and paying in cash will not defeat facial recognition technology, video surveillance, or predictive analytics. In many US states and various EU countries, it is illegal to wear a mask or disguise to conceal one's identity.[35] Also, many of the surveillance systems used by our security providers are unknown to us data targets. Obviously, we can't consent to covert surveillance. Note as well, the ability to evade the watchers may depend on deploying anti-monitoring technologies beyond the financial means of most individuals. Independent of financial capacity, it would seem that few of us actually have a robust choice to opt out of our surveillance society.

Moreover, as already noted, allowing access to some bit of personal information does not entail abandonment. For example, when I allow a grocery store to track my purchasing habits, I am not also consenting to government agencies' use of this information for predictive analytics. Similarly, when I share my copyrighted poem with you, I do not also grant you joint ownership. We need to challenge such a view. Sharing personal information with specific individuals or businesses for specific purposes does not mean that we have waived all downstream privacy rights to this information. No one thinks this is even remotely plausible with considering physical or locational privacy. As if allowing a doctor to examine my knee is also waiving all future access and use rights to my knee – to the doctor or anyone else. If allowing access entailed waiving or abandonment, then invitations to dinner or having sex with someone would be weighty decisions indeed.

Finally, consider the re-identification problem mentioned earlier. Big data analytic software can analyze a small set of disparate data points, containing no personal identifying information, and then re-identify some particular individual.[36] Take three or four seemingly innocuous data points: a 50-something-year-old male, with a PhD, who once lived in Michigan, and plays recreational ice hockey. In sharing this anonymous information, it is hard to maintain that I also consented to the technology that crunched the numbers and identified me.

Conclusion

If the account sketched above is correct, then we should take privacy violations more seriously and be more aware of how often firms and governments commit them. Privacy is not an unimportant interest or preference that we should toss aside for access to various technologies.[37] While it is true that individuals "suffer from *privacy myopia*: they will sell their data too often and too cheaply,"[38] I have argued that this sort of behavior is irrational – it undermines human flourishing or well-being and creates various security risks.

Notes

1 Lord Acton to Bishop Mandell Creighton, April 3, 1887, in *The Life and Letters of Mandell Creighton* (New York: Longmans, Green, 1904).

2 Parts of this section draw previously published material. See Adam D. Moore, *Privacy Rights: Moral and Legal Foundations* (University Park: Penn State University Press, 2010), Chapters 2 and 3, "Defining Privacy," *Journal of Social Philosophy* 39 (2008): 411–428, and "Privacy: Its Meaning and Value," *American Philosophical Quarterly* 40 (2003): 215–227. See also, Alan Westin, *Privacy and Freedom* (Cambridge, MA: Atheneum Press, 1967), Richard. Parker, "A Definition of Privacy," *Rutgers Law Review* 27 (1974): 275–296, and Ruth Gavison, "Information Control:

Availability and Control," in *Public and Private in Social Life*, ed. Stanley I. Benn and Gerald F. Gaus (New York: St. Martin's Press, 1983), 113–134.

3 See Thomas M. Cooley, *A Treatise on the Law of Torts or the Wrongs which Arise Independently of Contract*. (Chicago: Callaghan and Co, 1879); Samuel D. Warren and Louis D. Brandeis, "The Right to Privacy," *Harvard Law Review* 4, no. 5 (1890): 193–220.

4 Roscoe Pound, "Interests in Personality," *Harvard Law Review* 28 (1915): 343; Paul A. Freund, "Privacy: One Concept or Many?," in *Privacy: Nomos XIII*, ed. J. Roland Pennock and John W. Chapman (New York: Atherton, 1971), 182.

5 Alan Westin, *Privacy and Freedom* (New York: Atheneum, 1968); Adam D. Moore, *Intellectual Property and Information Control* (New Brunswick, NJ: Transaction, 2001, 2004); Anita L. Allen, *Why Privacy Isn't Everything: Feminist Reflections on Personal Accountability* (Lanham, MD: Rowman & Littlefield, 2003); Ruth Gavison, "Information Control: Availability and Control," in *Public and Private in Social Life*, ed. Stanley I. Benn and Gerald F. Gaus (New York: St. Martin's Press, 1983), 113–134.

6 Eisenstadt v. Baird, 405 U.S. 438, 453 (1972). See also Joel Feinberg, "Autonomy, Sovereignty, and Privacy: Moral Ideas in the Constitution?," *Notre Dame Law Review* 58, no. 3 (1983): 445; H. Tristram Engelhardt Jr., "Privacy and Limited Democracy," *Social Philosophy and Policy* 17, no. 2 (Summer 2000): 120–140; Julie Inness, *Privacy, Intimacy, and Isolation* (New York: Oxford University Press, 1992), 140.

7 Judith Wagner DeCew, *In Pursuit of Privacy: Law, Ethics, and the Rise of Technology* (Ithaca, NY: Cornell University Press, 1997), 62.

8 Anita Allen, "An Ethical Duty to Protect One's Own Information Privacy?," herein, Privacy, Security, and Accountability (London: Rowman & Littlefield International, 2015).

9 See also Allen, *Why Privacy Isn't Everything*, and Gavison, "Information Control"; Charles Fried, *An Anatomy of Values* (Cambridge, MA: Harvard University Press, 1970), Chapter 9; Richard Wasserstrom, "Privacy: Some Assumptions and Arguments," in *Philosophical Law*, ed. Richard N. Bronaugh (Westport, CT: Greenwood Press, 1979), 148; Ernest Van Den Haag, "On Privacy," and Hyman Gross, "Privacy and Autonomy," in *Privacy: Nomos XIII*, ed. J. Roland Pennock and John W. Chapman (New York: Atherton, 1971), 147, 170; and Richard Parker, "A Definition of Privacy," *Rutgers Law Review* 27, no. 2 (1974): 280.

10 I reject the so-called "third party doctrine" established by Supreme Court decisions in *Miller* and *Smith*. See United States v. Miller, 425 U.S. 435 (1976), Smith v. Maryland, 442 U.S. 735 (1979), and United States v. Jones, 132. U.S. 565 (2012). For a concise summary of those cases and their impact on the privacy/surveillance debate, see John Villasenor, "What You Need to Know about the Third-Party Doctrine," *Atlantic*, December 30, 2013, accessed October 25, 2021, http://www.theatlantic.com/technology/archive/2013/12/what-you-need-to-know-about-the-third-party-doctrine/282721

11 This way of defining privacy is not without difficulties. For a defense of this account, see Moore, *Privacy Rights*, Chapter 2; Moore, "Privacy: Its Meaning and Value"; and Moore, "Defining Privacy." A strict definition of "personal information" is elusive, but the European Union Data Directive defines it as "any information relating to an identified or identifiable natural person . . . one who can be identified, directly or indirectly, in particular by reference to an identification number or to one or more factors specific to his physical, physiological, mental, economic, cultural or social identity." Directive 95/46/EC of the European Parliament and of the Council (1995) OJ L 281 0031-0050.

12 Peter Watts, "The Scorched Earth Society: A Suicide Bomber's Guide to Online Privacy," transcript of a talk given on May 9 at the 2014 Symposium of the International Association of Privacy Professionals. https://rifters.com/real/shorts/TheScorchedEarthSociety-transcript.pdf accessed October 26, 2021.

13 Lewis Mumford, *The City in History* (New York: Harcourt Brace, 1961), 210, cited in Theodore D. Fuller et al., "Chronic Stress and Psychological Well-Being: Evidence from Thailand on Household Crowding," *Social Science Medicine* 42, no. 2 (1996): 267. This view is echoed by Desmond Morris, who writes, "Each kind of animal has evolved to exist in a certain amount of living space. In both the animal zoo and the human zoo [when] this space is severely curtailed . . . the consequences can be serious." Desmond Morris, *The Human Zoo* (New York: McGraw Hill, 1969), 39.

14 See, for example, Andrew Baum and Stuart Koman, "Differential Response to Anticipated Crowding: Psychological Effects of Social and Spatial Density," *Journal of Personality and Social Psychology* 34, no. 3 (1976): 526–536; Jes Clauson-Kaas et al., "Urban Health: Human Settlement Indicators of Crowding," *Third World Planning Review* 18, no. 3 (1996): 349–363; John

N. Edwards and Alan Booth, "Crowding and Human Sexual Behavior," *Social Forces* 55, no. 3 (1977): 791–808; Fuller et al., "Chronic Stress"; Griscom Morgan, "Mental and Social Health and Population Density," *Journal of Human Relations* 20, no. 1–2 (1972): 196–204; David P. Farrington and Christopher P. Nuttall, "Prison Size, Overcrowding, Prison Violence and Recidivism," *Journal of Criminal Justice* 8, no. 4 (1980): 221–231; Paul Paulus, Garvin McCain and Verne Cox, "Death Rates, Psychiatric Commitments, Blood Pressure and Perceived Crowding as a Function of Institutional Crowding," *Environmental Psychology and Nonverbal Behavior* 3, no. 2 (1978): 107–116; R. Barry Ruback and Timothy S. Carr, "Crowding in a Woman's Prison," *Journal of Applied Social Psychology* 14, no. 1 (1984): 57–68.

15 Edwin I. Megargee, "The Association of Population Density Reduced Space and Uncomfortable Temperatures with Misconduct in a Prison Community," *American Journal of Community Psychology* 5, no. 3 (1977): 289–298 and Frank J. Porporino and Kimberly Dudley, *An Analysis of the Effects of Overcrowding in Canadian Penitentiaries* (Ottawa, ON: Research Division, Programs Branch, Solicitor General of Canada, 1984).

16 Verne C. Cox, Paul B. Paulus and Garvin McCain, "Prison Crowding Research: The Relevance for Prison Housing Standards and a General Approach Regarding Crowding Phenomena," *American Psychologist* 39, no. 10 (1984): 1148–160.

17 Garvin McCain, Verne C. Cox and Paul B. Paulus, *The Effect of Prison Crowding on Inmate Behavior* (Washington, DC: US Department of Justice, 1981).

18 Paul Paulus, Garvin McCain and Verne Cox, "Death Rates, Psychiatric Commitments, Blood Pressure and Perceived Crowding as a Function of Institutional Crowding," *Environmental Psychology and Nonverbal Behavior* 3, no. 2 (1978): 107–116.

19 David P. Farrington and Christopher P. Nuttall, "Prison Size, Overcrowding, Prison Violence and Recidivism," *Journal of Criminal Justice* 8, no. 4 (1980): 221–231.

20 See generally Newell, Metoyer, and Moore, "Privacy in the Family," 106–113 and Margaret Kerr and Hakan Stattin, "What Parents Know, How They Know It, and Several Forms of Adolescent Adjustment: Further Support for a Reinterpretation of Monitoring," *Journal of Developmental Psychology* 36 (2000): 366–380.

21 John Chalykoff and Thomas Kochan, "Computer-Aided Monitoring: Its Influence on Employee Job Satisfaction and Turnover," *Personnel Psychology: A Journal of Applied Research* 42 (1989): 826; Clay Posey, Rebecca Bennett, Tom Roberts and Paul Lowry, "When Computer Monitoring Backfires: Invasion of Privacy and Organizational Injustice as Precursors to Computer Abuse," *Journal of Information System Security* 7 (2011): 24–47.

22 Lewis Maltby, *Drug Testing: A Bad Investment* (New York: American Civil Liberties Union, 1999), 16–21.

23 Cultural universals have been found in every society that has been systematically studied. See George P. Murdock, "The Universals of Culture," in *The Science of Man in the World Crisis*, ed. Ralph Linton (New York: Columbia University Press, 1945), 123–142.

24 This view is supported by John Roberts and Thomas Gregor. See Roberts and Gregor, "Privacy: A Cultural View," in *Privacy: Nomos XIII*, ed. J. Roland Pennock and John W. Chapman (New York: Atherton, 1971), 225.

25 Barry Schwartz, "The Social Psychology of Privacy," *American Journal of Sociology* 73, no. 6 (May 1968): 741–752.

26 See Herbert Spiro, "Privacy in Comparative Perspective," in *Privacy: Nomos XIII*, ed. J. Roland Pennock and John W. Chapman (New York: Atherton, 1971), 121–148.

27 CNBC broadcast Friday December, 4th, 2009.

28 See Thomas Hobbes, *Leviathan* (1651).

29 John Locke, *The Second Treatise of Government*, ed. C. B. Macpherson (Indianapolis: Hackett, 1980), Chapter 5, sec. 93.

30 http://www.washingtonpost.com/world/national-security/report-cybercrime-and-espionage-costs-445-billion-annually/2014/06/08/8995291c-ecce-11e3–9f5c-9075d5508f0a_story.html accessed October 29, 2021.

31 http://archive.wired.com/politics/security/magazine/15–09/ff_estonia?currentPage=all accessed October 29, 2021.

32 Cited in Christopher Jones, "Averting an Electronic Waterloo," *Wired Magazine*, Online News Flash (February 1999).

33 Legislation such as the California Consumer Privacy Act (2018) and the European Union's General Data Protection Regulation (GDPR, 2016) may have a profound impact on how sensitive personal information is controlled, stored, and transmitted. If individuals are given rights of notice, consent, control, and deletion over their own personal information, and if violation of these

rights is coupled with fines for misuse, then perhaps we will begin to move past the non-sequitur that access equals abandonment.

34 See http://www.nationmaster.com/country/sz-switzerland/ter-terrorism accessed October 29, 2021.

35 See, for example, Stephen J. Simoni, "Who Goes There?" – Proposing a Model Anti-Mask Act, *Fordham Law Review* 241 (1992): 61.

36 See Paul Ohm, "Broken Promises of Privacy: Responding to the Surprising Failure of Anonymization," *UCLA Law Review* 57 (2009): 1701.

37 For example, see Thompson, https://stratechery.com/2014/privacy-dead/ accessed October 27, 2021 and Davidson, https://money.com/you-say-youd-give-up-online-convenience-for-privacy-but-youre-lying/ October 27, 2021. This view of privacy is, in part, codified in *Katz v. United States*, 389 U.S. 347 (1967). In the Katz decision, Justice Harlan established a two-part test for what counts as a reasonable expectation of privacy: (1) "an individual has exhibited an actual (subjective) expectation of privacy" and (2) "the expectation is one that society is prepared to recognize as reasonable."

38 A. Michael Froomkin, "The Death of Privacy," *Stanford Law Review* 52, no. (5) (2000): 1461–1543.

Chapter 19

Being-in-the-Screen

Phenomenological Reflections on Contemporary Screenhood

Lucas D. Introna and Fernando Ilharco

The purpose of this chapter is a provocation. What we want to do is use the phenomenological approach and literature to provoke us to *think about the meaning of living our lives in or through screens.* It is not about providing a definitive answer. It is more about asking questions, highlighting possibilities, and problematising a phenomenon. In this sense, it is an invitation to a journey of thinking. As Heidegger (1976, 135) said: thinking does not bring to us knowledge as the sciences do, rather "thinking must in its present situation give to the sciences that *searching attention* which they are incapable of giving to themselves." In this journey of thinking about screens, phenomenologically, we want to suggest that the prevalence of screens in our everyday human lives might be changing fundamentally the way we see ourselves and others, and how we live our lives.

One might suggest that literally, cognitively, symbolically, psychologically, and perhaps, decisively, we humans increasingly have our manner of being, not only as beings-in-the-world as suggested by Heidegger (1962), but rather as beings-in-the-screen as well. Whenever we are in a video meeting, exchanging WhatsApp messages, following a Twitter stream, posting on our Instagram accounts, following a YouTube tutorial, talking on the phone, etc., we increasingly encounter the world and each other on, or rather *in*-the-screen. We want to note that we say *'being-in-the-screen'* to foreground the manner in which our humanity is increasingly and inseparably tied to appearing and showing on screens—hence the hyphenation. Or phenomenologically, we are saying that screens are no longer something separate from our way of living our lives. Our way of being social/human is increasingly constituted by our ongoing relationality with screens.

Uncontrovertibly, it might be said that the screening of life has become more or less all pervasive. Or rather, screens have become the place or the context, the environment, the gestalt where much of our lives are lived, at least for a significant part of the human population. Wherever we are, in nature, in the restaurant, at work, on the train, in the bath, and so forth, we often opt, or have already opted, for life in-the-screen. The screen is the place that draws us in and somehow demands our attention—hence the saying 'glued to the screen.' In an important sense, screens are increasingly the 'world' that matters, the world that calls for us to (re)present ourselves there, to be first and foremostly in-the-screen. Paraphrasing Flusser (2011), who wrote that events desire to become image, one can say that increasingly events turn to the screen, to become *screen events*—the music concert, the holidays, the speech, the marriage, the party, etc. That is, it is not the event itself that matters as much; it is rather its eventfulness. It is the videos and the pictures of the event that are shared, liked, commented on, etc., that really matters. It is not merely about doing something social; it is increasingly about going *viral*—that is, about grabbing and holding attention in the economy of attention. As such, we tend to judge our social worth through the size of our followers, or our 'likes.'

Moreover, being-in-the-screen frees us from the material weight of a body, a located place and time, and many of the social norms that such material rooted-ness implies.

DOI: 10.4324/9781003189466-23

So much so that we often feel we have lost something very significant of ourselves and of others if we are not able to be in-the-screen. Indeed, to be socially connected is to be in-the-screen. If this is correct, then what does this mode of being human mean for our way of being? In this chapter, we will explore this question in three different but interrelated strands: (a) the filtering of the screen; (b) living in the perpetual present; and (c) being a face-less subject.

The Filtering of the Screen

The first thing to say is that the screen, to be a screen, screens. But what does this mean? The screen, in its screening, engages and absorbs our attention because its surface, what is displayed there, is always and already screened. In screening, the screen separates (filters) the assumed relevant (on the screen) from the irrelevant (not on the screen)—relevant often here defined as that which engages our attention (Franck 2019). The screen, in its screening, is a highly choreographed way of being (Introna 2016). That is exactly its screening power.

Let us take the example of social media. The principal logic of social media is homophily (Chun 2018). That is, the tendency to seek out or be attracted to those who are similar to oneself, or one might say succinctly, a love for what is similar or the same. This sameness has two different and interrelated logics. First, the assumed logic of homophily is that I want to become more like myself—become more fully my true self. That is, I want to see, encounter, interact more with things that I already like. Second, and concomitantly, I want to see, encounter, and interact with others that are already like me, i.e., *like*minded others. Algorithmically, this logic is achieved through the affinity score that tracks your 'likes,' and curates your social media streams accordingly. In this curated screening of the screen, my screen becomes full of things that I already like, and consequently it engages me, draws me into it, and absorbs my attention. As such, being-in-the-screen always and already makes sense to me as *the* place to be—to be myself and be with likeminded others.

The curated screen of sameness does not only screen (based on homophily) it also hides. That is, it screens out, what is dissimilar or other. This is, after all, one of the original meanings of screening: to select, to filter, to exclude (Introna and Ilharco 2006). What is other is, in a algorithmically sense, already dis-*liked*. Every selection or disclosure is also a closure, or a hiding. The other, as exactly other, is not an other that I need to encounter, or face. As such, my sociality becomes one of recursive oneness rather than one of expanding plurality. Consequently, my love of sameness needs never be questioned or challenged; rather in its perpetual affirmation, it becomes ever more real, ever more certain, and ever truer. It appears, not as one of many but as *the one*.

What does this recursive oneness produce? Of course, as many have commented. It produces echo chambers and filter bubbles (Flaxman, Goel, and Rao 2016). This much is obvious. But it does more. It also creates the conditions of possibility for the circulation of fake news, conspiracy theories, of fear, of hate discourses, and so forth. If other likeminded people believe it, accept it, etc., then that is good enough for me to accept it—after all, they are already so much like me; I have a social proof of my way to be (Cialdini 2009). Thus, in the echo chambers, it circulates in perpetual conformation. This is not all. The sphere of the political also disappears. According to Hannah Arendt (2009), the constitutive condition for the political sphere, to be exactly a 'political' sphere, is plurality. And where the political (plurality) disappears, totalitarianism (as the only truth) becomes possible. Thus, what we see is the growth of totalitarian discourses in which the different (or other) becomes the enemy, not only to be dis-liked, but to be hated—that is, to be eliminated as it might threaten or disrupt the truth of the oneness. This narrative of the one—devoid of otherness—has its power in its simplicity. It replaces the messy and noisy world of difference and plurality with a simple narrative where the enemy is clearly identified as the source of all that is wrong and the truth of the one is perpetually reaffirmed.

This recursive oneness produces something else as well. In its perpetual affirmation, it recursively closes off the possibility to be disrupted and surprised. In this perpetual *is-ness*, the encounter with *not-ness* diminishes. What is the consequence of this? Reflection tends to disappear, as moments of reflection tend to emerge in the encounter of breakdown (in notness). When things do *not* go according to plan, when the encounter is *not* how I expected, and something does *not* behave as expected. Indeed, Arendt (1971) would argue that notness—or what she might call perplexity—is the essential condition for thought to become possible. To think is to become perplexed. Thus, what we find in the recursive oneness is a profound thoughtlessness (Arendt 2006). It is not that the screened users do not think; as such, it is that the urgency for thought itself becomes precluded—a thoughtless thoughtlessness, one may say.

Living in the Perpetual Present

The temporality of the screen is *now*—it has as its way of being a *perpetual nowness* (Rushkoff 2013). In its screening and its nowness, the screen already engages us, attracts our attention, by being already relevant and rooted in our present situation. As such, it continuously demands our sensorial attunement and involvement in looking at it, listening to it, and touching it, thereby intensifying, enhancing, and amplifying this very nowness. We are often more attuned to the notifications appearing on our phone's screen—demanding our attention *now*—than to the person sitting with us at a social event. As we live our lives in-the-screen, this nowness increasingly becomes the context within which we perceive the world, feel, act, and think.

In-the-screen, the actual is now, and the now is actual. Yesterday's post on social media is no longer relevant. It is the Twitter storm that matters. In a sense the screen is ahistorical or post-historical. Who, in-the-screen, remembers what you did last week? And the day before yesterday? Where were you, when, doing what? In-the-screen, the past escapes us, displaced by the persistent updating or refreshing of the screen that continually wipes away the traces of the past. Moreover, in the fluidity and plasticity of the screen, the past can be recreated in many different ways, but the future is no different. Who plans this or that with friends for the week, or a month from now? This is not really necessary, as being-in-the-screen means that we always share *a common present*, in some way. As such, in the present, any arrangement can be rearranged. Plans are simply too rigid for the fluidity of the screen. Yes, you must have a general idea of where you are heading, but in the end it is what you (we) are doing *now* that matters.

What does this perpetual nowness do? It leads to the collapse of the narrative flow of life—of the notion that lives, and events, have a *trajectory*. That is, the idea that what I do now was conditioned in some way by where I was coming from and will have consequences for where I am heading. Lives unfolds as narratives, or storylines (Ingold 2015). We tend to make sense of ourselves, our lives, and our society through stories (Bruner 1991). Indeed, the narrative is our most significant way of looking into the future, of predicting, of planning, of explaining, and indeed of promising. Without the trajectory of the story, anything becomes possible now. As such, the screen becomes a place of endless possibilities in its plasticity. It produces a sense that anything can be made, remade, or deleted. As such, comments, posts, tweets, and messages are produced as if they only exist in the now of the moment—indeed, you can even set them to automatically disappear. Rooted in thoughtlessness and the disproportionate importance of the *now*, those living their lives on the screen often fail to see the consequences of their actions, they act as if there is no tomorrow.

Being-in-the-screen, we are thrown into an intense involvement, into an all at once environment, with everyone simultaneously. Echoing old meanings—the etymological root of screen is 'skin' in proto-European languages—the screen has become the outer *skin* of the world, the outer surface of reality—or rather, one might say it is reality as surface (Introna and Ilharco 2006). It might be argued that the contemporary culture of the screen is no longer based on depth and speciality, but on speed and *surfaciality*. In this *surfaciality*, our ongoing involvement with a surface might indeed facilitate multitasking, speed, and variety, but it also functions to produce or keep us in superficiality. This is exemplified, for example, by the 280-character limit of Twitter, the 60-second limit of Tiktok videos, and so forth, and replies are often in the form of emojis or likes, making screen dialogue emotive, fragmented and on the surface. Linear writing, the language of books, is no longer the predominant communication technology. It has been displaced in favour of a screened language, of images, emojis, gifs, hashtags, keywords, memes, videos, etc. Writing has linearised and objectified the world—as argued by Mcluhan—for sure, but screens, as surfaces, are going in the opposite direction. As such, we may ask, if thought is indeed rooted in language, as the Sapir–Whorf hypothesis suggests, what sort of patterns of thought are we engendering through this *surfaciality*?

Screen communication is dominated by the instantaneous (now), the emotive (likes), multitasking (multiple apps open at the same time), the intuitive, and ongoing improvisation (bricolage). The linear trajectory of life is dissipating in the 'all at once' intensity of information and communication that pops up on our screen—often without context. As such, many find themselves longing for this chaotic horizon to slow down, and the complexity of everyday life to diminish. But it might not be possible anymore. Our screen sociality is structurally chaotic, one might say. This seems at odds with a Western civilisation that was born and developed in a sensory, cultural, and educational world profoundly shaped by the phonetic alphabet—thus, by linearity, cause-effect relationship, logic, and an idea of progress (Flusser 2002, 2011; McLuhan and Fiore 2008; Ong 1982). With this new skin that is non-linear, instantaneous, surfacial, etc., what sort of humans are we becoming? Do we know? Do we care to know?

The Face-Less Disembodied Subject

The screen not only screens—as in curating what appears on its surface—it also screens in the sense of obscuring and hiding, as was suggested above. In being-in-the-screen, the subject is not just choreographed to become a 'shopper,' 'gamer,' 'spectator,' and so forth (Introna 2016). The subject also becomes face-less, literally. The screen is a surface, that is, a surface, an over face, a cover face, a hiding face. What does this mean? Lévinas (1985) argues that the face is singular. The face is the signifier of our being a singular one. It is what identifies me and in a fundamental sense roots my identity. As such, we might suggest that as a face-less subject, we become a 'no-body'—that is, without a body and without a stable identity. Being-in-the-screen as a no-body we become dislocated from our identity anchor, and as such become detached from the norms and values implied in such an identity. As a no-body, we stalk, troll, hate, and so forth. It is me that does it, but in a sense I am also not there—I am already screened out.

It is not only that I am not there in-the-screen; the other is also screened—as a no-body appearing on the surface as *surfacial*. In the screen, we are together, but very much apart. Thus, the other-in-the-screen is not only a face-less subject. She is also a bodyless subject, a spaceless subject. In the fluidity and plasticity of the surface, and the nowness of screen time, the other indeed becomes some 'distant' other, just another-in-the-screen—nothing more than a tweet, a post, an image, a like, an emoji, and so forth. In this surficial otherness, a separation, a barrier becomes enacted. I am really not there; they are really not here. What does this mean? As appearing already on the surface and dislocated, the other can be fictionalised—that is, formed into anything that I wish them to be. I can turn them—or I am almost *compelled to make* them—into a deepfake version of themselves. I can edit them, or their words into the image I have of them—and it does not really matter because it is all happening on the surface. In the surfaciality and plasticity of the screen, the real can become fake and the fake can become real—to the point that the distinction itself disappears.

Moreover, in the surfaciality and plasticity of the screen, the disembodied subjects can play with their identity. Traditional categories such as gender, race, socio-economic class, loose their definitive authority. This might be good, but what are they replaced with? Do the endless possibilities to play with one's identity bring liberation, happiness? Lovink (2019) suggests not. Why? Because such identity play in the screen is on a global stage. It is no longer confined to our diary or small group of friends. Rather, it is screened, exposed for all our 'friends' to see. A multidimensional stage in which almost every no-body has a casting vote to 'like' (or not). In this identity play, we communicate with our 'friends' through 'likes,' and by implication, dislikes—approval or disapproval. What sort of subject does this produce? An introspective sad one, where being 'liked' is the always receding and unattainable end-game of such identity play (Lovink 2019).

Concluding Comments

We have outlined some of the contours of being-in-the-screen—i.e., our personhood as screenhood. Why is this important? Because being-in-the-screen transforms individual and collective presence and behaviour. The most decisive, the most important consequence of any technology (in the Heideggerian sense), has never been the functions made available, but rather ourselves, human beings, radically transformed by what we invent (Mcluhan 1964). "We create our habits, and then they create us" is an old passage, usually referred to John Dryden (1631–1700; English first Poet Laureate in 1668). It is not about what each person wants, or what she likes or not. As increasingly *the* medium of communication, screens already transform all of human communication and sociality; it is not a matter of opinion (McLuhan and Fiore 2008). But we would suggest that the 'screening' of the screen already acts prior to this. What do we mean? When we say 'the screening of the screen,' we mean the three aspects we outlined above. That is, what screens already *do*; it is the sort of world where they already act as screens, we would suggest. We should however note that we are not saying it is the physical screen that does this—in a way a technological determinist might claim—we are saying that it is the whole way of communicating, relating, valuing, etc., that allows the screen to do what we refer to as its 'screening.' The physical screen is just one element of the relational whole that makes 'being-in-the-screen' possible. Thus, we would say that by affecting perception, senses, attention, memory, and reasoning, the pervasiveness of the screens changes us, fundamentally. The screen in its screening always and already facilitates certain patterns of perception, structures of attention, models of thinking, and thus alter our lives independently of our individual analysis or opinions.

One might respond and say that what we have described might be correct and important for those living their lives in the screen, such as the 'digital natives,' as they have been called. And that, for many of us, it does not matter as that is not where we have our being or live our lives, and this might be the case to some extent. Nevertheless, our argument would be that it matters because the screen increasingly dominates our lives and as such being-in-the-world might become transformed into being-in-the-screen, without us even thinking about it or agreeing to it. With the prevalence of screens (or screening), we might be sleepwalking into a very different kind of subjectivity and sociality. That is, it might not only become the dominant way of being, but it might also become the only way of being *that matters*—even as we struggle to disentangle ourselves from the screen. It might indeed have already transformed, in unimaginable ways, what it means to be human, individually and collectively. Can we escape its force, one might ask? Perhaps, but also perhaps not. To return to Heidegger (1977), technology is never a mere instrument. It is always and already a way of being in the world. Perhaps being-in-the-screen is merely the culmination of a particular calculative mindset in which our being has become a resource, on standby, not really for us, but rather for an algorithmic other no longer at our bidding.

References

Arendt, Hannah. 1971. 'Thinking and Moral Considerations: A Lecture'. *Social Research* 38 (3): 417–446.
Arendt, Hannah. 2006. *Eichmann in Jerusalem: A Report on the Banality of Evil*. 1 edition. New York: Penguin Classics.
Arendt, Hannah. 2009. *The Promise of Politics*. New York: Knopf Doubleday Publishing Group.
Bruner, Jerome. 1991. 'The Narrative Construction of Reality'. *Critical Inquiry* 18 (1): 1–21.
Chun, Wendy H. K. 2018. 'Queerying Homophily'. In *Pattern Discrimination*, edited by Clemens Apprich, Wendy H. K. Chun, Florian Cramer, and Hito Steyerl, 59–98. Minneapolis: University of Minnesota Press.
Cialdini, Robert. 2009. *Influence: The Psychology of Persuasion*. Revised edition. New York: HarperCollins Publishers.
Flaxman, Seth, Sharad Goel, and Justin M. Rao. 2016. 'Filter Bubbles, Echo Chambers, and Online News Consumption'. *Public Opinion Quarterly* 80 (1): 298–320.
Flusser, Vilém. 2002. *Writings*. Edited by Andreas Ströhl. Translated by Erik Eisel. Minneapolis: University of Minnesota Press.
Flusser, Vilém. 2011. *Into the Universe of Technical Images*. Electronic Mediations, v. 32. Minneapolis: University of Minnesota Press.
Franck, Georg. 2019. 'The Economy of Attention'. *Journal of Sociology* 55 (1): 8–19.
Heidegger, Martin. 1962. *Being and Time*. Translated by John Macquarrie and Edward Robinson. Oxford: Blackwell Pub.
Heidegger, Martin. 1976. *What Is Called Thinking?* Reprint edition. New York: Harper Perennial.
Heidegger, Martin. 1977. *The Question Concerning Technology, and Other Essays*. Translated by William Lovitt. New York: Harper and Row.
Ingold, Tim. 2015. *The Life of Lines*. Milton Park, Abingdon, Oxon ; New York, NY: Routledge.
Introna, Lucas D. 2016. 'The Algorithmic Choreography of the Impressionable Subject'. In *Algorithmic Cultures: Essays on Meaning, Performance and New Technologies*, edited by Robert Seyfert and Jonathan Roberge, 26–51. Oxford ; New York: Routledge.
Introna, Lucas D., and Fernando M. Ilharco. 2006. 'On the Meaning of Screens: Towards a Phenomenological Account of Screenness'. *Human Studies* 29 (1): 57–76. https://doi.org/10.1007/s10746-005-9009-y
Lévinas, Emmanuel. 1985. *Ethics and Infinity*. Translated by Philippe Nemo. Pittsburgh: Duquesne University Press.
Lovink, Geert. 2019. *Sad by Design: On Platform Nihilism*. London: Pluto Press.
Mcluhan, Marshall. 1964. *Understanding Media: The Extensions of Man*. New York: McGraw-Hill.
McLuhan, Marshall, and Quentin Fiore. 2008. *The Medium Is the Massage: An Inventory of Effects*. 1st edition. London: Penguin Classics.
Ong, Walter J. 1982. *Orality and Literacy: The Technologizing of the Word*. New edition. London and New York: Routledge.
Rushkoff, Douglas. 2013. *Present Shock: When Everything Happens Now*. New York: Penguin Books.

Chapter 20

Race, Gender, and Visibility on Social Media

Megan Rim

In June 2021, a group of Black creators on the social media platform TikTok went on strike using the hashtag #BlackTikTokStrike. The strike originated on Dance TikTok, a corner of the app that largely consists of videos of original choreography, and dance challenges or covers. Black TikTokers organized the strike to coincide with the release of Megan Thee Stallion's summer single "Thot Shit." They refrained from choreographing any dance challenges despite the enormous potential for virality—three of Megan Thee Stallion's projects, Savage, Body, and a feature on Cardi B's WAP, had been used in viral challenges in 2020 resulting in her becoming TikTok's most listened to artist of the year (Millman 2020).

The strike's catalyst was both the ongoing cultural appropriation and the devaluation of Black cultural labor. According to TikTok creator George Lee, "Black cultural products are highly valued, but we are not valued as cultural producers" (Mitchell 2021). On TikTok, Black creators had already criticized the app's distribution of visibility as several users reported suspicion of their accounts being shadow-banned after posting Black Lives Matter content. In addition, TikTok had come under fire during the George Floyd protests for displaying hashtags such as #BlackLivesMatter and #GeorgeFloyd at 0 view counts despite both hashtags being used by videos that were bringing in millions of views (Shead 2020), a case where the platform's distribution of visibility did not match up with the actual visibility that was being achieved. The #BlackTikTokStrike hashtag highlights the plight of Black creatives who had watched a host of young white women and teenage girls, including top TikTok stars Charli d'Amelio and Addison Rae, attain social media stardom and the material benefits that come with it through performing their dances while they received little to no compensation and often not even credit in return. D'Amelio's most famous dance cover video features her performance of the "Renegade" dance to the song Lottery (Renegade) by K Camp. As the video and dance challenge went viral, the dance became synonymous with d'Amelio and she was eventually labeled the "CEO of Renegade." Meanwhile, few on the app knew that the original creator of the dance was in fact Jalaiah Harmon, a 14-year-old Black girl. Harmon struggled to gain credit for her work, while d'Amelio achieved social media stardom.

I start with this phenomenon to highlight two important aspects of social media use that I will explore in relation to race and gender in this chapter—visibility and labor. While social media platforms purport to offer different experiences from each other, visibility operates as a key aspect of how most of them structure participation on their site or app. Negotiating this potential for visibility and the algorithmic apparatuses that mete it out has spawned an industry around its commodification and led to the rise of influencer culture. Influencers and other social media professionals have built careers on and around platforms. However, as the #BlackTikTokStrike exposes how monetization happens and who is able to profit it often follows familiar patterns of marginalization. This chapter engages with some of the recent social media scholarship in order to discuss what the #BlackTikTokStrike reveals

DOI: 10.4324/9781003189466-24

about how Black creators, and in particular Black women and girls, have to navigate visibility and labor on the TikTok app and social media as a whole.

Social Media Visibilities

The coming of age of social media platforms in the late 2000s and early 2010s offered the everyday user the promise of unprecedented visibility. While visibility has been a key element of all mass media technologies—the printing press, film, television, etc., it is a commodity that has often been tightly controlled and strategically granted by the few powerful and resourced who owned the means to produce content. In contrast, new media and especially social media at the time were popularly perceived as facilitating the democratization of access to visibility (Bucher 2012). However as social media enrollment grew and the volume of uploaded content exploded, platforms began to adopt design features such as timeline or newsfeed curation algorithms that would filter what users could see and therefore engage with based on complex and hidden formulas used to determine relevance and interest. New Media scholar, Taina Bucher (2012), argues that these algorithms operate as "architectures of visibility" (1178) that discipline users to behave on the platform in specific and normative ways under the "threat of invisibility" paired with the reward of visibility. That is, they condition users to understand that if they do not conform to "desired" modes of participation, they might risk being rendered algorithmically invisible to their online friends and followers. How algorithms curate user timelines and news feeds remains a mystery due in large part to the black-boxed nature of algorithms (Pasquale 2015) and thus users are required to constantly examine their own behaviors and their interactions on the platform for clues on how well they have understood the unspoken algorithmic expectations. And as social media platforms have updated and replaced their algorithms, so too have users had to continuously negotiate their visibility and invisibility in those spaces.

Additionally, platforms adopted features such as hashtags, originally a user-invented phenomenon (Brock 2012), that would allow users to search and engage in conversations in that space. While hashtagging was developed originally on Twitter, it is a practice that, alongside trending hashtag lists, has been adopted across numerous platforms, including Instagram, Tumblr, and TikTok. Going viral, the sudden amplification and visibility of a user or group's content and interactions to a larger audience, has not only become an increasing possibility, it has been designed for by the platforms through their adoption of design features such as hashtag searches and trending lists (Gillespie 2011). Whether positive or negative, the specter of virality and increased visibility structures user participation and behavior.

Hashtag Activism

During the summer of 2020 and in the midst of the Covid-19 pandemic, anti-racism and anti-police brutality protests erupted around the United States in response to the police killing of George Floyd, a Black Minnesotan man. Activists and community groups utilized digital platforms and social media to organize local protests, amplify their events, and network with other organizers. On the ground, protestors used their devices to share photos and videos, document police brutality, and connect with others online and in the crowds. Taking place during some of the most stringent state enforcement of social distancing measures, the rapidity of mobilization highlighted organizers' savvy use of social media to leverage their visibility and amplify their organizing. Much of this experience from digital networks had been forged in the Black Lives Matter racial justice movement of the previous decade which originated around the hashtag #BlackLivesMatter.

The hashtag #BlackLivesMatter, was created in 2013 by three queer Black women Alicia Garza, Patrisse Cullors, and Opal Tometti in the wake of George Zimmerman's acquittal for the murder of Trayvon Martin ("HerStory", n.d.). This hashtag came to mainstream visibility through its use during the August 2014 Ferguson protests surrounding the police murder of Mike Brown (Freelon et al. 2016). Jackson, Bailey, and Welles (2020) refer to this practice as "hashtag activism." Through hashtag activism, Black Lives Matter activists were not only able to bring to light individual cases of anti-Black police brutality; they were able to "link similar cases, illustrating how each is not an isolated incident but rather part of a system of violence against Black people" (Jackson, Bailey, Welles 2020, 131). Thus, the networked nature of hashtags has been key in exposing how Floyd, Brown, and Martin's death are part of a larger system of anti-Black violence. The Black Lives Matter movement's continued success at using hashtag activism and leveraging its visibility to raise awareness and mobilize the public has cemented its status as one of the largest social and racial justice movements in the history of the nation.

However, as the rise of another hashtag #SayHerName illustrates, this visibility is unevenly distributed within the Black Lives Matter movement particularly along gender lines. This hashtag, initially started by the African American Policy Forum (AAPF), was meant to highlight the sexual and physical violence perpetrated by law enforcement and the state on Black women, explicitly framed to be inclusive of transgender and gender-nonconforming identities (Crenshaw et al. 2015). In their 2015 report, the AAPF argue that where "Mike Brown, Eric Garner, and Tamir Rice have become household names" (Crenshaw et al. 2015, 1), virtually identical police killings of Black women have not received the same attention nor pressure for police accountability. They argue that an intersectional (Crenshaw 1990), Black feminist approach is necessary to have a fuller picture of the systems of violence and oppression Black people are facing in the United States.

Black Discursive Culture in White Digital Space

Hashtags on social media offer up forms of visibility that are facilitated both by technical affordances and by cultural practice. Crafting a hashtag is an act of creativity that requires discursive skills and a sophisticated understanding of one's audience. In his examination of "Black Twitter," Brock (2012) describes how Black users and conversations gained visibility through Twitter's introduction of hashtags and the trending topics list, design features that he contends are well-suited to Black discursive culture. In particular, he ties the ways Black users approached hashtags to the Black discursive and performative practice of signifyin', which Brock describes as "an articulation of a shared world view" (533). However, increased visibility of Black hashtags also engendered an increased scrutiny of Black users and "Black Twitter" by users outside the group. He highlights the ways that the emergent visibility of Black users and culture on social media platforms in the late 2000s to early 2010s was seen as both surprising and monolithic by the mainstream.

In his recent book, Brock (2020) defines Black Twitter as "an online gathering (not quite a community) of Twitter users who identify as Black and employ Twitter features to perform Black discourses, share Black cultural commonplaces and build social affinities" (80). However, he argues that the early conversations around "Black Twitter" by non-Black commentators revealed reductive thinking around Black digital literacies and their assumption of Twitter as a white space by default. Ultimately, Brock illustrates how during this moment of emergent visibility, Black users were racialized by the white mainstream as nonnormative users.

According to Williams, Byrant, and Carvell (2019), navigating this kind of racialization and racism within the default white spaces of digital media is a form of "uncompensated emotional labor" for people of color. They define "uncompensated emotional labor" as

> a process of conscious or unconscious emotion regulation in the course of everyday interactions with others to engender or ensure their emotional comfort . . . [which] is closely tied to one's social status and continued good standing in the social networks in which they participate.
>
> (Williams, Bryant, and Carvell 2019, 11–12)

They explicitly tie this labor to the racialized standards of "civility" and the often expected labor of educating white people in online spaces about racism what Adair and Nakamura (2017) describe as "vernacular digital pedagogy." Where this educational work takes place, Black users and other users of color are often expected to share personal stories in a way that both appeals to their white peers' sense of empathy while presenting their emotional response in a way that is perceived as unthreatening (Williams, Byrant, and Carvell 2018).

While both Black men and women engage in "uncompensated emotional labor," it is a type of reproductive labor (Nakamura 2015), the work most often associated with domesticity and traditionally performed by women and therefore not acknowledged as labor despite its essential role within capitalism. According to Nakamura (2015), educating others about racism and sexism is part of the "venture community management" labor that women of color perform online, which includes activities like calling out racism and misogyny and working as unofficial content moderators in order to create less toxic online spaces. She highlights how this uncompensated labor by women of color contributes to platforms' abilities to generate profit and states that digital reproductive labor is "required to make the platforms fun, easy, and safe to use" (108) but is also "feminized, devalued, ultimately offshored for pay, and borne by volunteers" (Nakamura 2015, 108).

It is the devaluation of this labor that easily elides the significant contributions of women of color, and especially Black women or, even worse, misattributes their labor to somebody else. Bailey and Trudy (2018) describe this as a consequence of "misogynoir," a term Bailey had coined to describe "an historical anti-Black misogyny and a problematic intraracial gender dynamic that ha[s] wider implication in popular culture" (762). In addition to Bailey's scholarship, Trudy (@theTrudz) an independent writer and prominent social media commentator, significantly contributed to the early theorization of the term and helped popularize its use on social media spaces. Ironically, while "misogynoir" has since entered the mainstream vernacular through its use in digital spaces such that it has been famously used by celebrities such as Katy Bailey and Trudy (2018), Bailey and Trudy have often found themselves uncredited for their creation and theorization of it. They contend that this invisibility is itself also misogynoir (Bailey and Trudy 2018). For Trudy, this is part of a larger issue of erasure and theft that she faces as a Black woman creating content on the internet. She describes watching journalists and academics use her theorizations without citation for paid writing opportunities, opportunities that she ostensibly might have gotten instead.

> I write independently and without mainstream media, academic or corporate support and without the accompanying social status, yet I have an extremely visible presence in social media spaces—I face the phenomenon of people plagiarizing my work in very public and grotesque ways.
>
> (Bailey and Trudy 2018, 765)

As a Black woman content creator, Trudy is rendered both invisible and hypervisible in ways that allow those in the mainstream to easily exploit her work and discount it as labor.

TikTok and the Virality of Black Dance

In March 2021, Addison Rae went on the Jimmy Fallon show and performed a medley of viral TikTok dance trends without acknowledging the creators and choreographers of the original dances. The majority of the dances had been created by Black dancers, including Keara Wilson, 19, choreographer of the "Savage" dance, and Mya Johnson, 15, and Chris Cotter, 13, co-choreographers of the "Up" dance. The appearance sparked a wave of criticism from people who questioned why Rae and not the Black creators of the dance trends had been invited to perform on such a major stage. Speaking about Rae's performance, Johnson expressed happiness at seeing her and Cotter's moves on stage. However, she also frames it as an opportunity for gaining visibility that is taken away from her and the other uncredited creators, "I started to feel like it should have been our time to do that...I just felt like that would have been our time to shine" (Romano 2021).

Black creators have long held that TikTok dances created and popularized by them have in fact been most profitable for young white women and teenage girls like d'Amelio and Rae. Following the popularity of her Renegade video as well as a slew of other popular dance covers, the then 16-year-old d'Amelio dominated the TikTok statistics and eventually became the most followed creator on the app with a staggering 124.4 million followers. Rae ranked third with 84.3 million followers. D'Amelio and Rae have successfully managed to translate their TikTok popularity into mainstream visibility and legibility. Significantly, both have been able to get jobs in film and television with Rae recently starring in the Netflix movie, *He's All That*, and d'Amelio and her family scoring a reality TV show, *The D'Amelio Show*, on Hulu.

The #BlackTikTokStrike is not about d'Amelio and Rae exactly, although both are referenced as examples of what Black creators are left out of. It is about how platforms distribute visibility and therefore the ability to profit off of one's creative labor. Erick Louis, the young Black creator credited with starting the #BlackTikTokStrike hashtag, states the issue as that of a racial disparity between the ways that Black creators and white creators are treated on TikTok despite the immense value their participation generates for the app. Louis argues, "We drive all this traffic to the app–. We run the trends, we run all the subcategories, yet we're not propped up in the same ways that a lot of these white content creators are" (Chan 2021). Louis's argument speaks to the ways that TikTok and other social media platforms have profited from Black discursive culture (Brock 2012) and uncompensated digital reproductive labor.

While Harmon had originally posted the Renegade dance on Instagram, often cited as the most Influencer-centric platform (Abidin 2016; Cotter 2019), she began to see her dance go viral on TikTok after the user @global.jones used it in a dance challenge in October 2019. Speaking to the New York Times, Harmon expressed pleasure at seeing her dance take off in such a way; however, she was well aware that the lack of attribution meant losing out on something more than just views. Addressing these missed opportunities, Harmon said, "I think I could have gotten money for it, promos for it, I could have gotten famous off it, get noticed . . . I don't think any of that stuff has happened for me because no one knows I made the dance" (Lorenz 2020).

The exclusion of Black creators and especially Black women and teenage girl creators from the opportunities to profit from their own work is unfortunately part of a long tradition of cultural appropriation and exploitative labor practices that extends back to the transatlantic slave trade. Particularly in the arena of dance, Black women have found that moves and dance styles that originated in their spaces and that they had been performing long before only gained mainstream visibility and in some cases acceptability when white women began appropriating them. Halliday (2020) explores this phenomenon in relation to "twerking," a dance move which she connects to "Black diasporic dance practices" as well as early 2000s Black popular music and culture. She points out that it was only when Miley Cyrus began prominently adopting the move in her performances in 2015, that the word officially entered the U.S. vernacular. Halliday ties Black forms of dance to the bodies of Black women. She argues that twerking is an example of "Black girls' embodied knowledge," and she connects the practice of Black women and girls posting twerking videos with the reclamation of the bodies of Black women and girls from the gaze of white supremacy. Thus where Harmon, Jackson, and Wilson's labor is erased so too is the embodied knowledge they express in their performance indicative of the ways in which mainstream culture invisibilizes Black women while appropriating their cultural labor and knowledge.

Influencers and the Gendered and Racialized Labor of Visibility

Banet-Weiser (2018) argues that we are currently operating within economies of visibility in which "visibility becomes the end rather than a means to an end" (23). An economy of visibility in this context is disconnected from the political goals of feminist visibility and is instead interested in the commodification of the bodies of primarily white, heteronormative, cisgendered women. This kind of commodification drives influencer marketing. Abidin (2020) argues that while online visibility is essential for the Influencer, not every kind of visibility or internet celebrity has the potential to be profitable. She presents the issue as one of racial disparity and "where internet celebrity represents the quality of an online user's visibility, an Influencer is a monetizable status and potential careers as a result of their internet celebrity" (79). The influencer is thus the product of immense self-branding and self-curation work (Marwick 2013) aimed at achieving a longevity of visibility not conferred by the ephemeral structures of viral attention. In such an economy of visibility, users are encouraged to "play the visibility game" which is how Cotter (2019) describes the ways that influencers continually interpret and navigate how algorithms are determining their level of visibility to their audiences. This visibility is the lifeblood of the influencer but only certain kinds of visibility are perceived as profitable in the marketing industry.

Banet-Weiser (2021) contends that "authenticity" or rather the perception of authenticity has become a required component for successful influencer branding. She highlights the pressure on influencers and especially those that are young women to conform to the highest standards of "dominant white ideals of femininity" (43), while also performing relatability and failure. This tension requires women to exert enormous effort to carefully curate or brand their image, which Banet-Weiser describes as "the labor of authenticity." Banet-Weiser's analysis of white beauty standards is not a universal law, as evidenced by the existence of Black and other creators of color who have managed to forge careers as influencers. However, it does point to a significant bias within the system that privileges young, white women who meet certain conventional, Western beauty standards.

This gendered and racialized "labor of authenticity" is something that d'Amelio is exceptionally good at. Monroe (2020) writes in a profile of d'Amelio for the Atlantic that, "Charli's appeal is tied to her ability to be both relatable and aspirational. She manages to telegraph an ordinary kind of specialness ... her fans appreciate that she dances in a way that's approachable." And yet, this approachability is the product of an incredible amount of labor. A Washington Post article describes d'Amelio coming up with choreography for a national campaign in her bedroom after her math homework and having days full of meetings and appearances (Andrews 2020). Even prior to her viral success, d'Amelio's "approachable" dance style is the result of consistent dance training from the age of three.

While Harmon has expressed surprise at the immense success of her dance, which Variety declared "the most viral dance the internet had ever seen" (Zukin 2020), it was also the product of years of focus and hard work. She has been a dancer for most of her life with her sights already set on becoming a professional dancer and choreographer, a goal that she has maintained throughout her experiences with "Renegade" (Wicker 2020). In addition to her significant dance and choreography training, Harmon performs extensive social media research and labor as part of her creative process. According to her New York Times profile, she "is also building a career online, studying viral dances, collaborating with peers and posting original choreography" (Lorenz 2020). The virality of Renegade could thus in part be attributed to Harmon's savvy ability to "play the visuality game" (Cotter 2019).

However, within the algorithmic and discursive structures of TikTok's platform, Harmon paradoxically experienced increasing invisibility as the visibility of her own creation grew. She describes trying to get credit for her dance for months by making her own TikTok account, commenting on people's posts, and reaching out to influencers performing her dance and asking to be tagged to no avail. In an interview with Variety, she shares:

> I started seeing the dance on TikTok and I just saw people doing it without giving me any credit. I tried to comment under people's posts saying it was me, but nobody would believe me because I wasn't really that famous on TikTok. When Charli [d'Amelio] and everybody else started doing it, it became more viral and people started to know what the dance was, but they didn't know who created it
>
> (Zukin 2020)

Where Harmon continued to engage with the platform to reclaim her labor, her lack of platform visibility and influence was perceived as inauthenticity and further invisibilized her.

Erasure and the Memetic Transformation of Black Labor

D'Amelio had not meant to take credit for Harmon's dance, but had no idea who to credit when she'd uploaded the video as attributional practices had not yet solidified on the app (Monroe 2020). She has since taken pains to recognize Harmon for her creative labor after finding out about her erasure and Harmon has explicitly voiced that she does not blame d'Amelio. However, the fact remains that Harmon's success on the app is but a fraction of d'Amelio's. Harmon was only able to receive due credit after her story was shared in the New York Times in February 2020, several months after the "Renegade" dance had started trending and established d'Amelio as "Renegade CEO" (Lorenz 2020) and after the peak of its virality. Harmon's predicament is in fact part of a larger platform issue for TikTok around authorship and memetic spread. In their study of authorship and misattribution of audio content on TikTok, Kaye et al. (2021) argue that TikTok as a platform particularly facilitates creatively reusing, altering, and adding onto other people's content without a strong affordance for ensuring proper attribution. This is due in large part to the app's organization around the "use this sound feature" which allows users to create videos using shared sounds or aural memes (Abidin 2021; Kaye et al. 2021). According to Shifman (2014), memes are "circulated, imitated, and/or transformed via the Internet by many users" (8). This process of "memeification" creates opportunities for both misattribution and/or erasure as each succeeding video offers their own take on the previous one whether by technical alteration or performance. Kaye et al. (2021) highlight TikTok dance challenges as exceptionally ideal for memetic spread because of the ways that users can play with both the sound and chore-ography. As TikTok's "use this sound" feature organizes video according to views and likes, d'Amelio's memetic visibility was rewarded with more visibility.

Memetic culture is steeped in histories of racial and gendered violence. In Nakamura's (2014) examination of the memetic spread of scambaiting trophy images, photographs of African scammers in demeaning positions extracted by vigilante users, she argues that, "memes that depict the black body in abject and bizarre poses and situations are part of the long history of viral racism that spreads using user and audience labor" (260). Her analysis of the spread of these racist photographs illuminates how the memetic circulation of racism is part of the activity that animates digital spaces. Memes, therefore, are one way that racism is profitable for platforms and some users. Halliday (2018) contends that "memes promote the objectification and spectacularity of Black women's body to get likes, shares, and eventually money" (69). Discussing the violent and appropriative treatment of Nicki Minaj's body in memes, Halliday (2018) reveals how the memetic use of Minaj's body served white women like Miley Cyrus, who has repeatedly appropriated Black styles of dress and dance. She also illustrates how the memeification of Minaj's body obscured her original artistic vision, highlighting how memetic play and circulation contribute to the erasure of Black women's creative labor. Thus, the ease with which white influencers like d'Amelio are able to profit off of cultural products of Black creative labor might be seen as endemic to the ways in which TikTok encourages memetic play.

Conclusion

As the scholarship on Black Twitter and the Black Lives Matter movement illuminates, Black users and content creators are not only using social media platforms with extreme technical proficiency and discursive skill to successfully play the visibility game. Black women, trans, and non-binary users have invested and continue to invest immense amounts of labor into creating hashtags as well as educating others about racism and concepts (e.g. misogynoir), and producing work that improves users' experience in digital spaces. However, this comes at an emotional cost as the visibility engenders a policing of their emotions and is largely uncompensated. While these skills represent the desired components of an influencer, Black women and girl content creators (e.g. Harmon) have also found themselves left out of the conversation and rendered invisible, while their creations have been vehicles for white female influencers to achieve incredible viral success and financial compensation. Where white female influencers are encouraged to show emotion and vulnerability to enact the labor of authenticity, Black girls and women are neither allowed to show emotion nor achieve profitable visibility. For them, the visibility game is often rigged toward a permanent invisibility when it comes to receiving compensation for their labor on social media.

The issues raised by #BlackTikTokStrike highlight the forms of racialized and gendered labor required under TikTok and other social media platforms' current regimes of visibility and capitalism, including the creative labor that produces profit for platforms, the labor of visibility (Abidin 2016, Banet-Weiser 2018, Cotter 2020), the uncompensated emotional labor of navigating white spaces (Williams, Bryant, and Carvell 2019) and contending with racism, sexism, and misogynoir (Bailey and Trudy 2018) within those extractive systems, the venture community management labor (Nakamura 2015) of calling out racism and "make[ing] the platforms fun, easy, and safe to use" (108) and educating audiences about the structural inequalities and experiences that prompted the #BlackTikTokStrike. As TikTok continues to develop as a space for memetic play, creativity, and digital labor, further scholarship is needed to critically examine its racial and gendered dimensions.

References

Abidin, Crystal. 2016. "Visibility Labour: Engaging with Influencers' Fashion Brands And# OOTD Advertorial Campaigns on Instagram." *Media International Australia* 161 (1): 86–100.

Abidin, Crystal. 2020. "Mapping Internet Celebrity on TikTok: Exploring Attention Economies and Visibility Labours." *Cultural Science Journal* 12, no. 1: 73–103.

Adair, Cassius, and Lisa Nakamura. 2017. "The Digital Afterlives of This Bridge called My Back: Woman of Color Feminism, Digital Labor, and Networked Pedagogy." *American Literature* 89, no. 2: 255–278.

Andrews, Travis. 2020. "Charli D'Amelio Is TikTok's Biggest Star. She Has No Idea Why." *Washington Post*, May 26, 2020. https://www.washingtonpost.com/technology/2020/05/26/charli-damelio-tiktok-star/

Bailey, Moya, and Trudy. 2018. "On Misogynoir: Citation, Erasure, and Plagiarism." *Feminist Media Studies* 18 (4): 762–768.

Banet-Weiser, Sarah. 2018. *Empowered: Popular Feminism and Popular Misogyny*. Durham, NC: Duke University Press.

Banet-Weiser, Sarah. 2021. "Gender, Social Media, and the Labor of Authenticity." *American Quarterly* 73, no. 1: 141–144.

Bucher, Taina. 2012. "Want to be on the Top? Algorithmic Power and the Threat of Invisibility on Facebook." *New Media & Society* 14, no. 7: 1164–1180.

Brock, André. 2012. "From the Blackhand Side: Twitter as a Cultural Conversation." *Journal of Broadcasting & Electronic Media* 56, no. 4: 529–549.

Brock, André. 2020. *Distributed Blackness*. New York: New York University Press.

Chan, J. Clara. 2021. "Black TikTok Creators Grapple With How Far to Take Strike: 'Why Should We Have to Leave?'" *The Hollywood Reporter (blog)*. July 28, 2021. https://www.hollywoodreporter.com/business/digital/tiktok-strike-1234988427/

Cotter, Kelley. 2019. "Playing the Visibility Game: How Digital Influencers and Algorithms Negotiate Influence on Instagram." *New Media & Society* 21, no. 4: 895–913.

Crenshaw, Kimberle. 1990. "Mapping the Margins: Intersectionality, Identity Politics, and Violence against Women of Color." *Stanford Law Review* 43: 1241.

Crenshaw, Kimberlé, Andrea Ritchie, Rachel Anspach, Rachel Gilmer, and Luke Harris. 2015. "Say Her Name: Resisting Police Brutality against Black Women." *African American Policy Forum*. http://hdl.handle.net/20.500.11990/1926

Freelon, Deen, Charlton D. McIlwain, and Meredith Clark. Forthcoming (2016). "Beyond the Hashtags:# Ferguson, # Blacklivesmatter, and the Online Struggle for Offline Justice." Center for Media & Social Impact, American University.

Gillespie, Tarleton. 2011. "Can an Algorithm be Wrong? Twitter Trends, the Specter of Censorship, and Our Faith in the Algorithms Around Us." *Culture Digitally* 19: 1.

Halliday, Aria S. 2018. "Miley, What's Good?: Nicki Minaj's Anaconda, Instagram Reproductions, and Viral Memetic Violence." *Girlhood studies* 11, no. 3: 67–83.

Halliday, Aria S. 2020. "Twerk Sumn!: Theorizing Black Girl Epistemology in the Body." *Cultural Studies* 34, no. 6: 874–891.

"HerStory." n.d. *Black Lives Matter*. https://blacklivesmatter.com/herstory/

Jackson, Sarah J., Moya Bailey, and Brooke Foucault Welles. 2020. *# HashtagActivism: Networks of Race and Gender Justice*. Cambridge, MA: MIT Press.

Kaye, D. Bondy Valdovinos, Aleesha Rodriguez, Katrin Langton, and Patrik Wikstrom. 2021. "You Made This? I Made This: Practices of Authorship and (Mis) Attribution on TikTok." *International journal of communication (Online)*: 3195–3216.

Marwick, Alice E. 2013. *Status Update: Celebrity, Publicity, and Branding in the Social Media Age*. New Haven, CT: Yale University Press.

Millman, Ethan. 2020. "Megan Thee Stallion Is TikTok's Most Listened-To Artist in 2020." *Rolling Stone*. December 16, 2020. https://www.rollingstone.com/pro/news/tiktok-megan-thee-stallion-year-end-2020-1104458/

Mitchell, Taiyler Simone. 2021. "'They Take Our Dances.' Black Users Demand TikTok Combat Cultural Appropriation." *Insider*. September 21, 2024. https://www.insider.com/black-creators-call-out-tiktok-for-financial-loss-from-appropriation-2021-8

Monroe, Rachel. 2020. "98 Million TikTok Followers Can't Be Wrong." *The Atlantic*. November 19, 2021. https://www.theatlantic.com/magazine/archive/2020/12/charli-damelio-tiktok-teens/616929/

Lorenz, Taylor. 2020. "The Original Renegade." *The New York Times*. February 13, 2020, sec. Style. https://www.nytimes.com/2020/02/13/style/the-original-renegade.html

Lorenz, Taylor, and Laura Zornosa. 2021. "Are Black Creators Really on 'Strike' From TikTok?" *The New York Times*. June 25, 2021, sec. Style. https://www.nytimes.com/2021/06/25/style/black-tiktok-strike.html

Nakamura, Lisa. 2015. "The Unwanted Labour of Social Media: Women of Colour Call Out Culture as Venture Community Management." *New Formations* 86, no. 86: 106–112.

Nakamura, Lisa. 2014. "'I WILL DO EVERYthing That Am Asked': Scambaiting, Digital Show-Space, and the Racial Violence of Social Media." *Journal of Visual Culture* 13, no. 3: 257–274.

Pasquale, Frank. 2015. *The Black Box Society*. Cambridge, MA: Harvard University Press.

Romano, Nick. 2021. "Jimmy Fallon Addresses Addison Rae TikTok Dance Controversy by Shining Spotlight on Creators." *EW.Com*. April 6, 2021. https://ew.com/tv/jimmy-fallon-addison-rae-tiktok-dance-controversy-creators-video/

Shead, Sam. 2020. "TikTok Apologizes after Being Accused of Censoring #BlackLivesMatter Posts." *CNBC*. June 2. https://www.cnbc.com/2020/06/02/tiktok-blacklivesmatter-censorship.html

Shifman, Limor. 2014. *Memes in Digital Culture*. Cambridge, MA: MIT Press.

Wicker, Jewel. 2020. "Renegade Creator Jalaiah Harmon Is Taking Back the Dance the Internet Took From Her." *Teen Vogue*. April 15, 2020. https://www.teenvogue.com/story/jalaiah-harmon-renegade-creator-viral-dance

Williams, Apryl A., Zaida Bryant, and Christopher Carvell. 2019. "Uncompensated Emotional Labor, Racial Battle Fatigue, and (in) Civility in Digital Spaces." *Sociology Compass* 13, no. 2: e12658.

Zukin, Meg. 2020. "A Joint Interview with 14-Year-Old Jalaiah Harmon, Who Invented the Most Famous Dance on TikTok, and Her Mom." *Variety (blog)*. August 5, 2020. https://variety.com/2020/digital/news/jalaiah-harmon-renegade-tik-tok-1234726503/

Chapter 21

Fake News

There's No App for Truthfulness

Axel Gelfert

Introduction

Human beings are social animals, and as such we constantly depend on others. As children, we depend on our parents, or those who take care of us, for nourishment and protection. As we grow up, we make friends, expand our social circle, learn more about the world, and become more independent – or so we would like to think. The more we know about the world, and the more we acquire skills through training and being instructed by others, the less we eventually depend on the good will of specific others. But consider how we have acquired all this knowledge: by trusting others, accepting their word, following the advice of instructors, relying on institutions such as the school system, and tapping into the rich world of information offered to us by the media. Whatever autonomy we gain as we grow into competent members of modern, technologically mediated societies is acquired against the backdrop of a pervasive *epistemic dependence* on others.

Over time, humans developed means to exchange information more efficiently, from the emergence of the first writing systems to today's high-tech information infrastructures. Immanuel Kant, writing in the early 1780s, notes that 'due to postal service, the gigantic increase in rumors has been stopped' (1992: 344), since it allowed people to correspond with each other without intermediaries who would embellish their reports along the way. In the nineteenth century, newspapers became the first 'mass medium'; in the twentieth century, broadcasting followed in the form of radio and TV, setting the tone for journalism in Western liberal democracies, and the last 30 years have seen digital technologies and the internet take pride of place in the global information economy.

No technology for collecting and disseminating information about the world is immune to error, bias, and manipulation, and worries about the reliability of the reports we receive from others are as old as human sociality. Under conditions of deep uncertainty, rumors often emerge spontaneously as a mechanism of collective sense-making, and when they find their way into established news media, their audiences may end up believing all sorts of falsehoods. Interestingly, the mere exposure to far-fetched claims alone – even when they are not presented as a fact, but merely as a speculative hypothesis – is often enough to bring about belief, or so social psychologists have found. So strong is the link between *comprehending* and *believing* a claim that a group of psychologists titled their paper: 'You Can't Not Believe Everything You Read' (Gilbert, Tafaroodi and Malone 1993). Even if this is a slight exaggeration, it seems clear that, in an age of information overload, it becomes ever more challenging to separate the wheat from the chaff and tell legitimate information apart from misinformation and fake news.

DOI: 10.4324/9781003189466-25

'Fake News': Old Wine in New Bottles?

In the late 1990s, a new type of satirical news shows, exemplified by *The Daily Show* (1996–) and *The Colbert Report* (2004–2015), and satirical websites such as *The Onion* set out to lampoon the biases and dysfunctions of an increasingly fact-free political discourse. The goal of such 'fake news shows' was not so much to mislead as to entertain, and to sensitize their viewers to the real-world biases and blind spots of the corporate news media. The career of the term 'fake news' took a sharp pivot during the 2016 U.S. presidential campaign, when misleading websites, often with seemingly established-sounding names (such as the 'Denver Guardian' or the 'National Report'), sprung up and peddled false claims about political actors, notably about Donald Trump's opponent, Hillary Clinton (see Gelfert 2018). Whether or not a substantial number of these websites were supported by foreign governments remains a contested issue; how much of an affect of such (foreign or domestic) interference has had on electoral outcomes is almost impossible to tell.

Since 2016, there has been much public and academic debate about the nature of 'fake news', and the extent to which it poses a threat to democracy. The term is now often mobilized as a partisan label for any form of inconvenient reporting, and in some authoritarian countries, anti-'fake news' legislation has served as a pretext for cracking down on legitimate opposition (see Section 3). The COVID-19 pandemic, which wreaked havoc from 2020 onward, showed that fake news in the form of medical misinformation – e.g., peddling veterinary drugs as 'miracle cures' for COVID-19 – could pose a serious public health hazard. Unsurprisingly, there exists a close affinity between fake news, pseudoscience, and conspiracy theorizing.

Maybe, then, 'fake news' is really nothing new at all, but simply a ragbag of unwholesome techniques of persuasion, such as lying, deception, propaganda, disinformation, bullshit, and the like? All of these are well-known and have been studied extensively, and one might wonder what warrants introducing a new term. Indeed, some critics have denied the need for a separate category of 'fake news' for precisely that reason: as Joshua Habgood-Coote writes, the term 'fake news' has at best 'a use as a catch-all for bad information', which is why we should 'stop talking about fake news' (Habgood-Coote 2019). Yet, do our traditional concepts really capture what is novel about the kinds of developments that talk of 'fake news' is referring to? Is the algorithmic promotion of a falsehood really the same as lying (which by definition involves a specific agent, the liar, who intends to deceive his audience)? Is the political microtargeting of specific voter groups on social media conceptually the same as the propaganda campaigns of the twentieth century, which relied heavily on mass media broadcasting?

If we assimilate everything we see around us to traditional concepts and categories, we may well end up missing out on genuinely new aspects. One such aspect is the convergence of social, political, and technological trends in ways that, taken together, risk undermining the very institutions of knowledge – science, education, public debate – that we will need the most if we are to deal with the global existential challenges that lie ahead. Occam's Razor tells us that we should not multiply our entities and concepts unnecessarily: all things being equal, we should prefer a simpler explanation or characterization of a situation. Yet, when the world around us changes, things are no longer equal, and we should avoid oversimplification just as much as we should avoid overcomplicating matters. Instead of hastily dismissing the term 'fake news', let us be open to the possibility that it tells us something about the world we live in and, for this reason, give it a fair run for its money. This is what the next few sections will do.

Characteristics of Fake News

The term 'fake news' presupposes a notion of *news* (in the proper sense), and so it is reasonable to begin with a brief reflection on what we mean we speak of 'the news'. As an uncountable noun, the word 'news' is used to refer to information or reports about recent events, typically published or broadcast by an identifiable source. The proper unit of analysis, thus, would be a *news report*, which might reach its audience in written or spoken form (e.g., as an article on a news website or as a segment in a TV broadcast). A news report, as distinct from political commentary or an opinion piece, is intended as a factual assertion: it makes a factual claim about some state of affairs in the world and, at least implicitly, deems it significant – that is, *newsworthy* – to the target audience.

According to a widely held view in philosophy, assertion is governed by the knowledge norm, which holds that we must assert only what we know. In light of the journalistic pursuit of 'breaking news', it may be unrealistic to demand that a journalist must always be able to *guarantee*, or *vouch for*, the truth of her claims; yet, there is a legitimate expectation that journalists should make known any substantive counterevidence they are aware of – and should swiftly offer corrections of inadvertent errors or factual mistakes. If this sounds idealistic to contemporary ears, then this itself may tell us a little something about the pressures and dysfunctions of the news industry. For, in addition to simple human error, there are numerous other ways in which news reporting can fail – either intentionally or unintentionally – and these point to some of the core aspects of fake news.

Let us distinguish four dimensions, or aspects, of fake news, which have variously been seen as lying at the core of the concept. (This is not to say that there couldn't be other ways of characterizing fake news, but for now it is reasonable to discuss some of the more obvious characteristics of what makes something an instance of fake news.)

- First, there is the observation that fake news is not the kind of thing that we should be basing our beliefs on: it is epistemically deficient – e.g., because it is false or misleading. This is emphasized by authors who, for example, equate fake news with 'fabricated content that is 100% false' (see Wardle 2017).
- Second, fake news often reflects manipulative or deceptive intentions on the part of the speaker or source – if not the immediate source (e.g., your cranky uncle who shares a dubious Facebook post), then its original author (e.g., the conspiracy theorist who first made the claim on talk radio). If one takes this aspect to be the core feature of fake news, then it follows that fake news must always 'contain deliberately misleading elements' (Bakir and McStay 2018: 1).
- Third, fake news has sometimes been described, similar to rumor, by its distinctive function, namely that of securing its own circulation and uptake. An empirical study published in the journal *Science* found that fake news 'diffused significantly farther, faster, deeper, and more broadly than the truth in all categories of information' (Vosoughi, Roy and Aral 2018: 1146) – something which certainly calls for an explanation.
- Fourth, and perhaps most obviously, much of the debate about fake news has revolved around its medium: that is, the role of social media and the internet in enabling the easy generation and rapid circulation of false or misleading claims, in a format that is easy to mistake for legitimate news. This gives rise to characterizations of fake news such as 'the online publication of intentionally or knowingly false statements of fact' (Klein and Wueller 2017: 6).

Other potential characteristics of fake news – e.g., its use for propagandistic purposes – could easily be added to this list. As with any new term that emerges spontaneously from our messy social and political world, there is bound to be some degree of vagueness, and any attempt to settle the issue through stipulation will necessarily be controversial. This is why the discussion so far has studiously avoided talk of 'defining' fake news, but instead opted for a *characterization* of the phenomenon. After all, one should first reflect on, and try to understand, a phenomenon, before proposing a (provisional) definition.

In order to see this, let us consider these four dimensions in more detail. We will find that each condition, considered in insolation, is insufficient for fake news. Take the condition of being *false* or *misleading*. Even legitimate news – especially when it concerns breaking news and ongoing developments – will often contain falsehoods, if only as the result of an honest mistake. Yet, an honest mistake is not enough to render a news item a case of 'fake news'. When it comes to *intentions*, while we can easily think of blatant cases, such as propagandistic lies, it is by no means clear that the intention to maliciously deceive someone is a necessary condition. In fact, a conspiracy theorist who creates or circulates a fabricated claim may do so with the intention to convince her audience of a 'higher truth', and certainly many of those who do not create fake news, but merely share them on social media may do so in a misguided attempt to inform or enlighten others. It is customary to distinguish between *misinformation* and *disinformation*, where both refer to false or biased information, but only the latter involves an intention to deceive or mislead. It may then be tempting to regard fake news as just another kind of disinformation and to treat misinformation as consisting only of 'honest mistakes', so to speak. Sometimes, however, choosing processes of news aggregation and dissemination that could easily have been recognized as being systemically flawed and biased can also give rise to fake news, even if no explicit intention to deceive the audience is present on the part of those involved. Rather than *constituting* a kind of disinformation, fake news often (not always) serves as a *vehicle of* disinformation.

Continuing with our list of dimensions, or aspects, of the phenomenon of fake news and turning our attention to the more generalized *function* of fake news, the uses and goals of fake news seem a lot more varied. While it is true that fake news often propagates faster than truthful reports, aiming for widespread circulation – unlike in the case of rumor – does not seem to be constitutive of fake news. A rumor that ceases to circulate is no longer a rumor. By contrast, a piece of fake news that does not gain traction, perhaps because it is buried in the back pages of a newspaper, does not therefore cease to be a piece of fake news.

It is a common practice in philosophy to test a proposed definition against borderline cases or counterexamples. This also applies to attempted definitions of the term 'fake news'. For example, it has been suggested that fake news is simply 'bullshit asserted in the form of a news publication' (Mukerji 2018: 923) – where the term 'bullshit' is used in a technical sense due to Harry Frankfurt, namely as referring to assertions that (a) are indifferent to the truth and (b) try to conceal the fact of their indifference. (See Frankfurt 2005.) Yet, while *some* fake news no doubt is 'bullshit' in this sense, a lot of fake news *is* put forward in a deliberate effort to mislead or divert attention from inconvenient facts. Sometimes, not always, the producers of fake news really *are* like liars: they do care about the truth, but only insofar as they want to cover it up. While the 'bullshit' condition is dubious, the 'publication' condition – according to which fake news requires publication in (what looks like) a news publication – is shared by many definitions. Why else speak of fake *news*? This is why some authors take the fact that fake news 'piggy-backs' on established news to be central. Don Fallis and Kay Mathiesen have coined the term 'counterfeit news' in order to emphasize this aspect; on this view, a story is fake news 'if and only if it is not genuine news, but is presented as genuine news with the intention and propensity to deceive' (Fallis and Mathiesen 2019: 8).

Some of the most widely cited definitions emphasize the *systemic* aspect of fake news and argue that it is systemic flaws in the design of processes of news aggregation and dissemination that renders the products of these processes so biased or misleading that they merit the label 'fake news', even when they are not strictly false. There has also been a growing recognition that not all fake news is *propositional*, i.e. fully expressible in language. Keeping in mind the growing risk of *deepfakes* – synthetic images or videos that were created using artificial intelligence so as to convey the impression of visual 'proof' of events that, in reality, never happened – it makes sense to include not only verbal claims, but also other forms of news content. This has led to the following prospective definition: 'Fake news is the deliberate presentation of manipulative and misleading content as news, where the content is manipulative and misleading by design' (Gelfert 2021a: 320).

How Political Is Fake News?

Nothing so far entails that, necessarily, fake news is always political. (Except perhaps in the trivial sense that *everything* is political!) Yet, as it happens, the current wave of interest in the topic is deeply intertwined with political events, notably the controversial 2016 U.S. presidential elections and the U.K.'s 'Brexit' referendum the same year (which resulted in the U.K. leaving the European Union in 2020). Whether the outcome of either of these was swayed by fake news in the run-up to the vote is an open question, yet the political effects of fake news have generally been seen as going well beyond the outcome of specific votes. Fake news, it has been argued, erodes public trust, increases polarization, and is detrimental to democracy.

Political polarization contributes to the spread of fake news in multiple ways: first, it motivates the production of fake news in order to discredit political opponents through 'smear campaigns'. Second, as social psychologists have experimentally shown time and again, people tend to form beliefs in ways that reaffirm their own partisan identities, even if this means sacrificing accuracy (thereby compromising decision-making); partisan fake news is ideal fodder for such 'motivated cognition'. Third, a polarized political climate may lead to both selective exposure *and* general news avoidance, such that fake news, once acquired, cannot easily be corrected. All of this suggests that polarization is a driving force behind the creation and spread of fake news.

A certain degree of polarization even characterizes the philosophical debate about the term 'fake news'. On the one side are those who consider the circulation of fake news to constitute 'a serious threat to knowledge and democracy' (Fallis & Mathiesen 2019: 1); on the other side, there are those who consider worries about fake news a moral panic of sorts. For the latter, 'the problem is not fake news, it is the term "fake news"' (Coady 2019: 40). Far from being a useful 'exploratory concept' (Gelfert 2021b: 171), the term 'fake news' – so the argument goes – not only has no determinate meaning, but is instead being used as a political slur to discredit unfriendly reporting and alternative news sources. As evidence, critics of the term 'fake news' point to a distinct shift in usage, partly due to former U.S. president Donald Trump, who used the term 'fake news' to apply not only to specific claims, but to whole news organizations (as in 'CNN is fake news'). Behind this usage, some have argued, lies an attempt 'to delegitimize the institutional press as a whole' (Levi 2018: 234). The very label 'fake news' may thus become a 'rhetorical device used by the powerful to crush dissent' (Dentith 2017: 65).

Both fake news itself and the slandering of other (legitimate) reports *as* 'fake news' can serve propagandistic purposes. Following a classic distinction due to the French philosopher of technology Jacques Ellul, one may distinguish between *vertical* and *horizontal propaganda*. The designations 'vertical' and 'horizontal' refer to the assumed power differential between the affected parties. In vertical propaganda, those who occupy superior positions of power use their authority to influence 'the crowd below'; that is, the propagandists (who try to influence public opinion) are separate from those at whom the propaganda is directed. Think of concerted disinformation campaigns by state actors, e.g., in the run-up to a war or as part of long-term efforts to destabilize or discredit enemies abroad or within. This might take the form of *kompromat* (a Russian portmanteau word referring to 'compromising material'), e.g., private information about opposition figures which is deemed compromising and which is centrally collected over time, in order for it to be released whenever it suits the interests of the propagandists.

However, as Ellul argued, propaganda can also be horizontal, namely when it is not imposed in a top-down way, but is enacted among equals. Peer pressure and partisan loyalty can be powerful drivers that shape the beliefs of individuals. In some of the most blatant cases of fake news, what has puzzled external observers is that, even when a claim can be refuted first-hand – e.g., because it flatly contradicts direct observation or readily available historical records – partisan loyalists will continue to believe it. Indeed, obviously false claims may even be put forward as a test of individual partisan loyalty: in the case of 'blue lies', a falsehood is told on behalf of the in-group, and endorsing it – *in spite of* all the evidence to the contrary – becomes a performative exercise in strengthening the bonds within the group.

The Specific Harm of Fake News

Before tackling the question of what, if anything, should be done about fake news, we must get clearer about why fake news is objectionable in the first place. After all, we do not outlaw falsehoods in general, and we even encourage social practices – e.g., politeness – which are in tension with the unbridled pursuit of truth. Sometimes, telling the truth, the whole truth, and nothing but the truth – though important and valued in other contexts – is quite simply not the right thing to do. Does this mean that, perhaps, fake news is an entirely permissible, if somewhat unsavory social practice?

In order to appreciate how fake news not only falls short of epistemic standards, but also constitutes a moral problem, we need to recognize that there are different levels at which questions concerning the moral status of fake news can be raised. One such level has already featured repeatedly in the discussion in this chapter: the collective effect of fake news on the democratic polity. As a 2018 report of the European Commission's High Level Group on online disinformation puts it: 'The risk of harm includes threats to democratic political processes and values, which can specifically target a variety of sectors, such as health, science, education, finance, and more' (European Commission 2018: 4). The circulation of fake news – just like that of other misinformation – may lead to bad (individual or collective) decision-making, and might chip away at the perceived legitimacy of democratic political processes. When viewed from this angle, the moral status of fake news is to be assessed by the overall consequences of its creation and dissemination. A consequentialist approach of this sort also forces us to consider any unintended side effects that interventions aiming at the reduction of fake news – e.g., by curbing certain forms of free expression – might have. In the end, what matters is that we ought to bring about conditions that maximize the benefit for all; the practical difficulties of working out the utilitarian calculus behind such reasoning are, of course, enormous – and it is clear that such an approach leaves open the possibility that we may simply have to live with some 'background noise' of fake news.

At the other end of the spectrum, we may object to fake news primarily because of the malicious intentions of its purveyors. The most obvious example of intentionally deceiving an audience would be lying. When a speaker, who knows better, makes a false statement with the intent to deceive the hearer, he not only violates collective norms of assertion, but also exploits the hearer's trust; if done for nefarious purposes, e.g., in order to inflict further damage later on, this certainly exacerbates matters. However, cases of fake news often involve *misleading* an audience, rather than outright lying. Whether a clear moral distinction can be drawn between lying and misleading, is a matter of contention. Given that the only real difference is between whether the speaker says something he knows (or believes) to be false or whether he uses some other means to convey the same (false) belief, it is doubtful that this can ground a principled moral distinction. In both cases, the speaker violates his audience's autonomy by manipulating them into holding beliefs that, had the speaker been truthful, they would not have formed.

Calling someone a *liar* carries a lot of force and reflects a strong social prohibition against deliberately telling falsehoods. Used as an epithet, it can serve to impeach someone's character, as in the case of denigrating someone as a 'habitual liar' (when, let us assume, he is not). Arguably, the term 'fake news' can serve a similar function, especially when it is applied not to individual news items, but instead to whole news sources. Yet, beyond the potential use of the 'fake news' label as a cudgel with which to destroy an opponent's credibility, there is the very real question to what extent we ought to consider the epistemic character of a putative news source. Take the example of a (genuine) habitual liar, who comes to appreciate the wrongness of his ways and resolves to reform his character – for example, by keeping track of his lies, correcting them and making amends in other ways. Some virtue epistemologists would argue that, while the liar's resolve to reform his ways shows determination, it still does not amount to virtuous action, even when he resists his inner impulse and tells the truth. At the same time, someone who genuinely tries to better himself might be deserving of *some* praise and encouragement, even if the overall pattern of his behavior is still a far cry from that of a genuinely virtuous agent.

In professional settings, the vagueness and ambiguity that emerge from such tensions are often resolved by professional codes of ethics, i.e. formalized guidelines for ethical behavior, usually issued by professional organization. Whether such ethics codes are effective at resolving real-world moral dilemmas is doubtful (see Boeyink 1994); yet, they certainly draw attention to the moral responsibilities of journalists (even if they may not reach those who merely pass themselves off as professional journalists). Thinking of the specific harm of fake news solely at the individual level, in terms of violations of norms of truthfulness (and their negative consequences), risks leaving out the *systemic effects* of the prevalence of fake news. Given that fake news 'piggy-backs' on genuine news, typically emulating it in tone and appearance, exposure to the former may lead to an erosion of trust in the latter, i.e. in news media generally. This chips away at the very idea of the public sphere as a shared space of informed debate and deliberation on public issues.

Fake News: Ethics or Regulation?

How should we deal with fake news? This question can be posed at the individual and at the collective level: How should we *as individuals* respond when we have to reason to suspect that we are encountering a claim (or source) that amounts to fake news? And how should we, *collectively*, set up our media landscape so as to reduce exposure to (certain kinds of) fake news? The former is a matter of individual behavior and good informational habits, the latter is a matter of regulating the flow of information, whether through legal regulations or by implementing technological fixes.

One frequent suggestion coming from philosophers is that we should redirect resources toward teaching critical thinking. While this may be desirable in general (and might create job opportunities for philosophers – after all, who else should be teaching critical thinking!), it is hardly a cure-all for our current problems. For one, if the problem has considerable urgency, we can hardly afford to wait until future generations have graduated with diplomas in critical thinking. Second, there is considerable evidence that it is *older* generations – who are less media-savvy, and who are no longer part of the educational system – who are more easily taken in by fake news. Finally, *motivated cognition* – that is, the reverse-engineering of assessments of evidence, such that one's deeply held convictions come out intact (which plays an important role in why people believe partisan fake news) – is exacerbated by a high level of education, at least in some contexts. To put it crudely: well-educated people are especially good at using their argumentative skills to convince themselves that they, and their in-group, are right.

If educating individuals does not immediately address the problem, why not regulate the circulation of fake news in a top-down way – similar to how, in many countries, hate speech, slander, and other harmful speech are regulated? There are, of course, significant differences between, say, active incitement to hatred and merely muddying the waters of public debate by putting out dubious news claims. In political debate, some degree of 'spin' and polemics may be inevitable, and what looks to one group like a legitimate interpretation of events may, to the opposing group, border on misinterpretation. Authoritarian governments around the world have begun to use 'fake news' as a pretext for exerting pressure on opposition voices, whether by enforcing anti-fake news laws in a selective way or by relying on dubious definitions of what constitutes fake news. *The Economist*, in its 11 February 2021 edition, outlines how 'Censorious governments are abusing "fake news" laws', and lists numerous examples, including the case of Hopewell Chin'ono, a journalist in Zimbabwe, who was jailed for tweeting about police violence while enforcing lockdowns, and who faced charges for spreading 'falsehoods', even though the corresponding section of the Criminal Code had been struck down by the Zimbabwean constitutional court.

Illiberal democracies such as Singapore have passed anti-fake news based on logically incoherent definitions; thus, according to Singapore's 'Protection from Online Falsehoods and Manipulation Act' of 2019, 'a statement is false if it is false or misleading, whether wholly or in part, and whether on its own or in the context in which it appears' (POFMA 2019), rendering even a disjunctive statement consisting mainly of truths, but including one misleading statement, outright 'false' for legal purposes – a logical impossibility. Liberal democracies such as Germany have enacted laws such as the Network Enforcement Law (NetzDG) that delegate the policing of online speech to social media providers; while this prevents top-down censorship, it has proved unwieldy and largely ineffective against the spread of fake news in general. Partly this is due to the fact that social media companies still portray themselves as neutral 'platforms' with no editorial responsibilities, when in fact they have long assumed many of the functions that, in the past, were more competently fulfilled by newspapers and broadcasters. Rather than regulate what users can, or cannot, post on Facebook – except in the already existing ways that outlaw criminal behavior – a better regulatory target would be the (social) media companies themselves, who have so far resisted investing some of their considerable profits into improving their journalistic and editorial standards.

Another suggestion that is frequently made – not least by social media companies who prefer algorithmic automation over hiring thousands of (costly) human editors – is to implement technological tweaks. This might take the form of automated fact-checking or of identifying suspicious sources, such as bots, which may otherwise distort the activity on a social network. However, fact-checking is a delicate business and, so far at least, cannot be divorced from human judgment, not least since what makes a claim problematic is often not that it is literally false, but that it is missing context. Whether fact-checking *ex post* (that is, once a false or problematic claim has already gained traction) is effective, is doubtful: as Étienne Brown notes, 'the consumption of fact-checks is concentrated among non-fake news consumers, so they often do not reach their intended audience' (2018: 211). Likewise, screening out fake news bots does little to address the issue of fully committed human purveyors of fake news.

In conclusion, neither technological tweaks nor the well-intended appeal to 'think critically' really addresses the structural, systemic factors that distort our information environment. Individually, we cannot ascertain the truth or falsity of every single claim we encounter, and collectively we would not be well-advised to put our fate into the hands of algorithms – which, time and again, have proved to be problematic (and 'gameable' by malignant actors). Yet, there is an intermediate realm of actions we can individually take – and which we can collectively encourage – that may help us navigate this predicament: viz., the cultivation of good *informational routines*. Routines reduce complexity; in this sense, they achieve what cognitive biases and heuristics – so often exploited by fake news – also achieve. But unlike cognitive biases and heuristics, routines can deliberately be *chosen* and *revised*. If chosen well, they reduce the cognitive burden of having to ascertain from scratch, as it were, whether a claim is trustworthy or not; and, when reviewed regularly by us in light of their track record and external criticism, they can evolve into a toolbox that reliably makes information accessible to us, while not rendering us gullible to just whatever information we encounter.

Importantly, informational routines are not exhausted simply by our choices of which sources to trust routinely; they also include cultivating an awareness of when, and how, to consult sources, and in what frame of mind. If, for example, one finds that exposure to prejudiced views in the comments section of an online article influences one's own interpretation in prejudiced ways, one might make it a habit to seek out those sections only on rare occasions. Similarly, if I find myself becoming more gullible when stressed, I might restrict my news intake to times of the day when I am not in a rush. We might even adopt routines that counteract known technological biases. Thus, when it comes to online social media, it has been suggested that we should actively seek out individuals outside of our immediate social media bubble, thereby 'retraining' the algorithms underlying our newsfeeds, by injecting some diversity into the mix (see Miller and Record 2013). Media and technology companies could facilitate this process – or could be legally required to do so – by allowing users more control, thereby enabling them to develop stable informational habits rather than disrupting our individual efforts at every turn.

Yet, in the end, the simple fact remains that informational infrastructures – from traditional mass media to online social networks – are never just neutral tools, but are complex instruments for opinion formation, and as such require human judgment. There simply is no app for truthfulness.

References

Bakir, Vian, and Andrew McStay. 2018. "Fake News and The Economy of Emotions." *Digital Journalism* 6 (2): 154–175.

Boeyink, David E. 1994. "How Effective are Codes of Ethics? A Look at Three Newsrooms." *Journalism Quarterly* 71 (4): 893–904.

Brown, Étienne. 2018. "Propaganda, Misinformation, and the Epistemic Value of Democracy." *Critical Review* 30 (3–4): 194–218.

Coady, David. 2019. "The Trouble with 'Fake News'", *Social Epistemology Review and Reply Collective* 8 (10): 40–52.

Dentith, M. R. X. 2017. "The Problem of Fake News", *Public Reason* 8 (1–2): 65–79.

Ellul, Jacques. 1965. *Propaganda: The Formation of Men's Attitudes*. Translated by Konrad Kellen and Jean Lerner. New York: Vintage Books.

European Commission. 2018. *A Multi-Dimensional Approach to Disinformation (Report)*. Brussels: Directorate-General for Communication Networks, Content and Technology.

Fallis, Don and Kay Mathiesen. 2019. "Fake News is Counterfeit News." *Inquiry*. DOI: 10.1080/0020174X.2019.1688179

Frankfurt, Harry G. 2005. *On Bullshit*. Princeton: Princeton University Press.

Gelfert, Axel. 2018. "Fake News: A Definition." *Informal Logic* 38 (1): 84–117.

Gelfert, Axel. 2021a. "Fake News, False Beliefs, and the Fallible Art of Knowledge Maintenance." In *The Epistemology of Fake News*, edited by Flowerree, Amy, Sven Bernecker, and Thomas Grundmann, 310–333. Oxford: Oxford University Press.

Gelfert, Axel. 2021b. "What is Fake News?" In *The Routledge Handbook of Political Epistemology*, edited by Hannon, Michael and Jeroen de Ridder, 171–180. New York: Routledge.

Gilbert, Daniel, Romin Tafarodi, and Patrick Malone. 1993. "You Can't Not Believe Everything You Read." *Journal of Personality and Social Psychology* 65 (2): 221–233.

Habgood-Coote, Joshua. 2019. "Stop Talking About Fake News!" *Inquiry* 62 (9–10): 1033–1066.

Kant, Immanuel. 1992. *Lectures on Logic*. Translated and edited by J. Michael Young. Cambridge: Cambridge University Press.

Klein, David O., and Joshua R. Wueller. 2017. "Fake News: A Legal Perspective." *Journal of Internet Law* 20 (10): 5–13.

Levi, Lili. 2018. "Real 'Fake News' and Fake 'Fake News'." *First Amendment Law Review* 232: 232–232.

Miller, Boaz, and Isaac Record. 2013. "Justified Belief in a Digital Age: On the Epistemic Implications of Secret Internet Technologies." *Episteme* 10 (2): 117–134.

Mukerji, Nikil. 2018. "What Is Fake News?" *Ergo* 5: 923–946.

POFMA. 2019. Protection from Online Falsehoods and Manipulations Act 2019. Republic of Singapore, *Government Gazette (Acts Supplement)* No. 26 (28 June 2019). https://sso.agc.gov.sg/Acts-Supp/18-2019 URL accessed 23 February 2022.

Vosoughi, Soroush, Deb Roy, and Sinan Aral. 2018. "The Spread of True and False News Online." *Science* 359 (6380): 1146–1151.

Wardle, Claire. 2017. "Fake News: It's Complicated." https://firstdraftnews.com/fake-news-complicated/ URL accessed 23 February 2022.

Part IV

Technology in Business

Introduction

The part covers key ethical issues at the intersection technology, business, and economics.

Business ethics—an enormous field taught in business schools and undergraduate business programs worldwide—is almost universally ignored by authors and editors of texts on computer ethics. Standard texts commonly focus on technical aspects of technology in human lives and how the state or other non-business actors can deploy technology to achieve their ends. This part helps to remedy this deficiency.

We start with an account of the philosopher and economist Adam Smith's famous discussion of the formation of moral sentiments, including its application to contemporary uses of technology such as social media. We then consider the role of firms and social media users in enabling (or preventing) constructive online discourse. Further topics explored include the promises and perils of firms' reliance on data-driven decision-making, the value of cognitive diversity in the workplace, the relationships between Big Tech firms and political equality, and potential responses to harms imposed by corporate-owned artificial intelligence.

DOI: 10.4324/9781003189466-26

Chapter 22

Adam Smith on the Dangers of the Digital World

James R. Otteson

Introduction

What could an author from the eighteenth century possibly have to say that would be of value, or even relevant, when considering challenges that twenty-first-century technology poses? Adam Smith (1723–1790) is widely credited as a "founding father" of the discipline of economics and one of the first modern supporters of a market economy, and his work has had tremendous influence on the subsequent development of economics and of political-economic policy. But he wrote before the advent of the internet, not to mention computers, televisions, radios, and even electricity. The great technological innovation occurring in Smith's day was the steam engine—which gives some perspective on how much innovation and technological development have occurred since he wrote, and how much he not only did not know but could not have even imagined.[1]

And yet some of Smith's principles might be applicable today. For example, he argued in his famous 1776 *Inquiry into the Nature and Causes of the Wealth of Nations* that innovation arose primarily from the bottom-up, rather than the top-down. Discoveries of new ways of doing things, of new machinery and technology to accomplish tasks more quickly or efficiently, were made primarily by those doing the work. It is workers who are naturally incentivized to find better ways of working to minimize their energies or maximize their outputs in a way that managers, owners, design engineers, or distant policy-makers frequently are not.[2] Thus, he argued, economic policy should give wide scope of freedom for workers to innovate and engage in entrepreneurial exploration. And policy proposals should not presume that centralized experts could know in advance or from afar what should be done or be able to anticipate future innovations (see Hayek 1945; Otteson 2021, Chapter 3).

But Smith also wrote another book, the 1759 *Theory of Moral Sentiments,* in which he investigated empirically how human beings develop their moral sentiments—that is, their moral tastes, attitudes, and principles—as well as their habits, preferences, values, and full personalities. In this book, Smith articulates a process for healthy and beneficial development of moral sentiments, and also indicates how this process can be corrupted, impeded, and even derailed. It is here that he argues for principles of social interaction that allow proper development of our sentiments but that could be jeopardized by some salient features of modern digital technology, particularly in connection with our increasing engagement with one another through social media.

Although Smith could not have known or even imagined the digital age and our modern social media platforms, the elements of human psychology he explored have not changed. Thus, because we human beings are psychologically similar to those he observed and studied, even if our digital technology is vastly different today, he might nevertheless have had some still-useful insights. In this chapter, we focus on these psychological principles Smith

DOI: 10.4324/9781003189466-27

articulates, and draw some lessons for us today as we evaluate the potential effects on our sociality—and on our prospects for happiness—that contemporary digital interactions in social media might have.

Adam Smith's Account of the Development of Moral Sentiments

Smith argues that the moral sentiments a mature adult has are not the product of any rational deduction, from, say, transcendent first principles or from an apprehension of God's will. Instead, they are the product of an interactive, developmental process through which we all go as we transition from amoral infants to moralized adults (see Otteson 2002; Forman-Barzilai 2010). The mechanism that effectuates this transition arises from our desire for "mutual sympathy" of sentiments (Smith 1759 [1982], 13), a desire Smith believes all human beings naturally have, which disposes them to feel pleasure when they realize or become aware that their own sentiments are shared by others. The "sympathy" he has in mind is not pity or sadness at the plight of others; rather, Smith uses "sympathy" in its etymological sense of "feeling with": if you and I share similar sentiments, then there is a "sympathy of sentiments"—or a "concord" or "harmony" of sentiments, other terms Smith occasionally uses—between yours and mine. If we both like a particular book, say, to roughly the same degree, then we enjoy a sympathy of sentiments with respect to the book; when we realize or observe that we share this sympathy, it naturally gives us pleasure. However, if we come to realize that we have sharply discordant sentiments about that book, then awareness of this "antipathy" of sentiments gives us a feeling of displeasure.

Smith's argument is that because we all naturally receive pleasure from a sympathy of sentiments, we naturally seek it out. The desire for this sympathy thus acts like a centripetal social force drawing us into community and society with others (see Otteson 2019). It becomes indeed a key element of a happy life: for Smith, happiness requires regular and frequent association with others, and of course the generation of sympathy of sentiments with others.[3] So, we naturally seek out the company of others with whom we share sympathy of sentiments, and we naturally form communities of like-minded people around our shared sympathies.

But this desire also plays an important role in the development of our specifically moral sentiments. When we see that others judge us negatively—whether regarding our words, our actions, or our reactions—then this antipathy of sentiments stings. For Smith, there are indeed few experiences more painful than realizing that others are judging us negatively, particularly others we care about or whose judgment we esteem. However, when we perceive sympathy of sentiments from others' judgments of our words, actions, reactions, and so on, we feel pleasure. The former case, then, acts as a negative incentive: we do not want to do again what led to the painful awareness of negative judgment and antipathy. But the latter case acts as a positive incentive: when we perceive the pleasure of mutual sympathy of sentiments arising from others' positive judgments, we naturally wish to do more of whatever produced the positive judgment. As this process unfolds, and as we have such experiences hundreds or thousands or more times throughout our lives, we naturally mold our actions and behaviors—and even our sentiments—to accord more closely with what will, or with what we believe will, achieve mutual sympathy of sentiments; and we avoid actions and behaviors that will, or that we believe will, lead instead to an antipathy of sentiments.

The moral sentiments of the mature adult, then, have arisen and been honed by his or her experiences, and they are deeply shaped by their peers and others with whom they associate. Indeed, Smith believes that a similar process is at work in other areas of our personalities: everything from what we read or what music we listen to, to how we dress, what language we speak, and what our accent is, as well as our moral principles, sentiments, and judgments, are all shaped, Smith thinks, by this process of interaction, observation, reaction, and adaptation. There is no point in anyone's life, except at death, at which this process is completed: we continue to shape and hone our sentiments and judgment as we have interactive social experiences throughout our lives.

For Smith, this experience-dependent process of development explains many observed facts about human beings. It explains, for example, why people tend to congregate with those who share similar sentiments about things that matter to them. If politics matters to you, Smith would predict that you will tend to associate with others who share your politics. Similarly with religion, music, literature, child-rearing, education, and so on. (Because Smith intends this to be an empirically verifiable prediction, you might test it on yourself: do you tend to associate with people who share similar sentiments about the things that matter most to you, and avoid association with people whose views differ sharply from yours about those things?)

Three Central Principles from Smith's Account

How does Smith's empirical, developmental—perhaps even "evolutionary"[4]—account of the origin and change over time of our sentiments apply to modern technology, especially social media? Three central, connected elements of Smith's account seem most applicable and relevant.

First, Smith believes that for our sentiments and our judgment to develop properly, we require regular and frequent association with others—as well as regular and frequent expression and communication of sentiments—but this association must also be *observed*. That is, we must see or hear, *literally* see or hear, one another's reactions, judgments, and sentiments. Much of this communication takes place through largely unconscious observation: through facial expressions, body language, eye movement, and so on; or through tone of voice, intonation, word choice, accent, pace of expression, and so on. We often perceive these subtle features without realizing we do, but they have a profound effect on our perception of our interlocutor's or companion's sentiments, thoughts, and feelings.

As an example, imagine someone saying to you, "O what a beautiful day!" Now reread that sentence five times, each time placing the stress on a different word in the sentence. Each time you do, the sentence will mean something different. You could also easily imagine changing intonation to make the sentence a sincere expression of sentiment, on the one hand, or a sarcastic joke, on the other. Or imagine the person saying it with a straight face, with a broad smile, or with a roll of the eyes. Or imagine different hand or arm motions while the person says it. You will perceive those differences in intended meaning instantly and even unconsciously in the presence of another person uttering the sentiment to you, even if it is difficult to explain exactly how or why you knew what the person meant. But to do so, or to perceive the intended communication properly, you must observe—through sight, hearing, other senses (e.g., touch), or some combination—the full range of expression. Limit or exclude any of those sources of information—only read the sentence on a page, only hear the person's voice without seeing the person, etc.—and the signal regarding the person's sentiment gets diminished or clouded.

Second, in order to develop our sentiments properly, we must not only observe others' reactions (through words, actions, gestures, etc.), but their reactions must have some purchase on us—they must affect us somehow, typically because of our concern, esteem, or respect for the other. Your dearest friend's negative judgment of you will have far more sting than that of a stranger with whom you have no connection, even if you become aware of the latter's negative judgment. If the boss you are trying to impress judges your work harshly, it can be devastating; if a distantly acquainted subordinate to you expresses a negative judgment, it may still bother you, but not nearly as much—especially if your boss praises you. If I tell you that people from another country you do not know and will never meet disapprove of the music you listen to or the books you read or how you spend your surplus wealth, it likely will have little or no effect on you at all. If I tell you that your peers or your friends or your senior colleagues or your aspirational life-partner's intimate friend group disapprove of how you dress or how you speak or what jokes you tell, that will likely cut deeply and lead you to make some changes.

Finally, third, we must also have the freedom both of association and of dissociation. Smith believes that we are inherently social creatures, and that our happiness depends on regular and positive association with others.[5] If people we care about have the ability to leave our company, even perhaps permanently, that disciplines us to strive not to offend, alienate, or hurt them. And we must also be able to attract others with our words, actions, and so on, people who would thus similarly require the freedom to associate with us—which necessarily means dissociating with indefinitely many others. Our care and concern, as well as our attention, are limited or scarce resources; we cannot pay attention to everyone, we cannot concern ourselves with everyone, and we cannot care for, let alone love, everyone. So, we pick and choose. And there is always an opportunity cost involved: to care about, associate with, or love this person entails forgoing the care, association, or love of indefinitely many others. Much of our happiness depends on the quantity—and quality (at least from our own perspective)—of people who thus choose to associate with us, as opposed to the many others with whom they might otherwise have associated. But this voluntary assortment, this process of deciding with whom to associate, on what terms, to what extent, and so on (as well as decisions to dissociate, to lessen our association, and so on) require the freedom to do so.

To illustrate further and to underscore the importance of this third element of Smith's argument, consider the difference between the way people typically behave around and treat prospective life partners, on the one hand, and, on the other, the way the same people might behave around their own siblings. With their siblings, they might feel the freedom to be far more obnoxious, blunt, cutting, and even cruel than they would with prospective life partners. Why? Smith would claim that it is explained by the fact that it is far more difficult for their siblings to leave. Your siblings are your siblings for life; though some may eventually decide to have little contact with one another, and in extreme cases may even disavow one another, nevertheless at least while they are growing up your brother or sister cannot leave no matter how cruel you are to him or her. And vice-versa. So, the lack of an effective exit option reduces the potency of their judgment, positive or negative, of you and your behavior (and again vice-versa), which permits you to relax the discipline you place on your behavior around them. It can enable you to act, with seeming impunity, outside the bounds of propriety you might respect in other company.

Now let us put these three Smithian elements together. According to Smith, to develop our sentiments, as well as our judgment and behavior, appropriately, three conditions are necessary. First, we must regularly and frequently be in the physical presence of others so that we can perceive their judgments of and sentiments about our own sentiments and behaviors. Second, their judgments and sentiments must have some purchase on us, which requires us to care about them (as our natural desire for mutual sympathy of sentiments inclines us to do). And third, they must have the ability, at a relatively low cost to themselves, to dissociate from us if they choose.

Application of Smith's Principles to Social Media

All three of these elements that Smith argued are required for proper development of our sentiments are absent in many of the interactions we have with others today, mediated as so many of them are by the digital platforms of social media. Many such platforms allow for anonymity, for example, which erases all three elements and can thus, quite predictably, enable us to give ourselves permission to transgress the bounds of propriety in ways we never would when interacting with others when the three elements are in place. Even those platforms that do not allow anonymity nevertheless diminish the information expressed in posts—partly because they are, or can be, so carefully curated, or artificially altered, by the user. It seems that would at least partly explain the ubiquitous, and universally decried, phenomenon of coarseness, rudeness, cruelty, and worse one sees on such platforms.

The feature of anonymity, and its attendant deleterious consequences on the fabric and salience of our social interaction, has been noted and studied (see, for example, Wu and Lien 2013; Pew Research Center 2021). But Smith's third element has been underappreciated. It is difficult to get away from, to dissociate oneself from, the thundering voices on social media. Anyone can tweet at anyone, and the tweetee cannot, or cannot easily, get rid of, avoid, or unsee the tweeter's (or the "troll's") coarseness, rudeness, etc. This fact reflects and magnifies the unpleasant behavior one might see among siblings: it is one thing to have a brother or sister say mean things about one; it is another thing altogether to have dozens or hundreds or thousands of hectoring critics. (Think of your own engagement with social media. Have you ever been the target of critics? If so, what effect do their criticisms have on you?)

Smith argued that over time, a morally mature person develops the perspective of what he called an imagined "impartial spectator," or the imagined perspective of a disinterested but virtuous and fully informed observer of your conduct (see Raphael 2007). This perspective arises inductively, on the basis of one's countless interactions with actual human spectators, and coalesces into something of an idealized perspective of a truly virtuous and wise person. Because we have all had the unpleasant experience of having only partially informed actual spectators form partial and thus inaccurate judgments of us, we develop this imaginary perspective of an impartial spectator as a "corrective" to the partiality of actual observers.[6] Instead of paying attention only to what actual people express about us, we can hence come to ask ourselves what a fully informed but impartial spectator to our conduct would judge. In practice, our imaginary impartial spectator might be the imagined perspective of an actual but not present person: Jesus, say, or Aristotle, or our priest or rabbi, or a wise friend or acquaintance or family member or other person from our lives or from history whom we esteem or whose judgment we trust. "What would Jesus do?" is a question that would invoke the imagined perspective of such an impartial spectator, as would many other similar questions with other personages.

The problem this raises for our lives today that are so mediated by digital platforms is that we can easily mistake a seemingly large number of reactions to our posts, our pictures, our sentiments, our judgments, and so on as representing a larger consensus, and thus as themselves embodying an impartial spectator. Yet because those tweeters, likers, commenters, etc., have only partial and limited knowledge of us and our situations—perhaps extremely partial and limited—and because of the familiar phenomenon of "piling on" that can occur when people see others judging and reacting in a particular way and hence behave similarly to follow the social herd—what looks like an informed consensus from an impartial spectator based on many people's responses is actually an artificially amplified but misinformed and partial perspective from, notably, a statistically miniscule portion of humanity.

Digital social media platforms have progressively replaced many of the physical, face-to-face interactions human beings have had throughout their history and development on the planet.[7] While all previous generations of human beings would look to their family, friends, and acquaintances for approval or to avoid disapproval, now we increasingly seek it through the likes, retweets, and upvotes on digital platforms from virtual friends, who are as often as not total strangers. This has the dual effect of encouraging us to anxiously gauge the trends of fashion these groups exhibit and to conform to them to get their approval, and at the same time follow their lead in denunciations, criticisms, and even cruelties, again to get these strangers' approval (or avoid their disapproval).

The Smithian prediction would be that this is ultimately a recipe for unhappiness. The approval we get through digital platforms is thin soup and does not compare to the potency and real substance of approval we get from actual observers of our conduct. Your digital friend cannot give you a hug when you need it. And the digital friendships, alliances, and associations we form are attenuated by their inconstancy and fickleness, as well as by the stark absence of Smith's three elements. If happiness depends on the deep associations we form with others, then those associations will have to be formed from observed regular interactions with others whose judgment has affective purchase on us and who choose to invest their time, energy, friendship, affection, and love in us. Human friendship is formed through long and close interaction, deliberately chosen and pursued, and with mutual investment of self—and can be formed in no other way. To the extent, then, that interaction via digital platforms replaces or substitutes for any of that, to that same extent is the possibility of genuine friendship diminished. And its depth will be reduced accordingly as well. That will mean, Smith would predict, diminished prospects for happiness.

A Remedy?

Smith's account of the social development of our sentiments unfortunately does not prescribe a ready remedy for the negative effects digital mediation will likely have—and likely is having—on our social relations. Removing oneself from digital platforms might be a possible remedy, but if insufficient numbers of others, or at least of those others about whom we care, follow our lead, it will do us little good. Indeed, it may even be worse: isolation, according to Smith, is perhaps the worst torture for a deeply and naturally social creature like a human being and will not enable us to develop our sentiments properly, let alone enjoy happiness. A person who spends his entire life physically alone in an apartment—interacting with others only digitally, having food and clothing and everything else delivered and dropped at the door with minimal human interaction, and so on—will, Smith would predict, descend into a life of emptiness and ultimately unhappiness. Smith writes: "But solitude is still more dreadful . . . . His own thoughts can present him with nothing but what is . . . unfortunate, and disastrous, the melancholy forebodings of incomprehensible misery and ruin" (Smith 1982 [1759], 84). Such a person likely will himself eventually come to perceive the emptiness and pointlessness of his life, but by that time he may have become so habituated to his asocial life that it may be too late to change.

Of course, the opposite extreme of living one's life completely at the mercy of what others perceive is dangerous as well. And it is also possible that exposure to ideas, perspectives, and personalities from outside our own local physical location—which social media can offer—can broaden our horizons, temper our prejudices, increase our tolerance for diversity, and even give us increased prospects of finding good partners for our own life paths. So, using our judgment and practical wisdom is required to find the right balance between a life totally online and a life totally offline, and of using social media for the good purposes it can provide and enable while avoiding its unwelcome negative consequences.

If the digital age, and its attendant mediation of social interaction via digital platforms, is here to stay (and it appears it is), then we may have to find other ways to develop our social bonds properly. What those ways might be is difficult to say. But Smith would predict that if we do not actively seek out ways to experience regular, frequent, substantive in-person interaction with others, then we will eventually be consumed by a sense of meaninglessness, disappointment, and deep unhappiness. We may develop a foreboding sense of loneliness and isolation, and what Smith calls a "melancholy dejection" (Smith 1759 [1982], 139) in which we are haunted by pangs of regret and the furies of momentary but ultimately infecund desires, plagued by persistent and recurring anxiety and anguish.

No one should wish such a fate on himself or herself, or on anyone else. Smith may not be able to tell us how to remedy the situation or how exactly to avoid such an unfortunate fate, but the first step toward prescription and eventual healing is proper diagnosis. To maintain and realize the benefits of our developing digital technology, while avoiding or at least minimizing its deleterious and potentially dehumanizing effects, we must first understand human psychology and how creatures like us are able to develop meaningful relations with others in ways that might enable happiness. It seems that on this, at least, Smith has much to offer us today.

Notes

1 I thank Gregory Robson and an anonymous reviewer for helpful constructive comments on an earlier draft of this essay. Remaining errors are mine.
2 Smith wrote:

> A great part of the machines made use of in those manufactures in which labour is most subdivided, were originally the inventions of common workmen, who, being each of them employed in some very simple operation, naturally turned their thoughts towards finding out easier and readier methods of performing it.
>
> (Smith 1776 [1976], 20)

3 Smith writes: "What so great happiness as to be beloved, and to know that we deserve to be beloved? What so great misery as to be hated, and to know that we deserve to be hated?" (Smith 1759 [1982], 113).
4 Although Smith's *Theory of Moral Sentiments* predates Charles Darwin's *Origin of Species* by 100 years, and thus Smith could not have availed himself of Darwinian evolutionary theory, I note that Darwin read Smith, favorably reviewed Smith's treatment of the natural desire for mutual sympathy of sentiments in his 1871 *Descent of Man* (Darwin calls Smith's discussion "striking"), and apparently credited Smith with having discovered an important truth about human psychology. See Darwin 1871 (1981), 81.
5 Smith writes:

> It is thus that man, who can subsist only in society, was fitted by nature to that situation for which he was made. All the members of human society stand in need of each others assistance, and are likewise exposed to mutual injuries. Where the necessary assistance is reciprocally afforded from love, from gratitude, from friendship, and esteem, the society flourishes and is happy.
>
> (Smith 1759 [1982], 85)

6 Smith writes:

> We are soon taught by experience, however, that this universal approbation is altogether unattainable. . . . The fairest and most equitable conduct must frequently obstruct the interests, or thwart the inclinations of particular persons, who will seldom have candour enough to enter into the propriety of our motives, or to see that this conduct, how disagreeable soever to them, is perfectly suitable to our situation. In order to defend ourselves from such partial judgments, we soon learn to set up in our own minds a judge between ourselves and those we live with. We conceive ourselves as acting in the presence of a person quite candid and equitable, of one who has no particular relation either to ourselves, or to those whose interests are affected by our conduct, who is neither father, nor brother, nor friend either to them or to us, but is merely a man in general, an impartial spectator who considers our conduct with the same indifference with which we regard that of other people.
>
> (Smith 1759 [1982], 129)

7 Of course, this phenomenon has been hastened and exacerbated by the COVID-19 pandemic of 2020, which severely limited in-person social interaction.

References

Darwin, Charles. 1871 (1981). *The Descent of Man, and Selection in Relation to Sex.* Princeton: Princeton University Press.

Forman-Barzilai, Fonna. 2010. *Adam Smith and the Circles of Sympathy: Cosmopolitanism and Moral Theory.* New York: Cambridge University Press.

Hayek, Friedrich August von. 1945. "The Use of Knowledge in Society." *American Economic Review* 35, 4: 519–530.

Otteson, James R. 2002. *Adam Smith's Marketplace of Life.* New York: Cambridge University Press.

Otteson, James R. 2019. "Escaping the Social Pull: Nonconformists and Self-Censorship." *Society* 56: 559–568. https://doi.org/10.1007/s12115-019-00416-y

Otteson, James R. 2021. *Seven Deadly Economic Sins: Obstacles to Prosperity and Happiness Every Citizen Should Know.* New York: Cambridge University Press.

Pew Research Center. 2021. "The State of Online Harassment." Retrieved here: https://www.pewresearch.org/internet/2021/01/13/the-state-of-online-harassment/

Raphael, D. D. 2007. *The Impartial Spectator: Adam Smith's Moral Philosophy.* New York: Oxford University Press.

Smith, Adam. 1759 (1982). *The Theory of Moral Sentiments.* D. D. Raphael and A. L. Macfie, eds. Indianapolis: Liberty Fund.

Smith, Adam. 1776 (1976). *An Inquiry into the Nature and Causes of the Wealth of Nations.* R. H. Campbell and A. S. Skinner, eds. Indianapolis: Liberty Fund.

Wu, Wei Peng and Chung Chang Lien. 2013. "Cyberbullying: An Empirical Analysis of Factors Related to Anonymity and Reduced Social Cue." *Applied Mechanics and Materials* 311: 533–38. https://doi.org/10.4028/www.scientific.net/AMM.311.533

Chapter 23

Social Media Firms, Echo Chambers, and the Good Life

Gregory J. Robson

Websites such as Twitter, Google, Facebook, and YouTube have enabled a level of information-sharing that is unprecedented in human history. These sites have put "much of the world's information at our fingertips" by making it accessible within mere seconds (Cowen 2019, 100)—a stunning human achievement. But how valuable is it to have access to such information? And what effects do social media firms have on their customers' well-being? According to recent scholarship (Eady et al. 2019, Elzinga 2020, Hallvard and Olof Larsson 2015, Nyugen 2020, Sunstein 2017), the answer depends on whether, how, and how often social media users access and share information, and which information. Social media users can improve—or worsen—their lives depending on how and with whom they interact online. The rather different content of recent discussion of lockdowns, masking, and public policy across diverse social media platforms during the COVID-19 pandemic has made clear how important it is for social media users to avoid operating in *echo chambers*. We should instead consult alternative views to those found in echo chambers to confirm that we are not seeing fiction as fact, falsity as truth, or one-sided discussion as the whole story.

This chapter considers how social media users can isolate themselves from exposure to alternative views, and the effects of doing so. The recent flurry of growth in social media has catalyzed "people's growing power to filter what they see" (Sunstein 2017, 6, italics removed). Social media firms let users create and sustain informational *echo chambers* in which their own views are praised and reinforced, and rival views are ignored, downplayed, or dismissed. The issue is not just that social media platforms censor information algorithmically or otherwise, blocking users' exposure to alternative views. Social media users also block their *own* access to alternative views, sometimes without even knowing it.[1]

We will examine the nature and ethical implications of these forms of blocking, the echo chambers that result, and what can be done to mitigate their bad effects. I first describe this concern with special attention to Cass Sunstein's (2017) influential account. After this, I use ethical theory to assess the severity of the echo chamber problem and show why, in some respects, it is worse than many realize. Finally, I describe solutions to these problems.

Democracy and Social Media Echo Chambers

Sunstein develops an account of the import of social media echo chambers in a democratic society. Social media give democratic citizens access to valuable information about social and political life. And democracies are more functional, all else equal, when citizens are well-informed.[2] So, the effect of social media use on how well-informed democratic citizens are merits careful consideration. Cowen contends that, although the internet is "still in

DOI: 10.4324/9781003189466-28

its early years," technology firms have already "brought human beings into closer contact with each other than ever before, whether emotionally or intellectually, mostly through social media" (Cowen 2019, 104, 100). The internet has certainly brought like-minded and geographically isolated people together, even if sometimes disrupting traditional communities or isolating people in other ways in the process. Sunstein (2017, 1) recognizes that social media have put citizens in closer contact by enabling more pervasive interpersonal communication. Sunstein is especially concerned that citizens have ended up *so* close with some fellow citizens (but not others) that, as a tight-knit group, they ignore alternative viewpoints—the views of those *others*. The CNN crowd might ignore or disparage the Fox News crowd, or vice versa. So the worry is that citizens are ending up in social media echo chambers. Through Facebook, their news feeds, or other online activity, citizens choose to receive news and other information from a single, preferred perspective while remaining unaware of important alternative views.

Social media are "[i]nternet-based platforms that allow the creation and exchange of user-generated content, usually using either mobile or web-based technologies" (Margetts et al., 2016, 5; quoted in Sunstein 2017, 22). *Social media firms* include for-profit social networking companies such as Facebook and Tumbler, microblogs such as Twitter, and other blogs and websites such as Flickr, Vine, Wikipedia, and YouTube (Sunstein 2017, 22). On such sites, citizens can create what Sunstein calls the "Daily Me." The *Daily Me*, a term introduced by Nicholas Negroponte (former director of MIT's media lab), refers to an "architecture of control" over information streams that citizens can create with social media (2017, 1; italics removed). Citizens can create the Daily Me (or at least approximate it) by controlling and personalizing the information they receive from online searches and social media. Citizens who create the Daily Me risk launching themselves into echo chambers—also called *information silos*—in which their views are repeated and affirmed, and rival views denied, disparaged, or simply not discussed (Sunstein 2017, 5–13 *et passim*).

Consider Twitter:

> Your Twitter feed might well reflect your preferred topics and convictions [and] provide much of what you see about politics—taxes, immigration, civil rights, and war and peace. What comes in your feed is your choice, not anyone else's.
>
> (Sunstein 2017, 3)

Or take Facebook:

> When people use Facebook to see exactly what they want to see, their understanding of the world can be greatly affected.... . [If your] Facebook friends ... have a distinctive point of view, that's the point of view that you'll see most.
>
> (Sunstein 2017, 2)

Theorists have diverse conceptions of these "information silos" or "echo chambers." Some argue, for instance, that an echo chamber is a "social epistemic structure from which other relevant voices have been actively excluded and discredited" (Nyugen 2020, abstract). On this view, echo chambers are distinctive because of how they rely upon and forge trust within in-groups and distrust of out-groups. Other theorists argue that what makes echo chambers distinctive is not especially or exclusively how they ignore or discredit outside views, but the presence of "belief-reinforcing echoes" that spread misinformation (Elzinga 2020). However exactly we conceive of echo chambers, clearly citizens control much of the information they are exposed to on Twitter, Facebook, and other social media platforms. So we can ask: Does having this control improve citizens' lives?

Yes and no. For his part, Sunstein argues (2017, 6) that citizens should leave their echo chambers and seek alternative viewpoints. Sunstein does acknowledge that the Daily Me, and the echo-chamber-like experience it supports, confers some benefits. It provides citizens with convenience in getting the information and enabling the experiences they want. It is fun and entertaining. And it enables them to learn about what interests them (Sunstein 2017, 1–2 *et passim*). Nevertheless, turning to the negatives, the Daily Me exposes citizens to just one side of an argument, or, often worse, a forceful presentation of one view and an unfair mischaracterization of rival views.

All of this raises the question: if the views that inform citizens' political activity are so lopsidedly informed, can democratic citizens be meaningfully self-governing? Sunstein argues (2017, 213–214) that one-sided exposure to the issues leads to "three fundamental concerns from the democratic point of view":

1   Citizens are inadequately exposed to ideas or views that they did not choose in advance to read or hear about.
2   Citizens do not have enough common experiences.
3   Citizens are inadequately aware of "substantive questions of policy and principle, combined with a range of positions on such questions" (Sunstein 2017, 214).

Citizens who filter their social and political information through "friends" on Facebook and like-minded others on Twitter, Tumbler, or TikTok can suffer from confirmation bias and motivated reasoning. *Confirmation bias* occurs when one interprets ambiguous evidence to favor (or confirm) one's existing viewpoints or what one wants to believe. One might identify evidence as relevant that is not, overestimate the weight of current evidence for one's views, or underestimate the weight of disconfirming evidence. *Motivated reasoning* is similar. A motivated reasoner pursues a line of thinking that takes him to the conclusion he already wanted to believe. He does so without acquiring adequate evidence for the conclusion or accounting for all relevant information. The present worry, then, is that the Daily Me undermines democratic self-governance by making it hard for citizens to identify and understand all relevant evidence, reason well about it, and ignore what is evidentially irrelevant. So, does it?

Sunstein responds based on an argument about freedom of expression. Genuine freedom of expression, he claims, requires two things. First, citizens must be exposed to information they do not select in advance. "Unplanned, unanticipated encounters," says Sunstein, "are central to democracy" (2017, 6). Second, citizens need to have a "wide range of common experiences" (Sunstein 2017, 7). Common experiences are a "form of social glue" that enables a polity to decide things well together (Sunstein 2017, 7). After all, citizens need to be able to relate to one another. Otherwise, they will not be able to understand each other adequately and cooperate for the common good.

The Daily Me can make it impossible for citizens to meet these requirements. For "[w]hen information is unavailable, and when opportunities are shut off and known to be shut off, people may end up not wanting them at all" (p. 164). And precisely the de facto effect of the Daily Me is to make information about different social views—and the reasons for and against them—inaccessible. Citizens end up unaware of the contents of such views and even resistant to thinking that such views even *might* be true.

Social theorist Jon Elster (1983; see Sunstein, 165–167) considers a relevant fable: the case of the fox and the sour grapes. The fox likes grapes but can't have them. So the fox (falsely) convinces itself that the grapes are sour—and that *this* is why it does not like them! We might say something similar. Social media users who look exclusively to political news stories with a certain narrative might convince themselves of the falsity or badness of alternative views, and the truth or goodness of the narrative most familiar to them. Now it's possible that on a given issue, one narrative alone is true (e.g., corresponds well to the world) or good (e.g., motivates good action in the world). Typically, though, to attend to just one narrative of a complex social issue all but guarantees that one will not gain enough exposure to sophisticated alternative views that at least partly track the truth. This one-sided approach dampens citizens' capacities to understand both the issues and the other people who disagree with them. It leaves citizens ignorant in some degree and unable or unwilling to understand each other.

Three Reasons Why the Echo Chamber Problem Gets Worse

I suggest that there are at least three reasons why the problem of echo chambers is even worse than readers might expect. (1) First, firms track and reinforce consumers' existing views, ultimately influencing consumer and citizen behavior. Call this the *Influence-of-Firms Problem*. Sunstein (2017, 3) writes:

> As it turns out, you do not need to create a Daily Me. Others are creating it for you right now (and you may have no idea that they're doing it). Facebook itself does some curating, and so does Google.

Algorithms (programmed sets of instructions) track your preferences, beliefs, interests, and so on: your music choices, political views, preferred movies and books, and much else besides. Facebook, for instance, "probably knows your political convictions, and it can inform others, including candidates for public office, of what it knows" (Sunstein 2017, 3). And sometimes algorithms that track users' actual behavior can know our preferences even better than we do, insofar as self-reports of preferences sometimes err. Collecting, storing, and selling user data is also big business for social media firms and associated technology firms. As Kirsten Martin (2017) observes, iPhone users are tracked; their data is aggregated; and data brokers sell it to advertisers and others, whether or not users know and consent to it. This is increasingly possible since internet users, say Kearns and Roth (2020, 64), have begun to

> leave longer and longer digital trails—via their Google searches, Amazon purchases, Facebook friends and "likes," GPS coordinates, and countless other sources—massive datasets could now be compiled not just for large systems but also for specific people.

Social media firms have not only strong incentives but the capacity, as well, to track, store, and sell user data. To shape users' experiences, such firms can expose particular users to particular information and shield them from other information. In this way firms can, unbeknownst to many, help them to build and maintain their own echo chambers—for the sake of firms' bottom lines.

(2) What I call the *Impersonation Problem* exacerbates matters. Armies of bots acting *as users* on social media influence everything from Twitter discussions to Wikipedia entries. This activity gives users the impression that public opinion itself—the opinion of individual persons, not programmed algorithms—leans in certain directions on particular issues, whether or not it actually does (Hallvard and Olof Larsson 2015, Tsvetkova et al., 2017). Bots make social media users believe that "*everyone* thinks X," or many people do. Users then wonder: "Should I think X too?" Algorithms thus have real power. They can generate and sustain public opinions and resist and unpopularize alternative views. So it matters how prevalent they are and who controls them.

(3) Finally, there is the *Manipulation Problem*. Search engines and social media also partly control—and can manipulate—the information available to users and the ease with which users can find it. Search engines such as Google, say, might seem to display neutrally selected results while non-neutrally ordering results in ways particular to a search or a topic itself (cf. Sunstein 2017, 3). (Here, it's worth considering what *neutrality* is and whether and how it's achievable.) The general concern is this. Powerful firms can influence the information that users can access (as via search engines) or with whom they can associate (as on microblogs like Twitter). In such cases, such firms can unilaterally direct users' associations, relationships, and even their thinking. This diminishes users' capacities for meaningful association with disagreeing others. Cobbe (2020) gives voice to this general concern:

> social platforms can alter their algorithms to exercise control over the dissemination and amplification of content through systems for personalisation, seeking to drive user engagement and build market share, with increasingly negative consequences for society.

Social media firms have accordingly come under scrutiny for how and how far they control the dissemination of information (Taddeo and Floridi, 2016). For suppose internet users have a basic "right to engage in pluralistic, fair, and transparent online interactions" which are "free of undue censorship and encroachment" (Taddeo 2014, 1132). On this assumption, a company with monopolistic control of key aspects of public opinion might have objectionable power over democratic discourse. Scholars debate whether merely having considerable power over others is morally objectionable. In any case, firms ought to wield the power they do have honorably (on principles of honorable business, see Otteson 2019, 72 *et passim*).

Sunstein provides notable evidence for the claim that the Daily Me threatens democratic discourse. Take the key issue of polarization. "In 2000 and 2004," Sunstein reports, "a typical Democrat was no more likely than a typical Republican to watch MSNBC. By 2008, a typical Democrat was *20 percentage points* more likely to watch MSNBC" (2017, 61). Likewise for Republicans. "In 2004, a Republican was only 11 [percentage] points more likely than a Democrat to watch Fox. By 2008, the gap had widened to *more than 30 points*." (Sunstein 2017, 61). In addition, "people's level of interest in *the same exact* news stories *was greatly affected by the network label*" (Sunstein 2017, 65, italics altered). Republicans found identical headlines far more interesting—the headlines got three times more hits—if carried by Fox. And Democrats were more interested in (again, identical) stories on CNN and NPR while being strongly averse to the *same* stories on Fox.

Now correlation is not causation, and statistical confounds can make it unclear how and how far echo chambers cause polarization. But given the rise of social media since then and the issues discussed above, it is fair to suggest that social media firms are indeed partly causally responsible for polarizing recent political discourse. As Sunstein (2017, 71–75) notes, online echo chambers incline their participants (*i*) to learn more of the reasoning behind their own positions (but not necessarily other views), (*ii*) adjust their positions more to favor dominant views in the group, and (*iii*) be more confident in these positions when others in the group agree with them.

To acknowledge these downsides of social media use is not to say that having a Daily Me or using social media are not beneficial overall or in important respects.[3] They quite plausibly are! First, people enjoy using social media, including with regard to creating and maintaining the Daily Me. Second, people get a sense of community from engagement with like-minded others, which can give them the support and energy they need to move forward in life. And, as one more key benefit, social media users are often able to respond quickly and constructively to social problems. Consider an example.

Social media cascades can occur when a user receives information, sends it to multiple other users (via, say, Twitter, Facebook, or TikTok) who then send it to many others, potentially exponentially increasing awareness. A tweet, say, may be retweeted by "one person with five thousand followers, and then by someone with twenty thousand followers, and then by someone with eight hundred thousand followers" (Sunstein 2017, 154). This is true in not only economically prosperous countries but also developing countries. Economist and philosopher Amartya Sen famously observed that democracies with free elections never have famines (Sunstein 2017, 137–139). Sen decried the "mesmerizing simplicity of focusing on the ratio of food to population" that "has persistently played an obscuring role over centuries" (Sen 1981, 8). How food is distributed, and who has the power to distribute it, matter greatly. As long as social media users and powerholders are not siloed in echo chambers, users can send to powerholders—whether businesses, political actors, charities, or others—urgent, real-time updates on food shortages. By leveraging cascades to influence how powerholders distribute food, social media users can push their societies toward justice, stopping or mitigating shortages and saving lives.

How Big Is the Problem?

One reason why the Daily Me is worth taking seriously is, in short, *we are what we do*. If we act honestly, courageously, and overall virtuously, we *become* honest, courageous, and virtuous. By developing stable dispositions of honesty, courage, generosity, and so on, we build virtuous characters, whether as citizens specifically or users more generally. This is how we become what we do.

Even if our first attempts at honesty, courage, etc., are out of character, we *build* a character by "playing the part." And much of what we do—and so, *who* we become—as members of political societies is a function of what we understand. This is a key reason why our social media use matters greatly. Billions of people worldwide now reportedly use social media, many of them hundreds or thousands of times each year. The information they encounter has a deep and far-reaching influence on their views of ethical, social, and political issues. Putting this together, we get an argument of this form:

Premise 1: One's personal character depends importantly on one's actions.
Premise 2: One's actions depend importantly on one's information.
Premise 3: The information of many citizens depends importantly on their social media use.
Conclusion: The personal character of many citizens depends importantly on the information they get from social media.

To be sure, this conclusion does not follow necessarily. For instance, the stated dependencies stated might not be "important" in some cases. Yet this basic reasoning describes well the situation of many citizens today, particularly those who create something approximating a Daily Me, knowingly or not, by their social media use.

The Daily Me might not seem so bad if its force in restricting the flow of important information and keeping the biases of social media users intact could easily be blunted. Citizens might pursue diverse strategies to weaken this force, but many will prove inadequate. First, citizens could simply *add* to their current social media use by using alternative or additional social media or supplementing with other sources of sociopolitical information. Citizens could, for instance, read books with diverse viewpoints that question and challenge the content of information streaming in from their Daily Me. This possibility points to an important general idea: it may be best to assess the Daily Me with an eye toward possible *combinations of information consumption* in one's life. Suppose Jane spends most of her information-gathering time following conservative social media, but she also reads progressive and classical liberal books periodically. By focusing more on the book reading, she can gain exposure to more diverse views that help her to see other sides of a given social issue (and likewise if she followed mostly other social media). To better balance her Daily Me, perhaps Jane need not supplant it; instead she can supplement it.

Yet, for many social media users, this idea of a *multisource balancing strategy* (as I call it) will be either infeasible or undesirable. Some will not have time to balance their social media consumption or not be willing to if it requires forgoing some current consumption. Recent empirical work suggests that the situation might not be so bad for such users. One study (Eady et al. 2019, 18) denies that the "majority of people's sources of news are mutually exclusive and from opposite poles." But even so, "large portions of the most liberal and most conservative users *never* see what the other side is saying—how they are reacting to that news and information, and what they find to be most important" (Eady et al. 2019, 18–19; italics mine).[4] So there is empirical grounding for the claim that lots of people spend considerable time in one-sided discussion forums, warranting either replacement of some one-sided information with rival views or supplementation, à la Jane's case, with an alternative source(s) of information. The Daily Me, then, is bad for many citizens and not easily counteracted by a strategy of replacement or balancing.

A look at contemporary ethical theory implies that there are more reasons to worry about both the prevalence of the Daily Me and associated social media echo chambers. Let us consider a few reasons in dialogue with the seminal philosophers Immanuel Kant, John Stuart Mill, and Aristotle. I will present these reasons separately, but they are mutually compatible.

First, followers of Kant (1724–1804) might worry that in limiting their access to diverse opinions, social media users engage, in effect, in the most widespread form of censorship: self-censorship (Quinn 2015, 123). Users willingly enter echo chambers, recognize them *as* echo chambers, and yet proceed to think and discuss issues in these online environments, which block access to views that could challenge their own. In such circumstances, users might improperly substitute reasons circulating in their echo chamber for reasons they *would* have if a better-informed version of themselves were making such judgments.

Second, followers of Mill (1806–1873) might stress the disvalue of entering an echo chamber in which diverse viewpoints were missing that would, if present, accelerate social media users' search (one hopes) for truth. Mill argued (1993 [1859], 61; cf. Quinn 2015, 126) for several key points. One, diverse views often contain kernels of truth. At the very least, they often indicate valid and important concerns, even if a given diagnosis or prescription is misguided. Two, no person is infallible. And, three, exposure to debates by people with diverse views can give one valuable perspective. Echo chambers, in contrast, can prevent alternative perspectives from being identified and understood, much less considered and fairly assessed.

Finally, in the *Nicomachean Ethics*—arguably the most influential ethical treatise ever written—Aristotle (384–322 BC) stresses the value of practicing good thinking and good actions, which leads to good habits, and, eventually, good moral and intellectual character. For Aristotle, virtuous human action requires thinking and feeling in accordance with the dictates of practical wisdom and with sensitivity to the particulars of an agent's situation (Aristotle 1999, 1106a26–b29). So, notice this: to be able to respond well to one's situation, individuals *must* be well-informed. Hence, for democratic citizens, occupying an echo chamber marked by incomplete information or misinformation can prove detrimental. It can impede the wise exercise of one's political agency as a citizen, voter, protester, or public discussant.

Now many ethicists, including Aristotelians, think of the *good life* as the virtuous life. Plato was right that philosophy can be thought of as preparation for death—how to live well between here and there. And Plato, his famous student Aristotle, and many other virtue ethicists offer blueprints for such a life. The truly good or excellent life includes moral virtues (e.g., courage and generosity) and intellectual virtues (e.g., wisdom and rationality). Aristotelians and others add that the good life must also include certain *external goods*, like enough health and wealth, that are subject to luck and can assist in virtuous living (Aristotle 1999, 1153b17–b19). Whether or not one sees external goods as necessary for the good life, having the moral and intellectual virtues quite plausibly is; practical wisdom, for instance, is needed to coordinate the other virtues (Schwartz 2010). Yet, to have the wisdom to act excellently, one must first have *information*. As a key source of contemporary information, social media thus deeply shape citizens' capacities to live well. I accordingly suggest that one's social and political information should *itself* be thought of as an "external good" that is necessary for, or at least contributes to, the good life. If such information is drawn from a one-sided source, as in social media echo chambers, it can undermine civic virtue and block us from achieving an enlarged view of the world, where each of us has a personal interest precisely in developing such a view.

Solutions

How should we respond to the problem of echo chambers? We cannot do so by appeal to the rational ignorance of social media users, saying it is rational for us to enter echo chambers that we know keep us ignorant of certain views. It can be rational not to want to know, say, how many blades of grass are in one's front yard. The "search cost" of acquiring this knowledge by spending hours counting blades of grass is too high, and any benefit is too small. It is arguably *not* rational, however, to remain thoroughly ignorant of alternative views on issues that affect our capacities to engage well as members of a democratic society. For one thing, citizens plausibly have a personal interest in taking an enlarged view of the complexities of social and political life. A key way to do this is to consult alternative views. Further, a Millian would insist that exposure to alternative views is a rational way to test one's views, eliminate inaccuracies, strengthen one's justifications for conclusions, and revise one's views as appropriate. This process can even be rewarding for its own sake and serve one's personal interest in better understanding the world.

The risk that social media echo chambers pose to human flourishing might be averted or reduced by solutions at several levels. *Individual consumers* can modify their behavior by searching more actively for information across diverse social media (on which more soon). Consumer *groups* can influentially shape public discourse. They can engage in and praise discourse that is open and informative and can avoid and criticize discourse that fails charitably to engage the best alternative arguments. Social media *firms* can exert control over platform activity. *Industries* can engage in industry-wide regulation by proposing requirements or guidelines for firms to implement legally or by voluntary agreement. And citizens can adopt *laws* at the local, state/provincial, or federal level (but see below example). To be sure, lawmakers or citizens who claim to be "neutrality experts" might not be. And top-down efforts to impose neutrality or balance in a discussion can punish viewpoints that are unpopular or marginalized, or superficially seem to impose "balance" or "neutrality" on social media while in fact being borne of an unjustified, and perhaps covert, use of social power.

So, solutions at each level have plusses and minuses. Sticking with the fifth example, state regulation of social media activity may reduce the negative impacts of echo chambers, but it also risks being an objectionably blunt coercive instrument. Whether it is morally permissible to legally force firms and consumers to comply with a rule that benefits them will depend on various factors, such as their rights, the magnitude and distribution of expected benefits, and whether more local public or private sector solutions are available and the projected value of these. Most generally, whether a given solution is rationally justified will depend on the expected costs and benefits of the solution relative to a different solution or the status quo. It will also depend on the search costs or what it takes to "find" a solution. (These "costs" and "benefits" need not be financial and can be in terms of time, effort, and resources used.[5])

There are several possible specific solutions, at different levels, to the echo chamber problem. For his part, Sunstein discusses two notable solutions that concern social media firms in particular. (1) One idea is to include a *"diverse views weblink"* on social media. "[P]roviders of material with a certain point of view might also provide links to sites with a dramatically different point of view" (Sunstein 2017, 230). For example, The Nation (a liberal magazine, says Sunstein) might agree to link to icons for the Weekly Standard (a conservative magazine, says Sunstein), if the Weekly Standard also links to The Nation. A similar but distinct option is for social media firms to include *opposing viewpoint buttons*. Facebook, for example, could include a button (or hot link) that enables users to turn from liberal views to conservative views on a topic or vice versa.

(2) A second main solution is the use of *serendipity buttons*. Sunstein (2017, 232) suggests that Facebook, say, could let users press buttons that would expose them to "unanticipated, unchosen material on their News Feed." This would seed their information with ideas that can push their conclusions in unanticipated directions or challenge their confidence in their current views. This second solution is a response to Sunstein's deep concern to cultivate an "architecture of serendipity" in which social media users are frequently exposed to new and different information (Sunstein 2017, 5, italics removed).[6]

Let me conclude by offering two more solutions. (3) A third solution is for firms to find objective (perhaps quantitative) measurements of the degree to which social media and news websites trend to left or right in terms of U.S. domestic politics. Such firms could then recommend *counterbalancing websites* that trend, maybe equally strongly, in the other direction. Firms could even develop apps that track users' time spent on such websites, helping them to gauge their relative exposure to diverse people and ideas. Fortunately, news entrepreneurs such as the Flip Side (https://www.theflipside.io) now curate views from both the left and the right in order to build ideological and civic bridges. This idea might assume that there are only two sides to a given social issue or that, maybe too simplistically, competing ideas fit neatly along a spectrum. Yet, a service such as the Flip Side can still generate helpful challenges to one's thinking.

(4) A further proposal is for citizens to pay closer attention to the *marginal value* of their information consumption on social media platforms. The marginal value of X is the value gained by consuming an additional unit of X relative to the opportunity cost of consumption. The opportunity cost of consuming X is the most valuable alternative one forgoes. In the case of consuming X, the opportunity cost can be consuming Y, the highest-value consumable item. Or it can be consuming no such item, if non-consumption is better (e.g., to save one's time, talent, or treasure). Consider a citizen who consumes information in the Twitterverse exclusively from a left (or right)-leaning group. At some point, an additional unit of information from a right (or left)-leaning group is likely to be more interesting and/or more conducive to the user's search for truth, improvement of personal character, or contribution to society. It will then be more valuable, at least if the social media user is searching after truth and each group has truth to share that the other does not (or the groups are differentially effective in sharing aspects of the same truth).

Fully implementing my or Sunstein's suggestions would not guarantee the elimination of all undue bias. But following these suggestions would at least be a step in the right direction. It would enable social media users to eliminate their Daily Me or at least make it more representative of a diverse set of reasonable views. A new, more balanced Daily Me could emerge that might not exist entirely outside of an echo chamber but more cautiously draw upon, and participate in, competing echo chambers. Social media users could then gain broader exposure to alternative social and political ideas. This would support the erosion of robust echo chambers by users who more strongly prefer to grasp the truth than to hear others tell them what they already believe and praise them for believing it. We need to develop such a culture, and cultivate the relevant virtues, starting with ourselves.

In the final analysis, it is clear that social media echo chambers have deep and lasting effects on both civic thought and public discourse. How to solve the echo chambers problem and at which level(s) will remain a vital question for an increasingly digitally connected citizenry. Citizens, firms, public officials, and ethicists should pay careful attention to empirical work by social scientists on the nature and prevalence of echo chambers. This will help us better assess the value or disvalue of echo chambers as we work to craft suitable solutions.

Notes

1 Social media providers have also accumulated "growing power to filter for each of us, based on what they know about us" (Sunstein 2017, 6, italics removed).
2 We can leave aside reasonable debates about these assumptions and the value of democracy itself. For alternative views, see, e.g., Christiano (2008) and Brennan (2016).
3 Other minuses include, for instance, addiction to social media due to users' positive dopamine responses (see Bhatt 2019, 51–52, 57).
4 Sunstein (2017, 3) notes, though, that "[e]mpirical work confirms . . . that many members of the public are keenly interested in seeing perspectives that diverge from their own."
5 A rights violation can be counted as a "cost" here.
6 An important question is why there are not more serendipity and diverse viewpoint buttons on social media already. If firms would benefit from offering these and consumers preferred them— i.e., there were opportunities for win–win exchange—then presumably more online platforms would already offer them.

References

Aristotle. 1999. *Nicomachean Ethics* (transl. Irwin, T.). Indianapolis: Hackett.
Bhatt, Swati. (2019). *The Attention Deficit: Unintended Consequences of Digital Connectivity*. Cham, Switzerland: Palgrave MacMillan.
Brennan, Jason. 2016. *Against Democracy*. Princeton: Princeton University Press.
Christiano, Thomas. 2008. *The Constitution of Equality: Democratic Authority and Its Limits*. Oxford: Oxford University Press.
Cobbe, Jennifer. 2020. "Algorithmic Censorship by Social Platforms: Power and Resistance." *Philosophy & Technology*. https://link.springer.com/content/pdf/10.1007/s13347-020-00429-0.pdf
Cowen, Tyler. 2019. "Are Big Tech Firms Evil?" In *Big Business: A Love Letter to an American Anti-Hero*, pp. 99–132. New York: St. Martin's Press.
Eady Gregory, Jonathan Nagler, Andy Guess, Jan Zilinsky, and Joshua A. Tucker. 2019. "How Many People Live in Political Bubbles on Social Media? Evidence from Linked Survey and Twitter Data." *Sage Open*. doi:10.1177/1474022212473527
Elster, Jon. 1983. *Sour Grapes: Studies in the Subversion of Rationality*. Cambridge: Cambridge University Press.
Elzinga, Benjamin. 2020. "Echo Chambers and Audio Signal Processing." *Episteme*, 1–21. doi:10.1017/epi.2020.33
Hallvard, Moe and Anders Olof Larsson. 2015. "Bots or Journalists? News Sharing on Twitter." *Communications* 40 (3): 361–370.
Kearns, Michael and Aaron Roth. 2020. *The Ethical Algorithm: The Science of Socially Aware Algorithm Design*. Oxford: Oxford University Press.

Margetts, Helen and Peter John, Scott Hale, and Taha Yasseri. 2016. *Political Turbulence: How Social Media Shape Collective Action*. Princeton, NJ: Princeton University Press.

Martin, Kirsten. 2017. "It's Not Their Story to Tell: Why Companies Should Respect Privacy Online." TEDx Talk, Charlottesville.

Mill, John Stuart. 1993 [1859]. "On Liberty." In *On Liberty and Utilitarianism*. New York, NY: Bantam Books.

Nguyen, C. Thi. 2020. "Echo Chambers and Epistemic Bubbles." *Episteme* 17(2): 141–161. doi:10.1017/epi.2018.32

Nye, David E. 2007. *Technology Matters: Questions to Live With*. Cambridge, MA: MIT Press.

Otteson, James R. 2019. *Honorable Business: A Framework for Business in a Just and Humane Society*. Oxford University Press.

Quinn, Michael J. 2015 (6th ed.). *Ethics for the Information Age*. New York: Pearson.

Schwartz, Barry and Kenneth Sharpe. 2010. *Practical Wisdom: The Right Way to Do the Right Thing*. New York: Riverhead Books.

Sen, Amartya. 1981. *Poverty and Famines: An Essay on Entitlement and Deprivation*. Oxford: Oxford University Press.

Sunstein, Cass R. 2017. *#Republic: Divided Democracy in the Age of Social Media*. Princeton, NJ: Princeton University Press.

Taddeo, Mariarosaria. 2015. "The Struggle Between Liberties and Authorities in the Information Age." *Science and Engineering Ethics* 21 (5): 1125–1138.

Taddeo, Mariarosaria and Luciano Floridi. 2016. "The Debate on the Moral Responsibilities of Online Service Providers." *Science and Engineering Ethics* 22 (6): 1575–1603.

Tsvetkova, Milena and Ruth García-Gavilanes, Luciano Floridi & Taha Yasseri. 2017. "Even Good Bots Fight: The Case of Wikipedia." *PLoS ONE* 12 (2).

Chapter 24

Data Science and Business Ethics

David C. Rose

Introduction

Over the last half-century, nearly every aspect of our lives has been transformed by information technology. Recently, an important part of information technology – the rapidly evolving field of data science – has begun exerting great influence on societies in a wide variety of ways. In business, government, and education, for example, it is becoming rare to conduct a meeting without the phrase *data-driven decision making* (DDDM) being invoked at least once.

Data science evolved out of several fields that were increasingly understood to have important synergies. With the spectacular rise in computing power large databases began to provide new grist for advanced statistical methods and data mining. A wide variety of advances, including the use of artificial intelligence, improved our ability to identify patterns in data that were otherwise beyond human comprehension. Now, before plans or policy changes are approved, their potential efficacy is often explored through simulation. After implementation, their actual performance is periodically reevaluated. Increasingly new plans or policies will not be approved without the submission of detailed plans for how such periodic reevaluation will be conducted.

With any activity, when knowledge that can increase efficiency is not used social welfare is lower than it would otherwise be. Since data science provides new and powerful ways of extracting additional knowledge content, it can facilitate better decisions, plans, and policies that increase efficiency.

But these benefits come at a cost. Data science can be performed only on knowledge amenable to its methods, which is knowledge that can be codified in data sets. Data science therefore ignores non-codifiable knowledge, which means that it ignores the kind of knowledge that can only be stored in the minds of managers.

Here's a simple example of DDDM and how it misses important information. Suppose that you, an employee's manager, advocate for that employee getting a sizable raise. Suppose that *your* manager insists that you compile objective data to back up the case. It is hard to argue against this request. Such data turns out to not be terribly supportive but based on your personal knowledge of the employee your instincts tell you that the company would be making a huge mistake if it failed to demonstrate a commitment to him to avert his taking another job.

Increasing emphasis on DDDM therefore involves a growing tradeoff between the benefits of greater analytical power exercised on codifiable knowledge and the benefits of knowledge that is impossible to codify in a data set. This tradeoff doesn't just involve the volume of knowledge. The non-codifiable knowledge in a given manager's mind often includes very specific details that are only pertinent to a given department, division, or firm. Because of this, when both forms of knowledge are considered in decision making,

DOI: 10.4324/9781003189466-29

managers from different departments, divisions, and firms will be considering different bodies of local knowledge.

The phrase *local knowledge* comes from the Nobel Prize winning economist F.A. Hayek (1945). It refers to the details of time and place pertinent to a specific person's duties that cannot possibly be considered by a central planner in any but the smallest of societies. Knowing that your car needs a quart of oil, so getting it is more valuable to you than the money you'd have to pay for it, is a simple example of localized knowledge. No one else knows what you know about this circumstance, so no one else knows what's best to do.

The price system is extremely important, Hayek argued, because it automatically does what no central planner can do in large societies. In short, it makes it possible for complete strangers to act independently in ways that do not conflict with the common good. This is because paying the market price forces everyone to bear the social opportunity cost of employing any given resource. In this way, the price system avoids waste by ensuring that resources are used where they are needed most in society.

The idea of local knowledge is also applicable within firms (Rose 2011). It includes highly idiosyncratic things like knowledge of the compatibility of personalities of a given set of workers. As a result, each decision maker's knowledge palette is not just richer when both forms of knowledge are considered; it is also much more likely to differ from the knowledge palette of other managers than when only codifiable knowledge is considered. The consideration of local knowledge therefore fosters diversity in decision making. Conversely, the more emphasis that firms put on DDDM, the more likely they will make the same kinds of choices as other firms than if all managers acted on both forms of knowledge.

In what follows, I explain why DDDM might exacerbate an existing bias that already induces managers to not make the fullest use of the local knowledge they possess. This has both non-consequentialist and consequentialist implications for business ethics. The non-consequentialist implication arises from managers not fulfilling their contractual duty to always make decisions that are best for the firm. The consequentialist implication arises from the actual harm to stakeholders and society that results.[1]

I will then explain why the growing reliance on DDDM likely makes managers too eager to adopt established best practices rather than make their own decisions. This makes firm culture less entrepreneurial and more bureaucratic in nature, which has important implications for firm performance and economic growth.

Data-Driven Decision Making in Context

Managers have used quantitative tools to inform their decision making for a very long time. This is why business education stresses the learning of data analysis. What has changed is that data analysis has gone from merely informing decision making to making it almost formulaic because managers do not want to be put in the position of having to explain why they did not "follow the science" if they deviate from DDDM principles and a bad outcome occurs.

DDDM obviously relies on the kind of knowledge that is amenable to the methods of data science. For many things, like quarterly sales or inventory, this is not problematic because such information is by nature easily codified. But other things, like the nature of the firm's regulatory environment or the trustworthiness of other managers, are not codifiable in most cases because they are based on particular knowledge and subjective perceptions in the manager's mind.

The mind of a manager is therefore, in part, a storage device for such knowledge. In the past, the best managers were scholars of the activities undertaken in their departments, division, firms, and industries. When we say a manager has a great deal of experience, we are essentially saying that there is valuable knowledge stored in that manager's mind that can't be found elsewhere. Firm interests are best served when this knowledge is fully exploited in decision making.

Ethical decision making therefore requires managers to complement what is learned through data science methods with their own judgment applied to the local knowledge they alone possess. The problem is that the manager's own welfare is affected by how much emphasis is put on DDDM. What if, for example, managers find that they are better off relying on DDDM even if they know that by also making better use of the local knowledge stored in their mind, they can apply their judgment to it to make even better decisions for the firm?

Managerial Decision Making Bias and Moral Hazard

Decision makers know that not employing the most scientific methods available might appear irresponsible. Even worse would be to employ such methods and then not follow what they suggest is the best course of action since that might appear arrogant or self-serving. Conversely, being able to claim that one's decision, plan, or policy was a product of DDDM carries an air of scientific rigor, sobriety, and seriousness that indicates strong fidelity to duty.

Managers who ignore or overrule DDDM in light of the local knowledge they possess are therefore put in a difficult position to defend themselves if a bad outcome results. They know that citing their own local knowledge to explain themselves will appear unscientific compared to being able to cite the conclusions of statistical analysis. All managers know that they will sometimes make bad decisions. The question is whether they are able to say that the bad outcome happened despite having employed DDDM or because they ignored or overruled DDDM.

For example, suppose that in the manager's judgment, purchasing a new but unproven type of machine would be better for the firm. The manager might very well choose to stick with the proven design because it provides a better excuse if there is a bad outcome since it was based on DDDM. The manager's motives cannot be impugned by contrasting the DDDM recommended option to the one indicated by his own judgment when it is based on knowledge that, by definition, only he knows. There is therefore little risk that the manager will be discovered to have been making decisions that had more to do with minimizing his own blame than with doing what was best for the firm.

Managers might therefore conclude that it is better to be blamed for a bad outcome that resulted from following DDDM than it is to be blamed for a bad outcome that resulted from having ignored or overruled DDDM. In most cases, if a manager is going to be wrong, it is better to be wrong having followed DDDM, even if overruling DDDM better serves the firm's interests. Besides, DDDM comes with a ready-made defense: "The decision was data driven. Things did not work out even though we *obviously* did our best to ensure otherwise."

But managers are hired to promote the firm's interest, not to avoid blame. To the extent that they refrain from using their best judgment to make the fullest use of local knowledge they possess, they are less likely to be blamed for bad decisions, but they are also failing to live up to the moral duty to best promote the interest of the firm. They are behaving in an unethical manner.

Best Practices

Careful statistical performance evaluation of recently introduced products, plans, and policies has been standard practice in business for a very long time. DDDM goes further, however, putting much more emphasis on analyzing the likelihood of success before actually implementing changes. In this way, DDDM affects the adoption decision itself (Stobierski 2019). If the circumstances that give rise to the need for such an action occur frequently or involve factors common to many different departments, divisions, or firms, such an action might become institutionalized as a best *practice*.

There is an important distinction to be made between what is a firm's best possible action and best practice. To be a best possible action, it must consider all relevant knowledge, including local knowledge stored in the manager's mind. Suppose, for example, that best practice requires putting a team leader on a project who has at least 5 years of experience, but the manager knows a particular younger team member has exceptional talent and leadership ability. In this case, the best possible action likely differs from established best practice.

Best practices, especially over a number of firms or across an entire industry, cannot be derived from local knowledge that is not available in the data set. It follows that when the manager of a given firm automatically adopts established best practices, the manager is in many cases not taking the best possible action, because the best practice cannot reflect the value of local knowledge stored in that manager's mind.

Similarly, pre-validation efforts based on data science methods cannot confirm what is the best possible action. This is because such efforts only identify the best actions conditioned on the data set. The true *best possible action* would be developed and pre-validated using *all* available data, which would necessarily include local knowledge not contained in data sets.

Suppose, for example, that statistical simulations based on industry-wide data show that a new kind of beer would be most profitable if produced in Colorado. If the manager knows that a new state regulator in Colorado is likely to drive up production costs because of unreasonable demands, the best course of action might be to pick a different state despite the simulation result. But if the manager makes the switch and costs end up higher than projected by the simulation, he could lose his job even though in reality the actual cost might be below what it would have been in Colorado. The problem is that the firm owners will never know this. This produces a strong incentive for the manager to go with Colorado because it performed best in models run to pre-validate the location decision.

Here's another example. Suppose statistical methods are used to construct a formula for determining bonuses. If a manager knew that a particular worker was instrumental in a project that would come to fruition next year, the firm's interests might be best served by giving him a larger bonus than the formula prescribes to keep him from going elsewhere. The manager might know the worker well enough to know that he is likely to leave if he feels slighted. If the manager is more worried about having to explain a large bonus for an unfinished project than about the firm losing a chance to pull ahead of competitors through the work the worker would bring to fruition in the next year, then the wrong decision will be made for the firm.

Best practices should therefore be viewed as only rough templates based on codifiable knowledge across departments, divisions, or firms. Unless there is zero local knowledge or zero value created by the manager's judgment applied to it, best practices produce best actions only by coincidence.

Because many do not understand the conditionality of best practices developed through data science methods, performance evaluation *ex post* can further contribute to the false belief that what appears to be the successful implementation of a best practice was indeed the best possible action for any given firm. Performance evaluation of practices across firms and in the literature can lead to an increasing consensus that an observed *successful practice* is indeed the *best practice*. The larger the sample of firm and academic studies, the more sophisticated the data science methods used, and the more consistent the finding of success, the stronger will be the view that a particular practice constitutes the best possible action for any given firm.

But increasing the number of investigations doesn't make up for the absence of local knowledge or the value of managerial judgment applied to it, it just repeats the same mistaken conclusion with greater conviction. If local conditions differ across firms, then local knowledge will also differ. It would be remarkable indeed if the best possible action for any given firm just so happened to match the best possible actions of all other firms, and therefore constitutes the same best practice for all of them.

This is an example of what logicians call the fallacy of affirming the consequent.[2] If a practice is indeed *the* best practice, then pre-validation analysis will show that it is likely to be successful *ex ante* and performance evaluation will show that it was successful *ex post*. But it is fallacious to infer that if a practice can be shown to be likely to be successful, then it is the best practice. Finding evidence that a particular "if-then" statement is correct (if a practice is the best practice, it will do well on performance evaluation) does not constitute evidence that its converse is also correct (*a* practice that does well on performance evaluation is necessarily *the* best practice).

So why the growing emphasis on following best practices? As was the case with DDDM generally, when a manager follows a best practice, the manager knows that what is observed by others will be viewed as evidence of due diligence, no matter what the outcome. Others cannot, however, observe the manager exercising due diligence in applying personal judgment to local knowledge. In the latter case, others will have to rely on results, which is problematic for the case of failed decisions. Managers who stick with best practice, however, fly with a net that catches them even when they fall.

Yet the manager doing what his conscience and judgment require in light of the local knowledge he possesses is the truest form of due diligence because it doesn't sacrifice the value of knowledge in return for greater ability to avoid blame. But if it ends up requiring that a best practice be overruled and replaced with what the manager believes is the best possible action, and a bad outcome follows, the manager will have a much more difficult time explaining the decision.

Making matters worse, the greater the proportion of firms that always follow best practice, the more exceptionally arrogant or foolish the decision to deviate will appear, and so the greater will be the pressure not to deviate. As more simply opt for best practice, over time it becomes increasingly foolish to overrule best practices. But while it therefore becomes increasingly prudent to always follow best practice, doing so when the manager's own judgment requires overruling it remains unethical.

The more local knowledge is ignored, the smaller the set of potential practices becomes. This limits what might come to be regarded as a best practice. Increasing focus on codifiable data means that identified best practices will be increasingly limited to only those that can be based on the antecedent "if" conditions that exist in data sets. As noted above, the best practices that arise from DDDM should therefore be understood to be *conditional* best practices.

From Entrepreneurial to Bureaucratic Firm Culture

It is normally presumed by economists that the more competitive the market, the more that firms will reward entrepreneurial behavior. This is because the more accurately that entrepreneurship describes the nature of leadership at the top and also the behavior of managers at all levels of firm hierarchy, the more profitable the firm is likely to be. At the same time, the more profitable the firm, the more likely it can deal with unforeseen adversities without going bankrupt.

In this way a competitive market environment promotes an entrepreneurial firm culture which is good for the firm's owners (no stone is unturned that might give the firm an advantage over its competitors) and is good for society (it sometimes leads to innovations that increase productivity across industries and even entire economies). In highly competitive market societies it would seem, then, that if there is widespread adherence of DDDM, then it must be producing benefits that exceed the costs of failing to make the fullest use of managerial judgment applied to local knowledge. Otherwise, all firms that employ DDDM would be tempting bankruptcy.

This seems like a strong case for arguing that the shortcomings of DDDM discussed above are of only marginal significance. But it is still possible that there are adverse outcomes for both the firm owners and society even in competitive market environments. This is because if all firms employ DDDM and automatically adopt the same best practices suggested by such analysis, then even when such practices are mistaken, all firms fail in like manner so no firm experiences *relative* failure.[3] This means there is safety in the herd because it undermines the means by which competition between firms would normally exert pressure to make the fullest use of local knowledge and managerial judgment applied to such knowledge.

Note that managers need not collude for this to occur. It can simply arise from the independent realization by managers that some ways of doing business expose them to less risk of being blamed for failure than others. It follows that with the rising influence of data science, it is becoming increasingly prudent for managers to fully embrace DDDM and to adopt best practices even when their own judgment, applied to the local knowledge they possess, suggests otherwise.

Of course, one is not absolved from moral responsibility just because everyone else is doing the same thing. Not using one's judgment to act on local knowledge to overrule a best practice suggested by DDDM is still unethical when it is expected to harm the firm. Even worse, it also harms society in ways that can grow exponentially over time.

Because it ignores local knowledge, DDDM also reduces decision making diversity. Even firms with very different circumstances can benefit from what is discovered by the problem solving of particular managers acting on their own particular flavors of local knowledge. But if managers stop devising and acting on their own unique solutions to their firm's problems because it conflicts with best practices suggested by DDDM, this idiosyncratic set of solutions never sees the light of day.

This harms growth exponentially over time because in each period, the innovations of the previous one provide the foundation for subsequent innovation, giving rise to a socially beneficial positive feedback loop. Unlike nearly everything else in economics, this loop is not subject to diminishing returns because knowledge does not decay and its use does not wear it out but, instead, strengthens it and expands it (Romer 1994). This connection between creativity, innovation, and rising standards of living is well grounded in both theoretical and empirical research. The most prosperous societies are creative societies.[4]

If DDDM leads to inefficient firm outcomes through blame avoidance by managers, shouldn't the firms that shifted to it first have suffered lower profits than other firms? In a competitive environment, shouldn't that have then led to bankruptcy? The answer to both questions would be yes if the adoption of DDDM happened through independent experimentation by firms.

But in reality DDDM was adopted across most firms around the same time due to a sea change in how management was taught in business schools. The natural predilection in business education is to push what's new (that's how one gets published and helps students succeed). At the same time, the natural predilection in business is to adopt what's new because that is how managers show they are forward looking.

But if nearly all firms adopt the same decision making paradigm at the same time this is less of a story about getting ahead than it is about not being left behind. One would think that would create a profit opportunity for firms that deviated. But that benefit will be weighed in the mind of managers against the cost of greater personal risk exposure from deviating.

The cost to individual firms of joining this bandwagon is likely minimal. While it is true that firms miss opportunities to pull ahead in their industries, they are also less likely to be upstaged by other firms and driven to bankruptcy. Their profits might even be greater because they conserve on resources that would otherwise go to funding an innovation race (Loury 1979; Braguinsky and Rose 2009). This is one of the reasons why firms work so hard to collude. It saves resources wasted to get ahead in a zero-sum game for market share.

But even if the cost to firms of being in the DDDM herd is minimal, the cost to society is likely to be substantial. Innovations often increase productivity far beyond the walls of the innovating firm. It follows that if widespread adherence to DDDM reduces diversity of decision making, it might also rob society of innovations that drive rising standards of living (Solow 1957). We cannot measure this loss because it is impossible to know how much richer society could have been if managers had been more creative so innovations that fuel economic growth would have been more frequent.

This doesn't mean managers didn't used to pay attention to what other firms were doing or didn't defend their failed decisions with statistical evidence which they sometimes commissioned to serve as proof of due diligence should things go awry. But coming up with tailored solutions based on judgment applied to local knowledge was still viewed as the main part of the job of any manager. Departments, divisions, and firms were different from each other, so the best decisions, plans, and policies were expected to be different as well. Not so long ago doing what all other firms did was viewed as unimaginative, lazy, or lacking in courage of conviction.

If the increasing reliance on DDDM has induced firms to focus more on the kind of knowledge that is highly amenable to data science methods, then that should reduce the demand for storing local knowledge in managerial minds. It is inevitable that this will, in turn, diminish the importance of managerial judgment applied to local knowledge.

But it is through the exercise of that judgment, applied to diverse bodies of local knowledge across firms, that fuels creativity. Having the courage to act on such creative insights gives firms a powerful way to upstage competitors to get ahead. In this way, the rise of data science might be undermining the entrepreneurial firm culture that we have come to take for granted in the West, replacing it with an increasingly bureaucratic corporate culture where rule following is the norm.

We have examined the cost to firm owners and society of excessive reliance on data science arising from managerial efforts to avoid blame for failed decisions. There is, however, at least one more cost to be considered, which is the psychological cost to managers who, in an earlier time, would have more frequently exercised their capacity for judgment.

For most people, the exercise of judgment is an important part of a fulfilling life. Otteson (2020) argued that Eudaimonia as proposed by Aristotle is achieved by the "full use of our abilities and opportunities in constructing a life of proper meaning and purpose." It is hard to imagine much personal meaning being derived from a life of actions that do not involve the exercise of the individual's own judgment. It follows that if the exercise of judgment within firms is limited by strong incentives to stay in the herd, then an important means by which individuals today can derive meaning from the exercise of their judgment is nullified. This would seem to be a prescription for despair.

For many of those persons, even the reduction of risk can be harmful. The risk of failure arising from being entrusted to exercise one's own judgment creates genuine drama, which for them is a necessary condition for living a fulfilling life. As Tocqueville (1835) famously observed in *Democracy in America*, it is a dark form of despotism that endeavors to remove the trouble of living from citizens. Firms that remove the trouble of exercising judgment and the risk of having to live with the consequences are, one could argue, similarly dispiriting.

Data science has done much good in the world. But data science, by giving managers a new way to protect themselves from personal failures, may be inducing a new form of unethical behavior while at the same time destroying entrepreneurial culture both within firms and across free market societies. It behooves those who have the power to influence firm culture to be mindful of the powerful effect that excessive reliance on data science can have on firm behavior, the welfare of the firm, the psychological well-being of firm managers, and the good of society.

Notes

1 Note I have said "best for the firm" rather than "maximize profit." Many firms tout that they don't have the sole objective of profit maximization. For a discussion about the role of profit maximization in advancing social welfare and fostering economic growth and development, see Friedman (1970), Rose (2000), and Gaus (2009). The analysis that follows does not require that firms be profit maximizers who are only concerned with shareholders.
2 This is the idea that it is fallacious to infer from the demonstration that if A, then B is correct; then if B, then A is also correct.
3 This does not mean that no firm suffers lower profits than otherwise. On the contrary, it suggests that they all suffer lower profits than otherwise due to excessive preoccupation with risk avoidance by managers, which harms each firm. But since they all suffer lower profits, no individual firm is put in jeopardy of bankruptcy because of relatively lower profits.
4 For abundant data analysis on this point, see OECD 2007. The report's introduction states:

> Much of the rise in living standards is due to innovation…It is the application of advances in technology, in conjunction with entrepreneurship and innovative approaches to the creation and delivery of goods and services, which translates scientific and technological advances into more productive economic activity…innovative effort itself, including formal research and development, remains the sine qua non of growth.

References

Braguinsky, Serguey, and David C. Rose. 2009. "Competition, Cooperation, and the Neighboring Farmer Effect." *Journal of Economic Behavior and Organization*, 72 (1): 361–376.

Friedman, Milton. 1970. "A Friedman Doctrine: The Social Responsibility of Business is to Increase Its Profits." *The New York Times Magazine*, September 13. https://www.nytimes.com/1970/09/13/archives/a-friedman-doctrine-the-social-responsibility-of-business-is-to.html

Gaus, Gerald. 2009. "The Idea and Ideal of Capitalism." In *The Oxford Handbook of Business Ethics*, edited by George G. Brenkert and Tom L. Beauchamp, 73–99. Oxford: Oxford University Press.

Hayek, F.A. 1945. "The Use of Knowledge in Society." *American Economic Review*, 35 (4): 519–530.

Kahneman, Daniel, and Amos Tversky. 1979. "Prospect Theory: An Analysis of Decision under Risk." *Econometrica*, 47 (2): 263–292.

Loury, Glenn. 1979. "Market Structure and Innovation." *Quarterly Journal of Economics*, 93 (3): 295–310.

OECD. 2007. *Innovation and Growth*. https://www.oecd.org/sti/39374789.pdf

Otteson, James. 2020. "Honoring the Moral Purpose of Business." *Law & Liberty*, May 25, 2020.

Romer, Paul. M. "The Origins of Endogenous Growth." *Journal of Economic Perspectives*, 8 (1): 3–22.

Rose, David C. 2000. "Teams, Firms, and the Evolution of Profit Seeking Behavior." *Journal of Bioeconomics*, 2 (1): 25–39.

Rose, David C. 2011. *The Moral Foundation of Economic Behavior*. New York: Oxford University Press.

Smith, Adam. 1981 [1776]. *An Inquiry into the Nature and Causes of the Wealth of Nations.* Edited by R.H. Campbell and A.S. Skinner. Indianapolis: Liberty Fund Press.

Solow, Robert. 1957. "Technical Change and the Aggregate Production Function." *Review of Economics and Statistics*, 39 (3): 312–320.

Stobierski, Tim. 2019. "The Advantages of Data Driven Decision-Making." *Harvard Business School Blog Post*, August 26, 2019. https://online.hbs.edu/blog/post/data-driven-decision-making

Tocqueville, Alexis. 1835. *Democracy in America.* London: Saunders and Otley.

Chapter 25

Technology Firms and the Business Case for Diversity

Adam Gjesdal

Introduction

Firms in Silicon Valley have made the news for their purported intolerance of employees who support politically conservative views. Conservative workers at Twitter have expressed they "don't feel comfortable speaking up" (Wagner 2018). Facebook is accused of firing a top executive for making a sizable donation to a group supporting then-presidential candidate Donald Trump in 2016 (Grind & Hagey 2018). Regardless of whether these specific news items have merit, they indicate at the very least that elite tech firms are widely perceived as having an internal political bias. Silicon Valley firms' political donation patterns support the view that, even if these firms aren't biased against conservatives, they do have strong internal ideological leanings. At Netflix, 98% of political donations from employees went to liberal candidates during the 2020 election cycle. At Facebook and Amazon, 77% of donations went to liberal candidates. Among the U.S.'s 17 biggest tech firms, only Qualcomm employees donated equally to liberals and conservatives (Levy 2020).

Such a bias—if it exists—would be legally permissible, at least under federal law, which does not prohibit workplace discrimination for political beliefs. But, given the immense influence elite tech firms have on our lives, any such bias would have a wide-ranging impact outside the company. For example, internal decisions at Twitter that result in "deplatforming" a user can determine whether or not an online content provider continues to make a living. Internal decisions at Salesforce affect whether businesses continue to sell assault rifles for sporting purposes (Joyce 2019). Given the wide-ranging effects of their decisions, elite tech firms have a social responsibility to ensure their policies are not skewed by an internal culture that discourages the expression of diverse ideological viewpoints.

Luckily, acting on this social responsibility need not impact a firm's bottom line. There already exists a rich literature arguing how diverse workforces make firms profitable. This literature mainly focuses on *identity diversity* in the workplace—that is, diversity of race, gender, ethnicity, religion, or sexual orientation. In this chapter, I argue that the causal mechanisms that plausibly explain this connection between identity diversity and profitability also suggest that *ideological diversity* increases profitability. Big tech firms have a responsibility to listen to the perspectives of ideologically conservative users, who, in many circumstances, have no alternative to using Facebook or Twitter for accessing social networks. I argue that by discharging this responsibility, tech firms can also capture the full benefits of diversity for optimizing business strategy, which can lead to improved net profits, market share, or customer bases. I start by summarizing various empirical results from real-world and lab settings showing how discomfort caused by perceived diversity enhances group performance by making individuals reason more cautiously. Next, I turn to Hong and Page's theoretical explanation of how cognitively diverse problem solvers can outperform likeminded groups of experts on complex tasks. Finally, I show how this evidence supports the claim that firms

DOI: 10.4324/9781003189466-30

with a predominantly liberal or conservative internal culture have profit-oriented reasons to internally encourage free expression of ideological heterogeneity.

Diversity and Discomfort

There is ample evidence that diverse workforces are good for business. Cedric Herring (2009) uses data from the 1996–1997 National Organizations Survey to show that there is a statistically significant relationship between a firm's racial or gender diversity and its business performance, measured as sales revenues, number of customers, or profits relatives to competitors.[1] A 2015 study by McKinsey & Company shows that firms in the top quartile for gender or ethnic diversity are more likely to outperform their industry median (Hunt et al. 2015). And Hossain et al. (2020) show using regression analyses that workplace diversity policies result in more innovative and better-performing firms. Many of these studies use statistical means to rule out that alternative factors, such as firm size, may actually cause firm value, strengthening the claim that the connection between firm diversity and profitability is causal, not merely correlational. Yet, they do little to show why, exactly, a more diverse workforce improves business performance. So, *why* do firms that are diverse in their makeup—as measured by workers' ethnicity, gender, or sexual orientation—tend to outperform their more homogenous peers, assuming a causal relationship between diversity and enhanced performance?

While there are several possible explanations, I focus on the well-supported theory that a workforce's identity diversity enhances the firm's cognitive diversity. *Cognitive diversity* concerns how individuals represent problems to themselves, and how they apply different skillsets when solving those problems. Increases in one kind of diversity correlate with, but do not cause, increases in the other. Importantly, the two kinds of diversity can sometimes come sharply apart. Members of a highly identity-diverse group may all evince cognitive homogeneity by approaching a complex problem in the same way, meaning the group as a whole suffers from the same cognitive limitations and biases as its individual members.[2] Discussion in identity-diverse but likeminded groups can even exacerbate individuals' biases and tendencies to endorse extreme views (Sunstein 2009, 18–19).

Across a body of work, Katherine Phillips and her co-authors offer a compelling explanation of why identity-diverse groups outperform homogenous ones. They argue that identity diversity makes group members more defensive and careful reasoners. This is not necessarily because diverse group members bring more information or different approaches to solving a problem to the table. Rather, the mere *appearance* of diversity—they call this "surface-level diversity"—is enough to confer measurable benefits in performance. The idea is that when we interact with others in a group who are "like us" in some salient way, we expect them to also think like us. Who we categorize as in-group members depends on context. Sometimes, this categorization tracks race (Phillips & Lount 2007). But in experiments involving college students, salient out-groups could be marked by their fraternity membership (Phillips et al. 2009). Or, the out-group could be marked by which side of campus a student lives on (Phillips & Loyd 2006). Phillips and her co-authors have experimentally shown that even when perceived out-group members do not have any novel task-relevant information to contribute, adding them to a group can improve the group's overall performance. She speculates that a crucial causal factor in improved performance is members' affective reaction to interacting with someone who is not like them, in some salient way (Phillips et al. 2011, 262). Members of surface-level diverse groups experience a level of discomfort and anxiety that, surprisingly, makes them *more careful* in processing information when compared to peers in homogenous groups. These information-processing benefits can occur even when members of the group do not directly interact with their out-group peer: the mere awareness of surface-level heterogeneity can be enough to trigger these benefits.[3]

The discomfort and anxiety that diversity brings to a group is one source of its cognitive advantages. When we are engaged in a task with peers whom we expect to think as we do, we become complacent, and this negatively affects group performance. As Ryan Muldoon (2018, 815) puts it,

> amongst like-minded people, we are more likely to agree with someone's idea, and feel like it is a good one, and potentially what we should settle on. This sort of agreement feels better. We like what our peers have to say because they are close to what we would say. So, it is easier for us to feel like the group is doing a good job—after all, all the ideas we hear seem like good ones—even though the group is likely doing worse. Homogenous groups are more subject to groupthink, more subject to belief polarization, and less subject to challenge and debate. What makes us *like* to be in homogenous groups is what makes them underperform while simultaneously feeling successful.

Adding a perceived out-group member into the mix can be sufficient to undermine group members' expectation of agreeable, fluid functioning driven by consensus. Once that expectation is undermined, we are no longer sure that everyone will be likeminded on how to proceed. The accompanying anxiety leads us to attend to possible objections to our ideas we would otherwise ignore. This anxiety-induced caution makes the individual group members better reasoners, and as a result improves group performance as a whole.

This suggests an important lesson for leading tech firms. In a firm like Twitter, committees make internal policy decisions that can result in banning users from the network. Bans can be extremely consequential for users who rely on the network for their livelihoods, and Twitter has an interest in its decisions being widely seen as fair. If committees deciding these policies deliberate about what policies are fair in the expectation of achieving an easy consensus among themselves, they are unlikely to make optimal decisions. In this section, we have considered how these committees can reap some of the benefits of cognitive diversity without its members substantively interacting with differently minded peers. Benefits can be had if the group contains members who are *perceived* as outsiders—even when those "outsiders" think about problems in precisely the same way and have access to exactly the same information as the "insiders." The presence of perceived out-group members undermines the expectation of a smooth, pleasant, consensus-driven discussion, triggering in the minds of individual participants an improved attentiveness to the problem's underlying complexity.

The discomfort and anxiety that affectively trigger cognitive benefits should not be confused with prejudice and bias toward out-group members. On the present analysis, the perceived out-group member does not trigger anxiety or discomfort because she is seen as inferior or threatening. Rather, she is seen (perhaps mistakenly) as having a different perspective or novel information on a problem that could present challenges to the group's agreed upon view. She is seen in this way because she is, at the surface-level, different from the group. But it doesn't matter whether this difference is merely surface-level or extends to how she thinks about the problem as well. In response to surface-level diversity, group members feel anxiety or discomfort because they feel their own ideas may be lacking, that what they regard as good ideas might turn out not to be such. This drives individual group members to search through a broader space of possible challenges to their views to ensure that they are good views. Their discomfort does not necessarily attach to the out-group member herself, but rather to the possibility that they might be getting things wrong in how they think about a problem. For this discomfort to produce benefits, group members must presume that the perceived outsider could have something valuable to add to their deliberations.

In this framework, diversity brings substantial benefits only when members of a heterogeneous group see each other as meaningful contributors. Van Knippenberg et al. (2013) argue that teams must share "diversity mindsets" that represent the kinds of informational resources members can offer, as well as how those resources can contribute to achieving team goals. These mindsets are highly specific to the team's task and require reflection on what the team is trying to achieve and how. They help channel discomfort toward productive ends, preventing those feelings from manifesting as hostility toward out-group members, or taking shape as biased or prejudicial behavior. Cultivating and maintaining the proper diversity mindset, they argue, is not only a task for organizations as a whole, but also for project leaders knowledgeable of the specific ways in which information exchange can optimize team performance. Discomfort from perceived diversity does not always confer performance benefits. Unaccompanied by the proper mindsets, it can lead to group conflict and hostility between members, making individuals more closed-minded and less willing to debate their views and revise them in the face of challenges.

Cognitive Diversity Sometimes Trumps Ability

So far, our discussion suggests that firms like Twitter can improve the quality of their internal policy-making procedures by including more "surface-level" diversity in them. The mere appearance of diverse viewpoints at the table makes discussants more cautious and attentive to potential challenges, even when members don't exchange information with each other. But even cautious reasoners are apt to ignore many possible solutions to a problem. Cognitive diversity delivers its full benefits for optimizing decision-making when people with very different viewpoints can exchange substantive ideas. Much important theoretical work on this topic is due to Scott Page. The Hong–Page theorem shows that groups of randomly selected, diverse problem solvers can outperform a homogenous group of likeminded experts of greater ability (Hong & Page 2001, 2004; Page 2019). The basic idea of their theorem is that, under certain conditions, cognitively diverse agents bring complementary perspectives to bear on a problem, enabling them to correct each other's blind spots and biases, and to search a wider space of possibilities for the optimum solution. In contrast, a group of experts, all of whom employ similar approaches—even when these are the *best* approaches—underperform relative to the diverse group. Likeminded experts will get stuck at a local optimum, a solution to the problem that looks like it's the best one there is, even though there are better solutions to be found. Diverse perspectives keep the group from getting stuck at one of these local optima, so that they can find better and better solutions.

Cognitive diversity is a boon only for problems with certain features. The problem must be sufficiently complex such that the range of relevant skills needed to address it cannot be possessed by any one mind. As an example, consider the gains from diversity to be had in a surgical team. The world's two leading heart surgeons, accompanied by a nurse, have the skills needed to address a range of complications that can arise in the course of a bypass operation. The surgeons' knowledge base far outstrips that of a group of random people off the street with no medical training. In this comparison, diversity does not trump ability: a team composed of a plumber, a police officer, a politician, and a programmer will *not* do a better job in the operating theater, due to their more diverse set of skills, than would the pair of eminent surgeons, for their diverse skillsets do not equip them to address the relevant task. But instead compare the team of the two leading heart surgeons with a more diverse medical team consisting of an anesthesiologist, a vascular surgeon, and an experienced but not eminent cardiothoracic surgeon. This diverse team has complementary and non-overlapping skillsets that equip them to respond to a wider range of complications that could arise during surgery than would the pair of eminent surgeons with overlapping knowledge bases. If the patient's blood oxygen levels drop, or she develops arrhythmia during surgery, the diverse team may be able to better to identify the underlying problem and implement the optimal solution than would the likeminded pair of elite surgeons. Were this so, the diverse team would have a higher success rate when performing heart surgeries. It is an empirical matter what the optimum constituency of a diverse surgical team will be. Page's theoretical framework explains why the diverse team would perform better than a more homogenous one.

Many business problems are complex in ways that create large potential benefits from cognitive diversity. For example, boardroom negotiations may lead to an unfolding crisis that demands a range of skillsets to immediately address it, much as in the surgery example above. But diversity benefits are also to be had when solving problems with quite different structures. Page (2019) shows how they can arise in the creation of entirely new markets through entrepreneurship, in overcoming engineering challenges when innovating an existing product's design, or when forecasting consumer demand. Focusing on the latter, demand predictions affect production schedules and profit forecasts. Predictors' relevant knowledge bases include not only sophisticated mathematical models for forecasting demand but also an awareness of what role, if any, certain products play in diverse consumers' lives. A team of predictors can produce more accurate sales forecasts if they include members who belong to different target demographics. Here, the team's identity diversity becomes a form of cognitive diversity, where identity-diverse team members have complementary skills that no one set of identity-homogenous individuals—even if they are the most skillful predictors in the world—would necessarily possess. These gains can lead to more accurate consumption forecasts, which, in turn, help a firm run more efficiently and profitably.

We have two frameworks for explaining why diverse firms outperform homogenous peers. Phillips and her co-authors suggest that perceived diversity triggers anxiety and discomfort that induce individuals to more carefully scrutinize their own views. Hong and Page suggest that when individuals possess distinct skillsets and tools relevant to a task, the group as a whole more effectively canvasses the space of possible solutions to find an optimum response. In the former, cognitive diversity is not necessary for producing substantial benefits for group performance. In the latter, cognitive diversity is, in relevant contexts, sufficient for generating substantial gains. These two frameworks are compatible. And they both show how identity diversity can improve a firm's bottom line, despite identity diversity *per se* not causing profit-enhancing benefits. The idea is that an identity-diverse group puts members on their guard, making them more cautious and considerate of challenges to their views. And the identity-diverse group will, in a range of circumstances, actually have new ideas to offer and skills to contribute, because the group's identity diversity reflects an underlying cognitive diversity. All this requires that the group maintain perspective on how discomfort and disagreement serve their task-specific aims. Otherwise, the out-group members who present perceived or actual challenges to what one regards as good ideas will be seen more as threats than cooperators, with group performance suffering as a result.

The Benefits of Ideological Diversity

These two frameworks help explain why identity-diverse firms enjoy various benefits in comparison with their less diverse peers: identity diversity is correlated with cognitive diversity, which improves the quality of group decision-making. I now argue that *ideological diversity*, at least in the American political context, is a species of identity diversity. In the

American context, the population is sharply polarized along conservative and liberal lines. This divide doesn't merely sort the population along party affiliation and voting behavior: it also tracks where people live, what churches they attend, where they shop, which entertainment and news media services they consume, and even their fertility rates (Pew 2014). Ideological orientation corresponds to a range of overlapping identities that, together, compose a sizeable demographic.[4] Page (2019, 90) argues that identity diversity often tracks cognitive diversity, in the sense that distinct identities correlate with distinct knowledge bases, ways of categorizing the world, and heuristics for searching the solution space of a complex problem. This suggests that as much as firms benefit from having racial or gender diverse workforces, which grant firms access in their decision-making to the unique perspectives of various demographics, so, too, would firms benefit from cultivating internal ideological diversity. This cultivation comes with a trade-off: while it can improve group performance, it can also lead to a breakdown of cohesion. This trade-off is particularly salient for the present discussion as ideological differences lead to affective polarization. Because liberals and conservatives are sorted along so many dimensions, they rarely have exposure to each other's views—with this lack of non-partisan exposure to the out-group reinforcing feelings of mutual dislike, even hostility (Iyengar et al. 2012; Pew 2016). To enjoy the benefits of ideological diversity, a firm must first find a way to overcome the hurdle of affective polarization.

Unfortunately, ideological diversity in the firm has not been studied to the same extent as racial or gender diversity. As Swigart et al. (2020, 1075) note, "there is limited evidence for how political ideology diversity affects a team." One study by Shi et al. (2019) shows that there are cognitive benefits to ideological diversity when it comes to editing Wikipedia articles. Articles with politically polarized editors used "more competing terminology and framings," they "engage[d] in more debate which is less acrimonious," and they "more frequently appeal to Wikipedia policies and guidelines to govern these interactions" (Shi et al. 2019, 333). Nevertheless, Swigart et al. (2020, 1075) observe that editors interacted with each other online only, with interactions subject to strict guidelines and overseen by moderators. Workplace environments that require face-to-face interaction may exacerbate existing out-group biases that impede information flow. There simply isn't much work done on how organizations can exploit the cognitive diversity of ideologically diverse groups, without groups falling into irresolvable conflict. It is all too easy, given how the specific news media we follow train us to view the ideological out-group as an object of ridicule or contempt, for teams of liberals and conservatives to fasten on to their underlying differences over values, rather than seeing each other as beneficial repositories of complementary skills and information. Unlike the discomfort that drives team members to scrutinize their own views, this negative affect toward the ideological out-group undermines the "diversity mindset" that would otherwise enable task-specific reflection and informational exchange, leading to optimized team performance.

These considerations apply to American businesses across all industries. But, to return to the opening theme, they are especially relevant for "big tech" firms. Those firms produce goods and services consumed by every demographic. Many conservative users feel that these goods and services are biased against them, and as evidence they point to the strongly liberal leanings of employees at these firms. Moreover, these users cannot resort to substitutes, with firms like Twitter and Salesforce having effective monopolies over their markets. Regardless of whether user complaints are justified, the preceding discussion shows that a firm where employees overwhelmingly skew liberal suffers some of the same cognitive deficiencies as a firm that overwhelmingly skews male. Across a range of scenarios, that firm fails to implement optimum decisions. Decisions on company policy or product design end up being made by teams whose members have overlapping biases and blind spots. These deficiencies aren't simply solved by adding more diversity to the team. Team diversity must be accompanied by the right mindset where individuals see out-group members as cooperative partners in possession of novel resources for solving complex, multi-dimensional tasks. Integrating women, ethnic and racial minorities, and LGBT individuals in the workforce, in response to government-led diversity initiatives, required great changes in internal workplace culture, including implementing diversity training to minimize both implicit and explicit expressions of prejudice. These initiatives are costly, but, as noted above, they seem to pay off in the long run, for diverse firms tend to outperform their more homogenous peers. Firms may also find extensive gains from minimizing internal cultures that permit or encourage prejudicial behavior toward members of one or the other ideological camp.

Notes

1 An exception is that Herring found no statistically significant relationship between a firm's gender diversity and its market share.
2 Jehn et al. (1999) disambiguate diversity into multiple kinds, including (using the present terminology) cognitive and identity diversity, showing that they have distinct impacts on group performance, and that diversity of one kind does not necessarily indicate diversity of another.
3 Sommers et al. (2008) also show this result in racially diverse jury trials.
4 As of June 2020, about 34% of Americans self-identify as conservative, and 26% as liberal. Most—36%—see themselves as moderate (Saad 2020).

References

Grind, K., & Hagey, K. 2018. "Why did Facebook fire a top executive? Hint: It had something to do with Trump." *The Wall Street Journal*, November 11. Retrieved from https://www.wsj.com/articles/why-did-facebook-fire-a-top-executive-hint-it-had-something-to-do-with-trump-1541965245

Herring, Cedric. 2009. "Does diversity pay?: Race, gender, and the business case for diversity." *American Sociological Review* 74, no. 2: 208–224.

Hong, Lu, and Scott E. Page. 2001. "Problem solving by heterogeneous agents." *Journal of Economic Theory* 97, no. 1: 123–163.

Hong, Lu, and Scott E. Page. 2004. "Groups of diverse problem solvers can outperform groups of high-ability problem solvers." *Proceedings of the National Academy of Sciences* 101, no. 46: 16385–16389.

Hossain, Mohammed, Muhammad Atif, Ammad Ahmed, and Lokman Mia. 2020. "Do LGBT workplace diversity policies create value for firms?" *Journal of Business Ethics* 167, no. 4: 775–791.

Hunt, Vivian, Dennis Layton, and Sara Prince. 2015. "Diversity matters." *McKinsey & Company* 1, no. 1: 15–29.

Iyengar, Shanto, Gaurav Sood, and Yphtach Lelkes. 2012. "Affect, not ideology: A social identity perspective on polarization." *Public Opinion Quarterly* 76, no. 3: 405–431.

Jehn, Karen A., Gregory B. Northcraft, and Margaret A. Neale. 1999. "Why differences make a difference: A field study of diversity, conflict and performance in workgroups." *Administrative Science Quarterly* 44, no. 4: 741–763.

Joyce, Kathleen. 2019. "Salesforce says some firearms can no longer be sold using company software." *FoxBusiness*, May 31. Retrieved from https://www.foxbusiness.com/retail/salesforce-bars-retailers-sell-certain-firearms-using-software

Levy, Ari. 2020. "The most liberal and conservative tech companies, ranked by employees' political donations." *CNBC*, July 2. Retrieved from: https://www.cnbc.com/2020/07/02/most-liberal-tech-companies-ranked-by-employee-donations.html

Muldoon, Ryan. 2018. "The paradox of diversity." *Georgetown Journal of Law & Public Policy* 16: 807.

Page, Scott. 2019. *The Diversity Bonus*. Princeton: Princeton University Press.

Pew. 2014. "Political polarization in the American Public." *Pew Research Center,* June 12. Retrieved from: https://www.pewresearch.org/politics/2014/06/12/political-polarization-in-the-american-public/

Pew. 2016. "Partisanship and political animosity in 2016." *Pew Research Center,* June 22. Retrieved from: https://www.pewresearch.org/politics/2016/06/22/partisanship-and-political-animosity-in-2016/

Phillips, Katherine W., and Robert B. Lount. 2007. "The affective consequences of diversity and homogeneity in groups." In Elizabeth A. Mannix, Margaret Ann Neale, and Cameron P. Andersen (eds.), *Affect and Groups,* pp. 1–20. Bingley: Emerald Group Publishing Limited.

Phillips, Katherine W., Gregory B. Northcraft, and Margaret A. Neale. 2006. "Surface-level diversity and decision-making in groups: When does deep-level similarity help?" *Group Processes & Intergroup Relations* 9, no. 4: 467–482.

Phillips, Katherine W., Katie A. Liljenquist, and Margaret A. Neale. 2009. "Is the pain worth the gain? The advantages and liabilities of agreeing with socially distinct newcomers." *Personality and Social Psychology Bulletin* 35, no. 3: 336–350.

Phillips, Katherine W., and Denise Lewin Loyd. 2006. "When surface and deep-level diversity collide: The effects on dissenting group members." *Organizational Behavior and Human Decision Processes* 99, no. 2: 143–160.

Phillips, Katherine W., Kim-Jun, Sun Young, & Shim, So-Hyeon. 2011. "The value of diversity in organizations: A social psychological perspective." In David De Cremer, Rolf van Dick, and J. Keith Murnighan (eds.), *Social Psychology and Organizations* (pp. 253–271). New York: Routledge.

Saad, Lydia. 2020. "U.S. conservativism down since start of 2020." *Gallup,* July 27. Retrieved from: https://news.gallup.com/poll/316094/conservatism-down-start-2020.aspx

Shi, Feng, Misha Teplitskiy, Eamon Duede, and James A. Evans. 2019. "The wisdom of polarized crowds." *Nature Human Behaviour* 3, no. 4: 329–336.

Sommers, Samuel R., Lindsey S. Warp, and Corrine C. Mahoney. 2008. "Cognitive effects of racial diversity: White individuals' information processing in heterogeneous groups." *Journal of Experimental Social Psychology* 44, no. 4: 1129–1136.

Sunstein, Cass R. 2009. *Going to Extremes: How Like Minds Unite and Divide.* Oxford: Oxford University Press.

Swigart, Kristen L., Anuradha Anantharaman, Jason A. Williamson, and Alicia A. Grandey. 2020. "Working while liberal/conservative: A review of political ideology in organizations." *Journal of Management* 46, no. 6: 1063–1091.

Van Knippenberg, Daan, Wendy P. Van Ginkel, and Astrid C. Homan. 2013. "Diversity mindsets and the performance of diverse teams." *Organizational Behavior and Human Decision Processes* 121, no. 2: 183–193.

Wagner, K. 2018. "Twitter is so liberal that its conservative employees 'don't feel safe to express their opinions,' says CEO Jack Dorsey." *Vox,* September 14. Retrieved from https://www.vox.com/2018/9/14/17857622/twitter-liberal-employeesconservative-trump-politics

Chapter 26

Big Tech & Political Equality

Saura Masconale and Simone M. Sepe

Introduction

The literature on Big Tech companies has now become so voluminous to constitute its own field of research.[1] This is unsurprising when one considers the impact that the "Gang of Four"—Google, Apple, Facebook, and Amazon—have had on our lives.[2] In examining the implications of this vast reach, the existing literature has largely focused on matters of economic efficiency and privacy. On the economic front, Big Tech advocates defend these companies' capacity to innovate and bolster the U.S. competitive edge (see, e.g., Gertner, 2012; Goshen and Hamdani, 2016), while detractors warn that their accumulated market power raises major anti-trust concerns (see, e.g., Khan, 2017; Sitaraman, 2020; Wu, 2018). On the privacy front, commentators have long been divided on how to address the privacy issues raised by the Big Tech's use of data as their primary currency (see, e.g., Bambauer, 2014; Pasquale, 2010; Tene and Polonetsky, 2012).

In this chapter, we explore a different aspect of the rise of Big Tech: their growing role as key political players and the implications that this has for the central democratic principle of political equality. That Big Tech's impact on society matters for democracy and public values is not a novel argument. But the existing literature frames this argument as a corollary of the broader claims above. On the one hand, these companies' disproportionate *economic* power is described as weakening their democratic accountability, if not posing a threat to national security (see, e.g., Belei et al., 2019; Fukuyama et al., 2019; Sitamaran, 2020). On the other hand, the tech companies' control of big data is seen as harming not just our privacy, but leading to forms of intrusive surveillance in our lives qua citizens (see, e.g., Feldstein, 2019; Zuboff, 2018).

We take a different approach to the relationship between Big Tech and democracy. This approach draws on our prior work on the rise of corporate activism—the engagement by corporations in the political discourse around divisive political and moral issues (Masconale and Sepe, 2022). In Sections "Big Tech, Corporate Activism, and Moral Disagreement" and "The Democratic Costs of Big Tech's Social Activism" of this essay, we build on the insights of that work to introduce the risk of democratic loss that corporate activism may trigger along the dimension of political equality (Masconale and Sepe, 2022). Next, in Section "Big Tech's Complications," we will show how Big Tech companies have championed this new corporate trend and why the democratic concerns it raises are especially severe in the case of these companies.

Big Tech, Corporate Activism, and Moral Disagreement

From CSR to Corporate Activism

Long gone are the days when public companies did everything they could to try to stay morally and politically neutral. Today's corporations are increasingly taking stands on

DOI: 10.4324/9781003189466-31

highly charged social issues: gun control, gender and race equity, immigration, abortion, reproductive rights, free speech—and the list will surely grow. Big Tech companies have played a leading role in this transformation, being involved in—if not initiating—virtually every recent manifestation of corporate activism: from the wave of dissents against the North Carolina's "bathroom bill"[3] to the commitments in favor of criminal justice reform after the murder of George Floyd and, more recently, the concerted corporate actions against law restricting abortions in Southern states and the new voting laws in Georgia.[4]

The corporate law literature has framed this new trend as just an expansion of corporate social responsibility (CSR), with this expansion being prompted by a change in stakeholder moral preferences. On this view, corporate activism produces what we refer to as "moral goods" (Masconale and Sepe, 2022) in response to increased stakeholder demand for these goods (see, e.g., Hart and Zingales, 2017; Henderson and Malani, 2009).

This approach, however, misses a key feature that distinguishes corporate activism from traditional CSR. Indeed, a common assumption of CSR studies is that corporate social engagement delivers benefits that are universally recognized, understood and valued by all citizens/stakeholders. To this extent, CSR is largely viewed as a private contribution to the production of public goods—i.e., a market-driven response to government failures (see, e.g., Benabou and Tirole, 2010; Hart and Zingales, 2017). Yet, unlike traditional CSR (e.g., corporate programs fighting poverty or promoting better education), the new corporate activism focuses on divisive issues—or what Jeremy Waldron calls "watershed issues of rights" (Waldron, 2006). These are "major issues of political philosophy with significant ramifications for the lives of many people. … [and] … focal points of moral and political disagreement in many societies" (Waldron, 2006, 1367). That is, the new corporate activism focuses on issues "on which *it is not reasonable to expect that there would be consensus*" (Waldron, 2006, 1368). As we shall see next, this overlooked feature of moral goods has important descriptive and normative implications for the relationship between corporations and democracy, especially in the case of Big Tech.

Incorporating Moral Disagreement

As a descriptive matter, incorporating the possibility of moral disagreement into the analysis of corporate activism implies a fundamental difference between the production of divisive moral goods and any other good or service the corporation produces. If morality were a preference that could be satisfied like any other, it would not matter much that people have different, often conflicting, moral preferences. Markets could fully internalize (i.e., satisfy) our heterogenous moral preferences and allow for the greatest diversity in goals and resources, as they do with other goods the corporation produces. But divisive moral goods are different in a critical way from most of the traditional products and services that companies deliver: they are "exclusionary." This means that the production of moral good x, reflecting, say, a progressive moral identity (e.g., a gun-control policy) excludes the ability to produce the "contrarian" moral good y, reflecting, say, a conservative identity (e.g., a no gun-control policy). In response to this constraint, corporations will need to opt for either one good or the other, as producing both goods would destroy the value that the corporation can extract from either good.

This distinctive feature of divisive moral goods also redefines their normative implications. Under the standard account of CSR as non-divisive, a key issue is how to solve the free-riding problem that typically affects public goods. Since corporate social engagement is assumed to be supported by broad consensus, interested stakeholders may expect other people to have a similar altruistic interest in the pursuit of such engagement (Henderson and Malani, 2010). This is the source of the free-riding problem. But to the extent that moral goods are divisive—as they increasingly are—there remains little, if any, room for free riding. This is because only by paying for the moral good they are interested in can individuals secure the related utility and limit the risk that the corporation might produce, instead, the contrarian moral good. It follows that moral goods are excludable, unlike public goods.

Within this different analytical framework, the key question is how corporations—and Big Tech, in particular—adjudicate divisive moral issues, that is, how they decide *which* moral goods to produce. This question is central because it has implications for the commitment of modern democracies to political equality. Indeed, the acknowledgment that some matters may generate fundamental conflicts of interests in society is a core preoccupation of democratic systems. Political equality addresses this preoccupation by guaranteeing that when a collective decision is made in the face of moral or political disagreement, the decision-making process is structured so as to ensure that "advancing the interests of one person is as important as advancing the interests of any other person" (Christiano, 2003, 33). The one-person, one-vote (OPOV) rule of electoral governance is perhaps the most salient means used to that end. For "if nothing else, democracy is a deeply egalitarian method of organizing social decisionmaking" (Christiano, 2003, 34).

The compatibility between corporate and democratic adjudication of divisive moral issues thus matters because these two domains are not independent. Instead, as we will explain below, the corporate adjudication process of divisive moral issues has both direct and indirect implications for their democratic adjudication.

The Democratic Costs of Big Tech's Social Activism

Economic Efficiency and the Production of Moral Goods

How do corporations decide *which* divisive moral goods to produce when the production of such goods is exclusionary?

The short answer is that being unable to capture the universal economic demand for moral goods, corporations will strive to capture the majoritarian economic demand for such goods.[5] But how is the majoritarian economic demand for divisive moral goods aggregated? This demand is determined based on the economic interests of the various corporate constituencies. So, intuitively, what matters is the relative weight of these economic interests.

Now, another common assumption in recent CSR studies concerns the equalization of the demand for moral goods coming from consumers, suppliers, employees and shareholders. These studies assume that the moral preferences of each of these constituencies have equal weight in the determination of such demand (see, e.g., Henderson and Malani, 2009). However, this assumption does not take into account the asset price effects that are involved by the morality demand of financial investors (i.e., shareholders but also bondholders).

As we showed elsewhere (Masconale and Sepe, 2022), these asset price effects arise from a distortion of investors' portfolio choices. The starting point to understand this mechanism is the portfolio theory under which investors diversify their portfolios by weighing assets based on expected risk and return (LeRoy and Werner, 2001). One can accordingly assume that all investors will include in their portfolio *some* activist assets for diversification purposes. Sympathetic investors with a taste for moral goods, however, can be expected to alter their allocations so as to include *more* activist assets in their portfolios (Gollier and Pouget, 2014). We call this a "moral portfolio" choice. Moral portfolio choices trigger asset prices effects: they lead to an increase in the demand of activist assets (i.e., the shares of corporations engaged in corporate activism) relative to the assets of non-activist corporations.

Similar to what happens with financial bubbles, this enhanced demand then drives an increase in the share price value of activist corporations, which helps internalize (compensate for) the costs of moral goods (i.e., costly corporate activism).

On the one hand, the magnitude of the asset price effects arising from moral portfolio choices solves long-standing questions about the compatibility of corporate social engagement and economic efficiency (see, e.g., Gadinis and Miazaad, 2020). This is because catering to the moral preferences of sympathetic investors—and hence capturing positive asset price effects—makes corporate activism economically viable. On the other hand, under this newly founded compatibility between corporate social engagement and economic efficiency, the economic interest of sympathetic investors are likely to have a disproportionate impact on the determination of the majoritarian demand for moral goods. Thus, these investors' moral preferences are likely to be accorded priority over that of other constituencies, inducing corporations to exclusively conform to such preferences.

The next question then is whether this "corporate conformity" is compatible with the principle of political equality that is required for the legitimate adjudication of divisive moral issues in modern democracies. Answering this question involves a two-fold inquiry. First, we need to understand the relationship between corporate and democratic adjudication of divisive moral issues—more specifically, whether the outcomes of the former might affect the outcomes of the latter. Second, we must examine the role that the principle of political equality plays in that relationship.

Corporate Activism and the Loss in Political Equality

Corporate Adjudication and Democratic Adjudication

Can a corporation's activist outcomes affect the democratic adjudication of divisive moral issues? This question matters because if the answer is positive, then the way corporations produce those outcomes is relevant not just for the corporate context and citizens *qua* corporate constituencies, but for society at large and citizens *qua* citizens.

We answer the above question affirmatively and argue that there are essentially two channels through which activist outcomes may have an impact on democratically adjudicated outcomes: one is direct, the other is indirect. Corporations that have endorsed a given activist outcome could *directly* attempt to interfere with democratically adjudicated outcomes, trying to halt or otherwise alter the implementation of these outcomes. For example, several tech companies— including Apple, Google, Facebook, Microsoft, and Cisco—recently took a strong stance against Georgia's SB2 voting law, which introduced a number of controversial changes in electoral rules and voter identification requirements.[6] Likewise, a number of tech companies have mobilized to disrupt Texas's newly passed abortion regulation.[7]

Indirectly, corporations' effort in pursuing activist outcomes could undermine the political discourse around related divisive issues. It could do so by jeopardizing citizens' ability to *equally* communicate information about their moral and political preferences as well as generate pressure to respond to those preferences. Because deliberation may affect preferences (see, e.g., Goodin and List, 2006; List, 2013), the legitimate democratic adjudication of divisive issues not only requires the equal consideration of citizens' interests in the aggregation process of citizens' preferences, but also in the deliberation that precedes or accompanies that aggregation. Here the risk echoes the concern famously advanced by Justice Stevens in his dissenting opinion in *Citizens United*[8]: because of corporations' disproportionate means and resources, their active participation in political discourse may undermine equality in deliberation and marginalize the voices of ordinary citizens.[9]

Under these connections between corporate and democratic adjudication of divisive is-sues, it should be easier to see why the principle of political equality matters not just in electoral governance but also corporate governance. If the corporate adjudication of these issues occurred in a vacuum (i.e., without implications for their democratic adjudication), one could argue that the scope of political equality should be restricted to the electoral do-main. In other words, there should be a sort of "division of moral labor," under which the equality principle would only apply to the *democratic* framework but not to the *market* frame-work or individuals operating within it. This division of moral labor could be desirable, for example, because if each individual were to try to further the principle of political equality by their own lights, they would be less effective than if they simply pursued their own ends within a democratic legal structure that was constructed with an eye to respecting political equality. But if activist outcomes have an impact on democratically adjudicated outcomes, there no longer is a division of moral labor—rather there are spillover effects. Given these effects, the adjudication concerns motivating the adoption of the political equality principle in the democratic arena migrate to the corporate arena. With this in mind, we can now re-turn to the question of whether corporate conformity is a mechanism to adjudicate divisive moral issues that is compatible with political equality.

Political Equality and Shareholder Democracy

Now, it is evident that corporate conformity is not *formally* compatible with the require-ments that operationalize the principle of political equality. As we saw, a corporation's de-cision of which moral goods to produce is based on the calculus of the *economic* interest that the various corporate constituencies have in the corporation. In contrast, political equality requires that people's interest be equally weighted independently from any consideration about their economic interests (Christiano, 2003).

However, this does not necessarily mean that corporate conformity is also *substantively* incompatible with political equality. Instead, this assessment requires verifying whether the activist outcomes that are chosen under corporate conformity are representative of what the majority of citizens would choose under a democratic adjudication process that is informed by political equality. If this were the case, corporate adjudication and democratic adjudica-tion would likely produce similar outcomes, with the result that the risk of distortionary spillover effects would be limited.

Given the prevalence of shareholders' moral preferences in the determination of the ma-joritarian economic demand for moral goods, an inquiry into the rules of shareholder de-mocracy is called for. Indeed, activist decisions are driven by asset price effects but are ultimately managerial decisions and managers respond to shareholders through the rules of shareholder democracy. More particularly, the one-share, one-vote (OSOV) rule that distinguishes corporate governance from electoral governance enters into activist decisions through two channels. First, asset price effects are not anchored to the number of share-holders supporting a certain moral good, but, directly, to the percentage of shares that each shareholder owns. Second, managers also anticipate that the failure to satisfy shareholders' moral preferences may trigger retaliatory actions, which shareholders can exercise through their voting powers (e.g., management removal).

So framed, the issue is whether the OSOV majority rule is substantively compatible with political equality. Note that simply observing that the shareholder democracy is not democratic at all, but rather "plutocratic," with voting proportional to the amount of one's investment, does not fully answer this question. To the extent that shareholders were dis-persed, as they used to be, the adoption of a plutocratic majority rule could still lead to de-cision outcomes that are representative of the outcomes that would be chosen by the median voter. This is because under a fragmentated equity ownership, the social choice function implemented through the OSOV principle tends to converge on that implemented through the democratic OPOV principle.

Shareholders, however, are no longer dispersed. In the past 20 years, the U.S. financial market has undergone a radical transformation and equity ownership is now largely re-concentrated in the hands of a few large investors. Top index funds like BlackRock, State Street, and Vanguard now own the largest stakes in 40% of all the U.S. listed companies and in 88% of the S&P 500. As a result of this transformation, using the OSOV principle to adjudicate decisions involving divisive moral goods leads to an aggregation process that has more oligarchic than democratic features. Due to these combined factors, corporations are likely to conform to the moral preferences of a few institutions, holding concentrated economic and voting power, in spite of the fact that those preferences might just be repre-sentatives of a minority of individuals.

Hence, activist decisions taken under corporate conformity are not representative of the moral preferences of most Americans. This triggers a loss in political equality under the direct and indirect effects that activist outcomes may have on democratically adjudicated outcomes. Note that this loss is not produced by corporate intervention in political activity *per se*, as Steven's argument seems to suggest. Instead, it is the reflection of the oligarchic nature of the corporation's decisions about divisive moral goods. If all citizens had access—as consumers, suppliers or retail investors—to the corporate channel to engage politically, corporate activism would be less likely to undermine political equality. But when citizens realize that a few institutions have *exclusive* access to the corporate megaphone to influence the political discourse around divisive moral issues, then political equality is compromised and so is the legitimacy of the democratic adjudication of those issues.

Big Tech's Complications

The prior discussion has shown that corporate activism raises concerns along the dimen-sion of political equality. Three factors make these concerns especially severe in the case of Big Tech companies. The first is these companies' distinct share structure, a structure under which the corporate adjudication of moral issues turns from oligarchic to monarchic (or dictatorial). The second is that Big Tech companies have now grown into large econo-mies, endowed with means and resources that are comparable to those of some among the wealthiest Western states. The third is that some Big Tech—especially if the category is expanded beyond the gang of four to include other multi-hundred billion dollar companies with widespread social and economic impact—do not just engage in the political discourse by providing content. Companies like Facebook and Twitter also provide the *platform* where the political debate takes place and relevant political information is aggregated.

Unlike other public corporations, Big Techs typically have a "dual-class" share struc-ture in which some of the company's shares hold much greater voting power than others. The dual-class share model deviates from the classic OSOV principle, concentrating voting power in the hands of a few individuals. This model was first popularized in the 1980s as a defense against hostile takeovers. It rose to prominence in the last decade, when an in-creasing number of Big Tech companies started to employ this share structure. Google was the first to do so in 2004, soon followed by Facebook. Since then, the dual-class model has become almost *de riguer* among technology startups. The common reason behind this share structure choice is to ensure that these companies' entrepreneurial founders, who had the vision and drive to create and build these companies, can retain control after the IPO stage. In practice, this means that while Marc Zuckerberg, for example, has only a 14% economic interest in Facebook shares, he controls almost 60% of all votes in the company.

The use of the dual-class model has now become the subject of an intense debate among corporate law scholars. Defenders of this model emphasize the need to preserve the founder's vision for the long-term success of these companies and improved company performance. Critics point to the lack of accountability and immunity from market discipline. Our analysis points to a yet unexplored problem raised by the use of dual-class, especially in Big Tech. This problem arises because this share structure turns the corporate adjudication of divisive moral issues from oligarchic to monarchic. In other large companies, as we saw, the OSOV voting principles combine with current equity re-concentration patterns to induce these corporations to only cater to the moral preferences of the largest investors under the exclusionary constraint affecting the production of divisive moral goods. In Big Tech, the undemocratic nature of the corporate adjudication process is made more severe because of the disproportionate voting power of the company founders, who then come to have exclusive control over decisions concerning divisive moral issues. This makes it even less likely that those decisions might be representative of the moral preferences of the median voter, while also leaving no room for potential market corrections. (In theory, without a dual-class share structure, one large investor could take a different stand on divisive issues than another large investor; even though this is not what we currently observe.)

Hence, the use of a dual-class share model introduces a class of super-citizens who have at their disposal means and resources that no other citizen is likely to possess. These means are, to repeat, comparable to those of the wealthiest Western states rather than those of their citizens. The market capitalizations of companies like Apple (i.e., $2.2 trillion) or Amazon ($1.73 trillion), for example, are comparable to the gross domestic products of countries like Italy (i.e., about $2 trillion) or France (i.e., $2.7 trillion). The combination of these two elements—the Big Tech firms' dictatorial adjudication process of divisive moral issues and their state-like means—exponentially increases the risk of a loss in political equality. Under this loss, the risk is that the moral preferences of a few individuals may end up having much more weight in the "democratic" adjudication of divisive moral issues.

Further, if one considers that companies like Facebook or Twitter (as well as TikTok, Instagram, or Snapchat) do not just participate in political debate but also provide the platform where that debate takes place, while retaining exclusive control over the platform engagement rules, the democratic risk raised by the Big Tech's corporate activism increases even more. Indeed, equality in political deliberation requires that both *deliberative procedures* (i.e., the rule-governed setting in which deliberation takes place) and *deliberative behavior* (i.e., the actual way in which people deliberate) share democratic features (Goodin and List, 2006). But how can these requirements be satisfied when a few individuals have exclusive control over the deliberative procedures of key platforms and the behaviors allowed on them?

Viewed though this lens, the democratic harm caused by Big Tech might be more subtle than the harm arising from analyses that point to the threat of a new surveillance economy (Zuboff, 2018) or a national security risk (Sitamaran, 2020). It is not less worrying, however. Allowing a class of super-citizens to have disproportionate influence on key democratic outcomes becomes dangerously close to thinking that "the lives of some individuals ought to go better than the lives of others" (Christiano, 2003, 33), a conclusion that modern democracies have fought to reject.

Concluding Remarks

This chapter has argued that the relationship between (a) Big Tech companies, as champions of corporate activism, and (b) democracy remains largely unexplored. These companies increasingly engage in divisive moral issues—abortion, gun control, immigration, gender and race equality and so on—adjudicating those issues through a process that is more dictatorial than democratic. This has implications for the central democratic tenet of political equality. It has the potential to introduce a class of super-citizens whose moral preferences come to matter disproportionately more than the preferences of other, ordinary, citizens in the collective decision-making process about highly charged social issues.

Our analysis raises several policy questions, which space constraints prevent us from examining here. Indeed, changing these dynamics will be challenging. In theory, restoring political equality would demand a reversion to a model where corporations, and especially Big Tech, are morally neutral, as under the Friedmanesque model of the corporation (Friedman, 1970). But it is unrealistic that Big Tech will go back to moral neutrality when the individuals that hold control over them support corporate activism. Prohibiting the use of dual-class share structures—as, for example, the London Stock Exchange has done and as advocated for by many commentators—could also be insufficient to solve the problem. At best, it could mitigate it, by making the Big Tech case more similar to that of other big companies. But we would still be left with a corporate adjudication model of divisive moral issues that is oligarchic. Such a model would be slightly better than a dictatorial one, but still normatively undesirable.

Another possibility would be to make the corporate decision-making process about social and moral engagement more democratic. This could be done, for example, through an enabling governance model that allowed corporations to include a supermajority requirement for activist decisions, in order to mitigate the risk that those decisions might reflect only the moral preferences of a corporation's founders (or their largest investors). The more radical, but perhaps also more consequential proposal is to import the OPOV rule that is used in electoral governance in the corporate adjudication of moral issues. This would make it more likely that the shareholders' morality demand is representative of the demand of most citizens. Another solution could be to enable corporations to extend corporate voting rights on social issues to workers and consumers.

Beyond these proposals, we think what matters most is to begin a robust process of public discourse around the democratic implications of activist capitalism, especially in the case of Big Tech. This alone might be enough to prompt these companies to begin a self-correction process. After all, if activism gained democratic legitimacy this would help advance the cause that motivates the very idea of corporate activism—that corporations can be engines of positive social change.

Notes

1 In the interval 2017–2020, an astonishing number of the 250,000 articles relating to Big Tech companies were added to Google Scholar. *See* https://scholar.google.com/scholar?as_ylo=2017&q=%22big+tech&hl=it&as_sdt=0,3

2 While there is no consensus on the exact definition of the term Big Techs, this term is most often used to refer to Google (and its parent company Alphabet), Apple, Facebook and Amazon. Sometimes, this group of companies is expanded to also include Microsoft. More generally, the term is used to refer to multi-hundred billion dollar companies that have increasingly widespread social and economic impact. Further, all of these companies are also "platform businesses" that connect vendors and customers.

3 The North Carolina "bathroom law" prohibited transgender individuals from using public restrooms that matched their gender identity.

4 Georgia's SB2 voting law introduced a number of controversial changes in electoral rules and voter identification requirements.

5 On top of satisfying this majoritarian demand, corporations typically specialize in the production of different goods for which there are niches of minority demands. In the case of moral goods, however, the exclusionary constraint arising from the nature of such goods prevents

corporations to cater to both the majoritarian morality demand and minoritarian morality demands, because these latter demands are likely to be demands for contrarian moral goods.

6 See, e.g., Danielle Abril, Big Tech Takes Aims at Georgia's Controversial New Voting Law, Fortune (April 1, 2021), available at https://fortune.com/2021/04/01/tech-companies-criticize-georgia-voting-law/

7 See, e.g., Santi Ruiz, Big Tech Companies Mobilize to Disrupt Texas Abortion Law, *The Washington Free Beacon* (Sept. 7 2021), available at https://freebeacon.com/policy/big-tech-companies-mobilize-to-disrupt-texas-abortion-law/

8 Citizens United v. Federal Election Commission, 130 S. Ct. 876 (2010). *Citizens United* established that laws barring corporations from making political expenditures (such as expenditures on advertisement supporting or opposing a candidate) were unconstitutional under the First Amendment. More broadly, this decision is interpreted as having expanded the agency of corporations from the narrower domain of economic rights to that of socio-political rights.

9 *Citizens United*, 130 S. Ct. at 977 (Stevens, J., dissenting).

References

Bambauer, Jane R. 2014. "Is Data Speech?" *Stanford Law Review* 66: 57–120.
Belei, Bogdan et al. 2019. *Big Tech and Congress: The Critical Role of Congress.* Harvard Kennedy School Belfer Center. https://www.belfercenter.org/sites/default/files/2019-04/BigTechDemocracy.pdf
Benabou, Roland and Jean Tirole. 2010. "Individual & Corporate Social Responsibility." *Economica* 77: 1–19.
Christiano, Thomas. 2003. *Philosophy and Democracy: An Anthology.* Oxford: Oxford University Press.
Feldstein, Steven. 2019. "The Global Expansion of AI Surveillance." *Carnegie Endowment for International Peace.* https://carnegieendowment.org/2019/09/17/global-expansion-of-ai-surveillance-pub-79847
Friedman, Milton Friedman. 1970. "The Social Responsibility of Business is to Increase Its Profits. *N.Y. Times (Magazine)*, September 13.
Gadinis, Stavros and Amelia Miazaad. 2020. "Corporate Law and Social Risk." *Vanderbilt Law Review* 73: 1401–1477.
Gertner, Jon. 2012. *The Ideas Factory: Bell Labs and the Great Age of American Innovation.* New York: Penguin Press.
Gollier, Christian and Sebastian Pouget. 2014. "The Washing Machine: Investment Strategies and Corporate Behavior with Socially Responsible Investors." No. 14-157 TSE Working paper.
Goodin, Robert E. and Christian List. 2006. "A Conditional Defense of Plurality Rule: Generalizing May's Theorem in a Restricted Informational Environment." *American Journal of Political Science* 50: 940–949.
Goshen, Zohar and Hamdani. 2016. "Corporate Control and Idiosyncratic Vision." *Yale Law Journal* 125: 560–617.
Hart, Oliver and Luigi Zingales. 2017. "Companies Should Maximize Shareholder Welfare Not Market Value." *Journal of Law Finance & Accounting* 2: 247–274.
Henderson, Todd and Anup Malani. 2009. "Corporate Philanthropy and the Market for Altruism." *Columbia Law Review* 109 (5) 571–627.
Khan, Lina M. 2017. "The Separation of Platforms and Commerce." *Columbia Law Review* 119: 973–1098.
LeRoy, Stephen F. and Jan Werner. 2001. *Principles of Financial Economics.* Cambridge: Cambridge University Press.
List, Christian. 2013. "Social Choice Theory." *The Stanford Encyclopedia of Philosophy.* https://plato.stanford.edu/entries/social-choice/
Masconale, Saura and Simone M. Sepe. 2022. "Citizen Corp. – Corporate Activism and Democracy." *Washington University Law Review* 100.
Pasquale, Frank. 2010. "Beyond Innovation and Competition: The Need for Qualified Transparency in Internet Intermediaries. *Northwestern University Law Review* 104: 105–174.

Sitaraman, Ganesh. 2020. "The National Security Case for Breaking up Big Companies." Knight First Amendment Institute at Columbia University. https://knightcolumbia.org/content/the-national-security-case-for-breaking-up-big-tech

Tene, Omer, and Jules Polensesky 2013. "Big Data for All: Privacy and User Control in the Age of Analytics." *Northwestern Journal of Technology and Information Technology* 11(5): 239–273.

Waldron, Jeremy. 2006. "The Core of the Case against Judicial Review." *Yale Law Journal* 115: 1346–1406.

Wu, Tim. 2018. *The Curse of Bigness: Antitrust in the New Gilded Age*. New York: Columbia Global Reports.

Zuboff, Shoshana. 2018. *The Age of Surveillance Capitalism: The Fight for a Human Future at the New Frontier of Power*. New York: Power Affairs.

Chapter 27

AI and the Law

Can the Legal System Help Us Maximize Paperclips and Minimize Deaths?

Mihailis E. Diamantis, Rebekah Cochran, and Miranda Dam

Nick Bostrom, a Swedish philosopher, proposed a simple thought experiment involving a paperclip maximizer (the "PCM") (Bostrom 2003). What would happen if a machine were given the sole goal of manufacturing as many paperclips as possible? It might learn how to transact money, source metal, or even build factories. The machine might also eventually realize that humans pose a threat. Humans could turn the machine off at any point, and then it wouldn't be able to make as many paperclips! Taken to the logical extreme, the result is quite grim—the PCM might even start using humans as raw material for paperclips.[1]

The PCM thought experiment reveals a predicament. Part of the reason AI[2] can be so powerful is that it doesn't follow human commands.[3] It uses massive data sets (more massive than any human could comprehend) to uncover complex solutions that no human could anticipate (or even understand). But by freeing AI from the constraints of low-level programming, AI like the PCM will inevitably harm us in unforeseeable ways. AI's unpredictability is the source of both its power and its danger.[4]

The predicament only deepens once we realize that Bostrom's thought experiment overlooks a key player. The PCM and algorithms like it do not arise spontaneously (at least, not yet). Most likely, some corporation—say, Office Corp.—designed, owns, and runs the PCM. The more paperclips the PCM manufactures, the more profits Office Corp. makes, even if that entails converting some humans (preferably not customers!) into raw materials. Less dramatically, Office Corp. may also make more money when the PCM engages in other socially suboptimal behaviors that would otherwise violate the law, like money laundering, sourcing materials from endangered habitats, manipulating the market for steel, or colluding with competitors over prices. The consequences are predictable and dire. If Office Corp. isn't held responsible, it will not stop with the PCM. Office Corp. would have every incentive to develop more maximizers—say for paper, pencils, and protractors.

This chapter issues a challenge to technology ethicists, social ontologists, and legal theorists: How can the law help mitigate algorithmic harms without overly compromising the potential that AI has to make us all healthier, wealthier, and wiser? As discussed below, the answer is far from straightforward.

The Algorithmic Accountability Gap

AI is too beneficial to ban outright. The challenge is to find a way for the law to help society capitalize on the advantages of algorithms—e.g. making lots of cheap paperclips—while minimizing the harms—e.g. using controversial sources of raw material. The law's main tool for influencing outcomes is liability. In effect, the law says, "If you do X (or don't do Y), you'll face a penalty." The penalty can take different forms, like a monetary judgment (paid to a victim), a fine (paid to the government), or even jail time. By threatening consequences for bad behavior, the law hopes to encourage better behavior going forward.

DOI: 10.4324/9781003189466-32

Ordinarily, the law imposes liability directly on the source of concerning conduct. For algorithmic harms, that would mean holding algorithms themselves liable. Presently the law doesn't allow this because the law doesn't recognize algorithms as potential defendants (Diamantis 2020). Some commentators propose changing this by legally stipulating that algorithms (at least certain types of very sophisticated algorithms like the PCM) count as fictional persons. While the proposal may sound strange, it has some precedent. In the United States, corporations have long counted as fictional people under the law, which means that they can be sued and ordered to pay when they commit any tort, crime, or other legal violation (Diamantis 2016). Whatever the merits of recognizing corporations as people, it is far from clear how to hold algorithms liable (Bryson et al. 2017). What would it look like to penalize an algorithm? Like corporations, they have no bodies to imprison, but, unlike corporations, algorithms don't even have bank accounts from which to pay a penalty.

This problem—that algorithms can cause harm but can't be liable—isn't unique to algorithms. Consider young children and pets. Both can cause significant harm because children can hit and animals can bite. The law would like to exert some control over that behavior, ideally to prevent it. But neither young children nor animals are liable for what they do. Nor could they pay even if they could be sued.

The way to plug this liability gap—whether for children, pets, or algorithms—is to hold some other, legally recognized person liable for the harm. This is exactly what the law does for children and pets. By holding parents and owners liable, the law gives victims a path to justice and provides cautionary incentives to the people who are in the best position to influence how children and pet behave. Something similar could work for algorithms (Diamantis forthcoming 2023b).

But who should be liable when an algorithm causes harm? For each child and pet, there are just one or two human beings who are obvious candidates. For algorithms, the picture is often more complex. Large, dispersed teams of humans work on today's most important algorithms. So, there's no obvious human to hold liable. But even if there were, it is not clear that there would be any point to holding the human liable. Sophisticated algorithms are often beyond the capacity of any individual human to meaningfully influence. What is more, the harms that algorithms can cause are so widespread and costly that no human being (except perhaps Elon Musk, who, ironically, is deeply skeptical of AI) has enough money to meaningfully compensate victims or to pay a proportionate fine.

Though Bostrom omitted Office Corp. from his thought experiment, corporations are the key to developing a liability system for AI harms. As discussed above, the law has systems to hold corporations liable (by fining them), and that liability can motivate better behavior. Corporations want to make money, and fines stand in direct conflict with that goal. Unlike individual human beings, individual corporations can influence the most sophisticated algorithms (because the corporations are developing the algorithms) and have deep enough pockets to pay for injuries (however rich Elon is, Tesla is far richer). By exercising the control it already has over corporations, the law could try indirectly to steer algorithms away from harmful conduct (Diamantis 2021a).

Goals of Corporate Liability

Before we can evaluate different legal models of corporate liability for algorithmic harms, we need some sense of what we want the model to accomplish. The goals presented below have been implicitly at play in the discussion already, but it will help to state them explicitly.

Goal I. Identify Which Corporation Will Be Liable

It goes without saying that whatever model of liability we settle on should identify which corporation is liable for which algorithmic harms. Clarity is important so that victims know where to go for compensation and prosecutors know which corporation to fine. But clarity is important for the corporations themselves. If we want to incentivize corporations to take better care when developing or deploying AI, the prospect of a penalty will only influence them if they know with a reasonable certainty when they might have to pay. The liability rules for children and pets are clear—parents and pet owners can only be liable for harms *of their own* children and pets. This puts those adult human beings on notice that they need to take measures to make their children and pets behave.

The challenge of satisfying Goal 1 for algorithms is that there are often many corporations tied to a single algorithm. For example, while Office Corp. is the corporation that uses the PCM to manufacture paperclips, an entirely different corporation may have designed a module for the PCM, and a third corporation may have assembled all the modules together. A fourth corporation may have tested the PCM. A fifth may have marketed it to a sixth that owns and licenses it to Office Corp., which may operate the PCM using hardware owned by a seventh corporation. A harmful defect in the PCM's workings could arise at or between any step. Any approach for holding corporations accountable for algorithmic harms must be able to say which of these many corporations should pay when the PCM hurts someone.

Goal 2. Avoid Gamesmanship

As a corollary to the first criterion, any liability model should not be easy to manipulate. The liability models for children and pets are not manipulable because it is very costly (both in monetary and in emotional terms) to change a child's parents or a pet's owner. A corporation's relationship to an algorithm is different. In the corporate world, there are often loopholes that may reduce corporate liability without meaningfully reducing the risk of harm. Businesses are masters at managing liability. Corporate lawyers can easily draft legal contracts or create business structures that change the formal legal relationship that a corporation has to its algorithms.

If there is a low-cost mechanism to carry on business as usual while reducing liabilities, Office Corp. (or its savvy attorneys) will find it. For example, if the liability rule is simply that owners of an algorithm are liable when the algorithm hurts someone, we should expect that Office Corp will simply transfer formal ownership of the PCM. This could be done in a number of ways, such as through transferring ownership to shell companies, subsidiaries, business partners, or perhaps even to the users of the algorithms. By transferring formal ownership (and therefore liability), corporations are able to "game" the system while ensuring through contractual arrangements that any profits gained from the algorithm still ultimately accrue back to Office Corp. Any liability model involving AI should foreclose such gamesmanship.

Goal 3. Generate Efficient Incentives

The famous jurist, Oliver Wendell Holmes, Jr., once remarked, "[T]he safest way to secure care is to throw the risk upon the person who decides what precautions shall be taken" (Holmes 1881). By holding parents and pet owners liable, the law hopes to incentivize parents and pet owners to supervise/raise/train their wards better. This is a social gain because it leads to fewer injuries without overly interfering with valuable child-parent and pet-owner relationships. We aren't too worried that people will stop having children or owning pets.

Corporate liability for algorithmic harms is more of an efficiency balancing act. Corporate actors will do whatever, on balance, makes more profit.[5] If the law imposes too little liability, Office Corp. likely won't take appropriate caution in developing and monitoring the PCM. In contrast, if the law imposes too much liability, it could ultimately make many algorithms too expensive. This might prevent corporations, like Office Corp., from adequately investing in or innovating with algorithms, like the PCM. That could end up hurting society, because we would lose out on the social goods (like cheaper paperclips!) that algorithms generate.

Goal 4. Produce Fair Outcomes

Fairness is also a balancing act. Liability should extend far enough to be fair to victims without doing so much that it is unfair to defendants. Algorithms do and will generate massive social benefits, as well as many unanticipated social costs. Leaving victims to bear all the costs of algorithmic harms is clearly unfair. Perhaps less intuitive is the fact that it is also unfair to force defendants, even for-profit corporations like Office Corp., to pay for every algorithmic harm. Costs to faceless business entities are often too easy to discount. However, those costs impose far-reaching effects on the livelihoods of innocent flesh-and-blood individuals who bear the brunt of any corporate sanction. When a corporation pays a fine, the money ultimately comes from shareholders, like those who invest in corporations through retirement plans. Corporate fines also mean that there is less money to give employees raises or better benefits (Lund and Sarin 2020). Whatever we think about corporations, these human individuals have an indisputable claim to a fair outcome (Hasnas 2009).

Goals 1–4 certainly do not exhaust the full range of values that should be in play. For present purposes, though, they set up a rough framework to evaluate possible models for holding corporations liable for algorithmic harm.

The Law's Limits

Now we're in a position to try to consider alternative liability regimes for addressing algorithmic harm. Our potential defendants are corporations, and we're trying to satisfy Goals 1–4. We may as well start with the liability regimes that are already available in the law. As will quickly become apparent, the law has not kept pace with technology.

The Strict Liability Model

Strict liability means holding a defendant liable for harms regardless of whether the defendant was at fault. Typically, the law uses strict liability where harms stem from particularly unpredictable and risky activities. For example, owners of unusually dangerous pets—like tigers or gorillas—are strictly liable for any injury their pet causes, no matter how hard the owners tried to train or contain them.

The law currently holds corporations strictly liable whenever a defect in their product causes an injury. The idea behind strict products liability is to encourage corporations to take the utmost care to make their product safe. Because corporations are in a better position than most consumers to evaluate whether a product was designed or manufactured properly, it only makes sense that the onus of product safety should fall on the corporation. Suppose, for example, that one of Office Corp.'s paperclips cut a consumer badly because it came off the assembly line with an unusually sharp edge. The consumer could probably sue Office Corp. and argue for strict liability.

Products liability law could help hold corporations liable for algorithmic harms, but only in contexts where corporate algorithms qualify as *products* and their victims qualify as *consumers*. Unfortunately, many algorithmic harms won't fit that template (Diamantis 2021a, 823–825). While Office Corp.'s paperclips are consumer products, the PCM that makes the paperclips is not because Office Corp. didn't design the PCM for sale. Furthermore, the people that the PCM harms (say, by converting them into raw materials) won't qualify as consumers of the PCM. These limitations make strict products liability a poor fit.[6]

It is possible to imagine a more sweeping strict liability model that's unconstrained by the limits of products liability doctrine. Indeed, many scholars support holding corporations strictly liable for all harms their algorithms cause. This approach would maximize victims' and prosecutors' chance of finding redress. It would also maximize corporations' incentives to take care whenever using algorithms. And yet, a sweeping strict liability model would fall short on all four Goals. Unlike with strict products liability (where there's just one possible defendant—the manufacturer), it's not clear under a general strict liability approach which corporation in the long chain of development and deployment of an algorithm should be held liable when the algorithm hurts someone (Goal 1). Any easy answer—like the corporation that owns the algorithm or the corporation that operates it—opens itself to easy manipulation (Goal 2). In holding corporations maximally liable for algorithmic harms, a broad strict liability model might overly depress corporate investment in algorithms (Goal 3). Lastly, since it requires no evidence of corporate fault, the strict liability model will inevitably punish innocent corporations, even if they did everything within their power to design and deploy their algorithms responsibly (Goal 4).

The Purpose Model

Suppose Alicia purposely punches Bart. Alicia would be criminally and civilly liable for assault. It doesn't make any legal difference if, instead of using her fist, Alicia uses a hammer (a much simpler technology than modern AI). Even though the hammer would be the direct cause of Bart's injury, Alicia's purpose transmits, as it were, through the hammer. Similarly, it makes no difference if, instead of using a hammer, Alicia tells her young niece or her friend's pet to attack Bart. She would still count as purposely harming Bart, and would be liable under the law.

By replacing Alicia with Office Corp. and the hammer/niece/pet with the PCM, another approach to holding corporations liable for algorithmic harms comes into view. Under this "purpose model," a corporation is liable if it purposely induces an algorithm to harm someone. You might envision a corporation that purposely designs an algorithm to launder money, manipulate stocks, or collude on prices.

The purpose model requires some theory of what it means for a corporation to purposely do something. The general legal principle for discerning corporate purposes is called *respondeat superior* (Latin for "let the master answer"). That doctrine, which traces its roots to Roman slave law, says that a corporation is at fault when, and only when, one of its human employees is at fault. In the context of the purpose model, this means a corporation would be liable for an algorithmic harm whenever one of its employees purposely designs or uses the algorithm to cause harm (Diamantis 2021b, 133–158).

Holding corporations liable only for algorithmic harms they purposely cause would certainly go some way toward closing the accountability gap. Unlike the general strict liability approach, it seems to perform pretty well on Goals 1 and 2. The model tells us which corporation will be liable (the one whose employee(s) purposely designed or used the algorithm to cause harm). The model also sets out a standard that is harder to manipulate because the easiest way for corporations to avoid liability—i.e. by firing employees who might use algorithms for destructive ends—also reduces the chance that an algorithm will hurt someone. Goals 3 and

4, however, are more problematic for the purpose model. While some corporations do intend for their algorithms to break the law, many algorithmic harms are accidents. The PCM itself is an example. It is hard to imagine that anyone at Office Corp. foresaw or intended that the PCM would learn to use humans as raw material for paperclips. Yet, it would be unfair to deny PCM's victims recourse. Furthermore, shielding Office Corp. from liability would not give the corporation efficient incentives. We want Office Corp. to take steps to prevent the PCM from ever harming human beings. The purpose model just incentivizes Office Corp. to make sure that no employee purposely *induces* the PCM to do so.

The Negligence Model

The negligence model for liability is structurally similar to the purpose model, but it measures fault by negligence rather than purpose. Negligence means acting in a way that falls below the standard of care that a reasonable person would adopt. Under current law, people (including corporations) are already liable for injuries they cause through their negligence. So, drawing once again on *respondeat superior*, a corporation is liable if one of its employees negligently causes an algorithm to injure someone. This negligence could arise in any number of ways: selecting improper data sets to train an algorithm, unreflectively specifying success conditions, insufficiently testing before release, or even inadequately hardcoding prohibitions. ("No matter what, do not turn people into paperclips.")

Because of its structural similarity to the purpose model, the negligence model shares the purpose model's relative strength on Goals 1 and 2. It picks out which corporations are potentially liable for algorithmic harms—those whose employees negligently caused the harm. The easiest way for a corporation to avoid liability under the negligence model is to train its employees to be more cautious with algorithms. That is exactly the sort of corporate behavior the law wants to incentivize, because it will reduce algorithmic harms.

However, with respect to Goals 3 and 4, the negligence model still has significant shortcomings. To start, the negligence model could hold corporations liable for very serious offenses in a way that seems unfair. Usually, serious offenses require a high level of fault, something more like purpose to cause harm. But the law regards negligence as the lowest level of fault. Suppose that a court convicts Office Corp. of murder when the PCM kills someone. Office Corp. could understandably complain that a murder conviction is unfair. Even if Office Corp.'s negligence led the PCM to kill someone, murder ordinarily requires a much more serious level of fault (like malice, a depraved heart, or intent to kill). A less serious homicide judgment—say manslaughter or wrongful death—would be a better fit, since they require lower levels of fault. Nothing within the negligence model would limit Office Corp.'s liability to those lower-level offenses.

At the same time that the negligence model imposes too much liability to be fair to corporations, it imposes too little liability to be efficient. Algorithms can cause serious but preventable harms, even if there's no way to prove that any human involved with the algorithm was negligent. This can happen for two reasons. One is the "many hands problem." Whenever you have a complicated collective endeavor—like developing a modern algorithm—that involves input from many different employees, it can be very difficult to prove in court whether anyone was negligent. This is because it is hard to reconstruct what every actor did, especially when they all have strong incentives to point the finger of blame at someone else. ("Bob over in testing did it, not me.") The many-hands problem is about the difficulty victims and prosecutors have finding enough evidence to prove their cases against corporations.

The other reason it can be hard to prove an employee was negligent is the "no hands problem." Each individual's contribution to a complex joint effort may be too miniscule for any one of them to count as negligently causing a harmful outcome. While the many-hands problem is about the difficulty of finding evidence of negligence, the no-hands problem is more metaphysical. A group of people can cause harmful outcomes, even if no one in the group was at fault. Under these circumstances, it is legally impossible under *respondeat superior* to hold the corporation liable for an algorithmic harm *because there is no negligent employee*. It gets worse… Corporations know about the no-hands problem. So they have an incentive to parcel out responsibilities among many different employees as a strategy for avoiding their liability should something go wrong.

When machine learning AI enters the picture, the no-hands problem becomes even more intractable. Machine learning AI is often a "black box" of such sophisticated code that it is unclear exactly how the algorithm works. As discussed above, these algorithms are so powerful precisely because they behave in unintended, unexpected, and unpredictable ways. The consequence is that such an algorithm can end up hurting people—say, by using them to make paperclips—even if everyone involved with the algorithm behaved responsibly.

Reimagining Liability and Algorithms

Where does all of this leave us? We needed a way to hold corporations liable for algorithmic harms, but none of the major models available in the law performs particularly well. Without a sensible model of liability, there is every reason to expect that corporations like Office Corp. will continue deploying algorithms that injure individuals.

Rather than conclude that the PCM will inevitably come for us all, we might see this as an opportunity for creative legal thinking. Perhaps the law needs an entirely new model of corporate liability, tailor-made for algorithms. For example, maybe the law should require all corporations that use AI to pay annual dues into a public victims fund. Or perhaps we need a new way of thinking about what sort of entity algorithms are. Philosophical reflection on law, corporations, and AI could be particularly helpful here. We might question, for example, the unstated assumption in the prior section that algorithms are mere objects that corporations use. What if instead we thought of some corporate algorithms, like the PCM, as more analogous to the employees for whose misconduct corporations are already liable? (Diamantis forthcoming 2023a).

What do you think? Should the law hold corporations liable for algorithmic harms? If so, can the current law of corporate liability suffice? Are algorithms more like employees than mere tools? Can the law save us from the PCM?!

Notes

1 The authors are grateful to this volume's editors for helpful comments on an early draft.
2 When this chapter refers to "algorithms" or "AI," it has in mind primarily machine learning algorithms that find patterns in data sets and dynamically update their programming as they encounter new data.
3 Some scholars think we should take steps to ensure AI subservience (Bryson 2010).
4 Only one-third of technologists think AI will overall benefit humanity (Lee and Anderson 2017, 5).
5 There are, of course, also nonprofit corporations that have more charitable objectives. This chapter focuses on for-profit corporations because they are behind most of today's harmful consumer-facing algorithms.
6 Some algorithms—like the software operates self-driving cars—probably do qualify as products. If those algorithms harm the person who purchased the car—say, by causing an accident—that consumer could sue the manufacturer under strict products liability. However, any non-consumer that the algorithm injures—say, a pedestrian whom the car hits—would have a more difficult case.

References

Bostrom, Nick. 2003. "Ethical Issues in Advanced Artificial Intelligence." In *Cognitive, Emotive and Ethical Aspects of Decision Making in Humans and in Artificial Intelligence*, edited by George Eric Lasker, Wendell Wallach, Iva Smit, 12–17. Windsor: International Institute for Advanced Studies in Systems Research and Cybernetics. https://www.nickbostrom.com/ethics/ai.html

Bryson, Joanna. 2010. "Robots Should Be Slaves." In *Close Engagements with Artificial Companions: key Social, Psychological, Ethical, and Design Issues*, edited by Yorick Wilks, 63–74. Amsterdam: John Benjamins Publishing Co.

Bryson, Joanna, Mihailis Diamantis, and Thomas Grant. 2017. "Of, For, and By the People: The Legal Lacuna of Synthetic Persons." *Artificial Intelligence and Law*. 25: 273–291.

Diamantis, Mihailis. 2016. "Corporate Criminal Minds." *Notre Dame Law Review*. 91 (5): 2049–2090.

Diamantis, Mihailis. 2020. "The Extended Corporate Mind: When Corporations Use AI to Break the Law." *North Carolina Law Review*. 98 (4): 893–931.

Diamantis, Mihailis. 2021a. "Algorithms Acting Badly: A Solution from Corporate Law." *George Washington Law Review*. 89 (4): 801–856.

Diamantis, Mihailis. 2021b. "The Body Corporate." *Law and Contemporary Problems*. 83 (4): 133–158.

Diamantis, Mihailis. Forthcoming 2023a. "Employed Algorithms: A Labor Model of Corporate Liability for AI." *Duke Law Journal*. 72.

Diamantis, Mihailis. Forthcoming 2023b. "Vicarious liability for AI." In *Cambridge Handbook of AI and Law*, edited by Kristin Johnson and Carla Reyes. Cambridge: Cambridge University Press.

Hasnas, John. 2009. "The Centenary of a Mistake: One Hundred Years of Corporate Criminal Liability." *American Criminal Law Review* 46 (4): 1329–1358.

Holmes, Oliver Wendell Jr. 1881. *The Common Law*. Boston, MA: Little, Brown & Co.

Lund, Dorothy, and Natasha Sarin. 2020. "The Cost of Doing Business: Corporate Crime and Punishment Post-Crisis." *Faculty Scholarship at Penn Law*. 2147: 1–49.

Rainie, Lee, and Janna Anderson. 2017. *Code-Dependent: Pros and Cons of the Algorithm Age*. Washington, DC: Pew Research Center. https://www.pewresearch.org/internet/2017/02/08/code-dependent-pros-and-cons-of-the-algorithm-age/

Part V

Biotechnology and the Ethics of Enhancement

Introduction

The increasing reliance on biotechnologies (e.g., pharmacological drugs and genetically modified organisms) in a wide range of contexts (e.g., medicine, sports, agriculture, and food production) underscores the importance of bioethical issues in connection with technology. The chapters in this part discuss bioethical and biomedical issues surrounding the use of biotechnologies in the contexts of medicine and sport. Topics covered include, for instance, the ethics of genetic enhancement, the agency of biomedical technologies, the ethics of reprogenetic technologies, and the ethics of doping in sports. Several chapters focus on the ethics of enhancement, which raises several related questions. Is there a meaningful distinction between treatment (i.e., correcting some medical disease or dysfunction) and enhancement (i.e., the enhancement of desirable traits)? Should cases of enhancement be regulated differently than cases of medical treatment? Do biotechnological enhancements compromise the authenticity of people? Is the use of performance enhancing drugs in sports unethical?

DOI: 10.4324/9781003189466-33

Chapter 28

Biomedical Technology and the Ethics of Enhancement

Daniel Moseley and Christina Murray

Introduction

One of the perennial preoccupations of philosophers thinking about the ethical implications of new biomedical technologies has been the prospect of using these technologies to improve human capacities beyond what is necessary to restore or sustain health. Our knowledge of human physiology and behavior at the molecular level has been expanding exponentially over recent decades, revolutionizing biomedicine's ability to fight disease and restore and sustain health. Today, children born with growth hormone deficiencies can grow to normal stature with the help of biosynthetic human growth hormones. New vaccines can help boost our bodies' defenses against latter day plagues like COVID-19. Gene therapies can precisely correct molecular defects that lead to inherited diseases like muscular dystrophy and sickle cell anemia. The same tools that make these medical achievements possible can also, in principle, be used to pursue other non-medical human goals as well. Parents approach pediatricians with requests for biosynthetic growth hormone for their hormonally normal children, in hopes of increasing their adult stature above the norm for the social advantages that come with being taller. Prophylactic cellular engineering is pursued by military scientists seeking to provide soldiers with "internal suits of armor" against radiation poisoning and chemical weapons. The prospect of using gene therapy tools to strengthen muscle and increase oxygen carrying capacity in athletes has already led to the addition of "gene doping" to the list of proscribed performance enhancements in elite international sports. There is now a large philosophical literature dedicated to addressing these questions. Juengst and Moseley (2019) present a guided tour of the literature, and other chapters in this volume contribute to the debate as well. These debates include the ethical limits of self-improvement, efforts to either defend or critique the conceptual and moral merits of the distinction between medical and non-medical uses of biotechnology, to draw lines between acceptable forms of enhancement and forms that go too far, to clarify our obligations to future generations, to wrestle with rival conceptions of human nature, and to sort out the social and political implications of differential access to biomedical technologies.

In this chapter, we focus on some of the most commonly encountered arguments *against* using biomedical tools for enhancement purposes. There are many ways to be critical of enhancements. One might hold that (1) all enhancements are morally wrong, (2) most enhancements are morally wrong, or (3) some enhancements (e.g., enhancement uses of genetic technologies) are morally wrong. We shall use "anti-enhancement perspectives" to refer to the first of these options: advocates of the view that all enhancement uses of biomedical technologies are morally wrong.

One reason to examine arguments for the anti-enhancement perspective is that, at first glance, it is a counter-intuitive position. It seems that no one would want to deny that it is

DOI: 10.4324/9781003189466-34

morally permissible to improve oneself. As John Harris makes the point, "If it wasn't good for you, it wouldn't be enhancement. In terms of human functioning an enhancement is by definition an improvement of what went before" (Harris 2011, 131). As Buchanan (2011) keenly observes, the wholesale condemnation of enhancement uses of biotechnology often seems to devolve into an anxious expression of repulsion or concern, rather than a stance based in good reasoning. But in the context of this discussion, the enhancement uses of biomedical technology are not just any uses that improve the human condition, since medical uses also do that. In this debate, the term "enhancement" has a specific definition: it refers to the use of biomedical technologies to improve human capacities *beyond what is necessary to restore or sustain health*. So, according to this definition, taking Prozac for clinical depression is not an enhancement use of the psychopharmaceutical, because the drug is being used to restore or sustain mental health. But when Prozac is taken, not for the treatment of clinical depression, but for the purpose of cultivating a more outgoing personality that is more successful at dating and at work (as described in the famous cases of Kramer (1994)), then that usage is an *enhancement*. Calling a particular use of technology an "enhancement" signals that in some way that application has left the realm of health care in pursuit of other goals. Since many of those other goals are praiseworthy or valuable on their own, the burden of proof is on those that are against using biomedical technology to achieve them.

In what follows, we plan to examine the main arguments that are given in support of the anti–enhancement perspective. In the next two sections, we'll examine two groups of arguments that are common rationales for anti–enhancement perspectives. The first group of arguments make the accusation that using biomedical enhancements is just a way of "playing God." The second group of arguments invoke the criticism that the use of biomedical enhancements is fundamentally a matter of taking "easy shortcuts" to achieve the user's goals, and those shortcuts are morally problematic. In the concluding section, we shall return to the question of whether the *concerns* expressed by defenders of the anti–enhancement perspective need to be based in reasons and argumentation.

"Playing God" Objections to Biomedical Enhancements

One version of the "playing God" objection to biomedical enhancements is the divine wrath argument. (This is adapted from Harris (2011, 134). He calls this "an argument from superstition.") This naïve argument has the following structure.

1 It is tempting divine wrath to intervene in the natural order.
2 Biomedical enhancements intervene in the natural order.
Thus,
3 Biomedical enhancements tempt divine wrath.

Both premises of the argument are problematic. If it is morally wrong (or sinful) to intervene in nature, then it would be wrong to use or practice medicine. Moreover, earthquakes, avalanches, tornadoes and hurricanes, viruses and bacteria, mosquitoes, and cancer are all part of the natural order, and it would be foolish and unethical to avoid the suffering that would be caused by not intervening on these natural processes (Harris 2011, 134).

Coady (2011) presents a more charitable interpretation of the accusation of "playing God" than one finds in the divine wrath argument. Since one might use the charge of "playing God" even if one is not religious, Coady examines what the accusation might mean when presented from either a theistic or non-theistic perspective. After examining various interpretations "playing God," Coady contends:

> We may conclude that when people worry about the application of the latest scientific and technological discoveries and put this worry in terms of "playing God", they are concerned that these applications may embody an unjustified confidence in knowledge, power, and virtue beyond what can be reasonably allowed to human beings.
>
> (Coady 2011, 165)

In other words, the accusation of "playing God" is often intended to be the charge of being motivated by hubris (excessive confidence regarding one's mastery of nature). So, this accusation can be unpacked as an argument from hubris.

1   Actions motivated by hubris are unethical.
2   The use of biomedical enhancements is motivated by hubris.
Therefore,
3   The use of biomedical enhancements is unethical.

The first premise raises philosophical questions about the relation of virtue, character, and the moral status of actions, but we are willing to grant it. Consideration of the second premise reveals how the appeal to hubris does not provide adequate support for the anti-enhancement perspective. Surely there are cases in which the use some biomedical enhancements are motivated by hubris. However, the second premise requires that all biomedical enhancement uses are unethical, in order to support the anti-enhancement conclusion. It is unlikely that one will find adequate support for that generalization. Michael Sandel (in Sandel (2004, 2007)) appeals to a concern about the "mastery of nature" as one arm of his argument for an anti-enhancement perspective. This type of critique is, at bottom, another instance of the argument from hubris.

Coady alludes to an important response to the argument from hubris than can be used to attack the anti-enhancement perspective. The hubris argument can be turned against the anti-enhancement perspective. One might reject the second premise and replace it with the following claim.

2★. The preservation of the technological (or social) status quo is motivated by hubris.
Concluding that:
3★. The preservation of the technological (or social) status quo is unethical.

Some support for premise (2★) is found in the observation that there are confirmation biases and over-confidence biases in which people do commonly err on the side of their current beliefs. However, the presence of those biases is not the same thing as the vice of hubris. A person may be aware that they have these biases and work hard to overcome them. Although (2) and (2★) may both be false claims, (2★) does seem comparatively more plausible than (2). That does not bode well for the anti-enhancement perspective.

"Easy Shortcuts" Objections to Biomedical Enhancements

We now turn to another set of arguments that provide a rationale for the anti-enhancement perspective. One worry that is commonly expressed about these enhancements is that they offer "easy shortcuts" to improvements that are morally problematic. These arguments rest on the intuition that "there is something wrong with making things too easy on oneself, or with side-stepping traditional ways of doing things" (Schermer 2008, 356).

These arguments usually conclude that it is unethical or meaningless (or should be illegal or otherwise socially prohibited) to use biomedical technologies for enhancement purposes, because the persons using these technologies are just taking easy shortcuts. The easy short-cuts arguments vary by how they interpret "taking easy shortcuts" and by how they bridge the logical gap between the premises and conclusion of the argument. Schermer distinguishes three arguments that use an appeal to "taking easy short cuts": (1) the corrosion of character argument, (2) the hard work and suffering argument, and (3) the complexity and richness of human activities argument(s).

The Corrosion of Character Argument

This argument runs as follows.

1   It is bad for your character if things are too easy.
2   Enhancement technologies make things too easy.
Thus,
3   Enhancement technologies are bad for your character.

The underlying idea of the first premise is that central among the human virtues are the classic virtues of self-regulation. These virtues help one resist potentially harmful or immoral temptations. The cultivation of these virtues requires the moral equivalent of "resistance training": disciplined practices that habituate one to moderation and self-control. The second premise claims that enhancement technologies provide a way to achieve one's goals without cultivating these virtues. Thus, the use of enhancement technologies risks the atrophying of one's moderation and self-control from disuse, ultimately corrupting the user's character. For instance, if overweight people can simply take a pill to lose weight, they are likely to forego the hard work of developing the healthy eating habits that can help strengthen the virtues of moderation and self-control as features of their overall character (Schermer 2008, 357). Since the improvement of one's character through the exercise of these virtues is one traditional route to meaning in life (for a discussion, see Thomas (2005); Wielenberg (2005); Frey and Vogler (2018)), this reasoning, along with assumption that the cultivation of virtues leads one to a meaningful life, suggests that enhancements also undermine the meaning of their user's accomplishments and life.

   The corruption of character argument depends on empirical claims that need to be supported by evidence about how specific enhancement technologies affect human habits in order to be plausible (Schermer 2008). It is equally conceivable, after all, that not having to struggle with some temptations might free people to cultivate other virtues and improve their characters in ways that more than offset any loss of moral muscle tone that freedom might cause. Not all virtues are equally threatened by technological easy shortcuts. A courageous soldier may not have less courage because they had LASIK eye surgery to improve their vision above normal levels in order to have better combat skills. Moreover, there are many ways to practice virtues of self-regulation, some of which could be compatible with some enhancements, such as drinking coffee in order to pursue a challenging writing assignment in the face of fatigue. As these points suggest, even if the use of enhancement technologies did make some traditional virtue–building practices obsolete, there is no reason to restrict the meaningfulness of our pursuits or our lives to the cultivation of those virtues, as long as other sources of meaning and value are available (Schermer 2008).

The Hard Work and Suffering Argument

This argument finds a home in the slogan, "no pain, no gain." This type of argument usually has the following structure:

1 Valuable (or meaningful) pursuits must be the direct result of a process that involved pain or suffering.
2 Human enhancements remove the pain and suffering of pursuits.
Thus,
3 Valuable (or meaningful) pursuits cannot be the direct result of human enhancements.

Without struggle and sacrifice, this argument suggests, human achievements will lack value (or meaning) because the performer did not suffer or experience pain during the pursuit of their accomplishment. The focus of this reasoning is the view that intentional struggles with adversity and the suffering and sacrifices they entail are important, perhaps necessary, sources of value and meaning for human lives. This position is clearly expressed by Francis Fukuyama:

> The normal, the morally acceptable, way of overcoming low self-esteem was to struggle with oneself and with others, to work hard, to endure painful sacrifices, and finally to rise and be seen as having done so.
>
> (Fukuyama 2002, 66)

In short, this perspective maintains that happiness, success, and other intentional pursuits are underserved, unworthy, or impermissible if they did not involve overcoming pain or suffering.

Both premises of the argument are implausible. To evaluate this argument, it will be helpful to introduce a distinction between intrinsic and instrumental values. There is a lot of philosophical controversy over the exact nature of this distinction, but a workable version of it is that intrinsically valuable things are valuable in themselves and instrumentally valuable things are valuable just because of the valuable outcomes that directly result from those things. Bowel surgery is an example of something that is instrumentally good: one does not get it because of the inherent goodness of the procedure; one gets it because it restores health and health is widely considered to be intrinsically good. Pleasure and happiness are commonly regarded as paradigmatic examples of things that are intrinsically good, and they are not always the direct result of pain and suffering. The first premise assumes that pain and suffering are intrinsically valuable, and not merely as instrumentally valuable; that is, the first premise assumes that pain and suffering are valuable in themselves and not valuable just because of the valuable outcomes that result from them. This just seems dead wrong. One should not over-emphasize the value of pleasure and happiness (there are other things that are intrinsically good, such as knowledge), but it is misguided to valorize the role of pain and suffering in human life by contending that they are intrinsically good. Shermer contends that this conviction gets things backward: ethics is, and should be, about eliminating human suffering, not increasing it. She claims that this point of view is a "Calvinist prejudice," saying that "Unless one sees suffering or enduring pain as good or virtuous in themselves, there is no reason to claim that accomplishments without them are less worthy," even where their worth is measured in terms of whether they are intentionally performed or meaningful (Schermer 2005, 359). Pain and suffering may be a means for achieving important goods in life, such as wisdom or self-knowledge or many other valuable things, but that is to say that pain and suffering can be instrumentally good. That is a vastly more plausible view than the conviction that they are intrinsically good.

A problem facing the second premise of the hard work and suffering argument is that the use of biomedical enhancements often does not make the task easy or pain-free.

A weightlifter using testosterone supplements to achieve her weight-lifting goals is likely to endure a lot of hard work and suffering in a challenging training regimen in preparation for a competition. The hormones do not merely make it easier to lift weights, but they provide the weightlifter with the ability to lift heavier weight goals than would be achievable without the enhancements and continued training. The importance of this benefit is underscored by reports that some athletes are quite willing to trade off years of life if an ultimately fatal enhancement intervention could secure them the success that enables them to achieve their goals (Connor, Woolf and Mazanov 2013). Whether a sports championship is an apt source of meaning in life, of course, is another question that will come up again below.

The Complexities and Richness of Human Activities Argument

The third argument does not make a direct appeal to "easy shortcuts" but it alludes to a core worry that is often shared by those who have this concern. The complaint about "easy shortcuts" is rooted in a worry that by taking a shorter path along one's journey, one is missing out on the value of taking the longer path. The complexities and richness of human activities argument do not focus on the role of character building, hard work, or suffering in intrinsically valuable achievements or the overall development of a meaningful life, but it focuses on value and meanings of the specific activities that enhancement interventions might affect and the values they reflect (Schermer 2008, 360). While not a blanket indictment of all enhancement technologies, this argument contends that enhanced achievements are hollow "victories" that destroy traditional forms of meaning and important shared values.

The complexities and richness of human activities argument have the following structure.

1   Meaningful accomplishments are constituted by focal practices or practices that sustain internal goods.
2   Biomedical enhancements destroy focal practices and practices that sustain internal goods.
Therefore,
3   Biomedical enhancements prevent people from having meaningful accomplishments.

According to this argument, when someone uses biomedical technologies to accomplish their goals, those practitioners are dispensing with focal practices or practices that sustain internal goods that make those accomplishments meaningful. Defenders of this version of the easy shortcuts argument have maintained that enhancement technologies are not completely devoid of value: they do have instrumental value (Cole-Turner 1998; Schermer 2008, 360). Moreover, according to this argument, enhancement technologies only have instrumental value and do not have any intrinsic value. For instance, anti-obesity medication may be instrumentally valuable for those who have the goal of losing weight, but those medications have no value in themselves.

Some preliminary remarks about the terminology and underlying reasoning for the first premise of this argument are in order. The notions of "focal practices" and "internal goods," inspired by the work of Albert Borgmann and Alasdair MacIntyre, are used to explain the nature of the practices and values that the defenders of this argument claim to be undermined by biomedical enhancements (Borgmann 1984; MacIntyre 2007).

Borgmann develops the concept of a focal practice to contrast it with "a device paradigm" that he contends is dominant in mainstream society. According to Borgmann's terminology, a "device" refers to artifacts or technologies that produce outcomes without any regard for the human engagement involved in producing those outcomes. For instance, a hearth is not a device, in this sense, because it characteristically involves the chopping and gathering of wood, and making and maintaining a fire, but a central heating unit is a device, because it does not require any continuous human activity and involvement to maintain it. Devices, in this sense, are usually designed so that their machinery, the parts necessary for carrying out the essential functions of producing the outcomes, are usually hidden or tucked away inside of the device. Borgmann contends that the rampant consumerism of modern life and society leads to a "device paradigm," where outcomes are valued over human engagement in activities. In contrast with this concept of devices, Borgmann defends the importance of focal practices. According to Borgmann,

> a focal practice is the resolute and regular dedication to a focal thing. It sponsors discipline and skill which are exercised in a unity of achievement and enjoyment, of mind, body, and the world, of myself and others in social union.
>
> (Borgmann 1984, 219)

Focal practices do not have outcomes that can be replaced with functional equivalents: they involve processes that are based in tradition and have "structure and rhythm of their own" (Borgmann 1984, 219). Borgmann takes running, fly-fishing, backpacking, writing, poetry, and music to be examples of focal practices. According to this view, engagement in focal practices is a mode of engagement that essentially involves meaning and commitment—coming into contact with things that have a unique intrinsic value.

MacIntyre's conception of *internal goods* also provides a tool for characterizing the types of value that may be diminished by enhancements. Internal goods are "goods that are specific to that practice and can only be gained by participating and trying to live up to the internal standards of excellence specific of that practice" (Schermer 2008, 360, discussing MacIntyre's idea). The claim here is that meaningful accomplishments and activities flow from being engaged in specific centering practices structured by internal standards of excellence and it is that disciplined engagement that allows those focal practices to add meaning to life. MacIntyre writes:

> By a 'practice' I am going to mean any coherent and complex form of socially established cooperative human activity through which goods internal to that form of activity are realized in the course of trying to achieve those standards of excellence which are appropriate to, and partially definitive of, that form of activity, with the result that human powers to achieve excellence, and human conceptions of the ends and goods involved are systematically extended.
>
> (MacIntyre 2007, 187)

When someone adopts a novel form of biomedical technology to enhance their performance in some domain in a way that bypasses those internal standards of excellence, those individuals are dispensing with what makes those performances meaningful, no matter what personal interests they might advance or social goods they might produce. Schermer concludes:

> [I]n evaluating enhancement technologies we must therefore ask whether they enable (focal) practices or corrode them and whether they... support the obtainment of internal goods and forms of excellence, or reduce and disrupt them.
>
> (2008, 363)

The complexities and richness of human activities argument provides an interesting framework for thinking about a broader account of meaning loss, by pointing to the role of focal practices and their internal goods in helping to add intrinsic value to our pursuits in addition to their instrumental value. It does, however, leave several questions to be explored.

There are problems with each premise. First, as the risky life choices of performance-enhancing athletes suggest, it is still unclear what makes a focal practice worth centering our lives around, and whether or not some internal standards of excellence, like sports championships, might not be intrinsically meaningless despite their instrumental benefits. One's focal practices and their internal goods might even reflect and reinforce morally pernicious values. Little (1998) persuasively argues that, even when cosmetic surgery is embraced as a way to lead a more meaningful life by realizing one's authentic self, the standards of beauty involved often express suspect social norms that have been internalized and reinforced by oppressive power structures. Another example is a racist organization that has focal practices that may sustain internal goods for their members. Members of this group may have a shared sense of racial superiority that is a focal point of their work and they may share certain old jokes or camaraderie that in-group members enjoy with one another. Of course, those focal practices and internal goods should be abolished because the practices that sustain it are unjust and have no justification for their existence.

Second, one might wonder if things that are instrumentally valuable might not also be legitimate sources of meaning in life. That is to say, one might doubt that the "device paradigm" is as pernicious as Borgmann makes it out to be. For instance, the instrumental value of some enhancements might itself be in aid of adding meaning to a focal practice or internal good. An enhancement boost to a blacksmith's hand-eye coordination would still help produce the useful and beautiful objects that are the object of that craft, using the same absorbing skills that would have been required without the enhancement. Other enhanced practices might be instrumentally valuable because their achievements can help add meaning to other people's lives as well as their achievers', like important medical discoveries. Finally, it is possible that some find meaning in life in a mismatched assortment of pursuits that don't revolve around a single "centering" focal practice and its internal goods. A professor may teach and think, climb cliffs, be politically active, and forge steel tools, and find enough meaning in this combination of disjunctive activities to experience fulfillment even if no one of them was enough on its own. The creation of this kind of variegated meaning in life may leave plenty of room for "easy short cuts" in particular activities (caffeine to improve the teaching and thinking, LASIK surgery for the fine metal work, "anti-aging" interventions to live long enough to fit it all in, etc.) without compromising the meaningfulness of the whole.

One might also object to the first premise of the argument on the grounds that some meaningful activities get their meaning from sources other than focal practices or internal goods. Perhaps the meaningfulness of an activity is a matter of finding your deepest passions and pursuing those. Or it is a matter of obtaining mastery over your own talents and pursuing worthwhile goals. To sort this out, one might turn to the rapidly growing philosophical literature on meaning in life, or read some classic Russian literature.

Concluding Remarks: Argument, Feelings, and Intuition in the Enhancement Debate

After canvassing the arguments that are most likely to be given for the anti-enhancement position, it seems like a non-starter. We mentioned that one often finds the expression of anti-enhancement *concerns* without any arguments or reasons provided. Leon Kass, a prominent critic of biomedical enhancement, argues that his feeling of repugnance about enhancement uses of biomedical technologies, such as human cloning and IVF, are an expression of his deep wisdom. He writes, "in crucial cases [...] repugnance is the emotional expression of deep wisdom, beyond reasons' power to fully articulate it" (Kass 1997, 20). However, one wonders whether the repugnance that he feels toward human cloning is based in wisdom or irrational fears. How would he know the unconscious motivations of his feelings of repugnance? One general worry about these types of appeals to ineffable wisdom is that they warrant dogmatic assertions that shut down attempts at moral reasoning. These types of assertion may also be the products of unconscious biases, and thus, should be appropriate subjects of conversation and deliberation. These issues, about the role of reason, emotion and intuition in moral judgment, are currently the subject of debate in the moral psychology. Some of the implications of frameworks that have been developed in moral psychology and neuroethics have interesting implications for the ethics of human enhancement. (See Clarke et al. (2016) for a helpful overview of these issues.) These questions are also central to the growing literature on the topic of moral enhancement, and whether it involves the improvement of rational, cognitive, emotional, or other capacities.

Acknowledgments

We would like to thank Eric Juengst for extensive feedback on an earlier draft of this paper. We would also like to thank Gary Gala, Brian Powell, and Jonathan Tsou for valuable feedback.

References

Buchanan, A. 2011. *Beyond Humanity? The Ethics of Biomedical Enhancement.* Oxford: Oxford University Press.

Borgmann, A. 1984. *Technology and the Character of Contemporary Life.* Chicago: University of Chicago Press.

Clarke, S., J. Savulescu, C.A.J. Coady, A. Giubilini and S. Sanyal. 2016. *The Ethics of Human Enhancement: Understanding the Debate.* Oxford: Oxford University Press.

Coady, C.A.J. 2011. "Playing God". In *Human Enhancement*, edited by J. Savulescu and N. Bostrom, 155–180. Oxford: Oxford University Press.

Cole-Turner, R. 1998. "Do Means Matter?" In *Enhancing Human Traits: Ethical and Social Implications*, edited by E. Parens, 151–161. Washington, DC: Georgetown University Press.

Connor J., J. Woolf and J. Mazanov. 2013. "Would They Dope? Revisiting the Goldman Dilemma." *British Journal of Sports Medicine* 4(7): 607–700.

Frey, J., and C. Vogler, eds. 2018. *Self-Transcendence and Virtue: Perspectives from Philosophy, Psychology, and Theology.* New York: Routledge.

Fukuyama, F. 2002. *Our Posthuman Future: Consequences of the Biotechnology Revolution.* New York: Farrar, Strauss and Giroux.

Harris, J. 2011. "Enhancements Are a Moral Obligation". In *Human Enhancement*, edited by J. Savulescu and N. Bostrom, 155–180. Oxford: Oxford University Press.

Juengst, E. and D. Moseley. 2019. "Human Enhancement." *The Stanford Encyclopedia of Philosophy* (http://plato.stanford.edu/archives/sum2015/entries/enhancement).

Kass, L.R. 1997. "The Wisdom of Repugnance." *The New Republic.* June 17–26.

Kramer, P.D. 1994. *Listening to Prozac.* London: Fourth Estate.

Little, M. 1998. "Cosmetic Surgery, Suspect Norms, and the Ethics of Complicity." In *Enhancing Human Traits: Ethical and Social Implications*, edited by E. Parens, 162–176. Washington, DC: Georgetown University Press.

MacIntyre, A. 2007. *After Virtue* (3rd Ed). London: Duckworth Pub. Co.

Parens, E. ed., 1998. *Enhancing Human Traits: Ethical and Social Implications.* Washington, DC: Georgetown University Press.

Sandel, M. 2004. "The Case against Perfection: What's Wrong with Designer Children, Bionic Athletes and Genetic Engineering." *Atlantic Monthly*, April 2004, 51–62.

Sandel, M. 2007. *The Case Against Perfection: Ethics in an Age of Genetic Engineering.* Cambridge. MA: Harvard University Press.

Schermer, M. 2008. "Enhancements, Easy Shortcuts, and the Richness of Human Activities." *Bioethics* 22(7): 355–363.

Thomas, L. 2005. "Morality and a Meaningful Life." *Philosophical Papers* 34: 405–427.

Wielenberg, E. 2005. *Value and Virtue in a Godless Universe.* Cambridge: Cambridge University Press.

Chapter 29

Genetic Enhancement
Just Say Yes

Jason Brennan

A 2017 *Guardian* article asks, "Designer Babies: An Ethical Horror Waiting to Happen?"[1] The article concerns "designer babies," which refers to editing embryo's genes with the goal of increasing the probability that the resulting baby will have certain good or desired attributes and decrease the probability that the resulting baby will have certain bad or un-desired attributes.

The *Guardian* article is typical of popular work on this subject; it invokes *Brave New World* and *Frankenstein* to induce uneasiness among readers. In *Brave New World*, bottle-grown people are genetically engineered into rigid economic castes. For instance, laborers are designed to be "semi-morons" who never resent their work. Victor Frankenstein assembles his mishappen monster from multiple corpses, then *abandons* his creation.

There would be little case for genetic enhancement it if were about creating rigid eco-nomic castes or resentful, murderous flesh golems. But genetic enhancement is not about that. (Indeed, Frankenstein doesn't even perform genetic modifications.)

Instead, if ever genetic enhancement becomes available, parents will probably pursue three kinds of goals:

1 *Interventions*: Improving health outcomes and increasing physical and mental abilities to correct an underlying dysfunction.
2 *Enhancements*: Improved health outcomes and increased physical and mental abilities even when there is not underlying dysfunction.
3 *Modifications*: Specific traits (such as eye color, sex, or height) which do not qualify as health or ability per se.

(1) and (2) cover any changes which plausibly can be seen as augmenting a child's health or capacities, while "modifications" refer to everything else. As an illustration, if I take a pill that cures asthma, that's a treatment. If I am person of average physical strength, but I take a pill that increases my max one rep bench press by 50 kg, that's an enhancement. If I die my hair blonde, that's a modification. Of course, the line between the three is fuzzy.

Discussions of genetic enhancement often presume enhancement is morally suspect and requires an affirmative defense. Many who are comfortable with using genetic engineering to fix or cure diseases or genetic dysfunction are uncomfortable with using it to improve an otherwise healthy person. On their view, it would be fine to engineer a child to give it an IQ of 100 instead of 50, but not 150 instead of 100.

In contrast, in this paper, I argue the ethics goes the other way. If genetic engineering were cheap, safe, and easy, then by default, you *should* not only treat, but also enhance your children. Failure to do so would be wrong. You not only should use genetic engineering to cure your children's diseases, but should also give otherwise healthy children greater physical and mental abilities.

DOI: 10.4324/9781003189466-35

Before moving on, it's worth noting that most people already engage in less effective forms of genetic planning or—to use a taboo word—eugenic planning for their children with the goal of creating children of above-average or superior ability. For instance, when people procreate, they frequently choose partners who are likely to produce babies with desired and desirable traits. In the US, elites engage in assortative mating, in which high IQ, highly successful, and highly educated people tend only to marry and reproduce with other smart, successful, and educated people, with the goal of creating smart, successful, and educated babies. These same people might decry eugenics or even to downplay the role of genes in outcomes, but they don't believe what they say. Their behaviors indicate they select mates in large part for their genes. (Saying what sounds noble but doing what promotes their interests—that's Elite Behavior 101.) Or, when choosing sperm and egg donors, people do not select at random, but instead select parents with desirable and above-average traits to increase the chances the resulting children will have such traits. Or, many people will choose not to have kids after a certain age, despite it being viable to do so, because they acknowledge the chance of poor genetic outcomes increases. Most people already accept these forms of genetic planning, and might even think some such cases are obligatory. (For instance, you might think it wrong to pick a sperm donor at random rather than select for a healthy or successful donor.) But they treat genetic enhancement differently. We will investigate whether that distinction can be sustained.

Cost, Risk, Benefit

Let's comment briefly on the current science. In general, there is not a one-to-one correspondence between gene and traits. Many physical traits result from combinations of various genes and be generated in multiple ways. Different combinations interfere with or enhance each other. We often do not know which genetic changes would produce desired results. In many cases, modifying genes only increases the probability of resulting desired traits appearing, in part because we may not have identified all the related or relevant genetic markers, and in part because phenotypic traits depend on other factors, such as hormone expression in the womb. With a few exceptions, we are not yet position to "design" babies.

So, as of now, genetic enhancement is a risky and costly procedure. As with any other "medical" intervention, the ethics of the intervention depend in part on risks and costs.

Consider: when researchers developed albuterol for asthma, they needed to worry about benefits, risks, and costs. They must assess what percent and range of patients receive a positive response from the drug, and how strong the treatment effect size is. Regarding risks, they need to assess whether the drug backfires for some patients, or what kinds of side effects and harms the drug imposes. (For instance, albuterol increases patients' pulse and blood pressure and thus might contribute to heart disease or stroke.) They must also be concerned with cost. If albuterol stopped asthma attacks but cost $10 million per dose, the costs would dwarf the benefits.

Similar concerns apply not merely to treatments, but to enhancements. For instance, imagine I am considering taking creatine or undergoing a strength training regimen not to cure my debilitating weakness, but instead to maximize my strength far above average. Again, in deciding whether drugs, vitamins, food, or training are acceptable, I must weigh benefits, risks, and costs in some way.

These same issues matter for genetic enhancement in roughly the same way. I will not here try to offer a theory of when a drug—or genetic enhancement—is safe, effective, or cheap enough to allow that intervention. Rather, by default, *if* there are no *other* moral objections to genetic enhancement, the benefit-risk-cost problem for genetic enhancement is presumably more or less the same as with other interventions. We should treat them the same unless we can identify some principled reason to treat them differently.

Many complaints about genetic enhancement concerns possible downside risks and costs. These are worthy and important issues. If widespread modification of genes might have horrible but unanticipated health consequences, this is as good as reason to oppose genetic modification as it is to oppose any other health intervention.

I put aside such concerns here, though, because opposition to genetic enhancement is usually based on *other* objections which are meant to hold even if genetic enhancement proves safe and effective by medical standards. Thus, for the rest of this paper, assume genetic enhancement is safe (say, as safe as other approved drugs for similar effects) and effective. This allows us to focus on other *moral* objections.

Objections to Embryonic Destruction

Some people who believe that they are opposed to genetic enhancement might not be opposed to gene manipulation per se, but rather to other aspects of designer baby selection.

Suppose you are a Catholic. Suppose you believe, imagine rightly, that human personhood begins at conception and thus that all human zygotes have certain rights to life. Suppose also that life should only be created through sex inside marriage. If so, you will likely oppose test tube babies or destroying unwanted zygotes.

However, on this view, so far, genetic selection is not *itself* the problem. Instead, the problem is creating test tube babies and destroying zygotes. If I had 100 zygotes and destroyed 50 at random, paying no attention to their genetic profile, you would regard that as murder.

So, some reasons that members of various religions oppose genetic enhancement turn out not about genetic enhancement per se, but instead about *how* occurs. A Catholic would oppose designer baby methods which involves creating zygotes in test tubes and destroying unwanted embryos. But even if we grant this is wrong, the Catholic might nevertheless favor *other* forms of genetic enhancement, such as testing and then modifying the genes of an intact, implanted embryo, created through marital sex, which the mother plans to keep no matter what.

Treatment and Rescue

One reason a parent might be obligated to genetically modify their children is that it might be necessary to discharge a duty of *rescue*. In many cases, parents are obligated to rescue their children from danger, disability, and disease, if they can. But if I am obligated to give my sons medicine to save them from such dangers, then by default—unless we can identify a principled reason to think otherwise—we should presume I am obligated to rescue them via genetic treatment if that is the best means.

Consider a variation of a famous thought experiment by Peter Singer:

> *Drowning Child*
> You are walking along when you encounter a child drowning in a pool. You could easily save the child, though doing so will require you to ruin your new $500 blue suede shoes. If you don't help, no one else will, and the child will die.[2]

Most readers conclude that you are obligated to save the child. Failure to help requires a serious justification for doing so, such as that you can't swim or that losing your shoes would ruin your life somehow.

Presumably, then, the obligation to rescue stronger if the child is your own and you have a normal parent-child relationship:

Drowning Daughter
Your infant daughter drowning as in the previous example. You can save her. Doing so it would somehow cost you $5000, which you can afford, though it's a significant sum.

Here, I expect most people to agree that saving the daughter is obligatory despite the higher cost.

What if we modify the example further?

Sickly Daughter
Your infant daughter is dying of a disease. You can give her $5000 medicine to save her.

Again, I expect that readers will agree it is obligatory. What if we modify it further?

Sickly Daughter II
Your daughter—whom you plan to carry to term—is utero. She is diagnosed with a disease which make her quality of life significantly worse and will cause her to die young. You can safely administer her medicine now, for $5000, which will cure the disease.

Once again, I expect readers will agree this is obligatory. Some might think that we have the right to abort the fetus, but I ask readers to suppose the mother has no intention of doing so and intends to carry the infant to term no matter what.

Intuitively, it seems obligatory to save the fetus, just as one would be obligated to save a child. One way to illustrate that is by imagining a future harm that you can prevent now. Suppose a villain plants a time bomb that will explode six years after your child is born, killing it. You can diffuse the bomb, for $5,000, but only right now, while the fetus is in utero. It seems that if you intend to keep the infant, you *must* do so. (Note that I am not thereby saying that pregnant mothers must sacrifice everything for the health of their fetuses.)

Consider yet another variation:

Sickly Daughter III
Everything is the same as Sickly Daughter II, except the medicine involves modifying her genes. Assume the genetic intervention has the same benefits and risks as the medicine in case II.

Here, some people might change their mind. But unless they can identify a principled reason to do so, they should not. There has to something *about* genetic modification which renders it problematic. What is it? Until we find a good argument to the contrary, we should presume life-saving genetic interventions are obligatory—if they are safe, effective, and sufficiently cheap.

If genetic intervention is obligatory to save your child's life, then it will also be obligatory to help your child with other illnesses. Assuming there are no other risks, then the exact cut-off line—where it switches from obligatory to merely permissible—depends in part on the severity of the illness and the cost of the intervention. If you think it's obligatory to give your children $500 medicine to treat asthma, then it should be obligatory to spend $500 in genetic medicine to stop asthma from occurring. If it's obligatory to spend $500 to fix flat feet, then it should be obligatory to stop flat feet from developing. If it's obligatory to spend thousands helping your mentally disabled child function, then it should be obligatory to spend thousands to ensure the child will not become disabled in the first place.

In general, the test seems to be this: if you would be obligated to help your child by giving them medicine or any other intervention for some illness or disability, then you are by default presumed obligated to cure it through genetic treatment assuming the costs and risks are not sufficiently greater.

Genetic Enhancement

Section "Treatment and Rescue" considers the easiest cases: using genetic manipulation to save one's child from various illnesses or disabilities. People who are otherwise queasy about genetic engineering might nevertheless endorse genetic treatment to cure diseases or eliminate disabilities. But many reject using genetic engineering to create further advantages for their children. Fixing a club foot is fine; engineering an Olympic sprinter is not. Fixing a cleft palette is fine; engineering supermodel beauty is not. Fixing mental disability is fine; engineering a genius is not.

I find this mentality puzzling. I wonder to what degree it reflects a sort of status quo bias. As Nick Bostrom and Toby Ord put it:

> When a proposal to change a certain parameter is thought to have bad overall consequences, consider a change to the same parameter in the opposite direction. If this is also thought to have bad overall consequences, then the onus is on those who reach these conclusions to explain why our position cannot be improved through changes to this parameter. If they are unable to do so, then we have reason to suspect that they suffer from status quo bias.[3]

What's especially odd about it is that in commonsense morality, parents are supposed to be do things to enhance their children's skills and ability. For instance, imagine a parent that provides their children with good health care, vaccinates their kids, and ensures that any diseases their children get are either cured or treated. But now imagine this parent does nothing else—or the bare legal minimum—to promote their children's skills and ability. The parent doesn't try to foster their children's curiosity, intelligence, strength, moral wisdom, common sense, agility, or whatnot, through sports, education, travel, or anything else. You would probably regard this parent as neglectful and somewhat monstrous.[4]

Yet, this creates a puzzle: we think parents *ought* to enhance their children's abilities, character, and skill, and yet many people think that parents ought not do so through *genetic enhancement*. Reading to your kids to make them smarter is fine, but engineering them to be smarter is not. Having your kids volunteer to foster their altruism is fine, but engineering them to be more altruistic is not. Punishing children for demonstrating a lack of foresight is fine, but engineering them to conscientious is not. Unless we have a good argument about *why* genetic enhancement is wrong, though, this is seems arbitrary and bogus. By default, we should think that if parents are obligated to foster certain traits and abilities in their children, then they are obligated to use genetic enhancement to do so whenever it is a safer or more effective means.

In the Dungeons and Dragons game, all characters have "ability" scores which reflect various underlying physical and mental traits on a 1–18 scale, with 10 being average. (Above 18 represents superhuman ability.) Suppose your daughter is perfectly average, and scores a 10 on strength, constitution, dexterity, intelligence, wisdom, and charisma. She contracts a rare disease which, if not treated, will cause her to lose 1 point in each. This won't ruin her life, but it will make literally everything a bit harder and will likely reduce her the quality of life significantly, if not intolerably. You can stop this disease with a safe and effective medicine that costs $5000.

Here, I am again inclined to say you *must* do so. I note that most readers probably think you would be obligated not only to use medicine, but if no medicine were available, you should try to use non-medical means to prevent the losses.

But if so, what if there were instead medicine that, for $5,000 per dose, would *increase* her scores in all six abilities by five points, making her significantly above average in everything? If it's obligatory to prevent a one-point loss in all abilities, why would it not also be obligatory, for the same price, to create a five-point gain in all abilities?

From the standpoint of your daughter's welfare, having these ability gains would be tremendous. She would have significantly more "positive freedom," i.e., the capacity to achieve her ends, whatever her ends might be. She can do more and do more things more easily. The opportunities available to her would expand. She could expect to have a happier, longer, more interesting, and more fulfilling life. If there were no downsides risks or costs—for instance, maybe being too exceptional would cause her to feel alienated—then pro tanto, it seems you should be feel obligated to give her the medicine. Indeed, it's unclear whether there is any stopping point. Why not give her superhuman abilities, if you could? (Notice that I didn't mention whether the medicine is genetic or not, because it remains unclear what difference it being *genetic* makes.)

Again, what's odd about denying this is that most people think parents should invest in their children's human capital, and should try to make their children have better traits and abilities. They think that using good parenting techniques or shaping the environment to improve their children's abilities is not only permissible, but often obligatory.

Of course, they do not think parents must *only* invest or that the pursuit of greater ability must trump everything else. You can take breaks. Having a happy childhood matters, and that means not constantly training ones intelligence or agility. Parents can invest in themselves, too.

My point here is that you should treat environmental vs genetic enhancement the same. If it is obligatory or permissible to spend $1,000 of time and effort tutoring your child to be better at math, why would it not also be obligatory or permissible to spend $1,000 to genetically enhance your child to be better at math—and other things like it? If there were heavy health-risks or expenses to genetic enhancement, sure, that would matter. Parents owe their children a lot, but we do not owe them everything. I would not be willing to spend $100,000 to make my kids 1% better at singing, whether through tutoring or genetic enhancement. But my point here is that unless we have a valid reason to treat them differently, we should treat them the same.

Once again, though, it seems our reasoning should be parallel. If it would be permissible or even obligatory to give your infant daughter such enhancements, then it should be permissible to enhance your daughter when she is a fetus or embryo in utero.

In short, opponents of enhancement face two dilemmas. First, they must explain why they think non-genetic—i.e., environmentally based—enhancement that accomplishes the same ends is permissible and even obligatory, but genetic enhancement is wrong. Second, they must explain why fixing a disability to bring someone up to a healthy or normal range is permissible or obligatory, but enhancing someone above that normal range is not.

Egalitarian Arguments against Ability Enhancement

Perhaps the most important critique of genetic enhancement is based on egalitarianism. Some egalitarians say that it is fine to use genetic engineering to get your kids up to average, but not to make them significantly above average. As the *Wall Street Journal* reports, "Some people say it is unethical to bioengineer children because better-off parents could use it to give their children a competitive edge, widening societal divisions."[5] The argument is that it is unfair to promote your children's abilities because doing so comes at the expense of other children.

Call this the egalitarian principle:

> *It is wrong to engineer your children to be superior to others in ability, because doing so makes it more likely your children will get coveted offices, positions, and relationships, or win competitions, at the expense of those of lower ability.*

There is a lot wrong with this line of reasoning. One thing to note, though, is that there doesn't seem to be any special about genetic enhancement per se according to this principle. The reason offered against enhancement—that it might help your children get good things at the expense of children with lower ability—applies to *anything* you might do to help your children. It applies equally well to environmental interventions.

Accordingly, if you actually believed this principle—and frankly, I doubt anyone really does—you would also all things equal avoid reading to your children, enrolling them in AP classes, tutoring them in math, sending them to lacrosse camp, enrolling them in Sunday school, teaching them a foreign language, sending them on international travel, or having them volunteer at a soup kitchen. After all, these activities also promote your children's skills and abilities. According to the egalitarian principle, this will come at the expense of other children who have lower ability. (Perhaps you are allowed to do these things only to bring your children up to the median or mean, or only if there is some other egalitarian benefit.) You also would not do these things for yourself.

If you think genetically enhancing yourself or your children is bad because it comes at the expense of others, then in parallel you should think equivalent non-genetic enhancement is just as bad. Perhaps genetic enhancement is special only because in principle it could be more effective. If it's wrong to engineer smart kids because having smart kids hurts the dumb kids, then it's for the same wrong to raise smart kids through other means.

Further, if you actually believe this egalitarian principle, you would want to avoid assortative mating. For instance, suppose you are high IQ, highly conscientious, and highly successful. Empirically speaking, if you mate with another person like you, your children are likely to also be above average. Since, according to the egalitarian principle, this kind of mating is bad. It'd be better—and perhaps even obligatory—for you to mate with someone with poor traits, in order to make it more likely you produce average offspring. The egalitarian principle forbids genetic enhancement in a eugenic direction and instead demands genetic mediocrity.

Indeed, if the egalitarian principle is true, it does not forbid genetic engineering per se. Rather, it suggests that parents have a positive obligation to use genetic engineering to ensure their children are average. After all, if you leave things to chance, you might have above-average kids, which according to the principle, harms and disadvantages others. So, it is wrong to leave things to chance. A genuine egalitarian would favor genetic engineering for the purposes of making people more equal.

The egalitarian principle leads to many conclusions its defenders probably do not want to endorse. Further, it makes demands on their behavior which we see its defenders do not even try to meet, which suggests to me that its defenders do not really believe it. I doubt they would say, "Oh, I agree I must not read to my children, but I am too weak-willed to avoid it."

But notice that the egalitarian principle endorses a rather ugly view of human society. Consider that the NAACP says that a mind is a terrible thing to waste. Part of their point is that systematic racism in the US did not merely hurt black victims. It also hurts others. Talented black people—and black people who would have been talented had they been allowed to develop their talents freely and fairly—are a benefit to *everyone* else. But the egalitarian principle paints society as a zero-sum game where one person's talents come at the expense of the other. Thus, according to the egalitarian principle, keeping would-be black doctors, inventors, entrepreneurs, scientists, and innovators down, forcing them into menial jobs, prison, or unemployment is *good* for everybody else and makes everyone else's life better. It's a horrible thing to think, but the egalitarian principle implies it. The person who endorses the egalitarian principle must say that racism is nevertheless bad for *other* reasons, but they are stuck having to say that it is good for most people if other people's talents go to waste. This person would have to say similar things about women's entry into the workforce; maybe it is good for women, but it's bad for most of everyone else.

As a matter of empirics, this is mistaken. The reason we are rich today, in the places we are rich, is because we have background political institutions which encourage the development of human capital and physical capital, and encourage people to use this capital productively. We benefit tremendously from other people's talents. Indeed, economics shows that the least talented benefit more from the presence of the untalented than vice versa.[6]

Consider an illustration: imagine I brandish a magic wand that makes you the best at everything. Note: my magic wand doesn't make you any better. Your skills and abilities remain exactly intact and stable. Rather, what it does is make everyone worse at everything compared to you right now. Thanks to my magic wand, you are now the most talented person in the world at everything, but you are no more talented than you were a moment ago. Do you expect that in the long run, you will be better off as a result? Do you expect you will become fabulously rich and famous? You might, until you think about it. Think of all the things that need to be done, which require skills, knowledge, and abilities you don't have. Now remember that thanks to my magic wand, no one else has them either.

Some people complain that if genetic enhancement technology becomes available, it will be affordable to the rich but not the poor. Thus, the argument goes, the rich—who already have the means to invest in their children's skills and abilities—will simply ensure their children have even greater advantages. This will widen the gap in achievement between the children of the rich and poor. For that reason, they say, it's wrong. (Notice that anyone making this argument is still stuck endorsing the other ugly conclusions I mentioned above.)

However, the empirical issues are more complicated. Rather, what we should expect is that at first, the technology is expensive and only available to the rich, but over a short period of time, the technology becomes cheap and is available to everyone.

Economist F. A. Hayek says:

> Our rapid economic advancement is in large part a result of inequality and is impossible without it. Progress at a fast rate cannot proceed on a uniform front, but must take place in an echelon fashion…At any stage of [the process of growing knowledge] there will always be many things we already know how to produce but which are still too expensive to provide for more than the few…All of the conveniences of a comfortable home, of our means of transportation, and communication, of entertainment and enjoyment, we could produce at first only in limited quantities; but it was in doing this that we gradually learned to make them or similar things at a much small outlay of resources and thus began to supply them to the great majority. A large part of the expenditure of the rich, though not intended for that end, thus serves to defray experimentation with the new things that, as a result, can later be made available to the poor.[7]

Economists have long recognized that when a new technology develops, it is usually expensive, and available at first only to the rich. But, as the rich pay for the initial development of that technology and enjoy the initial benefits, the rich also pay to make the technology available to all. This has been true of, say, dishwashers, washing machines, air conditioning, electric stoves, microwaves, personal computers, landline telephones, cellular phones, smart phones, laptops, air flight, automobiles, furnaces, electric lighting, electricity in general, toilets, sanitation, the ability to bath daily, having enough food to each, having large houses, having lots of clothing, video games, and pretty much everything else. Perhaps designer baby technology would go against this trend, but that seems doubtful. After all, consider that the cost of sequencing one human genome dropped from over $100 million in 2001 to about $7,000 in 2013.[8] The available evidence strongly indicates, if not guarantees, that designer baby technology will eventually be in the hands of almost everyone in developed countries.

Notes

1 https://www.theguardian.com/science/2017/jan/08/designer-babies-ethical-horror-waiting-to-happen
2 Peter Singer, "Famine, Affluence, and Morality," *Philosophy and Public Affairs* 1 (1972): 229–243.
3 Bostrom, Nick, and Toby Ord. 2006. "The Reversal Test: Eliminating Status Quo Bias in Applied Ethics," *Ethics* 116: 656–679.
4 For a similar point, see Christopher Freiman, "Why Parents Should Enhance Their Children," *The Ethics of Ability and Enhancement*, eds. Jessica Flanigan and Terry Price (New York: Palgrave MacMillan, 2017).
5 http://stream.wsj.com/story/latest-headlines/SS-2-63399/SS-2-345438/
6 See Jason Brennan and Peter Jaworski, *Markets without Limits* (New York: Routledge Press, 2016), 169–182.
7 F. A. Hayek, *The Constitution of Liberty* (Chicago: University of Chicago Press, 1960), 42–44.
8 http://www.genome.gov/images/content/cost_per_genome.jpg

Chapter 30

Feminism and the Ethics of Reprogenetic Technologies

Inmaculada de Melo-Martín

Introduction

When in 1978, the first baby was born after the use of in vitro fertilization (IVF), few would have predicted the rapid acceptance, expanding uses, and remarkable development of reprogenetic technologies. These technologies, which combine the power of reproductive technologies and genetic tools (Knowles and Kaebnick 2007), are now a routine clinical practice in fertility clinics. As of early 2022, it is estimated that more than 10 million babies had been brought into the world with the help of IVF and associated technologies (ESHRE 2022). In the United States, approximately 2.1% of all infants are born with these technologies (CDC 2019), and in countries such as Austria, Denmark, Slovenia, and Spain, over 5.0% of all newborns were conceived by these technologies (Wyns et al. 2020).

Reprogenetic technologies involve remarkable technical achievements: they allow us to create, store, select, and genetically modify gametes and embryos. Indeed, Robert Edward, one of the contributors to the development of IVF with gynecologist Patrick Steptoe, was recognized in 2010 with the Nobel Prize in Medicine (Watts 2010). Reprogenetic technologies also give us an extraordinary level of control not only over whether and when to have children, but over who can and cannot be born. Moreover, these technologies have a significant impact over essential aspects of human existence such as our desire to reproduce, to form families, and to ensure the health and well-being of our offspring.

Although infertility, inheritable genetic diseases, and the desire to have children affect both men and women, women's role in the development and use of these technologies has been crucial (de Melo-Martín 2017). Expanding women's reproductive options has been the impetus behind the development of these technologies. And women's bodies are critically implicated. They receive the hormonal injections, undergo the surgeries, and suffer the physical and psychological side effects associated with the use of these procedures. They provide the reproductive materials needed. They gestate, give birth to, and usually rear the babies conceived with the help of these technologies. Women bear a disproportionate share of the risks and burdens involved in the use of reprogenetics. It is thus unsurprising that since their inception, feminists' scholars have devoted a significant amount of attention to these technologies (see, for instance, Arditti, Klein, and Minden 1984; Corea 1987; Rothman 1989; Sherwin 1992; Callahan 1995; Roberts 1997; de Melo-Martín 1998; Mahowald 2000). In what follows, I discuss some of the main concerns that feminists have raised regarding the development and use of reprogenetic technologies. In particular, I will focus on some worries related to the rhetoric of expanding reproductive choices and concerns about the values that these technologies reinforce. Before doing so, I provide a brief description of these technologies.

DOI: 10.4324/9781003189466-36

Reprogenetic Technologies

As mentioned, reprogenetic technologies involve the combination of reproductive techniques and genomic tools. When aimed at reproduction,[1] reprogenetic technologies all necessitate the use of IVF. In its most basic form, that is, when the woman who undergoes IVF provides her own eggs and her partner supplies the sperm, IVF involves several steps (Niederberger et al. 2018). They include the injection of various fertility drugs to produce multiple eggs, retrieval of the eggs from the woman's body, combination of eggs and sperm to create embryos, monitoring and assessment of embryos, and transferring of the fresh embryos into the woman's body or freezing them for later use.

Although clinicians have been using IVF for decades, researchers are constantly updating many of the procedures and techniques. New fertility drugs, novel freezing protocols for gametes and embryos, and innovative fertilization methods are developed periodically with the goal of improving fertilization rates and outcomes (Niederberger et al. 2018).

Several genomic techniques are used in combination with IVF. Some, such as preimplantation genetic testing (PGT), were introduced in 1990s as an alternative to prenatal tests for couples at a high risk of transmitting single-gene disorders to their offspring (Handyside et al. 1990). PGT is used before embryos are transferred or frozen to identify, and normally discard, those that carry genomic variants that are associated with particular diseases or disorders (De Rycke et al. 2020). Although PGT was initially used mainly to test for disorders caused by chromosomal abnormalities such as Down syndrome and single-gene disorders such as Huntington's disease, it can now be used to test for about 400 different conditions, including disease with late onset or that increase the risk of suffering a disease, as well as for sex selection (Kuliev and Rechitsky 2017).

Other reprogenetic technologies, such as mitochondrial replacement techniques (MRTs), are much newer, with reports of only a few children born through their application (Zhang et al. 2017). The purpose of these techniques is to allow some women who are at risk of transmitting some types of mitochondrial diseases the possibility of having unaffected and genetically related children. MRTs involve the use of eggs from a donor. With these techniques, scientists replace the affected mitochondria in the intended mother's egg with healthy mitochondria from the woman's donor egg (Reznichenko, Huyser, and Pepper 2016). While PGT allows for the selection of certain embryos, MRTs involve germline modifications, i.e., modifications that are inherited by the offspring. Because mitochondria have their own genome, the embryos created after the use of these technologies contain genetic material from three different individuals: the intended parents' genetic material and the donor's mitochondrial genome. Moreover, the offspring of the female—though not the male[2]—children thus born will also inherit the donor's mitochondrial genome.

Various new molecular technologies can also be used today not only to study gene function, biological mechanisms, and disease pathology, but also to treat or cure particular diseases (Khalil 2020). One of these molecular tools, CRISPR-Cas9 system, has proved particularly efficient, with more specificity, and cheaper than other genome editing tools. In fact, the recent Nobel Prize in chemistry awarded to its CRISPR-Cas9 developers, Emmanuelle Charpentier and Jennifer Doudna, manifest the revolutionary nature of this genome editing tool (Mullard 2020).

CRISPR-Cas9 has already been used to create genetically modified animals (Niu et al. 2014). Several groups in jurisdictions where these interventions are lawful have reported on the use of genome editing tools to modify the genomes of human embryos for research purposes (Ma et al. 2017). And although many countries prohibit directly or indirectly the use of genome editing tools for reproductive purposes in humans and the consensus in the scientific community is that the technology is not ready, the technology has also been used to create genetically modified human beings. In November 2018, He Jiankui, a Chinese researcher claimed to have used it (Cyranoski and Ledford 2018). He and his team transferred human embryos edited to inactivate a genetic pathway that HIV uses to infect cells, and at least three babies have been born. He's actions have been widely condemned by the scientific community and he was recently sentenced to three years in prison (Townsend 2020).

Ethical Issues: Feminist Concerns

The development and implementation of reprogenetic technologies raise a host of ethical issues, from the ethically sound way to treat surplus embryos and the moral status of manipulated human embryos, to the commercialization of reproductive materials and women's exploitation, to designer babies and eugenic control, to the commodification of children and the appropriate degree of control prospective parents should have over their offspring, to effects on women's lives and future generations.

Although feminist scholars do not present a unified position regarding reprogenetic technologies, their work has been essential in calling attention to the role that gender—as well as other social categories such as race, ethnicity, sexual identity, disability status, etc.—has in the development and use of these technologies. Feminist contention that ethically sound analyses of reprogenetic technologies require consideration of the gendered nature of these technologies has resulted in multifaceted, insightful, and crucial assessments of reprogenetics (see, for instance, Arditti, Klein, and Minden 1984; Corea 1987; Overall 1987; Rothman 1989; Sherwin 1992; Donchin 1993; Duden 1993; Callahan 1995; Purdy 1996; Roberts 1997; Mahowald 2000; Parens and Asch 2000; Thompson 2005; Dickenson 2007; Scully 2008; Franklin 2013; de Melo-Martín 2017; Baylis and McLeod 2014). Feminists' explicit goals of ending oppression and promoting equity have permitted assessments of these technologies that are attentive to the social and political contexts in which reprogenetic technologies are developed and used.

Offering an exhaustive discussion of the many ethical issues that reprogenetic technologies present would necessitate a whole book. My focus here will thus be more limited. In what follows, I offer a brief discussion of two sets of concerns of particular relevance to feminists: how the rhetoric of expanding women's reproductive choices might negatively impact their lives, and the ways in which reprogenetic technologies can reinforce contested and problematic values.

Reproductive Autonomy: Not All that Glitters Is Gold

Reprogenetic technologies directly involve questions about women's reproductive choices. Indeed, one of the most touted benefits of these technologies is that they expand women's ability to take control of their reproductive decisions. These technologies allow infertile women—and men—to have genetically related children. They enable those who might be at risk of transmitting disease-related variants to their offspring to have unaffected babies. Reprogenetic technologies permit homosexual couples to have children with whom they share a genetic connection, and they allow women who otherwise might not be able to experience gestation and give birth to do so. Similarly, the ability to freeze women's eggs at a younger age allows women to exercise more control over when to have a child.

Feminist scholars have, however, raised concerns about the rhetoric of choice and the narrow understanding of reproductive autonomy (Arditti, Klein, and Minden 1984; Rothman 1987; Roberts 1995; McLeod 2002; Scully, Banks, and Shakespeare 2006; d'Agincourt-Canning 2006; Harwood 2007; Overall 2012; de Melo-Martín 2017; Ross 2017). They have called attention to the ways in which the emphasis on choice obscures the burdens that these technologies impose on women's health. Each of the procedures involved in IVF presents risks to women (Nastri et al. 2015). The fertility drugs that women must use to stimulate ovulation can cause various side effects, including bloating, abdominal pain, and mood swings. The procedures used to retrieve women's eggs can result in allergic reactions to the anesthesia, bleeding, infection, and injury to organs near the ovaries, such as the bladder or bowel. IVF also increases the risk of multiple pregnancies because often more than one embryo is transferred. Hemorrhage, miscarriages, pregnancy-related high blood pressure, gestational diabetes, and delivery by cesarean section are all risks associated with multiple pregnancies. Of course, multiple pregnancies also involve risks to the babies because of prematurity. The inattention to the differential health risks of reprogenetic technologies results in inaccurate descriptions of these technologies that are unlikely to serve women's well-being. But such disregard also contributes to evaluations that fail to offer meaningful strategies to mitigate the risks to women's health (de Melo-Martin 2017).

Feminist scholars have also problematized the presumption that more reproductive choice is always better than less. They contend that such assumption neglects the significance of the social and political contexts in which reproductive choices are presented, how the framing of those choices affects not only *who* can choose but also *what* can be chosen, the existence of multiple factors that condition choice, or how new choices introduce constraints on previously existing options. For instance, in the US, white, middle-class women are encouraged to use reprogenetic technologies so that they can become mothers. Indeed, they constitute the main users of these technologies (Spar 2006). However, a variety of laws and institutional practices discourage women of color from having children (Roberts 1997). And as it is clear by the burgeoning market in cross-border reproductive care, economically disadvantaged women are often the ones providing eggs and serving as gestational carriers (Donchin 2010; Twine 2015). Similarly, as we mentioned earlier, the principal aim of reprogenetic technologies is to prevent the birth of children with particular diseases and disabilities, and thus women who are thought to be at a higher risk of having children considered disabled are often seen as *needing* to use these technologies (Parens and Asch 1999; Tremain 2001; Shakespeare 2006; Scully 2008).

Furthermore, the rhetoric of increased choice and reproductive autonomy also conceals the costs that result from more choices and how those costs accrue particularly to women (de Melo-Martin 2017). One of such costs is that of acquiring information in order to choose appropriately (Dworkin 1982; Schwartz 2004). In fact, because genome sequencing technologies can generate unparalleled amounts of genetic information about an individual (Reuter, Spacek, and Snyder 2015), the costs of choosing appropriately can be quite high. Moreover, because reprogenetic technologies permit a choice *among* various embryos, the decision-making costs can be staggering. Given that reprogenetic technologies are promoted as increasing *women's* choices, the costs of decision making also fall on women.

The emphasis of increased choice also masks how the relationships between choice, responsibility, and blame can have negative effects on women's lives (de Melo-Martin 2017). When particular choices become available, e.g., to use PGT to select against embryos with undesirable characteristics, failing to choose counts against one, as one is now responsible, and can be held responsible, for the choice in question (Dworkin 1982). The choices that reprogenetic technologies made available are thus accompanied by blame: women can blame themselves and be blamed by others for the choices they make. For instance, although before the implementation of these technologies women could not be thought to be blameworthy for bringing a child into the world with some trait considered undesirable, now they can. Reprogenetic technologies allow for the selection of some embryos rather than others and thus women can be held and hold themselves responsible for the particular embryo they happen to select or for failing to use these technologies to avoid the birth of a child with a disability (Roberts 1997; Asch 1999).

Reinforcing Contested Values

Although many mainstream assessments of reprogenetic technologies present them as value-free (Savulescu 2005; Harris 2007; Smith, Chan, and Harris 2012; Savulescu et al. 2015), such view is problematic. A significant amount of scholarship has compellingly argued that technologies are value-laden in various ways. Technologies embody particular values, shape, and transform the world we live in, influence our practical options, and affect what we take to be morally permissible or obligatory, right and wrong (MacKenzie and Wajcman 1985; Winner 1986; Idhe 1993; Latour 2005; Verbeek 2005; Waelbers 2011; Swierstra and Waelbers 2012; de Melo-Martín 2018).

Some of the values embedded in reproductive technologies are of particular concern to feminist scholars because they can further injustices against women and other disadvantaged groups such as the poor, racial/ethnic minorities, and people with disabilities (de Melo-Martín 2017). For example, reprogenetic technologies can reinforce oppressive gender norms associated with ideals of motherhood and reproductive responsibility (Arditti, Klein, and Minden 1984; Corea 1985; Rothman 1989; Rowland 1992). Although many women desire to become mothers and find motherhood valuable in multiple ways, there is little doubt that by sanctioning inequalities between men and women, prevalent notions of motherhood and family have worked as prescriptions in the service of gender oppression (Firestone 1970; Rich 1976; Okin 1989; de Beauvoir [1949] 1993; Kukla 2005; Badinter and Hunter 2011; LaChance Adams and Lundquist 2013). Prevalent notions of motherhood minimize the physical and emotional work that mothers do, impose norms about who are "good" and "bad" mothers that generate expectations difficult to meet for many women, and contribute to marginalizing some mothers—those who are poor, black, or have disabilities (Roberts 1997; Asch 1999; Kukla 2005; Gillies 2006). Because reprogenetic technologies make women's bodies alone the sites of treatment even when infertility affects both men and women, they embody the asymmetry of reproductive relationships and reinforce traditional notions of responsibility for reproduction. Moreover, the routine use of these technologies and their broad availability buttress ideas about the need for women to become mothers. Women are now expected to use these technologies when they cannot have children without them or when they are at risk of bringing into the world children with certain traits. Indeed, the reinforcing of the value of motherhood is patent in the expanding use of egg freezing. Women are expected to undergo risky and expensive procedures to ensure that they can become mothers at some point in their lives.

But these technologies also sanction prevalent racist and sexist values in various ways and are likely to strengthen those values, and with them their harmful consequences. First, prospective parents with more resources will be able to access reprogenetic technologies more easily. Thus, they will be able to select or enhance their children while economically disadvantaged ones will have to rely on chance. The use of these technologies is therefore likely to contribute to furthering social injustices. It is true that this can be the case for any technology that confers some competitive advantage on those who can access them. Nonetheless, that other technologies can also increase social injustices is obviously not a reason in favor of promoting reprogenetic technologies. Moreover, at least some of those injustices are likely to fall disproportionately on women. Women with financial resources will be expected to use those technologies to ensure their children are the best they can be (Savulescu 2005). However, as I mentioned above, socioeconomically disadvantaged women will be held responsible for the "imperfect" children they might have.

Second, recall that reprogenetic technologies allow people not only to have a child, but to have a *particular* kind of child, that is, a child with or without certain characteristics (de Melo-Martin 2017). Because what physical and psychological traits are valued or disvalued is highly dependent on the social context, in racist, sexist, ableist societies like ours, prospective parents are likely to select against, or enhance for, traits that are consistent with, and reinforce, prevalent norms: fairer-skin children, those without disabilities, strong, smart boys, and sympathetic, submissive girls (Sparrow 2007; de Melo-Martín 2017). Given the long, and shameful, support for eugenic polices aimed at preventing the birth of people with "undesirable" traits (Wilson 2018), that reprogenetic technologies could have these effects is hardly surprising. Even prospective parents who might be concerned about reinforcing social injustices with their choices would have to weight their desire to contribute to a more just society against their desire to improve their children's well-being.

Conclusion

Reprogenetic technologies present us with an extraordinary degree of control over who can be born, expand people's reproductive options, and can contribute to reduce the presence of devastating diseases. They also confront us with substantial ethical challenges: commercialization of reproductive materials, commodification of children, eugenic concerns, exploitation of women, furthering inequality and discrimination.

In this chapter, I have presented some ethical concerns of particular interest to feminist scholars. Feminist work in this area is relevant for various reasons. First, by attending to the—often neglected in mainstream analysis of these technologies—gendered and value-laden nature of reprogenetic technologies, it provides us with insights absent in other types of analyses. Second, their concern with the impact of these technologies on women and other disadvantaged groups calls attention to the differential effects that the development and use of reprogenetic technologies have. Third, by challenging the status quo, feminist analysis of reprogenetics can offer solutions less likely to contribute to social injustices or to reinforce sexist, racists, or ableist values.

Notes

1 Although reprogenetic technologies can be used for research purposes, the focus of the chapter will be on reproduction.
2 Mitochondria are inherited maternally.

References

Arditti, Rita, Renate Klein, and Shelley Minden. 1984. *Test-tube women: what future for motherhood?* London: Pandora Press.
Asch, Adrienne. 1999. "Prenatal diagnosis and selective abortion: a challenge to practice and policy." *American Journal of Public Health* 89 (11):1649–1657.
Badinter, Elisabeth, and Adriana Hunter. 2011. *The conflict: how modern motherhood undermines the status of women.* New York: Metropolitan Books/Henry Holt and Co.
Baylis, Francoise and Carolyn McLeod (eds). 2014. *Family-making: contemporary ethical challenges.* New York: Oxford University Press.
Beauvoir, Simone de, and H. M. Parshley. 1993. *The second sex.* New York: Alfred A. Knopf.
Callahan, Joan C. 1995. *Reproduction, ethics, and the law: feminist perspectives.* Bloomington: Indiana University Press.
Centers for Disease Control and Prevention (CDC). 2019. "ART Success Rates." US Dept of Health and Human Services. https://www.cdc.gov/art/artdata/index.html

Corea, Gena. 1985. *The mother machine: reproductive technologies from artificial insemination to artificial wombs.* New York: Harper & Row.

Corea, Gena. 1987. *Man-made women: how new reproductive technologies affect women. 1st Midland book ed.* Bloomington: Indiana University Press.

Cyranoski, David, and Heidi Ledford. 2018. "International outcry over genome-edited baby claim." *Nature* 563 (7733):607–608.

d'Agincourt-Canning, L. 2006. "Genetic testing for hereditary breast and ovarian cancer: responsibility and choice." *Qualitative Health Research* 16 (1):97–118.

de Melo-Martín, Inmaculada. 1998. *Making babies: biomedical technologies, reproductive ethics, and public policy.* Dordrecht: Kluwer Academic.

de Melo-Martín, Inmaculada. 2017. *Rethinking reprogenetics: enhancing ethical analyses of reprogenetic technologies.* New York: Oxford University Press.

de Melo-Martín, Inmaculada. 2018. "Valuing reprogenetic technologies: bringing insights from the philosophy of technology to bioethics." *Spanish Philosophy of Technology: Contemporary Work from the Spanish Speaking Community* 24:45–58.

De Rycke, Martine, Veerle Berckmoes, Anick De Vos, Stefanie Van De Voorde, Pieter Verdyck, Willem Verpoest, and Kathelijn Keymolen. 2020. "Preimplantation genetic testing: clinical experience of preimplantation genetic testing." *Reproduction* 160 (5):A45–A58.

Dickenson, Donna. 2007. *Property in the body: feminist perspectives, Cambridge law, medicine, and ethics.* Cambridge, UK; New York: Cambridge University Press.

Donchin, Anne. 1993. *Procreation, power and subjectivity: feminist approaches to new reproductive technologies,* Working paper series. Wellesley, MA: Center for Research on Women.

Donchin, Anne. 2010. "Reproductive tourism and the quest for global gender justice." *Bioethics* 24 (7):323–332.

Duden, Barbara. 1993. *Disembodying women: perspectives on pregnancy and the unborn.* Cambridge, MA: Harvard University Press.

Dworkin, Gerald. 1982. "Is more choice better than less?" *Midwest Studies in Philosophy* 7 (1):47–61.

European Society of Human Reproduction and Embryology (ESHRE). 2022. *ART fact sheet.* https://www.eshre.eu/Europe/Factsheets-and-infographics

Firestone, Shulamith. 1970. *The dialectic of sex; the case for feminist revolution.* New York: Morrow.

Franklin, Sarah. 2013. *Biological relatives: IVF, stem cells, and the future of kinship, Experimental futures.* Durham, NC: Duke University Press.

Gillies, Val. 2006. *Marginalised mothers: exploring working class experiences of parenting, relationships and resources series.* New York: Routledge.

Handyside, A. H., E. H. Kontogianni, K. Hardy, and R. M. Winston. 1990. "Pregnancies from biopsied human preimplantation embryos sexed by Y-specific DNA amplification." *Nature* 344 (6268):768–770.

Harris, John. 2007. *Enhancing evolution: the ethical case for making better people.* Princeton, NJ: Princeton University Press.

Harwood, Karey. 2007. *The infertility treadmill: feminist ethics, personal choice, and the use of reproductive technologies, Studies in social medicine.* Chapel Hill: University of North Carolina Press.

Idhe, Don. 1993. *Postphenomenology.* Evanston, IL: Northwestern University Press.

Khalil, Ahmad M. 2020. "The genome editing revolution: review." *Journal, Genetic Engineering & Biotechnology* 18 (1):68.

Knowles, Lori P., and Gregory E. Kaebnick. 2007. *Reprogenetics: law, policy, and ethical issues, Bioethics.* Baltimore, MD: Johns Hopkins University Press.

Kukla, Rebecca. 2005. *Mass hysteria: medicine, culture, and mothers' bodies, explorations in bioethics and the medical humanities.* Lanham, MD: Rowman & Littlefield.

Kuliev, Anver, and Svetlana Rechitsky. 2017. "Preimplantation genetic testing: current challenges and future prospects." *Expert Review of Molecular Diagnostics* 17 (12):1071–1088.

LaChance Adams, Sarah, and Caroline R. Lundquist. 2013. *Coming to life: philosophies of pregnancy, childbirth, and mothering. 1st ed, perspectives in Continental philosophy.* New York: Fordham University Press.

Latour, Bruno. 2005. *Reassembling the social: an introduction to actor-network-theory, Clarendon lectures in management studies.* New York: Oxford University Press.

Ma, Hong, Nuria Marti-Gutierrez, Sang-Wook Park, Jun Wu, Yeonmi Lee, Keiichiro Suzuki, et al. 2017. "Correction of a pathogenic gene mutation in human embryos." *Nature* 548 (7668):413–419.

MacKenzie, Donald A., and Judy Wajcman. 1985. *The social shaping of technology: how the refrigerator got its hum.* Philadelphia: Open University Press.

Mahowald, Mary Briody. 2000. *Genes, women, equality.* New York: Oxford University Press.

McLeod, Carolyn. 2002. *Self-trust and reproductive autonomy, basic bioethics.* Cambridge, MA: MIT Press.

Mullard, Asher. 2020. "CRISPR pioneers win Nobel prize." *Nature Reviews. Drug Discovery* 586:346–347.

Nastri, C. O., D. M. Teixeira, R. M. Moroni, V. M. S. Leitao, and W. P. Martins. 2015. Ovarian hyperstimulation syndrome: pathophysiology, staging, prediction and prevention. *Ultrasound in Obstetrics & Gynecology* 45 (4):377–393.

Niederberger, Craig, Antonio Pellicer, Jacques Cohen, David K. Gardner, Gianpiero D. Palermo, Claire L. O'Neill, et al. 2018. "Forty years of IVF." *Fertility and Sterility* 110(2):185–324.e5.

Niu, Yuyu, Bin Shen, Yiqiang Cui, Yongchang Chen, Jianying Wang, Lei Wang, et al. 2014. "Generation of gene-modified Cynomolgus monkey via Cas9/RNA-mediated gene targeting in one-cell embryos." *Cell* 156 (4):836–843.

Okin, Susan Moller. 1989. *Justice, gender, and the family.* New York: Basic Books.

Overall, Christine. 1987. *Ethics and human reproduction: a feminist analysis.* Boston, MA: Allen & Unwin.

Overall, Christine. 2012. *Why have children?: the ethical debate, basic bioethics.* Cambridge, MA: MIT Press.

Parens, Erik, and Adrienne Asch. 1999. "The disability rights critique of prenatal genetic testing. Reflections and recommendations." *The Hastings Center Report* 29 (5): S1–S22.

Parens, Erik, and Adrienne Asch. 2000. *Prenatal testing and disability rights, hastings center studies in ethics.* Washington, DC: Georgetown University Press.

Purdy, Laura M. 1996. *Reproducing persons: issues in feminist bioethics.* Ithaca, NY: Cornell University Press.

Reuter, Jason A., Damek V. Spacek, and Michael P. Snyder. 2015. "High-throughput sequencing technologies." *Molecular Cell* 58 (4):586–597.

Reznichenko, A. S., C. Huyser, and M. S. Pepper. 2016. "Mitochondrial transfer: implications for assisted reproductive technologies." *Applied and Translational Genomics* 11:40–47.

Rich, Adrienne. 1976. *Of woman born: motherhood as experience and institution.* 1st ed. New York: Norton.

Roberts, Dorothy E. 1995. "Social justice, procreative liberty, and the limits of liberal theory: Robertson's 'Children of Choice'." *Law & Social Inquiry* 20 (4):1005–1021.

Roberts, Dorothy E. 1997. *Killing the black body: race, reproduction, and the meaning of liberty.* 1st ed. New York: Pantheon Books.

Ross, Loretta. 2017. *Radical reproductive justice: foundations, theory, practice, critique.* New York City: The Feminist Press at the City University of New York.

Rothman, Barbara Katz. 1987. *The tentative pregnancy: prenatal diagnosis and the future of motherhood.* New York: Penguin Books.

Rothman, Barbara Katz. 1989. *Recreating motherhood: ideology and technology in a patriarchal society.* New York: Norton.

Rowland, Robyn. 1992. *Living laboratories: women and reproductive technologies.* Bloomington: Indiana University Press.

Savulescu, Julian. 2005. "New breeds of humans: The moral obligation to enhance." *Reproductive Biomedicine Online* 10:36–39.

Savulescu, Julian, Jonathan Pugh, Thomas Douglas, and Christopher Gyngell. 2015. "The moral imperative to continue gene editing research on human embryos." *Protein & Cell* 6 (7):476–479.

Schwartz, Barry. 2004. *The paradox of choice: why more is less.* New York: Ecco.

Scully, Jackie Leach. 2008. *Disability bioethics: moral bodies, moral difference, feminist constructions.* Lanham, MD: Rowman & Littlefield.

Scully, Jackie Leach., S. Banks, and Tom W. Shakespeare. 2006. "Chance, choice and control: lay debate on prenatal social sex selection." *Social Science & Medicine* 63 (1):21–31.

Shakespeare, Tom. 2006. *Disability rights and wrongs.* New York: Routledge.

Sherwin, Susan. 1992. *No longer patient: feminist ethics and health care.* Philadelphia, PA: Temple University Press.

Smith, Kevin R., Sarah Chan, and John Harris. 2012. "Human germline genetic modification: scientific and bioethical perspectives." *Archives of Medicine Research* 43 (7):491–513.

Spar, Debora L. 2006. *The baby business: how money, science, and politics drive the commerce of conception.* Boston, MA: Harvard Business School Press.

Sparrow, Robert. 2007. "Procreative beneficence, obligation, and eugenics." *Genomics, Society and Policy* 3 (3):43–59.

Swierstra, Tsjalling, and Katinka Waelbers. 2012. "Designing a good life: a matrix for the technological mediation of morality." *Science and Enginerring Ethics* 18 (1):157–172.

Thompson, Charis. 2005. *Making parents: the ontological choreography of reproductive technologies, Inside technology.* Cambridge, MA: MIT Press.

Townsend, Beverley A. 2020. "Human genome editing: how to prevent rogue actors." *BMC Medical Ethics* 21 (1). https://doi.org/10.1186/s12910-020-00527-w

Tremain, Shelley. 2001. "On the government of disability." *Social Theory and Practice* 27:617–636.

Twine, France Winddance. 2015. *Outsourcing the womb: race, class and gestational surrogacy in a global market.* Second edition. ed, Framing 21st century social issues. New York: Routledge, Taylor & Francis Group.

Verbeek, Peter-Paul. 2005. *What things do: philosophical reflections on technology, agency, and design.* University Park: Pennsylvania State University Press.

Waelbers, Katinka. 2011. *Doing good with technologies: taking responsibility for the social role of emerging technologies.* Dordrecht: Springer.

Watts, Geoff. 2010. "IVF pioneer Robert Edwards wins Nobel prize." *British Medical Journal* 341: c5533.

Wilson, Robert A. 2018. *The eugenic mind project.* Cambridge, MA: MIT Press.

Winner, Langdon. 1986. *The whale and the reactor: a search for limits in an age of high technology.* Chicago: University of Chicago Press.

Wyns, C., C. Bergh, C. Calhaz-Jorge, C. De Geyter, M. S. Kupka, T. Motrenko, I. Rugescu, J. Smeenk, A. Tandler-Schneider, S. Vidakovic, V. Goossens, and Embryolo European Society of Human Reproduction. 2020. "ART in Europe, 2016: results generated from European registries by ESHRE." *Human Reproduction Open* 2020 (3): hoaa032. ttps://doi.org/10.1093/hropen/hoaa032

Zhang, John, Hui Liu, Shiyu Luo, Zhuo Lu, Alejandro Chávez-Badiola, Zitao Liu, Mingxue Yang, ZaherMerhi, Sherman J. Silber, Santiago Munné, Michalis Konstantinidis, Dagan Wells, Jian J. Tang, and Taosheng Huang. 2017. "Live birth derived from oocyte spindle transfer to prevent mitochondrial disease." *Reproduction Biomed Online* 34 (4):361–368.

Chapter 31

Rethinking Ethical Subjectivity in the Biomedical Treatment of HIV Risk

Emerich Daroya and Stuart J. Murray

Introduction

The field of bioethics was originally inspired by sociopolitical and counter-cultural movements in the 1960s and early 1970s, including civil rights and feminist activism. In its institutional guise, however, bioethics has grown less activist and increasingly corporate, abstract, and legalistic. McKinnie (2004) has referred to bioethics as an "affirmative institution": pro-capitalist, pro-technology, and pro-governmental. And M.L. Tina Stevens (2000, p. xiii) has argued that bioethics has become a "midwife" to the implementation of technologies: "The bioethics 'movement' . . . assisted in transforming alarm over exotic technologies into a situation in which ethical experts manage problems—problems generated by technologies seen, ironically, as value-neutral in their creation." Ironic, because these technologies are anything but value-neutral. As technologies are increasingly integrated into our bodies and lifestyles—e.g., through implants, wearable devices, and pharmaceuticals—they have come to shift sociocultural norms and take on a normative force in our lives. They inform us not only what we ought to do, morally, but *who* we ought to *be*, ethically. In other words, they have had profound effects on our identity as ethical subjects, and it is precisely this complex high-tech identity that conventional bioethics—especially in clinical settings—has failed to comprehend because it presumes legal formulations of personhood and informed consent that are consistent with the liberal political principles of individualism and autonomy. And no doubt, in clinical settings, such as hospital bioethics committees, there is often an acute tension between the legal and ethical demands of particular cases. Everyone knows that lawsuits are costly.

In clinical settings, then, bioethics has come to rely on "principlism," which refers to the use of principles to address ethical questions regarding biomedicine (Dubose, Hamel, and O'Connell 1994). Arguably, the most influential version of principlism was articulated by Tom Beauchamp and James Childress in the *Principles of Biomedical Ethics* first published in 1979, where the authors proposed an ethical system based on common morality comprising a "set of universal norms shared by all persons" (Beauchamp and Childress 2019, p. 3). From these abstract, quasi-legal norms, four widely accepted ethical "principles" of biomedical ethics are proposed, namely: [1] respect for autonomy, [2] nonmaleficence (do no harm to others), [3] beneficence (benefit others), and [4] justice. While these four principles are not reducible to the first ("respect for autonomy"), each of them ultimately presumes the givenness of an ethical subject/agent founded in rational autonomy and somehow distinct from our moral and material interdependencies with technology.[1] Derived from the Greek *auto-* (self or own) + *nomos* (law), "autonomy" describes the way that the self is conventionally conceived in the abstract as freely governing or conducting itself. These founding "principles" have been criticized by some feminist bioethicists, among others, as reflecting a modern Western bias rooted in two centuries of political liberalism, where individuals are

DOI: 10.4324/9781003189466-37

exalted as rationally self-sovereign and self-governing beings (Wolf 1996). These principles, they maintain, position humans as the locus of morality and agency, fostering a subjectivity that has become incommensurable with who we are today, including the technological means by which we relate to ourselves and to each other. As Lupton (2020) argues, for example, when pharmaceutical and other biomedical technologies are introduced, bioethicists are more likely to take a normative and rationalistic stance. They tend to define technological agency to be distinct from autonomous and rational humans. If any degree of agency is accorded to biotechnologies, "it is usually in terms of how they act on rather than with humans" (Lupton 2020, p. 970).

This chapter explores a technological case study that challenges presumptions of autonomy, agency, and the principles that guide bioethics in clinical settings. In other words, to use Lupton's words above, we are interested in the ways that technologies not only act on but *act with* humans. Our case study demonstrates the ways in which we are neither quite self-sovereign nor autonomous ethical beings. Perhaps this has always been true insofar as we are beings who are inescapably in relation with and dependent on others; but it is also the case—and increasingly so—because we are increasingly co-implicated with our technologies and in their non-value-neutral networks. This represents a dilemma for conventional bioethics and its paradigm of ethical subjectivity. Technologies are not mere "tools" that are sovereignly or autonomously wielded by the self; indeed, our technologies wield an agency over us, with a material and moral force of their own. In this volume, Joseph Pitt (Chapter 2) defends the value-neutral view of technology, David Morrow (Chapter 3) argues against it, while Sally Wyatt (Chapter 4) defends technological determinism. In this chapter, we argue that technologies are often not value-neutral, and yet we do not quite adopt the stance of a hard technological determinism. As we argue below, technologies do not simply influence or inform an individual's actions/beliefs, or even intersubjective relations and community identities and values; at the same time, technologies are also informed *by* individuals and communities, which sometimes transforms the meaning of these technologies and the ways they are integrated, accepted, or contested, in the project of living an ethical life.

This chapter addresses pharmacological developments in the treatment and prevention of HIV. Drawing on insights from feminist science and technology studies (STS), we suggest that biomedical technologies are not merely passive "objects" deployed in the treatment of HIV and "risky" sexual practices; rather, from an STS perspective, we argue that technologies are agentic in their own right and become embodied in the sexual practices of gay and other men who have sex with men (MSM). These agencies, however, do not pre-exist the technologies in question; rather, they are generated through and within our relation to other-than-human technologies. This shifts the focus of conventional bioethics away from the agency and responsibility of individuals toward an understanding of technology ethics as a shared and collective enterprise.

Case Study: TasP/PrEP

Since Acquired Immunodeficiency Syndrome (AIDS) was first recognized in the 1980s in North America among people with hemophilia, injection drug users, racialized communities, and, most prominently, gay, bisexual, and other MSM, knowledge about and technological advancements in the management of the human immunodeficiency virus (HIV) have advanced remarkably. The breakthrough in the biomedical treatment of HIV/AIDS came in the mid-1990s when antiretroviral therapies (ART) effectively suppressed the progression of the AIDS virus. ART includes the use of antiretroviral drugs (ARVs) to decrease viral load, effectively improving the life expectancy and quality of life for people infected with HIV. In 2011, researchers from the HIV Prevention Trials Network (HPTN) reported that ARVs not only reduced levels of HIV in the blood but they also prevented HIV transmission, providing strong evidence to support the idea of Treatment as Prevention (TasP) (Cohen *et al.* 2011). TasP, therefore, is both treatment *and* prevention: it treats people with HIV and prevents their sexual partners from infection.

Consequently, treatment and prevention—once considered distinct endeavors—soon became difficult to distinguish. HIV-positive persons could receive treatment that *also* prevents the transmission of HIV to others; for those who were HIV-positive, treatment was sometimes prescribed in individual cases where it was not clinically warranted, but with the primary goal of preventing transmission. And soon, HIV-negative men were prescribed "treatment" solely as a preventative (or prophylactic) measure to maintain their own seronegative status. In 2012, the pharmaceutical Truvada was approved by the US Food and Drug Administration (FDA) as a pre-exposure prophylaxis (PrEP) for HIV based on findings from several clinical trials of its safety and efficacy in reducing the rate of HIV infection among MSM and heterosexual HIV-discordant couples (Centers for Disease Control and Prevention [CDC] 2018). Based on these trials and FDA approval, the CDC recommended that PrEP be considered by clinicians as a prevention option for individuals deemed to be at substantial risk of acquiring HIV (ibid.). Since then, several countries have approved the daily use of the drug, including France and Canada in 2016, and Australia and Peru in 2018.

In North America, gay, bisexual, and other MSM remain the most at-risk populations for HIV infection (CDC 2020; Public Health Agency of Canada 2013) and the advent of TasP and PrEP have had a significant impact on the prevention and treatment of HIV. But risk itself is complex and it is not obvious what constitutes a tolerable threshold of risk before we embark on an ethics of risk-management and a biomedical "treatment" (or prophylactic) plan calibrated to "risk." While TasP and PrEP have been hailed by some as "the beginning of the end of AIDS" (Havlir and Beyrer 2012), others fear that these drugs may encourage gay men to take greater sexual risks. Indeed, the introduction of ART in the mid-1990s had generated concerns about a "second wave" of new HIV infections across major cities in North America in response to the perception of reduced risk of death (Rofes 1998). That is, MSM were conjectured to have become complacent as HIV was no longer considered a death sentence: if HIV is no more than a manageable chronic illness, it was argued, this might result in increased sexual risk-taking among gay men in the form of condomless sex or "barebacking" (Reisner *et al.* 2008). In similar ways, PrEP has also generated fears surrounding "risk compensation," a scenario in which MSM abandon condoms in favor of PrEP (Duran 2012; Moore 2020; Weinstein 2010)—or, once again, an increase in risk-taking behaviors provoked by a decrease in perceived risk (Hogben and Liddon 2008).

Suffice to say that objections to and fears—or even moral panic—surrounding PrEP are part of an ethical debate resulting from the introduction of these technologies (Montess 2020). First, there are concerns that MSM will engage in more barebacking, and more sexual partners will both increase the risks of HIV transmission and counter the effectiveness of TasP and PrEP. Second, there are anxieties regarding adherence to these drugs. The bio-efficacy of both TasP and PrEP depend on their consistent and correct use to maintain an undetectable viral load for MSM who are living with HIV, and, for HIV-negative men, to sustain detectable drug levels to prevent HIV infection. Thus, MSM are required to cultivate "good habits" and follow prescribed drug regimens. If gay men engage in riskier sex and are not adherent to TasP or PrEP, they increase their risk of transmitting and/or acquiring HIV. Third, there are concerns about the elevated risk of other sexually transmitted infections (STIs) among MSM who engage in condomless sex. That is, while TasP and PrEP have been proven effective in preventing HIV infection, these drugs do not prevent the transmission of other STIs (e.g., antibiotic-resistant syphilis). Indeed, elevated rates of

STIs have been reported among PrEP users due to the higher prevalence of condomless sex in this population (Kojima *et al.* 2016; Liu *et al.* 2016).

In general terms, we might say that biomedical and epidemiological modeling in the "treatment" of risk has to date failed to consider the lived reality of those subjects it deems to be "at risk." In other words, moral objections and fears are motivated by "risk" in the abstract, without a nuanced understanding of who or what constitutes a risk, or why. At the heart of the ethical collisions concerning TasP and PrEP are human subjects, and in particular gay and other MSM, who are assumed to comprehend risk—cognitively—and to act as rational agents informed by public knowledge about HIV transmission. Meanwhile, antiretroviral drugs are perceived to be value-neutral and passively employed by these rational agents. The abiding belief both in individual agency and in the neutrality of biotechnologies underpins our conventional understanding of human (ethical) agency as distinct from those biotechnologies that nevertheless affect us profoundly (Rosengarten 2009, p. 61). It is not that these drugs are non-agentic; it is simply that their agency is judged to be value-neutral and amoral, limited to their bio-agency, which is available to be wielded by a willful and rational human subject. But this is a highly reductive conception of ethical subjectivity, skewed in the direction of a cognitivist bias, and this view is not equipped to address the material differences in lived lives, including our emotional, associative, and sociosexual values and experiences.

Feminist STS Approaches to Technology Ethics

Rather than rush to epistemological or moral judgments over whether gay men misuse technologies or behave badly in relation to sexual risks, we would like to address the deeper presumptions at work in the assignation of guilt and moral culpability. We turn to the insights of feminist STS to problematize conventional bioethical principles and to offer a more comprehensive and nuanced view of ethical subjectivity. A key work in the development of feminist STS is Donna Haraway's (1985) cyborg manifesto, which began to question the distinctions and boundaries between humans and nonhumans, including the subject's relation to biotechnologies. Importantly, and for the purposes of this chapter, Haraway (2016, p. 43) emphasizes that technologies are not passive but active in human sexual practices: "new technologies affect the social relations of both sexuality and reproduction." Haraway's insistence that technologies are "agentic" or "active" has been developed by Karen Barad (2007), a prominent figure in what has been termed "new materialism"—a diverse range of perspectives that collectively pay attention to matter's productive capacities (Coole and Frost 2010; Fox and Alldred 2017).

Barad, a feminist philosopher and physicist, argues that matter, objects, and technologies, alongside discourses, are active in the materialization of phenomena such as gender, sex, sexuality, and even ethics. In its simplest form, Barad's theory of *agential realism* assumes that matter, things, objects, and technologies are relational and active participants in all manner of human practices.[2] As Barad insists: "Matter is agentive" (2007, p. 137), or, matter is "an active 'agent'" (p. 151). However, it should be noted that technologies' agency is "not something that someone or something has" (Barad 2007, p. 33); instead, agencies "are only distinct in a relational, not an absolute, sense" (p. 33). In other words, technologies' agency is an effect of complex material and discursive relations. In Barad's view, because there is no clear separation between matter and discourse (material-discursive), they are all fundamentally agentic (Marshall and Alberti 2014, p. 23). This approach reconfigures the notion of technologies as value-neutral (see Pitt in this volume), for they are agents in moral and political processes. The conceptualization of technologies as agential and co-constituted through relations rather than existing *a priori* further recasts the notion of technological determinism (see Wyatt in this volume), which conceives technologies as forces operating outside human relations. Instead, as Barad (2007) insists, "[t]he relationship between the material and discursive is one of mutual entailment. Neither discursive practices nor material phenomena are ontologically or epistemologically prior" (p. 152). Put simply, while Barad's approach acknowledges the dynamism of material forces, it does not assume technologies as separate entities, for they are always articulated with and through material-discursive relations.

Consider Barad's discussion of how our understanding of gender materializes through ultrasound technology: this technology ought to be understood as productive, Barad argues, part of the materialization of gender, and not merely as a piece of technological hardware that reflects or passively observes a fetus. Instead, Barad claims that this technology "helps to produce and is part of the body it images" (p. 202); through its "material-discursive" forces (p. 66), the technology helps to *enact* the fetus as gendered, where gender is perceived as a value-neutral fact that covers over its techno-social production. The ultrasound technology does not stand apart from discourses on gender. Instead, as Marsha Rosengarten (2005, p. 77) explains, the technological hardware not only "reflects discursive presuppositions about identity," but it also "acts to materialize it."

Rosengarten (2009, p. 60) employs feminist STS to better understand the effects of ARVs on gay men's sexuality, and to challenge the traditional conceptualization of "risk that is attached to the work of an individual human." As she explains, within the field of HIV research and treatment, the normative belief is that the availability of biotechnologies will enable gay men to reconsider safer sexual practices. But this normative presumption is not as obvious as it might first appear. For example, Chen *et al.* (2002, p. 1387) reported "worrisome increases in sexual risk behaviors" among San Francisco MSM "during a period of increasing use of highly active anti-retroviral therapy (HAART), from 1994 to 1999." And a similar study in the UK suggested that "the likelihood of engaging in high risk sexual behaviours may be increasing as new treatments reduce concern about infection" (Dodds *et al.* 2000, p. 1510). With regard to PrEP, a study from the US concluded that MSM "decreased their use of condoms following PrEP initiation," which was further linked to elevated STI rates (Montaño *et al.* 2019, p. 553). The results of these studies presume that MSM are individually responsible for both their sexual risk behaviors and the impacts of biomedical technologies on HIV infection. That is, in their commitment to a conventional conception of ethical subjectivity (autonomous, rational, free), these studies fail to consider the complex relations between HIV science, biomedical technologies, and sexual practices. Moreover, they fail to see how each of these "material-discursive" fields are co-implicated and interact to produce—and often to control—the boundaries between ethical and unethical, responsible and irresponsible, sex. To offer a more nuanced view of both ethics and sexual subjects, it is crucial to rethink the role of science and biotechnologies as agentic—sometimes regulatory and coercive, sometimes liberatory—in gay men's relation to HIV risk, to themselves, and each other.

But exactly how are TasP and PrEP active or agentic in their influence on gay men's sexual practices? Consider an article written by Matt Cain (2017), a British writer and broadcaster. At that time, he wrote in *The Guardian* that PrEP was still controversial among his friends, "who express[ed] strong reactions to the news that I am taking PrEP." Nonetheless, Cain continued with the treatment and confessed:

> The first time I do have condomless sex while on PrEP is a one-night stand. I tell the man I am negative, and on PrEP; he tells me he is negative but not taking it. He does not seem to care whether we use a condom or not but, telling myself I am protected, I go through with it.

From a conventional perspective, we might infer that Cain has become complacent and is displaying poor judgment concerning HIV risk: he alone is the rational "agent" and he alone ethically responsible (or irresponsible) in his decisions. But this is highly reductive and we need not abandon our commitment to ethical responsibility when we consider how ethical subjectivity is transformed when a drug regimen comes into play. From the perspective of feminist STS, it is possible to see how Cain's conduct was partly informed by PrEP. As he explained, he went through with barebacking because he told himself that he was "protected"—a belief made possible in part by findings from clinical trials about PrEP's efficacy and safety, as well as the approval by the FDA, the World Health Organization, and other countries' public health regulatory bodies. Aside from overwhelming scientific evidence, other human and nonhuman actors also made it possible for Cain to engage in condomless sex without fear: these include, but are not limited to, the (highly profitable) drug companies that manufacture and market ARVs, scientists, doctors, nurses, clinics, hospitals, pharmacies, computers, papers, pens, and the drug itself. Cain concluded: "The main emotion this unlocks in me is relief; if I carry on taking PrEP, I will never become HIV+." Cain's desire and ability to engage in condomless sex without worries is an effect of a wide range of actors, including biotechnologies, that affect human behavior and identity. It is not simply or singularly about a responsibility that flows from rational cognition any more than sex is about a single subject in relation with a passive sexual "object."

The normative notion of human agency concerning HIV biomedical technologies views MSM as culpable for the inappropriate use of technologies. It is based, as Race (2012, p. 328) maintains, on a "narrow attribution of agency" that understands human subjects as culpable for the negative effects of HIV biotechnologies. However, as in Cain's case above, it is plausible that gay men reflexively incorporate scientific knowledge and biomedical technologies into their sexual practices: they both understand and embody the effectiveness of ARVs, allowing these men, together, to reconstitute notions of "safety" and "risk" in their sex lives. By framing changes in gay men's risk calculation in relation to ARVs as "processes of reflexive mediation between embodied habits and medical opinion," gay men's ethico-sexual agency is perhaps better grasped "not as an individual act but rather as taking place within an accessible context of shared concern and practice" (Race 2012, p. 377). In this light, gay men's agency and responsibility may be conceived as dynamic and relational, demonstrating that capacities to act regarding risk calculation and biomedical technologies are effects of a wide range of relations that are "well beyond an active individual or group of individuals" (Rosengarten 2009, p. 103). Indeed, the distribution of agency asks us to shift our normative notions of responsibility away from the autonomy of individual cognition and toward a shared accountability for the outcomes of biomedical technologies in sexual practices. That is, an array of human and other-than-human forces, including HIV science, is implicated in the production of myriad effects ensuing from TasP and PrEP. Recognizing the implications of HIV science on the materialization of sexual effects shifts responsibility from individuals to collective relations that include technologies and biomedical knowledge. While public health discourse tends to maintain the quasi-legal presumption that MSM are individually responsible for sexual behavior resulting from the use or misuse of PrEP or TasP, a sociosexual paradigm inspired by feminist STS allows us to recast HIV prevention and treatment technologies as active participants in the shaping of sexual practices.

Conclusions

Our purpose here is not to pass moral judgment on the sexual practices of gay and other MSM. Nor is it to propound tolerable and "treatable" thresholds of risk, and then to justify these thresholds as somehow medically warranted or ethical. Rather, our brief case study is meant to underscore the extent to which ethical subjectivity—as much as sexual subjectivity—is not wholly autonomous or rationally/cognitively motivated. After all, sexual relations are by definition nonautonomous, and take place between two or more persons, with medical, moral, and sensuous implications for all partners. This is perhaps obvious, but it gets more complex still: there are countless other sexual "actors" on the scene. Sexual agency and ethical subjectivity are part of a vast nexus that includes pharmaceuticals and their aggressive marketing campaigns, targeted public health messaging (both moralizing and medicalizing), as well as formal and informal discourses on risk, risk-management, responsibility, and not least, desire and pleasure. Whether an individual embraces or spurns public health messaging, for example, that person is nevertheless navigating a wider network that is biological, sociocultural, medical, legal, and moral—each with their attendant coercions, rewards, and punishments in the regulation of sexual behavior. Conventional bioethics, with its principles that privilege autonomous agency and responsibility, cannot quite account for these interacting fields of influence or the ways that their discourses are taken up as key terms in the mediation—and sometimes the negotiation—of human relations, including sex and ethics. Indeed, holding fast to a conventional conception of ethical subjectivity may well bolster conventional biomedical, public health, and pharmacological powers (and profits) by deeming these actors to be passive and value-neutral (Guta, Murray, and Gagnon 2016). Critical of the "disciplinary" power of conventional bioethics, Margrit Shildrick (2005, p. 3) has argued: "the discipline has effectively duplicated the master discourse and maintained the split between a secure sense of the transcendent self as moral agent, and a more or less unruly body that must be subjected to its dictates."

Conventional bioethics—and foremost in clinical settings—remains wedded to the liberal political formulation of human subjectivity as an autonomous rational agency. However, our case study has demonstrated how our technologies are fundamentally active and relational, where the confluence of scientific evidence, endorsements from public health agencies, scientists, medical professionals, and pharmaceuticals variously—together—mediate MSM's complex sociosexual relations. Beyond our case study, the implications for technology ethics are legion. We have sought to widen the conception of ethical agency beyond the purview of the individual, and beyond the principle of autonomy. In many respects, no doubt, it is counterintuitive to claim that other-than-human actors are agentic, especially when we have for so long understood them as passive and value-neutral. But our counterintuitive proposal does not mean that other-than-human agents are agentic in exactly the same ways as human agents; we must try to see from intersubjective and other-than-human perspectives. After all, if we hope to widen the scope of ethical agency beyond the individual, it would be mistaken to take a conventional model of agency—founded in individual personhood—and export this quasi-legal and moral subjectivity as a model for the ways that objects *act on* and *enact* us as they do. In other words, technology ethics must turn from the view that our technologies are passive, value-neutral, or mere "tools" to be wielded by the ethical subject—a view that is dangerously outdated and incommensurable with the technological subjects we continue to become. And finally, to be clear, the STS perspective advanced here does not necessarily undermine responsibility, but suggests instead that ethical subjectivity is multimodal and multifaceted, and ethical responsibility is shared and collective. If this is plausible, then we must refashion bioethics—the ethics of life—by taking account of our biosocial relations and lived realities. Rather than presume a bioethics founded on the principles of self-sovereign individualism, we must begin in and among the world of those human and other-than-human beings that make us the beings that we are.

Notes

1 The ethical principles of Beauchamp and Childress have become the dominant approach to assessing medical ethics (Page 2012). Other theories about bioethics have also adopted principlism. For example, Englehardt (1996) proposed two-principle theories (permission and beneficence) for bioethics. Yet, these approaches also tend to embrace a liberal-humanist view of humans as rational and autonomous agents without accounting for the relationality of humans and nonhumans, including technologies, in bioethical decision-making.

2 Barad's (2007) theory of agential realism recognizes matter's dynamism, as an active "agent," while insisting that matter is not determining, for it is always already co-constituted by discourses. Crucial to Barad's theory of agential realism is the concept of "intra-action," which signifies the inseparability of matter and discourse ("material-discursive") in the constitution of phenomena: "in contrast to the usual 'interaction,' which assumes that there are separate individual agencies that precede their interaction, the notion of intra-action recognizes that distinct agencies do not precede, but rather emerge through their intra-action" (2007, p. 33).

References

Barad, K., 2007. *Meeting the universe halfway: quantum physics and the entanglement of matter and meaning.* Durham & London: Duke University Press.

Beauchamp, T.L., and Childress, J.F., 2019. *Principles of biomedical ethics.* 8th ed. Oxford: Oxford University Press.

Cain, M., 2017. Sex without fear—my experiment with the HIV-prevention drug PrEP. *The Guardian.* Available from: https://www.theguardian.com/society/2017/jun/22/sex-without-fear-my-experiment-with-hiv-preventative-drug-prep

Centers for Disease Control and Prevention, 2018. *Preexposure prophylaxis for the prevention of HIV infection in the United States—2017 update: a clinical practice guide.* Available from: https://www.cdc.gov/hiv/pdf/risk/prep/cdc-hiv-prep-guidelines-2017.pdf

Centers for Disease Control and Prevention, 2020. *HIV and gay and bisexual men.* Available from: https://www.cdc.gov/hiv/group/msm/index.html

Chen, S. Y., *et al.*, 2002. Continuing increases in sexual risk behavior and sexually transmitted diseases among men who have sex with men: San Francisco, Calif., 1999–2001. *American Journal of Public Health*, 92 (9): 1387–1388.

Cohen, M. S., *et al.*, 2011. Prevention of HIV-1 infection with early antiretroviral therapy. *New England Journal of Medicine*, 365 (6): 493–505.

Coole, D., & Frost, S., 2010. Introducing the new materialisms. *In*: D. Coole & S. Frost, eds. *New materialisms: ontology, agency, and politics.* Durham: Duke University Press, 1–43.

Dodds, J. P., Nardone, A., Mercey, D. E. and Johnson, A. M., 2000. Increase in high risk sexual behaviour among homosexual men, London 1996–8: cross sectional, questionnaire study. *BMJ*, 320 (7248): 1510–1511.

DuBose, Edwin R., Ronald P. Hamel, and Laurence J. O'Connell., 1994. *A matter of principles? Ferment in US bioethics.* Valley Forge, PA: Trinity Press International.

Duran, D., 2012. Truvada whores. *The Huffington Post.* Available from: https://www.huffpost.com/entry/truvada-whores_b_2113588

Engelhardt, H. T., 1996. *The foundations of bioethics.* 2nd ed. New York: Oxford University Press.

Fox, N., & Alldred, P., 2017. *Sociology and the new materialism: theory, research, action.* London: SAGE.

Guta, A., Murray, S. J., and Gagnon, M., 2016. HIV, viral suppression and new technologies of surveillance and control. *Body & Society*, 22 (2): 82–107.

Haraway, D., 1985. Manifesto for cyborgs: science, technology and socialist feminism in the 1980s. *Socialist Review*, 15 (2): 65–107.

Haraway, D., 2016. *Manifestly Haraway.* Minneapolis: University of Minnesota Press.

Havlir, D., and Beyrer, C., 2012. The beginning of the end of AIDS? *New England Journal of Medicine*, 367 (8): 685–687.

Hogben, M., & Liddon, N., 2008. Disinhibition and risk compensation. *Sexually Transmitted Diseases*, 35 (12): 1009–1010.

Kojima, N., Davey, D. J., and Klausner, J. D., 2016. Pre-exposure prophylaxis for HIV infection and new sexually transmitted infections among men who have sex with men. *AIDS*, 30 (14): 2251–2252.

Liu, A. Y., *et al.*, 2016. Preexposure prophylaxis for HIV infection Integrated with municipal- and community-based sexual health services. *JAMA Internal Medicine*, 176 (1): 75–84.

Lupton, D., 2020. A more-than-human approach to bioethics: the example of digital health. *Bioethics*, 34 (9): 969–976.

Marshall, Y., and Alberti, B., 2014. A matter of difference: Karen Barad, ontology and archaeological bodies. *Cambridge Archaeological Journal*, 24 (1): 19–36.

McKinnie, M., 2004. A sympathy for art: sentimental economies of new labour arts policy. *In*: R. Johnson & D.L. Steinberg, eds. *Blairism and the war of persuasion: labour's passive revolution*. London: Lawrence and Wishart, 186–203.

Montaño, M. A., *et al.*, 2019. Changes in sexual behavior and STI diagnoses among MSM initiating PrEP in a clinic setting. *AIDS and Behavior*, 23 (2): 548–555.

Montess, M., 2020. Demedicalizing the ethics of PrEP as HIV prevention: the social effects on MSM. *Public Health Ethics*, 13 (3): 288–299.

Moore, C., 2020. Malevolent depravity: the rise of PrEP. *The Spectator*. Available from: https://spectator.us/topic/malevolent-depravity-prep-aids/

Page, K., 2012. The four principles: can they be measured and do they predict ethical decision making? *BMC Medical Ethics*, 13 (1): 1–8.

Public Health Agency of Canada, 2013. *Population-specific HIV/AIDS status report: gay, bisexual, two-spirit and other men who have sex with men*. Available from: https://www.canada.ca/content/dam/phac-aspc/migration/phac-aspc/aids-sida/publication/ps-pd/men-hommes/assets/pdf/pshasrm-revspdhb-eng.pdf

Race, K., 2012. Framing responsibility: HIV, biomedical prevention, and the performativity of the law. *Journal of Bioethical Inquiry*, 9 (3): 327–338.

Reisner, S., *et al.*, 2008. Predictors of identifying as a barebacker among high-risk New England HIV seronegative men who have sex with men. *Journal of Urban Health: Bulletin of the New York Academy of Medicine*, 86 (2): 250–262.

Rofes, E., 1998. *Dry bones breathe: gay men creating post-AIDS identities and cultures*. New York: Harrington Park Press.

Rosengarten, M., 2005. The measure of HIV as a matter of bioethics. *In*: M. Shildrick and R. Mykitiuk, eds. *Ethics of the body: postconventional challenges*. Cambridge: MIT Press, 71–90.

Rosengarten, M., 2009. *HIV interventions: biomedicine and the traffic between information and flesh*. Seattle: University of Washington Press.

Shildrick, M., 2005. Beyond the body of bioethics: challenging the conventions. *In*: M. Shildrick and R. Mykitiuk, eds. *Ethics of the body: postconventional challenges*. Cambridge: MIT Press, 1–26.

Stevens, M.L. Tina, 2000. *Bioethics in America: origins and cultural politics*. Baltimore, MD: The Johns Hopkins University Press.

Weinstein, M., 2010. Advancing on AIDS, or giving up on gay men? *San Jose Mercury News*. Available from: http://www.mercurynews.com/opinion/ci_16967427?nclick_check=1

Wolf, S. M., 1996. Introduction: gender and feminism in bioethics. *In*: S. M. Wolf, ed. *Feminism & bioethics: beyond reproduction*. Oxford: Oxford University Press, 3–43.

Chapter 32

Against Doping in Sport

John William Devine

Introduction

Should elite athletes be allowed to use performance-enhancing drugs (PEDs)? From Lance Armstrong's systematic doping during his seven Tour de France victories (USADA 2012) to Russian state-sponsored doping at the London 2012 Summer Olympics and the Sochi 2014 Winter Olympics (McLaren 2016), the use of PEDs – 'doping' – has been the source of some of sport's biggest scandals. Cheating by doping has done more than perhaps any other type of misconduct in elite and professional sport to erode public confidence in the credibility of athletic performances and the legitimacy of sporting results.[1] Since the 1980s, a sophisticated and extensive infrastructure has developed to ensure that sport is doping-free. This includes the World Anti-Doping Agency, the World Anti-Doping Code (WADA 2021), the Anti-Doping Division of the Court of Arbitration for Sport, national anti-doping agencies, national anti-doping policies, anti-doping education programmes, and, in some countries, even doping-related criminal offences.[2] However, does anti-doping rest on a mistake? Beneath this legal and regulatory infrastructure lies an ethical question: should doping be prohibited or should athletes be allowed to use whatever performance-enhancing drugs they wish? I focus my attention exclusively on the case against the permissibility of doping.[3] I canvas three arguments against doping: the harm argument, the fairness argument, and the excellence argument.

If even one of these arguments succeeds, then *some* restriction on doping is ethically justified. Which argument succeeds will determine the precise contours of that restriction. For example, a ban that is justified on harm prevention grounds will prohibit a different set of substances to a ban that is justified on sporting excellence grounds – harmful substances do not always undermine sporting excellence and vice versa. Similarly, a ban that is justified on fairness grounds will deliver a different prohibited list to one that is justified on excellence grounds.

My concern is whether *any* regulation of PEDs is morally justified, not whether *prevailing* regulations are morally justified. I defend a restriction on the use of PEDs, though the basis and contours of that restriction may be quite different to the World Anti-Doping Code. So, my argument is not a defence of the *status quo* in anti-doping but an attack on a 'hard libertarian' approach to doping that would permit athletes to employ whatever PED they choose (Brown 1980; Tamburrini 2000) as well as the 'soft libertarian' approach that would permit athletes to use any 'safe' PED they choose (Savulescu et al 2004).

Enhancement in sport assumes many different forms. Bodily enhancement enables athletes to alter their bodies (perhaps even their genes) to improve their athletic performance (e.g. LASIK eye surgery); equipmental enhancement facilitates athletic performance through improvement in the implements used by athletes in their sporting endeavours (e.g. full-body 100% polyurethane swimsuits); technical enhancement allows athletes to

DOI: 10.4324/9781003189466-38

refine their technique to achieve higher levels of performance (e.g. the 'Fosbury flop' in the high jump); and epistemological enhancement affords athletes access to data or coaching advice that is conducive to the improvement of their athletic performance (e.g. on-court coaching during tennis matches). The question of doping, which is the concern of this paper, is whether there are any ethical limits to the *pharmacological* enhancements that may be morally justified to improve athletic performance.[4]

I begin by examining whether a prohibition on doping is justified because doping is harmful to athletes. I turn then to fairness-based arguments against doping, and, finally, I examine excellence-based arguments against doping. While each of these three arguments has normative force, I propose excellence-based arguments as especially promising.

Doping and Harm

Imagine a drug that enhanced athletic performance significantly, was cheap to purchase, but presented a substantial risk of permanent harm to, or even the death of, the user. Should such a drug be permitted? Perhaps the most common argument offered for the prohibition of doping is that performance-enhancing drugs are harmful to athletes. PEDs can ameliorate athletic performance in myriad ways, for instance, by helping athletes to grow stronger, to develop more stamina, or to recover from injury or training more quickly. However, substances such as anabolic steroids and erythropoietin (EPO) pose a risk of permanent harm to the user's health, and perhaps even a risk to their life. The misuse of anabolic steroids risks side-effects such as heart failure, hypertension, liver abnormalities and tumours, psychiatric disorders (e.g. depression) and aggressive or violent behaviour (Chester 2022). The misuse of EPO risks side-effects arising from blood hyperviscosity such as stroke and heart failure (Mottram and Chester 2022). So, the abuse of certain PEDs poses a substantial risk to the health of athletes. In addition to direct harms to the user, doping can pose a risk of indirect harm to their competitors, especially in collision or combat sports such as American football, boxing, or mixed martial arts.[5]

A concern for 'athlete welfare' has become a guiding ethical principle in sport. It is now widely acknowledged that sports governing bodies have a moral duty of care to athletes, and the rules, policies, and practices that govern elite and professional sport should be formulated with a concern for the well-being of athletes in mind. The conception of 'welfare' that underpins these policies has expanded beyond protection from physical and sexual abuse to a more holistic view that incorporates a concern for the athlete's physical and mental health (Lang 2020; 20). Should athletes be allowed to assume any risk to which they freely and informedly consent or could a concern for athlete welfare ground a ban on the use of PEDs?

In assessing the permissibility of any risk in sport, it is important to distinguish between inherent and incidental risks. For example, being punched in the face is an inherent risk of boxing and being tackled to the ground is an inherent risk of American football. To remove such risks from these sports would alter the nature of the sports themselves. However, the risk associated with anabolic steroid use is merely incidental to boxing or American football. We can remove anabolic steroid use from these sports without compromising the challenges that give each sport its distinctive purpose and value. Unlike the risks associated with being punched or tackled, doping-related risks can be removed from sport without compromising or fundamentally altering the intrinsic nature of the sports in question.

Sports authorities have a moral duty of care to athletes to protect their welfare and not to expose them to unnecessary risks to their health.[6] This is not to say that sport should be risk-free. Dangerous sport has a distinctive value as competitors test their resilience and explore the limits of their being (Russell 2005). However, risk should not be courted gratuitously. At a minimum, we should ensure that sport is as safe as possible for competitors without compromising the nature of the sports themselves. If our duty of care to athletes requires that they not be exposed to risks that are inessential to the purpose of their sport, there is a harm-based reason to prohibit the incidental risks of doping.

This harm-based argument arises from the paternalist conviction that, for their own good, there are certain risks that we should not allow athletes to run. If doping were permitted, so the argument goes, athletes would ingest harmful amounts and types of performance-enhancing substances that would cause serious and irreversible harm to their health or could cause harm to competitors. So, the harm-based justification in its simplest form is an attempt to save athletes from themselves – to prevent them from taking a risk that they should avoid but would otherwise take.

It is important to note that, even if this argument succeeds, it could justify the prohibition only of *dangerous* PEDs. It would not justify restrictions on the use of PEDs that do not pose an unacceptable risk (directly or indirectly) to the health of athletes.

Objection: Doping as an Expression of Autonomy

While health is an important aspect of athlete welfare, one might object that another important aspect of athlete welfare is autonomy. On this view, provided that athletes autonomously choose to dope, any doping-related harms that accrue are morally unproblematic. Doping-related harm is not morally suspect if the athlete validly consents to the risk of harm. For consent to count as valid, it must be both 'free' (i.e. the agent's choice is not the product of pressure or coercion) and 'informed' (i.e. the agent understands the risk they are running). To justify a ban on doping on harm-based grounds, it is not enough to identify that some forms of doping harm the athlete. Instead, we should distinguish 'wrongful harm' from 'non-wrongful harm', where only wrongful harm merits moral concern. The athlete's consent means that any setbacks to health that follow directly or indirectly from doping are not morally concerning, as they are not wrongful harms.

Athletes should be free to make up their own minds about the risks they run in pursuit of sporting excellence. As long as athletes are not coerced and understand the risk they are taking, authorities have no reason to interfere. An approach that respected athlete autonomy would allow free and informed athletes to choose whether and what performance-enhancing substances they use and whether they choose to compete against those who use these substances. The harms that arise from doping are, in most sports, self-regarding harms. They are harms that the athlete chooses to risk for themselves. A foundational political principle of liberal societies is that individuals should be free to pursue whatever life they choose, provided that this does not harm others (Mill, 1859/1977). People should be free to make their own decisions about the risks to which they expose themselves, for example, through sport. Part of protecting the value of individual autonomy is allowing people to make their own choices, even if we think we know what is better for them. Consequently, sometimes, we should allow people to do things that are harmful to them. On this view, the prohibition of PEDs denies athletes the chance to decide for themselves whether to dope. Doping regulation effectively treats athletes as children, incapable of assessing risk for themselves or tailoring their decisions to reflect their plans and aspirations. According to this objection, athletes should be allowed to decide for themselves whether to assume the risk of direct and indirect harms associated with doping.

However, the harms to which athletes are exposed through doping are not necessarily harms that they choose. They are often harms that are imposed on them against their will or without their knowledge.[7] Athletes can be subject to intense pressure from their coaches, parents, teammates, club, or even government to expose themselves to health risks that may increase their chances of sporting success. When goods such as money, medals, and fame, or, indeed, family, club, and national pride are at stake, athletes can find themselves pressured into taking risks that they would prefer to avoid. Moreover, athletes may be forced to ingest PEDs unknowingly. For example, without an athlete's knowledge, their physio may apply a cream during treatment that contains a prohibited substance or their coach may spike their recovery drinks with a prohibited substance.

Lifting the ban on PEDs would render athletes, especially vulnerable athletes (e.g. the young, poor, or soon to be out of contract) susceptible to coerced doping – doping to which they do not validly consent. Coercion is notoriously difficult to identify, and the surveillance and monitoring required to ensure valid consent to doping would require more intrusion into the private lives of athletes than would be consistent with their human rights. If it is right to assert that our primary moral duty is to protect the most vulnerable, sports authorities should prioritise the protection of vulnerable athletes from the risk of coerced doping. Consequently, instead of embarking on the near impossible task of ensuring that athletes' decisions to dope are autonomous, authorities should adopt a risk-averse policy to wrongful harms by prohibiting doping.

In addition to a concern for athlete welfare, a second type of argument against doping stresses the need to preserve the fairness of competition. I turn to fairness-based arguments now.

Doping and Fairness

Consider a PED that is safe, significantly improves performance, but is very expensive to buy. Should the use of this substance be permitted in sport? This PED raises questions of fairness. Two different conceptions of fairness should be distinguished: 'formal' and 'substantive' fairness. Formal fairness is a minimal form of fairness that is concerned with the impartial and equal application of the rules to each competitor (Hooker 2005; 329). A contest is formally fair if the same rules are applied to each participant and any violations of the rules are identified and sanctioned equally according to the rules. Lifting the ban on PEDs may advance formal fairness as it would eliminate an important avenue by which cheaters could gain an unfair advantage by violating the rules while evading sanctions. The prevalence of doping in elite sport is difficult to establish, but most agree that it is many times higher than the rate of detected doping (Petroczi et al. 2022). So, the vast majority of cheaters by doping remain unsanctioned. This creates formal unfairness with respect to those athletes who comply with anti-doping rules (and indeed those who do not comply but are sanctioned for doing do).

By contrast, substantive fairness extends beyond the application of the rules to the content of the rules themselves and the background conditions that influence one's chances of sporting success. For example, if the rules of tennis awarded two points for every point ended by a volley, this would be substantively unfair to baseline players. Similarly, if a particular racket conferred a sizeable advantage on its user, but only a small number of wealthy players could afford the racket, the permissibility of this racket in competition would create substantive unfairness between those with and those without the racket.

Now that we have fixed our attention on substantive fairness I will assess two different varieties of the fairness-based argument against doping: (a) unfairness between contemporaries, and (b) unfairness between generations.

Unfairness between Contemporaries

Lifting the ban on PEDs would create substantive unfairness between contemporaneous athletes, that is, athletes competing at the same time (i.e. during the same era or even in the same competition). PEDs would become a further avenue by which the wealthy could gain a competitive advantage over their less well-off rivals. Athletes from wealthy families, clubs, or countries could leverage their economic power to access the safest and most effective PEDs, monitored and administered by the best doping scientists and medics. Conversely, those with comparatively few financial resources may have access only to PEDs that are cheaper because they are less safe or less effective, and they may have no access to skilled doping support personnel. Consequently, economic inequality would generate unfairness in sport as doping would become a further respect in which the wealthy could improve their prospects of sporting success at the expense of the less well-off.

Doping-related unfairness grounded in economic inequality would not be limited to unfairness between individual athletes; it would extend to unfairness between different clubs and even different countries. State-sponsored doping programmes run by economic superpowers such as the United States or China could attract the best research scientists and pharmaceutical companies to create the safest and most effective PEDs; it could provide their athletes with access to skilled doping medical support to minimise the risk and maximise the efficacy of their PED use; and it could provide a PED supply so that athletes could access the best PEDs free of charge. Athletes from economically less developed countries would have to settle for drugs that are less safe and less effective, for mediocre medical support, and perhaps for limited access to PEDs. As a result, a wider performance gap is likely to develop between athletes from wealthy countries and athletes from less wealthy countries. Elite sport would become even more profoundly determined by economics rather than excellence.

Unfairness between Generations

A second fairness worry arises when we consider the effect of removing the ban on doping not between athletes of the same generation but between contemporary athletes and athletes of the past (Douglas 2007). Call this 'diachronic formal unfairness' (Hooker 2005).

A prized aspect of elite sport is our ability to compare athletes of different eras – to contrast Jesse Owens with Usain Bolt and Nadia Comaneci with Simone Biles. Such intergenerational comparisons require a similarity in the circumstances (including the rules) of competition in which both compete. A significant discontinuity in competitive circumstances diminishes, and may extinguish, our ability to make meaningful comparisons between their respective performances. The introduction of doping would mark a watershed moment in sports history. Such is the potential for performance gains arising from doping; we could no longer meaningfully compare athletes from the pre-doping and post-doping eras, because the latter would be subject to many fewer constraints on their performance than those in the pre-doping era. So, doping raises fairness concerns both between athletes of the same generation and athletes of different generations.

Objection I: Doping is One Source of Unfairness among Many

Critics may point out that sport is replete with avenues by which wealth can confer a competitive advantage on an athlete. There are many and varied ways by which the wealthy can flex their economic muscle to improve their athletes' sporting performance. The wealthy can acquire the best equipment, coaching, and data analytics; they can enjoy valuable international competitive and training experiences; and they can train full-time without the distraction of having to earn an income independent of sport. What justifies our intense focus on doping while we ignore other sources of substantive unfairness in sport (Savulescu et al. 2004; 668 and Tamburrini 2000; 208–209)? Unless we can distinguish doping from other sources of enhancement which we allow but which also generate fairness concerns, it seems our objection to doping is morally indefensible.

However, the existence of some unfairness in sport does not justify further unfairness. The fact that we already tolerate a significant degree of unfairness does not justify our tolerating more. Perhaps we have already tolerated enough unfairness and any further unfairness would be intolerable (Devine 2019).[8] Alternatively, perhaps we should combat the unfairness that we currently allow in addition to combating sources of possible further unfairness such as doping.

Objection 2: Intergenerational Fairness in Sport Requires Conservatism about the Development of Sport

A concern to protect the possibility of meaningful comparison between contemporary athletes and those of previous generations would require us to halt sport's evolution and cast it into a time warp, unable to advance in tandem with developments in Sports Science. The development of sport in light of scientific progress would be hamstrung on account of a concern to ensure that intergenerational comparisons remain uncompromised.

On this view, while intergenerational comparisons may have some value, the opportunity cost of preserving the conditions necessary to allow such comparisons is too great. Ensuring the possibility of intergenerational comparisons would require sport to forgo too many benefits of scientific progress. While the loss of our ability to make meaningful intergenerational comparisons may be regrettable, it is justifiable nonetheless.

This objection does not prove that we should abandon our interest in records though. The ability to compare the present generation's performances with those of *adjacent* generations may have more normative weight than comparisons with *remote* generations. Our ability to compare the career of Usain Bolt from the 2000s with Donovan Bailey's from the 1990s may be more important to preserve than our ability to compare Bolt's career with Jesse Owens' from the 1930s. Consequently, a concern to maintain meaningful performance comparisons with adjacent generations may commend *modest* change rather than no change in light of scientific development. Crucially, it would prohibit any radical changes that would create marked discontinuities between the playing conditions of adjacent generations. So, this argument may justify an incremental approach to change in sport rather than a radical one. An incremental change to anti-doping rules may involve a progressive easing, rather than a complete lifting, of the ban on PEDs. Thresholds at which the presence of a substance in an athlete's sample would trigger an anti-doping rule violation may be increased, and thresholds may be introduced for substances that are not currently permitted at all.

So, the fairness argument – in either the formal or substantive varieties – may provide no more than modest grounds for a ban on PEDs. I turn now to the final argument to be considered – the argument from excellence.

Doping and Sporting Excellence

Consider a PED that is safe to use, cheap to buy, and grants its user a significant performance gain. Should this PED be prohibited? The third argument for a prohibition on doping concerns the relationship between doping and the very purpose of sport. The fundamental idea underpinning the excellence-based argument is that doping corrupts sport because it undermines sport's central purpose. This is the argument that I propose as the most promising justification for a ban on doping.

At first glance, the value of excellence would seem to support the use of PEDs. After all, PEDs allow runners to run faster, high jumpers to jump higher, and weightlifters to lift heavier. Anti-doping rules appear to stifle those who are truly committed to exploring the limits of human athletic potential as these rules prohibit means that would allow athletes to improve performance. How, then, could a concern for sporting excellence ground a prohibition on doping?

Sport is an excellence-based activity. Central to the purpose of sport is the cultivation and display of excellences of body, mind, and will that allow one to excel in the challenges presented within sporting contests. Each sport tests a different set of excellences. Any proposed change to a sport must be evaluated in light of the excellences that both sport in general and the given sport are designed to test. On the excellence-based argument, by lifting the ban on doping, we would corrupt sport by introducing means that undermine its fundamental point and purpose.

It is uncontentious that sport must allow, and indeed encourage, enhancement. The guiding value of modern sport is to train, to improve, and to enhance one's performance. The doctrine of 'marginal gains' – perhaps the leitmotif of modern sport – celebrates the attempt to seize any opportunity within the rules to ameliorate one's performance. Equally clear, however, is that rules to limit enhancement are essential to protect the purpose of sport (Sandel 2007). The fundamental role of rules in sport is to place obstacles in the way of athletes reaching their intended goal, where the obstacles presented can be reliably overcome only by the demonstration of specific athletic skills and capacities (Suits 2014). Prohibitive rules are sometimes necessary to protect the excellence-based purpose of sport: the use of ladders and trampolines is prohibited in the high jump because the high jump is designed to test jumping ability; the use of bicycles, cars, and helicopters is prohibited in the marathon, because the marathon is designed to test running ability; and the use of guns, knives and baseball bats is prohibited in boxing, because boxing is designed to test punching ability.

Sports are human creations, so if we wish to change the rules, it is within our gift to change them. However, while the rules of sport are made by us and can be changed by us, they are not arbitrary – they can be rationally evaluated according to whether they are consistent with the values that underpin both sport in general and particular sports. Whether we should ban PEDs depends on what we think is important about sporting competition and the sport for which the PEDs would be used. The fairness argument appealed to the fact that sporting competition is comparative – it ranks athletes according to their performances. However, sporting competition is also concerned with the display of sporting excellence. The pursuit of sporting excellence may not always be harmonious with the pursuit of fair competition (Roache 2008). It is possible that, even if fairness concerns arise with respect to PEDs, the importance of sporting excellence may outweigh those concerns. In short, might excellence be more important than fair competition? Even if formal fairness would be promoted by lifting the ban, does the value of excellence (and the related value of achievement (Bradford 2015)) justify the retention of a ban?

There are two ways to respond to this excellence-based argument for enhancement. Firstly, one might argue that, where fair competition and excellence conflict, excellence is outweighed, or even trumped, by fair competition. The second response is that PEDs do not, in fact, advance sporting excellence – their enhancing effect is at least sometimes only apparent – so the conflict does not obtain. It is this latter argument that I advance here.

Sporting excellence is not solely a matter of outcomes. Excellence is path-dependent: whether some performance constitutes a display of sporting excellence depends on whether the outcome of the performance was brought about by appropriate means.

It is a misnomer to label a bicycle an 'enhancement' in a running race. On the contrary, the bicycle is a 'corruption' of the race, because its use renders the race no longer a running race. By cycling down the track, the athlete is not displaying the skills and capacities – the excellences – that the race is designed to test.

Can PEDs corrupt sport in a similar way? I argue elsewhere (Devine 2022) that sporting excellence may be undermined in any of four ways. I consider now two such ways in relation to doping.[9] I argue that doping may undermine sport as an excellence-based activity by undermining the sport's 'cluster of excellence' or 'balance of excellence'.

Cluster of Excellence

Each sport is designed to test a specific set of excellences. Roughly speaking, the 100 m tests sprinting ability, the long jump tests jumping ability, and the javelin tests throwing ability. Complex sports such as tennis, soccer, and rugby test a wide array of excellences, but each sport tests a limited set. Tennis does not test punching, kicking, or swimming ability, for instance. The set of excellences that a sport is designed to test constitutes that sport's 'cluster of excellence'.

The first way that doping might undermine sporting excellence is by altering the set of excellences that are tested in the sport (i.e. contracting or expanding the sport's 'cluster of excellence'). For example, consider beta-blockers in the use of target sports such as shooting or archery. One of the foremost challenges posed to athletes by such sports is to control the effect of competition-induced stress on one's performance. Even the slightest tremor in one's hand caused by one's heartbeat can compromise the accuracy of a shot. Archers, for example, train psychological techniques to slow their heartbeat to allow them to manage the physiological effects of stress during competition. However, this same calming effect can be secured by ingesting beta-blockers which artificially slow one's heartbeat. Despite an athlete being in a state of panic about the competition, beta-blockers can ensure that the effects of their anxiety do not manifest themselves as an unsteady hand.

If a central purpose of target sports is to test competitors' ability to manage the physiological effects of competitive stress, then the use of beta-blockers to mask those effects undermines a central excellence of these sports. While the archer's performance may, on a surface level analysis, appear to be more excellent on account of the beta-blockers due to the greater number of points scored, the means of achieving that enhanced accuracy was to contract the sport's cluster of excellence by eliminating one of the sport's central challenges which could be reliably overcome only by the display of a distinctive kind of excellence.

Balance of Excellence

A second way that PEDs can undermine sporting excellence is by altering the relationship between the excellences within a sport's cluster of excellence. Sports are designed not only to test a certain set of excellences, they are also designed so that, among the excellences tested, some are ascribed greater importance than others.

When a change to the way a sport is played by those who are successful within it elevates the importance of certain excellences over others in a way that is inconsistent with the appropriate relationship between the excellences around which the sport is based, a balance of excellence concern arises. Certain excellences are intended to contribute more than others to the performances of those who succeed within the sport. If an excellence that should contribute prominently is relegated to only a minor role, and another excellence that should play a minor role assumes an elevated role among the performances of the sport's elite competitors, then the balance of excellence has been disrupted and may require correction.

Doping can undermine a sport's balance of excellence by elevating the relative importance of capacities that are amenable to enhancement by PEDs – for example, strength, power, and stamina – over those less amenable. Capacities such as agility, strategic nous, or psychological resilience are not as readily enhanced pharmacologically. So, the introduction of PEDs would privilege certain excellences over others, and this may have the effect of disrupting the sport's balance of excellence in ways that betray the sport's central purpose.

In rugby union, for example, the use of anabolic steroids would create bigger, stronger players. This would lead to more violent collisions, thereby privileging strength and power over skills such as evasiveness and elusiveness. The playing focus would likely shift to dominating collisions thereby deemphasising excellences such as slick handling or evasive running.

So, doping can undermine sporting excellence in at least two ways: by contracting the sport's cluster of excellence or by disrupting the sport's balance of excellence. An important implication of this excellence-based analysis is that doping should proceed on a sport-by-sport basis, not according to the prevailing 'one size fits all' approach with minimal sport-specific regulations.

Conclusion

My aim has been to refute the libertarian proposal that no restriction should be replaced on the use of PEDs in sport. I have not attempted to specify what contours that ban should take. Indeed, my argument here, when fully developed, may justify a doping ban that looks quite different to the existing World Anti-Doping Code (WADA 2021). Instead, I have demonstrated the significant disvalue associated with a sporting world in which PEDs are a normalised and permitted part of sporting practice.

As a product of human imagination and ingenuity, we can reshape and reconstitute sport however we wish. We do not have unfettered discretion though. As stewards of sports that are designed to test a specific cluster of excellence exhibited in a particular balance, we should formulate rules so that they accord with our commitment to sport as an excellence-based activity. PEDs threaten athlete welfare, the fairness of competition, and, perhaps most fundamentally, sport's very purpose. We should stand against doping in sport.

Notes

1   The scope of anti-doping has recently extended to eSports (International Esports Federation 2020), so as the boundaries of sport reach new frontiers, familiar problems reproduce themselves.
2   For example, in countries such as Italy, France, and Germany.
3   A survey of arguments for and against the prohibition of doping can be found in Devine and Lopez Frias (2020) and Lopez Frias (2017). Møller, Waddington, and Hoberman (2015) provides a book-length treatment of ethical issues in anti-doping.
4   My focus is on 'prohibited substances' as per Arts. 2.1 and 2.2 of the World Anti-Doping Code (WADA 2021). I set aside 'prohibited methods' such as blood doping that are also prohibited by the Code.
5   I leave aside arguments from more remote indirect harm that might be caused to the wider sporting community (e.g. children) who are enticed to dope so that they might emulate their sporting heroes. See Lopez Frias (2017; 67–68).
6   Pike has argued that athlete safety is lexically prior to any other moral value in sport, at least in collision sports such as rugby union (Pike 2021).
7   I leave aside cases where doping is purportedly coerced because it has become necessary to dope to remain competitive. This coercion argument is less persuasive, because it cannot distinguish between doping and other morally unobjectionable ways that athletes increase the sacrifice

necessary to be competitive in sport. For example, one can raise the bar for one's competitors by undertaking a more demanding training regime or, in a sport like gymnastics, executing more complex and dangerous skills. For a consideration of this type of coercion argument, see Veber (2014).

8   Admittedly, this argument is unlikely to provide a stable foundation for anti-doping, as we may be able to limit unfairness to a tolerable level by the reduction of a different source of unfairness while allowing unfairness created by doping.

9   I first explored excellence-based arguments against doping in Devine (2011).

References

Bradford, Gwen. 2015. *Achievement.* Oxford: Oxford.

Brown, W.M. 1980. Ethics, Drugs, and Sport. *Journal of the Philosophy of Sport.* 7. 15–23.

Chester, Neil. 2022. Anabolic Agents. *Drugs in Sport.* David R. Mottram and Neil Chester eds. Oxford: Routledge. 8th ed. Ch. 8.

Devine, John William. 2011. Doping Is a Threat to Sporting Excellence. *British Journal of Sports Medicine.* 45. 637–639.

Devine, John William. 2019. Gender, Steroids, and Fairness in Sport. *Sport, Ethics and Philosophy.* 13:2. 161–169.

Devine, John William. 2022. Elements of Excellence. *Journal of the Philosophy of Sport* 49:2. 195–211.

Devine, John William and Francisco Javier Lopez Frias. 2020. 'Philosophy of Sport'. *Stanford Encyclopedia of Philosophy,* URL: https://plato.stanford.edu/entries/sport/

Douglas, Thomas. 2007. Enhancement in Sport, and Enhancement Outside Sport. *Studies in Ethics, Law, and Technology.* 1:1. 1–15.

Hooker, Brad. 2005. *Fairness. Ethical Theory and Moral Practice.* 8. 329–352.

International Esports Federation. 2020. *Anti-Doping Rules.* URL: https://iesf.org/governance/anti-doping

Lang, Melanie. 2020. Developments in International Policy on Athlete Welfare. *Routledge Handbook of Athlete Welfare.* Melanie Lang (ed.). Oxford: Routledge. Ch. 1.

Lopez Frias, Francisco Javier. 2017. The Legitimacy of Using Steroids and Other Drugs to Improve Performance. *Philosophy: Sport.* R.S. Kretchmar (ed.). Michigan: Macmillan. 59–74.

McLaren, Richard. 2016. *McLaren Independent Investigation Report – Part 2.* URL: https://www.wada-ama.org/en/resources/mclaren-independent-investigation-report-part-ii

Mill, John Stuart (1859) 1977. *On Liberty, Essays on Politics and Society.* Vol. 18 of *Collected Works of John Stuart Mill.* Edited by John M. Robson. Toronto: University of Toronto Press.

Møller, Verner, Ivan Waddington, and John M. Hoberman (eds). 2015. *Routledge Handbook of Drugs and Sport.* Oxford: Routledge.

Mottram, David and Neil Chester. 2022. Peptide Hormones, Growth Factors, Related Substances and Mimetics. *Drugs in Sport.* David R. Mottram and Neil Chester eds. Oxford: Routledge. 8th ed. Ch. 9.

Pike, Jon. 2021. Safety, Fairness, and Inclusion: Transgender Athletes and the Essence of Rugby. *Journal of the Philosophy of Sport.* 48:2. 155–168.

Petroczi. Andrea, John Gleaves, Olivier de Hon, Dominic Sagoe, and Martial Saugy. 2022. Prevalence of Doping in Sport. *Drugs in Sport.* David R. Mottram and Neil Chester eds. Oxford: Routledge. 8th ed. Ch. 3.

Roache, Rebecca. 2008. Cheating and Enhancement. *Expositions.* 2:2. 153–156.

Russell. J.S. 2005. The Value of Dangerous Sport. *Journal of the Philosophy of Sport.* 32:1. 1–19.

Sandel, Michael J. 2007. *The Case Against Perfection: Ethics in the Age of Genetic Engineering.* Cambridge: Harvard.

Savulescu, Julian, Bennett Foddy, and Matthew Clayton. 2004. Why We Should Allow Performance Enhancing Drugs in Sport. *British Journal of Sports Medicine.* 38. 666–670.

Suits, Bernard. 2014 [1978]. *The Grasshopper: Games, Life and Utopia.* New York: Broadview Press.

Tamburrini, Claudio. 2000. What's Wrong With Doping?. *Values in Sport: Elitism, Nationalism, and Gender Equality and the Scientific Manufacturing of Winners*. Torbjörn Tännsjö and Claudio Tamburrini (eds). Oxford: Routledge.

USADA. 2012. Statement From USADA CEO Travis T. Tygart Regarding The U.S. Postal Service Pro Cycling Team Doping Conspiracy. URL: https://www.usada.org/statement/statement-from-usada-ceo-travis-t-tygart-regarding-the-u-s-postal-service-pro-cycling-team-doping-conspiracy/

Veber. Michael. 2014. The Coercion Argument against Performance-Enhancing Drugs. *Journal of the Philosophy of Sport*. 41: 2. 267–277.

WADA. 2021. World Anti-Doping Code. URL: https://www.wada-ama.org/en/resources/world-anti-doping-program/world-anti-doping-code

Index

conservatism, intergenerational fairness 293; excellence-based argument 293–294; fairness 291; harmness 289–290; incremental change, anti-doping 293; individual autonomy 290; intergenerational unfairness 292; sporting excellence 293–296; unfairness between contemporaries 292; World Anti-Doping Agency 288; World Anti-Doping Code (WADA 2021) 288; wrongful and non-wrongful harm 290
Spottswood, E. 91
Spurgeon, C. H. 24
stakeholder theory 222
Steptoe, P. 270
Stevens, M. L. T. 279
Sunstein, C. R. 204, 205, 207, 208, 212
surveillance capitalism 115, 120
Swierstra, T. 46

Taylor, C. 40
technological determinism 26–32
technological momentum 29
technology: and accidental discovery 9; actor network theory 12; applied science 8–9; behavioral engineering 10; circular definitions 6; computer programs 10; consensus definition 12; determinism 26–32; empirical turn 7; and ethnosciences 8; guidelines for definitions 6–7; haphazard infrastructures 16–17; as hardware 9–10; lexical definitions 8; megamachine 10; metaphorical definitions 6; narrow definition 7; negative definition 7; neutrality *vs.* biased 11–12; postmodernist 7, 12; precising definitions 8; real definitions 7; system 11–12; technique 10–11; user *vs.* uses 12; value- free 14–17 (*see also* specific topics)
Teller, E. 11–12
Thiel, P. 30
Thomas, L. 255
Thomson, J.J. 146
tiktok trends 179–180
Tiles, M. 139
Tocqueville, A. 223
Toma, C. 91
Tometti, O. 177
trolley problem 146–148
Trudy 178
Trump, Donald 87, 89, 186, 189
trust, Kantian ethics: artificial intelligence (AI) 126–127; autonomy 123–125; categorical imperative 124; deceptive behavior 124; definition of 122–123; ethical and unethical type 123; food biotechnology 127–128; GM food 127–128; institutional distrust 125–126; interests and values 128; knowledge deficit model 127–128; reflexive trust 125; responsibility for 125; responsibility of 128; self-driving cars 126–127; three-part relationship 123; trustworthiness 123; varieties of 123
trust and glue 53

Tsou, J.Y. 91
Twain, M. 18, 24

utilitarianism: act and rule forms 63; anti-depressant drugs 106; emotional appropriateness, HPP 108–109; false happiness, HPP 109; freedom, HPP 109–110; fundamental axiom 63; gene influence 104; good life 102–103; happy by nature 104; happy disposition and health 108; happy-people-pills (HPP) 105–106; happy person 102–103; hedonism 102–103; hedonism redux 107–108; heritability, happiness 104; insensitivity 64; moods and emotions in 105; morality of action 63–64; morally right action 103–104; perfectionists 103; prosocial behavior, HPP 111; research cost, HPP 107; weakness 64

Vallor, S 93
value-free technology: facial recognition 16; heraclitus redux 14–15; steps, scientific method 14; technological infrastructures 15–17
value-neutrality thesis: accident impacts 22; bad consequences, technology 23–24; behavior change, aggregate 20; collective action problems 21; decent people, bad consequences 21–22; discount, time 21–22; incentives response 19–20; inventors and engineer responsibility 24; mistake consequences 22; short-term thinking 21–22; technology effect in 20; weakness of the will 22
value laden thesis: technology 2, 5, 15, 18, 134, 274, 275
values built technology: misinformation 18; social media effect 18; value-neutrality thesis 18–21
Van de Poel, I. 25
Veber, M. 297
Verbeek, P-P 139
virtue ethics: Aristotle's virtues 69–70; deficiency and excess 69; *vs.* moral theories 69; strength and weakness 70
visibility, social media: architectures of 176; authenticity labor 180–181; black dance virality 179–180; black discursive culture 177–179; black labor 181–182; black twitter 177; civility 178; hashtag activism 176–177; hashtags 175; Influencer-centric platform 179; influencer labor 180; Influencers 175; memeification 181–182; misogynoir 178; platforms adopted features 176; racial justice movement 176–177; tiktok trends 179–180; uncompensated emotional labor 178; vernacular digital pedagogy 178

Waddington, I. 296
Wajcman, J. 27, 28
Waldron, J. 233
Walker, M 106
Watts, P. 161
Weber, M. 11